# Sartre & Flaubert

# HAZEL E. BARNES
# Sartre & Flaubert

The University of Chicago Press • Chicago and London

The University of Chicago Press, Chicago 60637
The University of Chicago Press, Ltd., London

©1981 by The University of Chicago
All rights reserved. Published 1981
Phoenix edition 1982
Printed in the United States of America
90 89 88 87 86 85 84 83 82    2 3 4 5

Library of Congress Cataloging in Publication Data

Barnes, Hazel Estella.
   Sartre and Flaubert.

   Bibliography: p. 437
   Includes index.
   1. Sartre, Jean Paul, 1905–1980. L'Idiot de la
famille.   2. Flaubert, Gustave, 1821–1880—Criticism
and interpretation.   I. Title.
PQ2247.S33B3       843'.8       80–26872
ISBN 0–226–03720–7 (cloth)
      0–226–03721–5 (paper)

*To Donald Sutherland in Memoriam*

# CONTENTS

# AUTHOR'S PREFACE

If Jean-Paul Sartre at the beginning of his career had produced a three-volume study of Flaubert, it might have been possible for a person writing a critical study of it to have some chance of arriving at an adequate perspective on the work as a whole and of singling out and commenting on its several significant contributions. At present the task is impossible for anyone. This final synthesis of Sartre's ideas both reflects his own lifetime of study and thought and rests upon all of his philosophy as it has been developed over half a century. It will take years of study by many scholars before someone might hope, relying on the work of his or her predecessors, to write something comprehensive and definitive. The problem is not simply the length of this book of nearly three thousand pages. Ideally the would-be critic should be an expert, not only on both Flaubert and Sartre himself, but on French literature and history, on psychoanalysis, and on Marxist theory. One confronts another question, in the form of a dilemma. It would be unrealistic to expect that very many potential readers have found time to read *L'Idiot de la famille* carefully, if at all. Should one write for the "saving remnant" of those who have? Or would it be better to assume that among those who have not read the biography, there is an interest in learning something about it before they tackle it for themselves?

I have attempted a compromise. This is not a condensed paraphrase of *The Family Idiot* in the sense that Catalano, Desan, and Cooper and Laing have published summaries with commentary on specific books by Sartre. But neither do I presume familiarity with the content of Sartre's three volumes. I think of it as a critical introduction to them. I have tried, within reasonable limits, to comment on what seem to me significant additions to Sartre's body of philosophical thought and important contributions to a better understanding of Flaubert. In this sense my book is, as its title indicates, about both Sartre and Flaubert. My twofold hope is that it may guide and influence more persons to read Sartre's book themselves and that it will be helpful to future scholars who may choose to study its specific problems with the detailed examination these deserve. I am only too keenly aware of the incompleteness of what I myself have done.

In my earlier writing on Sartre I had reason to be deeply appreciative of the work of Sartrean scholars. Now I wish to express my particular gratitude to those who have written on Flaubert. I am especially grateful for the information and insight I have found in the books of Benjamin Bart, Victor Brombert, Jean Bruneau, Philip Spencer, Enid Starkie, and Francis Steegmuller.

I am glad to express my sincere thanks to the John Simon Guggenheim Memorial Foundation, which granted me a fellowship for the academic year 1977–78, and to the Council on Research and Creative Work at the University of Colorado, which has also supported me in this undertaking as it has generously done in the past.

I take special pleasure in thanking two other persons: Luzie Mason, who transcribed for me handwritten notes by Sartre; and Doris J. Schwalbe, who read my manuscript as it progressed and who offered valuable suggestions for improving it.

Finally I want to acknowledge a debt of gratitude to Jean-Paul Sartre. In the fall of 1977 he sent to me a copy of his notes for volume 4 of *L'Idiot de la famille*. Just a few days before his final hospitalization in 1980 he confirmed in writing permission for me to use material from these notes in my book. This was an act of the greatest kindness.

Hazel E. Barnes

# INTRODUCTION

## Approaching *The Family Idiot*

Is *The Family Idiot* a biography of Gustave Flaubert or a novel? Is it Jean-Paul Sartre's autobiography in disguise? Is it a book about literature? Is it a philosophical work? It has been called all of these. Sartre has talked at some length about his attitude toward it and recognizes that the work is difficult to classify. His remarks, spoken on various occasions, have not been altogether consistent and have sometimes led reviewers astray. Critics have agreed on only one thing: *The Family Idiot* is too long. Three volumes of 2801 pages (and a projected fourth volume), and these not intended even to cover *all* of Flaubert's life and works, have earned for Sartre charges of self-indulgence and lack of consideration for his readers—though almost all serious reviewers have testified to the extraordinary richness of the opus.

*The Family Idiot,* quite apart from the problem of length, could not possibly serve as a satisfactory introduction to Flaubert for one not already acquainted with him. Reading one of the standard biographies is a prerequisite for understanding Sartre's study. Yet the work is not addressed primarily to Flaubert scholars, nor is it exclusively about Flaubert. A large part of it is devoted to the discussion of the literary situation in the mid-nineteenth century, viewed as a response to the writers of the preceding century and a half and as an anticipation of literary developments down to 1900, examined also as a reflection of historical events and changing attitudes in society. This does not mean that what we have is simply an extensive treatment of "Flaubert and his time." In a number of respects the work defies the traditional criteria of biography. It relies heavily on hypotheses concerning matters on which there can be no objective evidence—the relations between the infant Gustave and his mother, for instance, and speculations as to the reasons behind Gustave's games with his sister and with his schoolmates. Flaubert scholars have pointed to errors in detail of a kind which the usual biographer would make a point of avoiding but which apparently do not bother Sartre.[1] The reader interested primarily in Sartre's philosophy rather than in Flaubert will find an abundance of encapsulated phenomenological studies on a wide variety of subjects, e.g., reading, mourning, the comic, the practical joke, the ontological status of the imaginary. And perhaps most surprising of all, Sartre admits freely that he wrote this biography to prove a point; he says that Flaubert is the expression, though not the example, of a thesis.[2]

The nature of the thesis and the goal Sartre hopes to achieve in the *The Family Idiot* are presented clearly and succinctly in his preface; the desire to write *a* biography dates back many years earlier. In *Being and Nothingness,* at the conclusion of his presentation of Existential Psychoanalysis, he wrote, "This psychoanalysis has not yet found its Freud. At most we can find the foreshadowing of it in certain particularly successful biographies. We hope to be able to attempt elsewhere two examples in relation to Flaubert and Dostoevsky."[3] We may note that from the start he thought of biography as a means of demonstrating a method and that Flaubert was an intended subject. The precipitating cause of the later study, Sartre tells us, was a challenge proposed by Roger Garaudy, "Let's take some person and try to explain him, I by Marxist methods and you by your existentialist methods."[4] Actually Sartre combined both approaches in a preliminary study then as he did in the finished work. He has stated that the wish to show how psychoanalysis and a Marxist sociology could be profitably combined was a major factor in his decision to write "the Flaubert," as he generally refers to it.

> Everyone knows and everyone admits that psychoanalysis and Marxism should be able to find the mediations necessary to allow a combination of the two....

Everybody, he goes on to say, agrees that psychoanalysis can be useful to the Marxist and that much may be gleaned also from traditional sociology.

> Everyone agrees on all this. Everyone in fact *says* it but who has tried to *do* it? I myself was in general repeating these irreproachable maxims in *Question de méthode*. The idea of the book on Flaubert was to abandon these theoretical disquisitions ... and to try to give a concrete example of how it might be done.[5]

In the preface Sartre uses different language, but the same idea dominates. He begins,

*The Family Idiot* is the sequel of *Question de méthode*. Its subject: what can be known of a man today. It seemed to me that the question could be answered only by the study of a concrete case: What do we know—for example—of Gustave Falubert. [1:7][6]

Some persons would say that the most likely answer to such a question is that when all the data have been collected and interpreted, the subject of the biography will still not be *known*. This will not be just because essential clues, never having been objectively documented, will be unavailable to us. The real danger is that we will be left with diverse pieces of information which simply do not add up to anything; perhaps the truth is that a person and his life are not a totality but a collection of quite disparate and unrelated actions and reactions. Sartre is convinced that this is not the case.

Do we not risk ending up with layers of heterogeneous and irreducible significations? This book attempts to prove that the irreducibility is only apparent and that each bit of information, put in its place, becomes the part of a whole which ceaselessly makes itself and, by the same stroke, reveals its profound homogeneity with all the others. [1:7]

This sentence will not surprise students of Sartre. The idea that the individual consciousness, as the unifier of its experiences, makes itself by an initial project or choice of a way of being goes back to *Being and Nothingness*. True, this subjectivity cannot be simultaneously lived and objectively known by itself. But even earlier, in *The Transcendence of the Ego,* Sartre argues that when the ego or psychic structure of the self is viewed as it has emerged over the past, as a history, then one's own ego is neither more nor less directly accessible to one's present consciousness than the Other's ego is. Both are objects. *The Critique of Dialectical Reason,* while it deals with the causes of alienation and the distortions and mystifications which impede communication, nevertheless maintains that man is not unknowable, he is simply not known. Now Sartre expresses the strong conviction that in principle, if the documentation is adequate, any person can be known, understood in his totality.

In seeking to establish the "knowability" of a person, Sartre is concerned not only with his or her unique qualities but with a man's or woman's basic homogeneity with other members of the species. The *Critique* argued that just as we cannot grasp the movement of history without some knowledge of the projects of the group and the individuals who make it, so the particular man can be understood only in terms of his insertion in the history of a particular society at a given place and time. Now Sartre declares,

> A man is never an individual. It would be better to call him *a
> singular universal* [*universel singulier*]; totalized and thereby uni-
> versalized by his period, he retotalizes it by reproducing himself
> in it as a singularity. Universal by the singular universality of
> human history, singular by the universalizing singularity of his
> projects, he demands to be studied from both sides. [1:7–8]

Sartre had expressed the same idea more concretely in *Search for a
Method*. "Valéry is a petty bourgeois intellectual, no doubt about
that. But not every petty bourgeois intellectual is Valéry."[7] Nor has
any other philosophical poet exerted quite the same influence on
society as Valéry. If we are to understand who Valéry was or Flaubert
or anyone else, we must study him as he has responded to the psychological conditioning of his early life in the family and to society at
large—both directly and through his parents. The method will be the
fusion of Marxist sociology and existential psychoanalysis that Sartre
outlined in *Search for a Method*.

In the preface Sartre declines to comment further on the method
itself, preferring to let us watch it develop in response to the requirements of the project in hand. The method, the germ of which
Sartre discovered in the work of Henri Lefebvre, may be described as
"regressive-progressive"; it is alternately (and in combination) horizontal and vertical, analytic and synthetic. If an anthropologist tries
to understand a particular tribal society, for example, he might begin
by studying analytically each of the present structures with all their
contradictions, tensions, and divergencies in subgroups, statements
from internal and external witnesses, etc. The resulting description
would have only provisional validity as a collection of data. It would
need to be supplemented by the study of the historical formation of
subgroups and structures. A progressive synthesis would, if
adequately formulated and applied, draw all the facts together so as
to let us comprehend the meaning of the life of the group as a totality
in which even unharmonious units played their part. The approach
to an individual subject of biography would be much the same except for the additional fact that here the psychoanalytic history of the
individual must be placed in the context of the socio-historical reality
of the contemporary society as a whole. The method in each case will
be characterized by a high degree of reflexivity. What ultimately
distinguishes this from other methods is, of course, the fact that the
sociological approach is also Marxist and both the Marxism and the
psychoanalysis considerably transformed by Sartrean existentialism.

Almost as an afterthought Sartre, in the preface, asks, "Why

Flaubert?" If we were limited to the reasons given here, we might well feel that the choice was fortuitous. First, the documentation is abundant: Flaubert's own books, memoirs, travel accounts, the recorded evidence of contemporary witnesses, and those marvelous volumes of correspondence in which Flaubert writes freely like "a neurotic speaking 'at random' on the psychoanalyst's couch." The second is a personal reason: Sartre's long acquaintance with Flaubert's writing, resulting in the feeling that he had an account to settle with the French novelist whose outlook on life and literature were in so many ways opposed to Sartre's own. A third explanation is that Flaubert offers us the opportunity to see how a man has objectified himself in his books. Sartre, as a writer and critic, would not allow us to try to explain or judge a book by reference to its author's life. The literary work "as the objectification of the person is, in fact, *more complete, more total* than the life." It does not find its whole explanation in the life, but it offers itself as a "hypothesis and a research tool to clarify the biography."[8] To discover how Flaubert has objectified himself in *Madame Bovary* is to raise a problem of interest in itself. "What then is the relation between the man and the work? I have never said until now. Nobody has, to my knowledge" (1:8). Finally, Sartre adds, Flaubert, "creator of the 'modern' novel, is at the crossroads of all our literary problems today." In short, he is important to us and relevant.

Sartre tells us that at one point he had hesitated between Flaubert and Robespierre.[9] I doubt that the hesitation was for long that the possibility of a biography of Robespierre was more than theoretical. Reasons for choosing Flaubert which Sartre has mentioned elsewhere indicate that there is something a bit disingenuous in that offhand "What do we know of Gustave Flaubert—for example?"

In an interview just before the publication of the first two volumes, Sartre's immediate response to the question, Why Flaubert? was, "Because he is the imaginary. With him, I am at the border, the barrier of dreams." He adds that *The Family Idiot* deals with the problem of the relation between the real and the imaginary; in this respect it is a sequel to *The Psychology of the Imagination* (1940). Sartre wanted to study Flaubert as a man who preferred the imaginary to the real and, through him, to ask the broader question, "What was the *imaginary social world* of the dreamy bourgeoisie of 1848?"[10] In a filmed interview he adds another connection with his early work on the imagination—concern with the problem of art. "It is the true relation of the artist with the imaginary which is the work of art; this is one of the meanings of the book on Flaubert."[11] Finally Sartre relates this work to his own autobiography.

> The reason why I produced *Les Mots* is the reason why I have studied Genet or Flaubert: how does a man become someone who writes, who wants to speak of the imaginary? This is what I sought to answer in my own case, as I sought it in that of others.[12]

In choosing Flaubert as his subject, Sartre committed himself not only to doing the biography of a writer, but to writing a book which is also about literature and about what it means to choose to be a creator of images.

I believe that examination of *The Family Idiot* will show that Flaubert was uniquely suited to allow Sartre to accomplish all of his goals in writing a biography. One may begin to suspect, too, that Sartre's underlying, perhaps unacknowledged hope was to produce a work which would stand as the culmination and totalization of his own thought. No wonder that some readers praise the book as being much more than a biography, while others claim that it is not a biography at all.

If we want to grasp Sartre's own intentions, I think it is important to look now at what he himself has said on how the work should be read and classified. In a prepublication interview Sartre suggested that *The Family Idiot* might be viewed as a novel. He spoke in response to a question as to why he had stopped writing novels himself.

> Because I have felt no urge to do so. Writers have always more or less chosen the imaginary. They have a need for a certain ration of fiction. Writing on Flaubert is enough for me by way of fiction—it might indeed be called a novel. Only I would like people to say that it was a true novel.[13]

He added that in his endeavor to comprehend Flaubert, he used hypotheses, which he considered as guided and controlled fictions, to enable him to explain, for example, contradictions in Flaubert's correspondence. "My hypotheses are in this sense a sort of invention of the personage." On a later occasion he remarked that the overall movement of his biography was like that of a novel.

> I would like my study to be read as a novel since it is, in fact, the story of an apprenticeship that leads to the failure of an entire life. At the same time I would like it to be read with the idea that it is the truth, that it is a *true* novel.[14]

Sartre says that Flaubert is presented as Sartre imagines him to have

been, but adds that since he has used rigorous methods, the resulting image should also be Flaubert "as he really was." For Sartre a
critical and intelligent interpretation is still the result of the process
of imagination. To me it seems that his words were not intended to
convey the idea that this biography was less reliable or more of an invention by the author than any other biography. Some critics, however, have seized upon his statement as a reason for complaining that
Sartre did not care whether his Flaubert resembled the one who
actually lived; others have claimed that with our realization today of
the limits of discourse, Sartre has invented a new form of biography
with criteria closer to those normally applied to pure fiction.[15]
In neither case would Sartre be judged to have demonstrated that
a well-documented life is "knowable." Even Michel Rybalka, whose
first-hand knowledge of Sartre is not surpassed by that of any other
scholar, has concluded, "Perhaps we could apply the term 'novelistic'
to Sartre's whole enterprise, and we can wonder whether, all things
considered, *L'Idiot* is not the only novel possible today."[16]

Evidently Sartre came to feel that his statements had been misinterpreted. In a later interview (1976) he firmly rejected the idea that
*The Family Idiot* might be considered a novel in any way that would
reflect pejoratively on its status as biography.

> Perhaps I exaggerated a bit when I said that it was *a novel*. I never
> thought of it as such when I was writing it, and the role of imagi-
> nation, which in fact is a liberating of the imaginary, is all the same
> recaptured by a truth which there was in the imaginary. In other
> words, I let my imagination run only to the extent that I had texts,
> for example, or prior reflections sufficiently numerous to give to
> imagination a truth value. So that basically this idea that it is a
> novel would be effaced from the moment that the work would be
> finished—which it isn't since it stops with the third volume. This
> novel is not in fact a novel. . . . I consider that Flaubert is, for these
> three volumes . . . a collection of truths about Flaubert. It isn't a
> lyric effusion [*un lyrisme*] that I'm doing on certain aspects of
> Flaubert, it is the truth about Flaubert that I have tried to write. I
> tried to write with my imagination as well as my reason, but it was
> because I think that imagination is a provider of truths at the level
> of structures.[17]

In the light of these remarks, I think Sartre has invited us to apply
to his "Flaubert" all of the criteria for validity which he would consider appropriate for any biography that claimed to understand the
person concerned and not merely to document the events of a life.
What he has written is not, in his opinion, fiction.

At the same time Sartre recognizes that *The Family Idiot* is more than a biography. Its concentration on the literary situation of a particular period, its critical analysis of Flaubert's fiction might well seem to qualify it as literary criticism. This possibility Sartre acknowledges but rejects. "I do not regard it as a work of literary criticism but as a philosophical work." Here, too, he feels he must qualify. *The Family Idiot* is not a philosophical treatise of the classic kind. Sartre "leaves to professors of philosophy" the task of setting a neatly defined goal to be reached by the application of precise principles in a series of carefully ordered chapters. In his study theoretical problems have been selected and discussed subject to their relevance to his central purpose: "To constitute the life of a man—of a dead man."[18] Still, Sartre has written what he believes to be philosophy, and I think only the narrowest of technicians would argue otherwise.

The inclusion of extensive sociological commentary and his methodological claims apparently led Sartre to fear that some persons might expect to apply to the book criteria appropriate to standard objective research in social science. He explains that in submitting it to Gallimard's Philosophical Library series, he was admitting that its approach is not "scientific." What he says in this connection illuminates his conviction as to what the approach of the biographer ought to be. "'Scientific' would imply a rigorous use of *concepts*. As a philosopher I try to be rigorous with *notions*."[19] To work with a concept, according to Sartre, is to define things from the outside insofar as is humanly possible—objectively, and atemporally. To employ a notion is to try to define things from the inside, to include the "time of the object," and the "time of knowledge." In short, it is "thought that carries time within itself."

> By notion I mean that global but structured comprehension of a human reality which introduces temporalization—as an oriented becoming—into the synthetic apperception which it wants to have of its object and simultaneously of itself. [2:1811]

Sartre clarifies his meaning with the example of "passivity," a central notion in his interpretation of Flaubert. It is important to distinguish between the passivity of the very young child and the passivity of the man engaged in writing *Madame Bovary*. But it is necessary, too, for Sartre to be aware of the specific form of his own discovery of the notion and its development within his methodological approach. The interiority of the subject's experience and that of the author overlap and stand in a dialectical relationship. Finally Sartre states that the difference between "concept" and "notion" is similar to the distinction he had made earlier between "knowledge" (*connaissance*) and comprehension (*compréhension*). "The attitude necessary for comprehending a person is empathy." Earlier Sartre had distinguished knowledge and comprehension in terms of an individual's awareness of self. One can *know* a practical conduct, but can only *conprehend* a passion. Referring to *le vécu*, the lived experience, the ongoing dialectical process of psychic life, he claims that it, too, can only be comprehended. One can achieve certain flashes of intuition, sudden "fulgurations," which reveal the essential flavor or quality or orientation of a life, but these are not analytic knowledge, nor can they be expressed in verbalized concepts. With respect to one's own self, Sartre attributed the impossibility to the fact that a totalizing consciousness cannot be simultaneously the consciousness totalized. Now in speaking of his attempt to know Flaubert, he says that comprehension must come first. That is, he must first try through an empathizing imagination to grasp Flaubert's reactions as they would have been lived by him within the gradual process of his personalization. There must, at this stage, be no judgment passed by the author, only an effort toward sympathetic understanding of the structures and meanings and values of Flaubert's life world. If successful, Sartre may comprehend or understand Flaubert. Are we to say that when this happens, we "know" Flaubert? Yes and no. We can—at least in principle—know all there is to know *about* Flaubert, but here, too, we must distinguish between knowledge and comprehension. To *know* him is to relate, from our own point of view, the structures of his life and person in a way that includes his own self-comprehension as he has expressed it indirectly in his writing and in his reported statements and actions. It is, of course, not to know him from the inside, anymore than we do with those living closest to us. But we may know and understand him in somewhat the sense that we do with the characters of a novel. We can, Sartre is convinced, know enough *about* him so that we can grasp the basic orientation of his life and relate to it in a meaningful, unified pattern all of the information we have concerning him and—theoretically—his entire life history.

Sartre considers that he has written a philosophical work which is also a biography. What are we to say of claims that this so-called biography is really an autobiography? Claude Burgelin declared, "Through Flaubert as intermediary, Sartre refers us to Sartre and 'What can be known of a man today?' refers to 'What can I say about me?'"[20] No other reviewer went as far as this, but many have felt that to greater or lesser degree Sartre attributed to Flaubert conflicts and preoccupations really his own or, at least, sought to discover in Flaubert's childhood a parallel to his own. In short, this view would find *The Family Idiot* not only a sequel to the *Critique* and *The Psychology of the Imagination* but a follow-up of *The Words*. This charge Sartre has firmly denied. Objectively, he declares, his childhood was totally different from Gustave Flaubert's. Sartre was loved, even pampered; Gustave was underloved (*mal aimé*). Sartre finds it unhelpful to say that he saw himself in Flaubert as he did in Genet. He is closer to Genet, has "very few points in common with Flaubert."[21] Of course, there are elements of himself in the book, but that is not the same thing. Obviously, too, if Sartre thinks that his "Flaubert" is a true portrait, he would not consider that it has been molded by his own self-image. It would be premature at this point to try to say whether or not Sartre has projected more of himself into his subject than he realized. But we may note that aside from the question of parallels in the childhood situations, one basic theme appears in *The Words* and *The Family Idiot:* the problem of why one chooses the imaginary, why one wishes to become a writer. It was Flaubert, among other great "immortals," who inspired in Jean-Paul his own early dreams of literary glory. While Flaubert devoted his life to Art, he knew the anguished doubts that come even to the true believer. Sartre's quarrel with literature has produced the loudest explosions since Plato banished the poets from his imaginary republic. *The Family Idiot* represents the final battle in this war between Sartre as writer and Sartre as committed philosopher. Flaubert as a "concrete case" is as much a means for this project as he is for Sartre's intention to prove the validity of a method.

Explaining why he decided to resume work on the study of Flaubert which he had first done in response to Garaudy's challenge in 1954 and then abandoned a year later, Sartre said that one important factor in the decision was his resolve for once in his life to finish something (referring to his unwritten Ethics, the unwritten second volume of the *Critique,* the unfinished novel sequence, an incomplete study of Tintoretto).[22] It is ironic that this time he was prevented by external factors, his illness and near-blindness. His reference to a fifth volume, which would have taken up the later years of Flaubert, was an afterthought, not part of the original plan. In truth, no matter how intrinsically interesting it might have been, it would have been a trifle redundant to the work as projected. By the end of volume 3

Sartre has made his point, which is that the essential pattern of Flaubert's life was fixed in 1844 and the fruits of it objectified in *Madame Bovary,* an examination of which would have constituted the fourth volume. Even without volume 4 the work as it stands has a formal unity. If one were to delete Sartre's occasional references to an intended sequel, I think an uninformed reader would not feel that the book had been cut off before the end.

The subtitle of *The Family Idiot* is *Gustave Flaubert from 1821 to 1857.* The second date is, of course, the date of the publication of *Madame Bovary.* Taken literally, the dates are misleading. Volume 2 ends with a long discussion of "The Legend of Saint Julian the Hospitaler," published in 1877; much of volume 3 concerns Flaubert's life in the Second Empire and his attitude toward its fall in 1870. In expressing Sartre's basic intention, the subtitle is well chosen; the later material is included only as supporting evidence for his thesis—that Flaubert decisively fixed the meaning of his life at the time of his nervous crisis in 1844 and did not essentially change thereafter. In *Madame Bovary,* Sartre believes, we have not only the fruition of Flaubert's aesthetic creed but the revelation of his chosen attitude toward life, despite and even by means of the apparent impersonalism.

Sartre wants to show that Flaubert became the writer he was in response to two lines of conditioning. Roughly these are respectively psychological and sociological, though Sartre never entirely excludes the latter in discussing the former. More specifically the one line represents the influence of the family, the other that of society and cultural tradition. His constitution (the result of the infant's relation with his mother) and his family situation led Gustave to choose the imaginary. His decision to become a writer came into conflict with the father's career expectations. A nervous attack and prolonged illness in 1844 both resolved the family problem and crystallized in Flaubert's mind his image of himself as an artist and his concept of what the life of a writer should be; his aesthetic creed reflects the internal struggle and its resolution. The way in which Gustave lived all this, outwardly and inwardly, forms the subject matter of the first two volumes. Sartre's approach is that of the literary psychoanalyst; he examines all relevant documents with special attention to Flaubert's early fiction, down to *November* and the first *Sentimental Education.* Volume 3 concentrates on the line of sociological conditioning. Leaving Flaubert temporarily, Sartre examines the literary tradition as it was confronted by a beginning writer in the 1840s. After a survey of the literature of the eighteenth and early nineteenth century (its essential qualities and the attitude of the writers to their role), Sartre argues that the literary sector of what he calls the "objective mind" exerted a set of contradictory demands to which only one response was fitting. This was the notion of "art for art's sake" and the accompanying aesthetic which we find exemplified in the books of Flaubert. Thus we find an "overdetermination," a double and reciprocal conditioning of Gustave as person and as writer. Sartre next proceeds to analyze the prevalent ideology of the nonliterary public. He claims that Flaubert's personal "neurosis" led him to produce in *Madame Bovary* a book which, erroneously taken to be a realistic novel, suited to perfection the requirements of the bourgeois ideology—despite the scandal—and satisfied the unacknowledged neurotic needs of its readers. Returning at last to Flaubert the man, Sartre tries to show why the high point of the novelist's life was the years in which he frequented court circles during the Second Empire and that his sense of outliving himself after its fall was intricately linked with the self-image and sense of destiny he had chosen for himself at the time of the nervous crisis in 1844.

In my critical examination of *The Family Idiot* I have thought it best, in parts one and two, to follow the overall pattern of its development, but I will not be adhering to Sartre's order of discussion section by section. In part three, "The Biographer as Literary Critic," I will focus on Sartre's discussion of two of Flaubert's works. The first chapter will take up "The Legend of Saint Julian the Hospitaler," which Sartre finds particularly valuable as a revelation of Flaubert's basic "wager" with life. The second chapter will be devoted to *Madame Bovary*. While disavowing any intention of writing the missing volume, I think Sartre has given us enough information so that we can see, at least in outline, how he would have read the novel and how he would have related it to Flaubert himself. The published volumes include a significant amount of commentary on certain passages, and Sartre has made some notes for volume 4, which, thanks to his kind generosity, I have been allowed to read. In the conclusion I will attempt to provide a summary response to certain questions that will have been considered throughout the preceding discussion and that I have already touched on in this introductory presentation:

First, can we accept Sartre's "Flaubert" as Flaubert? We must attempt to determine how seriously Sartre's portrait challenges the traditional picture of the novelist and to decide whether the evidence and argument are sufficiently convincing to support a new view of him. Is *The Family Idiot* truly biography, or is it a novel or autobiography as has been suggested?

Second, in what ways has Sartre enriched and modified our understanding of Flaubert's novels and short stories? Will *Madame Bovary* henceforth seem the same book to us?

Third, how do we relate *The Family Idiot* to the rest of Sartre's work? In *Being and Nothingness* he remarked that very few persons are privileged to greet their death as a resolving chord. Sartre, despite his not having finished *The Family Idiot* as planned, seems almost to be one of them. Virtually all of his philosophical concerns are present in this last major work. Is it a tying up of loose ends, a rounding off? Does it contradict or radically modify what preceded? Does it open up new paths for others to follow? Does it solve the problem of the relation between Sartre the philosopher and Sartre the creative writer?

Obviously, much time and many books will be required before a fully adequate answer to all of these questions can even begin to emerge. I have attempted to provide a starting point.

# PART ONE

The Author of *Madame Bovary*

# CHAPTER ONE

## The Child in the Family

### THE SECRET WOUND

At a point midway in his discussion of Flaubert's early development Sartre remarks that any reader at about 1860, if he were asked, "Who *is* Gustave Flaubert?" would obviously not reply—or at least not at first—"He *is* a frustrated and jealous younger brother or one underloved or a passive agent." The response would certainly be, "He *is* a novelist" or "He *is* the author of *Madame Bovary*" (1:657–58). For the reader, Flaubert's being is his being-a-writer. And for Sartre, too. That is not to say that Flaubert's being is to be identified with his public persona. Rather Sartre claims that Flaubert *"made himself* a writer in order to resolve his inner conflicts"—those conflicts that derived from the fact that in his childhood his family situation led him to become "a frustrated and jealous younger brother," "one underloved," "a passive agent." These still remain and play their part in the author's self-objectification which we know as *Madame Bovary*.

In the opening chapter, called "A Problem," Sartre begins with an account of the first specific problem encountered by the child Gustave Flaubert. This leads naturally to Sartre's statement of the problem of his own book and the reason for its title: "We must seek to understand this scandal: an idiot who becomes a genius" (1:51). Flaubert's niece, Caroline Commanville, records that Flaubert had considerable difficulty in learning to read. His mother finally gave up the attempt to teach him; after tearful and stormy scenes, Flaubert learned from the local priest. The family felt that he was retarded. Hence Sartre's title, *The Family Idiot*. In treating this incident, Sartre demonstrates the nature of his method and sets forth several of the main themes of the book. The method is to combine by turn two procedures: regressive (also analytic) and progressive (also synthetic). Most of the first chapter is regressive. Sartre analyzes the frustratingly small collection of data we possess about Flaubert's early childhood, checks it against significant commentary from Flaubert's later years, and forms interpretive hypotheses.

He begins by challenging the accuracy of the niece's report, which after all was secondhand, based on statements made to her years after the event by Flaubert. Mme Commanville says Gustave's failure came when he was nine years old. Sartre points to the fact that we have a well-composed letter written by Flaubert when he was nine, and he argues reasonably enough that the niece's narrative has been compressed, that the difficulty extended over a longer period, and that probably Flaubert was only seven when the trouble began. Was he retarded? Obviously not, Sartre says, at least not if by retardation we mean lack of mental capacity. He seeks an explanation in other conduct ascribed to the young Gustave—his credulity, his passivity, his animal-like stupidity, his habit of falling into *hébétudes,* states of seeming stupor when he would lie or sit quietly for long periods with apparently little or no awareness of what was going on about him.

Sartre quotes from Commanville,

> The child was of a tranquil nature, meditative, and with a naïveté of which he maintained traces all his life. My grandmother told me that he stayed for long hours, a finger in his mouth, absorbed, with an air almost stupid. When he was six, an old servant... pestered by the child and amused by his innocence, told him, "Go look in the kitchen to see if I'm there." And the child went in to inquire of the cook. "Pierre told me to come to see if he was here." He didn't understand that they wanted to trick him, and in the midst of the laughter he remained dreamy, glimpsing a mystery. [1:17]

Sartre comments at some length on what is revealed in this portrait of a small child. Instead of simply accepting the incident as indicating a lack of understanding on Gustave's part, Sartre asks how it might have come about that he would act upon a supposition which contradicted even his small but definitive experience of the world. He suggests that like many other children, Gustave was frequently subjected to the teasing of parents who told him things which were false but probable:

> that his paymates had not arrived—when they were waiting for him behind the door, that his father had left "to make his rounds" without taking him—whereas the head physician was standing behind him, ready to pick him up and carry him into the carriage. All parents are jokers; duped since childhood, their pleasure is to

dupe their own kids—nicely. They never for a moment suspect that they are driving their children crazy. [1:19–20]

Sartre hastens to add that such conduct is not necessarily deleterious. Other factors enter in to determine how the child will react to spoken words. In Flaubert's case there were the stupors, those odd retreats from the surrounding world when Gustave took on an *air presque bête*. The adjective *bête* means stupid or foolish; as a noun it designates a simpleton or a fool, but also an animal. It has connotations of untamed, natural, innocent. Sartre argues that *bête* and related words held a special significance for Flaubert, one which included all of these meanings. On one occasion he said that the better part of him was poetry—"c'est la *bête*." Sartre writes,

> How many times Gustave will repeat in his correspondence: animals [*les bêtes*], idiots, mad fools, children come to me because they know that "I am one of theirs" [1:35]

Many small children, Sartre claims, like to pretend that they are little animals. This is because they sense that in one way their situation with respect to the adults is not so different from that of domestic dogs and cats around them. They do not really understand the language of the grownups, scarcely distinguish the meaning of words directly addressed to them from the caresses or slaps which similarly convey commands, affection, or disapproval. Young Gustave, Sartre argues, seems to have been able to love people and to feel that he was loved by them "only on the level of a common subhumanity" (1:25).

Still employing the analytic, regressive method, Sartre looks for corroboration and illumination for all these themes—the difficulty with words, the stupors, the animal stupidity—in a juvenile work by Flaubert, *Quidquid Volueris* (*Whatever You Wish*), written when he was fifteen. This is the story of Djalioh, the offspring of a woman and an orangutan. The man responsible for Djalioh's existence was M. Paul, whose motives were decidedly dubious. In part he was motivated by the desire to win a bet which he had made that he could pass off an ape as a man, also by the wish to settle once and for all the debate at the scientific academy as to whether an ape and a human could produce offspring. More passionately, M. Paul, wanting to avenge himself on a slave who had rejected his sexual advances, locked her and the animal together in a room. The woman died in giving birth to Djalioh who, sixteen years later in Europe, passed for human although he caused a feeling of uneasy repugnance in all who saw him. Djalioh secretly loved Adèle, the fiancée and later wife of

M. Paul. Two years after the marriage Djalioh, overwhelmed with accumulated desire and frustration, killed their child, then sexually attacked Adèle so violently that she died. Djalioh, now behaving almost totally like an animal, leapt about the room and fatally hurt himself by striking his head against the marble fireplace. His polished skeleton was displayed in a museum. Despite certain crudities and naïve reflections on the part of its young author, *Quidquid Volueris* is remarkably well constructed and is still able to sustain the reader's interest. Its subject matter, of course, is one quite likely to appeal to a teenager. At the same time there are innumerable other situations and plot possibilities open to an adolescent writer, and it may be significant that Flaubert chose this particular one.

Sartre finds the story filled with autobiographical implications. In Djalioh he sees the child Gustave, not quite animal and not yet fully human, unable to communicate with the adults who form his world. Djalioh has not been taught to read or write. He never speaks. At one point he starts to bring forth some utterance, but those who hear him think it is a sigh. Yet there are suggestions that he does not lack the capacity to produce the appropriate syllables; the problem is rather that the quality of what he feels cannot be put into words. When he is alone with nature, Djalioh experiences an ecstatic pantheistic expansion which is almost mystic. In Flaubert's description of these states Sartre finds the clue to Gustave's animal stupors, the *hébétudes* described by Commanville. He points to one passage in particular:

> Oh! his heart was vast and immense, but vast like the sea, immense and empty as his solitude ... and his whole soul expanded before nature like a rose which blossoms forth in the sun; and he trembled in all his limbs with an inner sensual delight, and his head between his two hands, he fell into a lethargic melancholy.[1]

There are other passages in Flaubert's early writings which suggest this sense of exaltation and feeling of being united with the totality of nature. Sartre notes that the idea of "expanding" (*se dilater*) is very close to that of "dissolving" (*se diluer*), and he claims that it finds its ultimate expression in *The Temptations of Saint Anthony* when the saint's pantheistic longing finally takes the form of desiring to become matter (1:25). The ultimate limit of expanding consciousness is loss of consciousness (1:42–44).

Sartre sees here, too, an anticipation of another of Flaubert's constant themes—the imagery of the high and the low, the fall from the suprahuman to the subhuman. The expanding of Djalioh's soul suggests first a horizontal enlarging but then, by a natural association, exaltation. The lifting up in a thrill of pleasure is followed immediately by a fall into a lethargic melancholy. None of this could be expressed in words by Djalioh—or by the young Gustave. Sartre reminds us that Flaubert in his early years held that poetry *was* the inexpressible; he never lost the belief that to some degree words were incapable of communicating the deepest feelings or the richest experiences. There always remained *"l'indisable."* [2]

Sartre concludes that the child Gustave is badly inserted into language; he remains passive in the active field of discourse. Like Djalioh he is unable to use words to communicate; he fails to see in them any possibility of reciprocity. Although in a certain sense he understands their objective significations, these meanings seem to be attached to them by the Other. As sounds coming to him from the Other (I am reminded of Homer's "winged" words), they resemble things which the Other imposes on him. "He does not speak, he *is spoken*" (1:49). At this stage the word seems to him a tool which others use to perform operations concerning him. His sense of himself as a vast, unlimited consciousness is delimited and stolen from him by the Other's use of words. "Culture, for him, is theft." Later, as Flaubert began to use words against the Other, it seemed to him that he must steal them. (We recall the bastard child Genet, who felt that he had to steal his being.) He must force these verbal tools to convey what they are not designed to express. From the original "bad" relation with words grew the later writer. Or as Sartre puts it, Gustave decided to write at age nine because "he could not read at seven" (1:40). In the beginning words were at most a means of pointing to objects, commands, directions. They were incommensurate with what he felt. Until the agonizing ordeal of being told to read, his sense of merging with natural surroundings was simple pleasure; afterward it became an escape.

This is still not to say why Gustave had trouble in reading, which involves solely the words of the Other, not one's own. In this connection Sartre introduces a new notion—Gustave's passivity. Accustomed to receive words, to use them at most as a directed response to those from whom the words first came, the child is asked suddenly to become an active agent in order to perform the act of reading. This he cannot do. For one is not wholly passive in reading, one acts upon the printed marks to make them live as a communication. Furthermore, for Gustave to read would be to leave that "sweet servile world of childhood" where the heavy stupors were allowed, if not encouraged. Sartre thinks that Gustave's autism and his passivity were inextricably connected.

Gustave's tendency to retreat from the world was not primarily the result of the richness of his inner life. Constant in Flaubert's writing, throughout his entire life, is the feeling of existence as ennui, the sense that life is a burden, that it is too fatiguing. He seems always to have the impression that something is fatally lacking in him. Sartre quotes from a letter written to Mlle Leroyer de Chantepie, who wrote to him admiringly after the publication of *Madame Bovary*.

> It is by means of work that I succeed in silencing my native melancholy. But the bedrock often reappears, that bedrock which nobody knows, the deep, always hidden wound. [1:47]

Sartre points out that the imagery is slightly confused. "A wound" suggests a specific injury, but the reference to a "native melancholy" evokes the idea of a defective nature. Flaubert seems to incline to the second; later on Sartre will show us the sense in which he believes that Gustave's constitution was indeed "wounded" by his treatment in infancy. The secret wound is Gustave's passivity. We must not see in it any "mark of an election"; yet we will watch how the later writer develops, not in spite of but by means of it. Some persons, Sartre tells us, are molded primarily by their histories, which relentlessly crush out the child they have been. Flaubert, on the contrary, "never got out of his childhood" (1:55–56).

Who or what is responsible for the wound? Is it the body? Is it a matter of physiology or of a malformation? Obviously, says Sartre, we can know nothing of the hazards of intrauterine life. In Flaubert's case we have no reliable evidence for his physical condition at any time. Even the cause of the famous nervous crisis is debated. And who is to say, asks Sartre, whether in any case the bodily dispositions are primary (1:50)? One thing seems sure. In his infancy Gustave's passivity expresses his relation with the members of his family.

> Thus the *apathy* is first the family lived at the most elementary psychosomatic level—that of respiration, of sucking, of the digestive functions and those of the sphincters—by a *protected* organism. In accordance with transformations which we will try to discern, Gustave assumes it so as to make of it a more evolved conduct and to assign to it a new function. Passive action becomes a tactic, an elastic defense against a danger better comprehended, the pure blind sense of injury [*ressentir*] becomes resentment [*ressentiment*]. [1:54]

At this point Sartre tells us that we have come as far as regressive analysis can bring us. If we are to advance further, we must resort to a progressive synthesis. Sartre has established the fact of Gustave's passive constitution, which effected a disturbed adjustment to language and a feeling of incapacity before life's demands. If we are going to understand how these things came about, we must try to grasp the quality of Gustave's life in infancy and during the first six years. Sartre recognizes the difficulties. Only external facts can be certainly established for any of that period. No third person has ever directly known the intimate relation between mother and child.

> Under these circumstances one must choose: either abandon the search or glean indications from everywhere, examine the documents from another perspective, in another light, and wrench from them other pieces of information. Of the alternatives, I choose the second. I know that the harvest will be meager. Yet if we are to learn any more details or discover the importance of certain facts which we had neglected, it will be necessary to attempt the progressive synthesis, to make conjectures on these six years which are missing to us and, in a word, to forge a comprehensive hypothesis which reunites the new facts to the troubles of the sixth [seventh?] year in a continuous movement. [1:56]

The validity of the reconstruction admittedly cannot be proved, but Sartre feels that he has at least a check on its verisimilitude. From the time he was thirteen, Gustave Flaubert wrote literary works, as well as letters, which we have at our disposal. The hypothesis may be tested for at least its probability by reference to what the subject himself has revealed of himself in his writing. We have seen already Sartre's use of *Quidquid Volueris* to explain the quality of Gustave's stupors.

Before proceeding to examine the specific details of Flaubert's family situation, Sartre makes one general point: we will look for the earliest influence in the relation between mother and child. It is there that the psychomatic is primary. "Maternal love," Sartre says, "is a relation and not a feeling" (1:57). The baby experiences itself as body through its contact with the mother's body. But the mother projects her whole person into what she does.

> It is *the whole mother* who projects herself into the flesh of her flesh. Her violence is perhaps only awkwardness; perhaps while her hands graze him, she does not cease to speak, to sing to the child who does not yet speak; perhaps he learns, as soon as he knows how to see, his own bodily unity by the smiles which she addresses to him; perhaps, on the contrary, she does what is necessary,

23

neither more nor less, awkwardly and conscientiously without un-clenching her teeth, too absorbed by a care which is displeasing to her. The consequences will be very different in the two instances. [1:58]

But in every case the infant will internalize the mother's activity as the passivity which conditions his every impulse. The mother be-comes *"la structure pathétique de l'affectivité"*; i.e., she provides the passive structure underlying the child's passional life.

Sartre says that the child's constitution is formed under the influence of his prehistory and his protohistory. Prehistory includes the objective structure of the family into which the child is born—the character and social situation of the parents, the number, age, and sex of the siblings. Protohistory refers to the early events—truly or falsely interpreted by the child—within which he slowly constructs what we would call the beginning of his biography, his history proper. It includes the preverbal relation with the parents, especially with the mother. Sartre's opening account of Flaubert's parents seems to be still regressive, but he has already moved into the pro-gressive synthetic by the time he begins to describe the attitude with which the newly born Gustave Flaubert was received and cared for. He anticipates the results in the statement that for Gustave, "His family is a well, he is at the bottom" (1:53). He can strive to rise to the top, but he cannot break down the structures that surround him.

There we have the basic problem. In presenting it, Sartre has touched on several things with which he will be concerned through-out the book. The importance of the relations between mother and in-fant in determining the child's constitution is something which he had hitherto never discussed. One gets the feeling in *Being and Nothing-ness* that the for-itself sprang forth from the ground of being in full maturity—like Athena from the forehead of Zeus. Jean Genet was first a child, to be sure, but Sartre never endowed him with a "con-stitution." This term is entirely new, and the whole idea seems to suggest a limitation on personal freedom which goes beyond even the pictures of alienated human reality in *The Critique of Dialectical Reason*. We may note also, though here it is only suggested, an in-creased importance assigned to a person's sense of his own body. The notion of "passivity," to which Sartre will attach great significance, has been introduced, though at this point it is employed primarily as simply a psychological quality. Finally, Sartre has raised the question of the nature of language as part of the *practico-inert*, the field of worked-over matter, into which we are inserted at our birth.

Sartre holds that the determining parent in Gustave's childhood development was his father, Dr. Achille-Cléophas Flaubert. Since, however, he holds that the mother was the figure responsible for the first tendencies implanted in the boy's emotional constitution, I will consider next what Sartre has told us of her.

## THE MOTHER

The chapter in which Sartre introduces Caroline Fleuriot Flaubert contains some of Sartre's finest writing. As critics have complained, it reads like a novel. The interpretations of Caroline's inner reactions fit the objective facts. The question is whether in real life the inner and outer may safely be assumed to fit together in the way that seems most probable. Even in a brief summation, I think we can see both the persuasiveness of Sartre's account and its novelistic quality.

Caroline was born of parents who loved each other passionately but were separated after less than a year of marriage when the mother died in childbirth. Sartre remarks that a widower frequently holds a grudge against the child "who kills his wife"; the surviving child often feels a sense of guilt. "We shall affirm that this was the case with poor Caroline; at any rate her father did not love her enough to want to survive; *he suffered his unhappiness in his body*" and died when his daughter was ten years old. Feeling obscurely that she was responsible for both deaths, Caroline "would marry only her father." She was entrusted to two ladies of Saint-Cyr, who agreed to care for her until she reached her majority; before that time came, both of them died. A cousin sent her to the home of a Dr. Laumonier, presumably a distant relative. "This child belongs to nobody; she passes from hand to hand; they prefer to die rather than to look after her." Caroline took refuge in her aristocratic ancestry, sustained only by her pride. Dr. Flaubert, a physician, met her in the Laumonier drawing room. Already well established, her elder by years, a man of old-fashioned manners, to her he was her father resuscitated. More like a father than a suitor, Achille-Cléophas decided that the Laumonier household was too loosely ordered and of a moral tone too light for his prospective bride; he had her removed to a pension where she stayed until the eve of their marriage. Caroline was happy to give him the total obedience he demanded, along with the love she had been unable to bestow on her father (1:82–84).

Madame Flaubert referred to the first seven years of her marriage

as the happiest of her life. These included the birth of Achille and of
two children who died. They preceded her move to the Hôtel-Dieu,
the hospital that Achille-Cléophas directed. This setting, in which
the youngsters were accustomed to see the sick being brought in, the
dead removed, where through a peephole they could watch the
medical students dissect corpses, might well have initiated a more
sombre period in Caroline's existence. Sartre feels that the move
there marked for her also a change in her relations with her
husband—his gradual withdrawal into absorbing professional interests and greater responsibilities, and then his infidelities. Gustave
Flaubert has recorded that on one occasion mother and children were
forced to wait in the street while his father went upstairs to chat with
a woman known to be his former mistress; his wife, Flaubert reports,
was neither jealous nor upset (1:96–97). Her husband was too proud
to lie to her. Sartre speculates that the doctor, out of a scornful refusal
to deceive, told his wife about his extramarital affairs. Caroline did
not cease to love him. When he died, she was inconsolable. Catholic
and vaguely deist, in contrast to his agnostic anticlericalism, she lost
her faith when he died, a faith which, Sartre points out, had not been
destroyed by the deaths of her newly born children.[3] It was as
though she felt that she might in some way keep her husband alive by
becoming like what he had been. Though Sartre does not make the
comparison, one may think of Charles Bovary after the death of Emma.
She "corrupted him from the grave," and he tried in his daily life to
exemplify her tastes as best he could. There is a similarity of reaction,
though one may wonder whether his mother's reaction led Flaubert
thus to describe Charles or whether the novel inspired Sartre in his
sketch of Caroline.

Other biographers before Sartre had suggested that Gustave was
jealous of his older brother, who succeeded, where Gustave failed, in
showing himself worthy to continue his father's career in medicine.
Sartre speculates that things might have been different and better for
Gustave if his sense of being rejected by his father had been con-
pensated by an exclusive and intense bond of affection between him
and his mother. Instead he was to find that his mother's love had
been reserved for another just as his father's was already bestowed
on his brother. Sartre, admittedly on very scanty evidence, claims
that Madame Flaubert was desperately anxious to have a daughter. In
the course of twelve years there were six children, only three of
whom lived, then none. To Sartre, particularly with respect to the
three years that included the births of Gustave, another boy who

died after six months, and a sister, named Caroline after her mother, this will for children seems almost "frenetic." He notes that the last three births occurred during the period at the Hôtel-Dieu when Madame Flaubert felt less happy in her husband's love; he suggests that her own unhappy childhood and her lack of intimacy with any female companion made her long for a girl upon whom she could lavish a new kind of affection, one whom she would make happy in compensation for her own lonely early years. Gustave came when Caroline was expected; almost before he was weaned the mother was pregnant again.

Sartre's hypothesis is that Caroline Flaubert, disappointed in her hope of a girl, and not really expecting that this boy would live any longer than the two who preceded him, looked upon him as a child without a future. "I imagine therefore that Madame Flaubert, a wife by vocation, was a mother by duty" (1:136). He pictures her as over-protective but without tenderness. She would anticipate the baby's needs and care for him skillfully. There would be nothing to stimulate a cry of pain or anger, but there would be no loving caresses. She would not speak to him with words whose intention he would grasp without language, would not assure him by smiles and facial movements that something was being expressed to which he was expected to respond. In short, the baby was given a mother's attention but not love, care but not caring. He experienced himself "as the object of the maternal cares but not their destination." He was the recipient of actions but never initiated them. Handled like a delicate instrument, he had no experience of human relations; he sensed the feeling that he was being raised with no expectancy of a future. His needs were filled, but the poverty of tenderness resembled undernourishment; it did not provoke in him any aggression. Most important of all, the infant developed no sense of his own value. For any baby, although hunger or some other need comes from within, his first emerging sense of himself as a separate being is necessarily bound up with his realization of himself as being cared for as an object. But "if the mother loves him, . . . he gradually discovers his being-an-object as his being-loved." As a "subjective object," he is not only the recipient of attentions but their goal. He is a value. Sartre claims that the well-loved child receives a precious gift which will affect his entire life.

This monster is an absolute monarch, always an end, never a means. Let a child be able once in his life, at three months, at six, to taste this happiness of pride, and he is a man. For the rest of his existence he will be able neither to revive the supreme pleasure of reigning nor to forget it. But he will preserve, even in misfortune, a kind of religious optimism which is based on the abstract, tranquil certitude of his value. Miserable, he is still one of the privileged. We shall see in any case that there is no common measure between an existence begun in this way and that of Flaubert. [1:136–37n.]

The child who is physically well cared for but deprived of maternal love is likely to develop a deep-rooted passivity, a psychosomatic pattern of conduct, which appears as a defect in his constitution. Sartre claims that the baby internalizes the attitude of such a mother as an inclination to submit to whatever happens without any external response, to receive what comes as inevitable or at least as something not to be overcome, just as the physical cripple or blind person must accept his deprivation as a given fact. He sees in this attitude the origin of Flaubert's later fainting fits, which in themselves are consent to passivity carried to the extreme although, as we shall see, they may represent a positive strategy in relation to his total behavior complex.

But was this really the relation between Gustave and his mother for those first two years? Sartre's next words bring us up short.

I admit this is a fable. Nothing proves that it was like this. . . . My narrative fits infants in general, not Gustave in particular. That doesn't matter. I wanted to pursue it to the end for this sole reason: the *real* explanation, I can imagine, without being the least disturbed, may be exactly the opposite of the one I invent. *In any case* it would have to pass by the paths which I indicate and would have to refute mine on the terrain which I have defined—the body, love. I have spoken of maternal love; it is this which fixes for the newborn the objective category of otherness; it is this which, during the first weeks, permits the child to feel as *other*, as soon as he can recognize it—the satiny flesh of the breast. [1:139–40]

Suppose we grant that Sartre is right in linking the mother's attitude with the child's discovery of himself as a body and with his affective disposition. Does this justify Sartre in basing his reconstruction of Flaubert's life on the assumption that "Gustave is immediately conditioned by his mother's indifference"? If the *particular* relation between mother and child is so decisive, then what we need are not reasons why it is so but specific evidence to show that either Caroline Flaubert cared for her child with a dutiful, cold resentment or, on the contrary, loved him deeply and overwhelmed him with smiles, caresses, and a multitude of verbal and bodily expressions of endearment. How are we to react to Sartre's cavalier admission of total lack of pertinent information? If he were interested only in outlining a method for biographical study or for psychotherapy, then we could agree that it doesn't matter whether in the case of Flaubert, for example, suspicions of maternal coldness are correct or not. But if the book is supposed among other things to demonstrate that the method can in this particular instance lead us to knowledge and understanding of the real Flaubert, then it matters very much whether or not Sartre's hypothesis is true to the fact.

I do not believe that this disturbing passage need make us conclude that a lack of evidence or even a possible falsification of the true facts at this crucial point has so vitiated Sartre's interpretation that there is no reason to read on—assuming that we do indeed want to learn something about Flaubert and not just about Sartre as some critics have suggested. At least this much may be said in Sartre's defense: he has not arbitrarily invented the novel of Caroline Flaubert and then wrenched known facts about her famous son so as to fit the hypothesis. Rather he has proceeded upon the basis of what Flaubert's own writings and the testimonies of his contemporaries have shown us to be recognizable characteristics of his personality, to find a hypothesis which would be in harmony with those facts. If we grant the importance of the first mother-child relation, some sort of hypothesis is not only permitted but obligatory. Our sense as to its rightness will depend on whether we feel that Sartre is successful in singling out Flaubert's passive constitution as the essential core of his existence. For the moment let us look simply at those things that Sartre believes to be directly consequent to the early deprivation of maternal love.

Gustave Flaubert developed a passive constitution because he was "underloved" (*mal-aimé*). In explaining the cause-and-effect relation between the lack of maternal love and passivity, Sartre begins by referring to the underloved infant's sense of nonvalorization. Every child, Sartre urges, ought to feel that he has been given a mandate to live. He should be instilled with the feeling that he is a movement toward a goal—like a "conscious arrow" with awareness of the intoxication of flight but a sureness with regard to his points of departure and the target. Feeling himself to be a supreme end, the child will consent to become the unique means of those who idolize him. To do so is his *raison d'être*. He has a mission and he is assured of reciprocity. "Live so as to fulfill us [*combler*], in order that we may be able to fulfill you in turn" (1:140). The baby develops the conviction that he is here *for* something.

That either humanity in general or the individual person is born with a mandate is so flagrantly in contradiction with what Sartre has written hitherto that this passage comes as a shock. In *The Words* Sartre bitterly reproaches himself for having cherished for fifty years his own conviction that he had been given the mandate to write. In *Being and Nothingness*, the statement, "Man is a useless passion," meant, among other things, that man is not *for* anything except that he is for himself in the sense that he and he alone makes himself what he becomes and creates his own values. Apparently in this passage Sartre himself was haunted by echoes of *Being and Nothingness*, for in making his present intention clear he uses one of his old analogies, that of the hammer. The underloved child, the one who is not enabled, through his mother's love, to feel that he has a mandate, does in fact thereby glimpse prematurely what he will later discover to be a "truth of reason." For the being of a hammer and the existence of a man have no common measure: the hammer is there for hammering; man is not there *for* anything; he is "thrown into the world" (1:143). This is one of the very few occasions when Sartre gives a positive value to feeling as opposed to reason; even here the concession to the emotional needs of the child is a step toward the discovery of a truth. "The truth [that man has neither a mandate nor a built-in purpose like the hammer] is intelligible only at the end of a long vagabond error; if it is imbibed *at the start*, it is only a true error."

When Sartre urges that children should be spared the unhappiness of knowing that they "exist without reason," he is not merely saying that they are too weak to bear the pain that must eventually come to all of us with our recognition of the truth of our existential condition. He means that if the child *feels* too early the truth of what he will someday *know*, he will miss two other true aspects of human reality. First, he will not realize himself as an active agent, will not know the meaning of praxis. If no response is expected of him, if the satisfaction of his needs is not related in any direct way to his attempt to express them, he will form no notion of himself as one who does things. The experience of being sovereign in his small universe accustoms the child to think of himself as called upon to give commands, to order, to arrange. In short, the delusion of being sole and absolute monarch prefigures, but without anguish, the existential situation in which the adult will discover that through his actions he must carve out his being in the world. Without the loving attention that makes him at once both loved object and cherished subjectivity, he is likely to view himself as only a passive thing in the world, only a recipient of action, wholly determined by what comes to him from the outside.[4]

As for the feeling of possessing a mandate, of having a mission—this experience by itself is neither true nor false. What is involved here is the sense that a life is meaningful and purposeful. Life taken by itself, Sartre holds now as in the 1940s, has no meaning. Human existence is contingent; the universe offers it no reason for being. But human reality provides a human meaning. "The meaning of a life comes to the living person by the human society which supports it and through the parents who engender it" (1:141). I think that Sartre is making two points here. First, the human person is by definition "*sinngebend*," a giver of meanings. His conduct is meaningful because it is always performed with some end in view. To live is to project oneself toward one kind of future rather than another. No life is without significance to the one who lives it or to those whom it touches, however slightly. Even the nameless dead, Sartre told us in *Being and Nothingness,* are not forgotten. By their individual and collective choices, as by their refusals to choose, they have made their historical period and the history of the human race what it has been. Sartre's second point is less a statement than a plea. When he says that parents engender a meaning and that society supports it, when he adds that in the same way they may also constitute non-meanings by sentencing human needs to remain unsatisfied, he is pleading for a community in which the intentional action of individuals will not be deviated, in which free action will not be alienated against the agent. To claim that every child has a right to that love which bestows upon him a mandate is not to lay claim to a nonhuman categorical imperative. It is not to impose upon the child a demand and a destiny which come from someone else. It is to urge that children be given the promise that their efforts to carve out their being in the world will be welcomed and sustained. It is tell them that they have a value and that what they do matters. It is simultaneously to announce to them their freedom and their responsibility.

It is the presence or absence of maternal love which is primarily responsible for either endowing the child with the gift of himself as a free agent or weighing him down with a passive constitution. Sartre states that he looks upon maternal love, "not as an emotion but as a relation." All the same, when he describes it and when he refers to

Flaubert as *un mal-aimé,* he leaves no doubt that it is indeed love he is talking about. Does this love bear any relation whatsoever to love as Sartre described it in *Being and Nothingness?* We must recall that in the earlier work there is a certain ambiguity as to whether the description of "concrete relations with others" applies to human relations as they must be or only to those in bad faith. Sartre himself has stated explicitly that one need not be tossed back and forth between the extreme alternatives of trying to lose one's subjectivity in the Other or exploiting the Other as object in order to guarantee oneself as sole subject.[5] At the same time he states quite definitely that conflict and not being-with (*mitsein*) is at the origin of all human relations, just as sexuality remains always an ingredient of them. I myself believe that for Sartre the subject-object conflict remains at the root and origin of human relations, but that love in good faith is possible as a triumph over that conflict. Be that as it may, I think we may see both a profound difference and points in common between the analysis of love in *Being and Nothingness,* where the examples are drawn from erotic love, and the discussion of maternal love in *The Family Idiot.*

One dissimilarity strikes us at once. In the earlier book love was defined as the desire to be loved. In the new context Sartre is not concerned with what the mother hopes to receive from the child; i.e., with her motives in loving. A mother might attempt to make her child wholly dependent on her and a projection of herself, but this would be to be in bad faith. If, on the other hand, Sartre meant to suggest that the mother ought to subordinate herself wholly to the child, making him her whole reason for living, he would rightly receive a monitory tap on the shoulder from Simone de Beauvoir. But Sartre is concerned with the mother who in loving her child is not putting her emotional needs first and who wants him to be a free and responsible human agent. Sartre's implied reproach, that the majority of children are—like Flaubert—*mal-aimés,* suggests that the relation of maternal love might depend partly upon a good or evil will as well as on the chances of a spontaneous upsurge of emotion.

In spite of this radical difference we can see a connection between the two analyses. In *Being and Nothingness* the lover wishes to preserve the Other's subjectivity even as he does everything possible to insure that the beloved will place the highest value on the lover's subjectivity in turn. The ideal would be a oneness-in-otherness in which each Other would freely and perfectly support the Other's image of himself without making himself an object. This is impossible since two people cannot become one while remaining two. Nevertheless Sartre does establish a certain reciprocity in his study of sexual desire and the caress. Through caresses, when there is mutual desire, each of the pair of lovers seeks insofar as possible to incarnate his/her consciousness in flesh. One may think of sexual desire as the desire to possess. In fact, Sartre does speak of one's longing to capture the Other's consciousness by lifting it from the surface of his flesh as one skims off the rich cream from the milk. But there is reciprocity as well since it is a mutual incarnation. Insofar as each consciousness has willed itself to be flesh, there is even a union of consciousness, though certainly not a merging or a oneness. In maternal love the mother's caress reveals the baby to himself as a "loved object." But if the caress is directed toward the infant as a total and valuable being, the caress serves here, too, to convey that it is a consciousness which is being sought and cherished. There is a solicitation of the child's subjectivity. Love is a language, Sartre said in *Being and Nothingness*. The mother's caress tells the child that he is valued and that a response from him is being sought. In his study of Flaubert, Sartre goes one step farther. Not only does touch convey the message from the mother's consciousness; its consequence for the child takes on a lasting endurance in the realm of the psychosomatic. The body plays an important role in Sartre's later thought as we will see throughout his discussion of Flaubert's development. In *Being and Nothingness* he carefully avoids any mind-body dualism. Although consciousness cannot be explained as an epiphenomenon of bodily functions, still it is *nothing except body*.[6] The body is the facticity of consciousness, its way of being-in-the-world. Thus we may say that as the child becomes conscious of being a body, it is his way of being-in-the-world that is revealed to him. This includes also, of course, his realization of himself as an Other in a world of Others.

Returning to Gustave Flaubert, we find that Sartre adds several corollaries to the passivity that comes from being deprived of maternal love. First, the child who senses himself as only a passive object experiences his life as "universal monotony; later he will call it 'ennui'" (1:144). In truth Flaubert complained of an undercurrent of ennui throughout all of his adult life. In writing about his adolescence, he called himself "a mushroom stuffed with ennui." Sartre finds the image apt in that it stresses the vegetative existence of the passively constituted. The comparison is also unflattering and indicates a dislike of self. That, too, is appropriate. The infant internalizes the lack of love, the nonvalorization as self-disgust. Sartre insists that Gustave Flaubert never learned to love himself and that here is the root of his well-known misanthropy. It is connected also, as we have seen, with his difficulty with language. "To speak is to act," but Gustave has not learned to act. Nor has he learned reciprocity, which is the essence of all true communication. Language and its meanings come solely from the Other, and so does his own meaning—or lack of it.

In describing the condition of Gustave in his first six years, Sartre introduces a startling comparison which binds together all of the preceding qualities and has particular relevance to Flaubert's sympathetic attitude toward "animality" (*bestialité*). He compares the small Gustave to a domesticated animal, especially to a lapdog in the living room. The passage follows the reference to Flaubert's lifelone ennui.

> Pure *"ennui de vivre"* is a pearl of culture. It appears evident that household animals suffer from ennui. They are homunculi, sorry reflections of their masters. Culture has penetrated them, ruining nature in them without replacing it. Language is their major frustration. They roughly understand its function but do not have the use of it. This restricts them to being *spoken*. We speak to them, we speak of them, they know it; this verbality potentiality, which is both manifest to them and denied to them, pierces through them, is installed in them as the limit of their powers. It is a disquieting privation which they forget in solitude and which denounces them *in their nature* when they find people again. I have seen fear and rage mount up in a dog. We were speaking of him, he knew it at once because our faces were turned toward him, snoozing there on the carpet, and because the sounds struck him full force as if we addressed ourselves to him. Yet we were talking to each other; he knew it, words appeared to designate him as our interlocutor and yet came to him blocked off. . . . This dog passed from anxiety to rage at having felt at his expense the strange reciprocal mystification which is the relation between man and animal. [1:144–45]

Sartre goes on to say that this rage must not be confused with rebellion. The dog summoned up anger in order "to simplify his problems" and soon calmed down, returning to lick hands and to please with clownish tricks. Sartre claims that at moments like the one described, the animal experiences a movement toward transcendence which is cut short. Somehow made to feel that immanence in nature is not enough, he is yet incapable of arriving at full self-reflection. "If Gustave shares this nostalgia with the animals, it is because he, too, has been domesticated." Love teaches, Sartre says; but if love is lacking, all that remains is animal training, a breaking-in (*dressage*) (1:146).

Bearing in mind both what seems to be Gustave's self-projection into the half-animal Djalioh (whose name, incidentally, was that of a dog in the Flaubert household[7]) and the adult Flaubert's statement that he had a special affinity with children and animals because he "resembled them," Sartre concludes that the little Gustave, like many children, felt himself to be a small animal. With both adults and children, Sartre claims, childhood is an animal category. For the child confronted by the first difficult demands from the outside world (e.g., learning to read), it is a category he is reluctant to abandon.

> Culture being recognized as the prerogative of the adult age, the child radically rejects it by making himself Nature forever; by the same token he finds a myth to explain his first resistance to acculturation: he is an animal, animals do not speak. [1:358]

The image of the lapdog sums up neatly Sartre's reconstruction of the small boy imbued with passivity as the result of his mother's conscientious but loveless care. Language seems to be something which points to him but in which he does not participate. He is not the initiator of meaningful action; his life is a repetition of movements without goals. As we may like to imagine happens with our domesticated pets, this external monotony is compensated by an inner life marked by a nonverbal contented sinking back into the bosom of nature. There is one other point of comparison. So far as we can tell, the animal has no clear self-image. Sartre claims that Gustave, because of his never realizing himself as an active agent, felt that his ego was imposed on him by the Other as words were. He was what others declared him to be. He was an actor whose role was given to him and who was nothing other than his role. *His ego was an alter ego.* R. D. Laing observes that the schizoid individual cannot relate to real persons but only to phantoms, to things, and to animals.[8] Sartre does not claim that Gustave was schizoid; the retreat into stupors and the affinity with animals are naturally linked in a child who has a tendency to retreat from the real world into an imaginary one. Passivity blurs our sense of the real, action sharpens it.

Sartre's passage on the dog's ennui and frustration is of special interest, quite apart from its connection with his immediate project. It is the sole instance in which he speaks directly of animals and hints at a possible metaphysics of nature. *Being and Nothingness* makes no mention of animals. Are they part of Being-in-itself, or are they at least a rudimentary form of Being-for-itself? I have always assumed that not having *self-consciousness*, they would be on the side of the In-itself, but they clearly possess *intentional consciousness*. There is a problem. In *The Family Idiot* Sartre seems to be saying that an animal may, especially after long association with humans, make an abortive movement toward transcending nature in a new self-awareness. Typically and even a little cynically, Sartre regards this as an impairment of the animal condition rather than an advance. The leap is never achieved.

> Without culture the animal would not be bored; it would live, that's all. Haunted by this absence, it lives—as an obliviating fall back into animality—the impossibility of surpassing itself. Nature is discovered in resignation. *L'ennui de vivre* is a consequence of man's oppression of the beasts; it is nature apprehending itself as the absurd terminus of a limiting process instead of realizing itself as a biological spontaneity. [1:146]

Some may object that Sartre is too anthropomorphic here and that to project metaphysical impulses into the mind of a dog is one degree worse than imagining Caroline Fleuriot's emotions before her marriage. But I prefer to see in it an indication that Sartre at least acknowledges the possibility, if not the need, of a metaphysics of nature which would link his ontology to scientific evolutionary theories.[9] This is one place where one might wish that he had not checked so quickly his impulse to digress from the subject in hand. As it stands, this brief discussion is as rich in suggestion and as tantalizing as the single sentence in the conclusion of *Being and Nothingness*, which hints that motion might be viewed as a first attempt on the part of Being-in-itself to found itself, an anticipation of the emergence of the self-conscious For-itself.[10]

While it would be premature at this stage of our discussion to ask whether Sartre's description of Gustave as a child underloved by his mother is a hypothesis which indeed seems to work out pragmatically in helping us to understand and explain the personality of the adolescent and adult revealed in his correspondence and in his literary works, I want to comment briefly on Sartre's presentation of the mother herself. I think we may distinguish between two kinds of novelistic devices which he uses. Often he simply invites us to let our own imaginations, under his guidance, restore to us the inner flavor of a situation or event which is established externally, to attempt a comprehension of the meaning of *le vécu*, the lived experience, as it must have been to the one who suffered it. This device is not a departure from the practice of our best biographers; there is no confusion in the reader's mind between what he is asked to accept as fact and what he is offered as empathetic interpretation. At other points Sartre uses as a fact with consequences an inner attitude, where the only possible evidence is the consequences themselves. Once again this is not an unheard-of procedure; we are accustomed to judge a person's motives by his actions, though we are admittedly sometimes mistaken. But when the psychological disposition is elaborately reconstructed and when the known facts are few and susceptible to a number of different explanations, one becomes uneasy. If the imaginative hypothesis is confined to a limited area, we may feel inclined to accept it as at least an interesting possibility and one which does no harm. But if it becomes a cornerstone of the interpretive edifice, then we are in the position of Socrates' student, who complained that after tentatively granting a number of uneasy admissions, he suddenly found himself confronting a proposition with totally inadequate support.

We find all of these techniques in Sartre's discussion of Caroline Fleuriot Flaubert. Sartre's colorful statement, 'They preferred to die rather than to look after her," and his suggestion that Caroline felt obscurely guilty for having caused the deaths are admittedly purely fictional representations of what was in the child's mind. But Sartre does not insist on the guilt or use it as an important motif in later discussion. If not taken too literally, his description fits poor Caroline's situation. How could she possibly not have felt herself to be an unwelcome burden? Her granddaughter testifies to the tradition that Caroline as a child was of "an eminently serious disposition." To say that "she would marry only her father" is going too far, but it is reasonable to infer that in her relation to Achille-Cléophas there was something of the child-wife. A certain silent, mournful resignation appears to have been characteristic of her. That she was submissive rather than assertive, still less rebellious, is in harmony with the evidence as is Sartre's picture of her as totally devoted to her husband. Sartre uses the tale of the doctor's visit to his former mistress, while his wife and children waited in the street, as an opportunity to speculate on the doctor's character: his caddishness and the strange combination of personal pride and respect for his wife which led him not to lie to her. The *London Times* reviewer objects that we know nothing about the duration of the visit nor of the husband's inner feelings. True. And it is possible that Gustave was deceived by his mother's apparent unconcern. But that is no reason to question, as the reviewer does, whether the incident ever actually occurred since "the only source is a casual reminiscence of Flaubert, who, on such points, was often less than precise."[11] It is hardly a likely thing for him to have invented. And it is Flaubert who tells us that his father did not conceal the truth because "he was too superior for that." Such an episode demands commentary and in this instance I think Sartre's speculations are justified.

A more important point is Sartre's claim that Madame Flaubert desperately wanted a girl and was disappointed when Gustave was born. There is no verbal evidence whatsoever for this. Sartre's argument that Caroline's frequent pregnancies producing five boys (including the three who died at birth or soon afterward) and the cessation of childbearing after the daughter's birth indicate an ardent desire for a girl is mildly persuasive but not really convincing. The giving of her own name to the baby might possibly be connected with the mother's wish to live her lost youth over again more happily in her daughter, though we must remember that the granddaughter was also called Caroline. By itself the hypothesis is plausible and innocuous. But when Sartre suggests that it was this longing for a daughter that was to a large degree responsible for the mother's not loving her son, he goes much beyond the evidence. If we find no further reason to accept Sartre's view of the probable relation between mother and infant, this one by itself will simply not do. Sartre is at his most fascinating, and his most outrageous and least excusable, in a footnote in which he links with Madame Flaubert's supposed desire for a girl, the deaths of her three children and her reception of Gustave.

> Of course the mortality rate at that time was severe. Still the disappearance of those three young males has always seemed to me suspicious. For lack of being "mothered" a child disappears—at one month, at three months. Can we imagine that the virtuous and "glacial" Caroline senior was the cause of their precipitate retreat? Alarmed by the preceding deaths, she would have made an effort for Gustave. It is to that that he would owe his life. Just in time. But subsequently she would have exclaimed, "Still another one!" The newborn, in the face of that welcome, would have hastened to return beneath the earth. [1:723]

Admittedly, Sartre does not try to force this hypothesis upon the reader; it is not essential to his argument. As a literary device, this suggestion without insistence is extremely effective in influencing our feelings about Caroline Flaubert. Ironically, it is exactly the kind of preposterous statement which would have elicited an appreciative guffaw from Gustave Flaubert himself—if it had been made about anyone other than his own mother. But Sartre's faintly comic treatment of the tragic deaths of the infants borders on the offensive. It inclines one to sympathize with Harry Levin's querulous outburst, "[The book] debases and trivializes whatever it touches."[12]

The most essential question, of course, is whether Flaubert's first relations with his mother were, in fact, responsible for his passive constitution and whether, indeed, this passivity was a basic stru-ature in the personality that developed in the course of maturing life. It is too early for us to try to answer this. Our next step is to consider what Sartre has said about Gustave's relations with his older brother and with their father.

## The Father and the Brother

Sartre believes that Gustave's mother was primarily responsible for his passive constitution and that his older brother, Achille, was the object of an intense jealousy which colored all of his reactions in his early years. But it was the father, Achille-Cléophas, who, in Sartre's opinion, was the determinant factor not only in Gustave's develop-ment but in the lives of the mother and Achille as well. Sartre's sketch of his origins and his character both differentiates the man and sets him in his period.

Achille-Cléophas Flaubert was born of rural stock, in a family whose male members had traditionally been veterinarians. Some-how they managed to send him to study at Paris where he did so well that he was given a grant from the state allowing him to complete his training as a physician and surgeon. He practiced in Rouen; in 1819, two years before Gustave was born, he was appointed director of the city hospital. Meanwhile he had married Caroline Fleuriot, who had on her mother's side connections with the minor nobility. Achille-Cléophas is a clear example of upward social mobility. Respected as a brilliant diagnostician, he not only treated the leading families of Rouen professionally, but was received at their dinner parties. Yet he was not really one of them. With an income below that required of voters, he could be only what Sartre calls a "passive citizen."[13] He himself seemed to emphasize rather than to downplay his agricultural origins. When the successful physician went on his rounds of house calls, he wore a goatskin jacket—like a peasant. He was grateful to the Bonapartist regime under which he had succeeded so well as a medical student; he was mildly liberal and critical of the government after the restoration of Charles X. But he was far from being a radical antimonarchist. Although he had friends among the wealthy industrialists, he himself invested his sizable earnings in land— as his fathers would have done. Most important, the Flaubert family structure displays signs of his split and of a certain social "hysteresis." This is the period of what Sartre calls the "conjugal family." Among the contemporary bourgeois, women were gradually assuming a certain importance, a position which if not fully liberated was at least influential and to some degree emancipated. Couples tended to have fewer children and to value them as individuals. But Dr. Flaubert was a paterfamilias of the old-fashioned kind, one who expected his wife to be subservient and his children to follow in paths marked out by himself. His wife was less honored, his children less free.

What sort of person was the doctor? Sartre describes him as one who was admired and liked by the citizens of Rouen, who found him both gentle and amiable. His students revered and feared him. Sartre speaks of his occasional melancholy, his frequent irritability and displays of temper. He seems to have been in some respects typical of scientists of his period. He aimed to achieve an objective, analytic, rational approach in life as in his work. Whether he embraced specifically the atheistic materialism of the eighteenth century is uncertain; he was certainly anticlerical. Sartre does not hesitate to refer to him as an atheist. He apparently shared in the prevailing attitude of the science of his day, which was to attempt to explain human beings mechanistically. Perhaps his philosophy of life may best be described as scientific naturalism. He made himself eminently bourgeois. As with most of his fellow citizens, his outlook was utilitarian, finding it natural that everyone should look to his own self-interest. And of course money was important.

> Science pays; that is just. The benefactor is humanity, a great man is recompensed by the money which is given to him. Therefore money is an honor. [1:79]

The bourgeois tended to place value on the strong individual; the scientific theory of the day was atomistic. The economic ideal was *laissez-faire,* with the law of supply and demand treated as one of the sacred laws of nature. Nowhere was there stress on community or on a totality in which the part found its meaning and enrichment in the whole. In the Flaubert family, life was lived around the idolized doctor, but it resembled "a solitude in common" (1:80).

As Sartre colorfully puts it, after the first mutant tears himself from the earth to perch on a limb, all birds have wings. Its descendants can flit from branch to branch, but who will admire them for that? The Flaubert children could hardly hope to repeat the doctor's ascent by moving into a still higher social class. We may now say that Gustave Flaubert ultimately finally surpassed his father, but this happened long after the latter's death. The paterfamilias naturally assumed that his sons would be physicians. Within the sphere of medicine the only reasonable hope for them was that they might seem not to lag too far behind their father. It is not unusual for a son to follow in his father's footsteps even today—whether freely or as the result of psychological pressure. Sartre, however, feels that it was Achille-Cléophas' clinging to his ancestral patterns which caused him to expect that his first-born would "inherit" the paternal position. Evidently this attitude would have profound effects upon Achille and upon Gustave, who was nine years younger.

Achille is the rightful successor of his father, not even the "chosen." Achille could be *deduced* like the consequence following logically from the first term of the series. "His father is sure of him; in this frightful certainty he engenders his son and by the same stroke kills him" (1:110). Achille cannot escape the crushing weight of his father's expectation. "A new Acneas, he lowers his head and takes Anchises on his back" (1:119). As a medical student he won highest honors. He worked with his father at Rouen and succeeded him as director of the hospital after his father's death. He appears never to have wanted anything else. Sartre notes that Achille, too, though in his home and his social habits he assumed a new sophistication, wore a goatskin jacket like his father's when he went on his rounds. He was not an original scientist; we are told that he often referred to his father as authority—"ipse dixit." Unless the father wished to be surpassed by his son, he could hardly have asked anything more.

Sartre is careful to point out that neither Achille's ability to succeed his father nor his inability to go beyond him is to be explained by native "intelligence." In *Being and Nothingness* Sartre insisted that the individual's consciousness is in no way determined by any of the great primary "givens" of heredity and environment. Now he still rejects the idea of genetic inheritance in the form of talent or special gifts, but he argues that society and the family play a role in deciding what is to be called "intelligent" and in eliciting appropriate responses from the individual.

> Achille did not owe to his exceptional intelligence the confidence which his father never ceased to place in him; he owed the rare qualities of his mind to the irrevocable decision which, from the time of his conception, perhaps even before that, had made him the princely heir of Science. [1:116]

In short, Achille was not born with a specifically endowed nature which led him to excel in sciences rather than to prefer literature as his brother did. Each boy responded to the situation in which he found himself. Sartre grants that in the case of creative thought which breaks away from established patterns, we may need to search for other reasons. (This is, in fact, what he has done with Gustave Flaubert.) But Achille produced nothing. He merely attained to "that character which we all have in common."

> Shall we say that this intelligence *imitates* or that it *borrows?* As you like. My opinion is that it is *awakened.* [1:117]

What happened, Sartre claims, is that under the favorable influence of parental love and expectant care, Achille opened his mind and heart to full development, in harmonious relation with his immediate environment. It was this very ease that resulted in his going no farther. Inheriting rather than earning the high esteem of the citizens of Rouen, he strove merely to retain it. Achille-Cléophas thirsted to achieve new scientific knowledge; Achille strove to keep abreast of the recent discoveries by others. It was enough for him to fill the place his father had created for him; he felt no need to enlarge it (1:106).

Somewhat unexpectedly Sartre asks, "Did Achille-Cléophas *love* him?" The answer he gives certainly has ironic overtones, but is somewhat sympathetic. As the father came to feel more and more that he could rely upon his son, he began to entrust to him an increasingly large proportion of the work to be done. Freed from full responsibility of caring for patients, Achille-Cléophas had time to work on a treatise on physiology by which he might perpetuate his name, and he took pleasure in acknowledging that this would not have been possible without Achille.

> We can imagine this reciprocity. The father was storing up for future joys for himself while preparing his son for future duties, for

future honors; the son could not fail to see himself as both the father's supreme end and the means of his glory. . . . Everything bound the two men together: past, future; at present each new illness was a collaboration. They discussed the case with deliberation, and the clinical idea arose in the head of either one indifferently. Is this to love? Yes. [1:120]

Love was "work in common, a precious confidence," not demonstrative, but intimate. The father had made the son, and he took pleasure in his handiwork.

The culmination came when the father, fatally ill, had to have an operation and insisted, against the wishes of his colleagues, that his son must perform it. A striking expression of family pride, Sartre says: "Only a Flaubert can take care of a Flaubert." Achille did so, and the doctor died. There was no reason to blame Achille, but it might suggest the son's ritualistic murder of the father. Sartre sees in it a rite of succession—"Save me or replace me" (1:121).

In the light of this feudal relation between the father and his first-born, it is not surprising that Sartre introduces the birth of Gustave in a chapter entitled "The Birth of a Younger Son." When Gustave at age seven was having trouble learning to read, Achille at sixteen was winning honors at school. The younger child was almost certainly reminded that the older one had learned easily when his mother taught him earlier. If Sartre is correct, however, overt feelings of jealousy probably did not manifest themselves until about the time of Gustave's reading fiasco. By an imaginative and yet reasonable use of hypothesis, Sartre attempts to reconstruct the family drama: for two years Gustave was almost exclusively in the hands of his mother; then Dr. Flaubert began to take an interest in him. He took the tiny boy along with him on his daily rounds. These three or four years Sartre refers to as the Golden Age. The nine years between Achille and himself prevented any sense of jealousy in Gustave. Achille was one of "the grownups"; moveover, for a large part of that time he must have been away at school.

What caused Gustave to feel that he had been expelled from Paradise? The failure with reading served to crystallize the difficulties, but it was a culmination rather than a first cause. Several things were involved. By now Gustave was beginning to perceive that he was expected to follow in Achille's path; comparisons unfavorable to him were being made; even before realizing the full consequences of what it meant to be the second son, he may have feared what lay before him. In addition Sartre suggests that the age of seven or thereabouts is a difficult period for any child—and for its parents. Just a bit earlier, at five or six, the child enters into an awkward, unattractive phase. Sartre writes,

> We know the effects of weaning on the nurseling; I believe that we can, at the thankless age of childhood, speak of a mother's counterweaning. At this time she discovers the radical otherness of the being she had taken for her reflection. [1:365]

The mother, Sartre says, finds herself illogically irritated by the timid yet inadequate thrusts toward independence. The docile infant is gone, but the child left in its place is incapable of looking after itself and still demands constant attention. From the child's point of view it is the others who have changed. He is scolded for behavior which formerly elicited a sympathetic laugh; he is called upon to perform for himself tasks which used to be done for him and which he finds difficult to do. In Gustave's case, Sartre implies the equivalent of a counterweaning initiated by the father. Dr. Flaubert suddenly gives up taking the little boy with him on his rounds. The father, Sartre suggests, who found it easy to think his own thoughts when accompanied by a tiny toddler, now finds himself inconvenienced by the babbling nuisance who demands his attention. Gustave feels he is in disgrace. The inability to read at first instruction brings on more tangible disapproval. Whether or not he actually hears the word "retarded," Gustave senses it in his father's attitude. From this point on, if Sartre is correct, Gustave Flaubert felt that he lived under a paternal malediction.

Now we can better understand the significance of the crisis with reading. Made passive by his mother and unaccustomed to internalize words so as to make them his own and thereby constitute from them a meaning, he is incapable of performing the action required for reading. Furthermore his reluctance to leave once and for all the Golden Age in which he might hope to have his father's love without having to prove himself worthy of it sets up a further internal block. He struggles and is made to feel still more inferior by the unfavorable comparison with Achille's earlier performance. Finally there is his sense of the father's judgment—"He is retarded." The child's love of the paterfamilias is rejected; he feels loved by neither parent. Henceforth Flaubert will carry with him an obscure sense that something essential is lacking in him and that he has been cursed because of it; he will be intensely jealous of the favored brother and will alternate between resentment and the feeling that his own condemnation is deserved because of some deep flaw within him.

Sartre points to emotional privation in respect to both parents as one of the factors that pushed Gustave toward a preference for the imaginary. The mediating term is the passivity. Although Sartre attributes the chief responsibility for Flaubert's constitution to his mother, he thinks that the father reinforced it. He claims that in the wake of the two boys' deaths, both parents refused to allow themselves to believe in his survival. This may have been partly responsible for the mother's first repression of tenderness. The father, too, would find no reason to think of the infant as a future agent with a destiny. As one who might well be fated not to live, Gustave was overprotected but underloved. If a baby's needs are anticipated rather than responded to, his sense of any relation between his actions and that which comes to him out of the environment is missing. In a statement made in an interview after publication, Sartre even more pointedly makes both parents responsible for Flaubert's passivity.

> It has two causes: the nurseling's handling by a mother with little love and the crisis Gustave met at age seven in learning to read, when his father took him in hand in an authoritarian and repressive way.[14]

Sartre goes on to say (or to imagine) that the father used Achille as a model and reproach to the younger son, thus giving him a sense of inferiority and intensifying his passivity.

Building upon this notion of passivity, Sartre claims that "it is a general fact that when we find ourselves confronting the impossibility of responding to the demands of the world by an act, the world loses its reality." The point is so important to him that he gives two examples. The first is an experience recorded by André Gide. In Venice Gide once found himself at night in a gondola in the middle of the lagoon. Threatened by gondoliers who were thinking of taking his money and possibly his life, he quite coolly sat there unconcerned in a mood of amused bewilderment. "Nothing was real, and the world was playing" (1:666).[15] There follows a reference to an event in Sartre's life. The occasion was during the war. He found himself in a situation in which he knew that if he remained stationary, the Germans would fire at him, while if he advanced the French would do so. Knowing that his safety no longer depended on him, he felt that all his acts were reduced to gestures, that he was playing a

role and that others would decide. Finally he concluded that the
Germans posed the worse danger since "they would not misfire."
But he says, "this opinion imposed by circumstances was so little
*mine* that it appeared as an integral part of the role which I had to
play" (1:667). In the case of the infant Gustave, Sartre claims that
even the satisfaction of his needs was tainted with an element of
unreality.

> Gustave is so constituted that, with his needs satisfied before they
> have even become manifest, desire, in him, does not arise as a de-
> mand for a concrete assuagement but as a dreamy waiting for a
> satisfation which will come or will not come and over which, in
> any case, he has no power. [1:666]

Sartre goes on to argue that there is no great difference between a
satisfaction which seems to come always by chance and a purely
imaginary satisfaction.

If this seems a bit dubious, we may turn for reinforcement to
another passage in which Sartre speaks of the child's need for emotional validation from his parents. By now the boy is aware of father
as well as mother.

> Filial love can be sincere; that is to say, *felt*. Filial piety, on the
> contrary, is a "display"; the child willingly lends himself to it; he
> says what the parents expect of him, remakes the gestures which
> have pleased them; he is giving a *presentation*. In this sense all
> bourgeois children are more or less actors. But when the parents
> respond to this "display" by another "display" and cover the little
> play-actor with caresses, the role tends to disappear. All this takes
> place in the intersubjective truth of family life. [1:674]

After Sartre's picture of Gustave's loveless infancy, one may be a bit
surprised to read that the child enjoyed this daily ceremony of love
during the Golden Age, but Sartre states that "the love which he bore
then for his parents was indissolubly a passion and an imperative."
During this blissful period he felt that he experienced what he ought
to experience because he was what he ought to be. At the same time
Sartre claims that Gustave, like other children, retained a bit of unreal play-acting in the expressions of his passions. "Doesn't he love
his father? On the contrary, he adores him. They have made him such
that he overdoes it a bit. We know why" (1:674). Since the average
reader will probably not know why, Sartre obligingly offers an explanation. Like other children, and even like adults, Gustave not
only exaggerates the expression of what he feels, but also mimes that

which he does not feel or at least does not feel yet. This is because "the emotion is not separable from the behavior which expresses it" (1:675). A child who is troubled may suddenly throw itself into its parent's arms, not because it feels an overwhelming impulse of tenderness, but because it wants to experience the renewal of that tenderness which will be awakened by the caresses. "In lovers, too, the amorous impulse arises, more often than is generally recognized, from dryness and emptiness." The reality of love is reaffirmed on both sides by the reciprocal gesture. This passage is quite consistent with what Sartre has written on the emotions ever since his early work, *The Transcendence of the Ego*. There he distinguished between the spontaneous impulse of attraction or repulsion and the "state" of love or hate. The state is an ideal unification of past, present, and future, which involves something like a faith or a vow so that one may speak of its abiding presence even at moments when the love or hate forms no part of the immediate intentions of consciousness.[16] The child's embrace of the parent, if the parent responds, both confirms the state and transforms it into living, spontaneously felt emotion. But what if the parent does not respond? The expected flow of emotion is not evoked. The initial gesture is suddenly revealed as nothing but a cold and empty play-acting. It is Sartre's view that this is what happened between the nervous doctor and his son, whose demonstrations seemed to the father exaggerated and annoying because they were overdemanding.

As Sartre interprets, Gustave's lack of emotional validation resulted in his feeling that his own emotions were permeated with unreality and that therefore he himself was somewhat unreal. Yet obviously he is real for others. Therefore he tries to coincide with the reality which they see. More than that, he would like to convince others to establish him as he would like to be. He wants at the very least "to see himself with their eyes, to live, as *subject*, the object which he is for them!" (1:678). He is not unlike the actor who labors by means of his words and gestures to persuade the audience to see him as what he plays. There is this similarity—that for both Gustave and the actor, the language he uses has been set down by others; it does not arise spontaneously from within himself to communicate his own message. And there is this difference—that the professional actor knows that he is Edmund Kean playing Hamlet or, in certain more alienated individuals, that he is John Brown playing Edmund Kean playing Hamlet; Flaubert knows only that he is the younger son in the Flaubert family, branded as inferior and with no destiny save to live out the unhappy fate that has been prescribed for him. In short, his subjective being is imaginary in his own eyes, and he must seek what he is objectively in the look of others.

Sartre finally concludes that Dr. Flaubert in relation to his son is "pathogenic" (2:1892). I assume that he means this in the sense that R. D. Laing, for example, explains schizoid reactions in the child as the result of the patterns of expected behavior established by other members of the family. For more than a hundred pages Sartre analyzes in detail six aspects of what he believes to be Gustave's inner response and gives evidence from Flaubert's writing to support the claim that these remain permanent qualities of his personality. I will summarize them briefly.

First, Sartre names *vassalage*. Flaubert responded to the semifeudal structure of the family by composing a fantasy (or at least by a reaction which implied some such fantasy) in which Achille-Cléophas was indeed *le Seigneur*, a sovereign lord who bestowed upon his vassals (his sons) their right to exist.

> Vassalage, for the child Flaubert, is the means chosen by an inessential being to gain the right to be essential by exploiting [*renchérissant*] his inessentiality. [1:336]

The vassal is necessary in order for the seigneur to realize himself—just as Hegel' slave is essential to the master, and vice versa. Gustave's sense of injury stemmed from the fact that his father, not playing the game, refused to let himself be adored. To this dream of vassalage Sartre attributes Flaubert's intense pride (reinforced by his mother's distant connections with nobility), his dislike of egalitarianism, his longing to be rich but refusal to make money by working for it. The climactic moment symbolizing Flaubert's acceptance as vassal was a true event. One day the duchess de Berry passed by as Dr. Flaubert stood there holding little Gustave in his arms. The Duchess stopped, held the child for a moment in her own arms, and kissed him.[17] This episode, Sartre claims, was the equivalent of a royal presentation, recognizing both father and son's place in the hierarchy of vassals and suzerains (1:600). When he was twenty-five, Flaubert found something "sublime, truly human" in the blind, fanatical devotion of one man to another as in the cult of the emperor (1:334). Much later, Sartre argues, the ideal of vassalage entered into Flaubert's complex attitude toward Napoleon III and his own position on the fringes of Napolean's court. The idea of the seigneur may easily be extended to the notion of God as supreme

Lord. Sartre finds in Flaubert, too, the feeling that his father was in some way equivalent of the Creator, the incarnation of God the Father. I must say that this whole concept of vassalage as a dominant ingredient in Flaubert's thinking and feeling seems to me the weakest part of Sartre's analysis. But in fairness it must be added that he does not intend us to think that Flaubert ever formulated the idea explicitly. What Sartre has tried to do is express verbally the *meaning* of unarticulated attitudes and resultant behavior.

Second, Flaubert assumed the existence in himself of a certain *insufficiency*. This was responsible for his difficulty in learning to read. As is typical of children in this kind of situation, Gustave felt that he was at fault even if he had been created lacking. Sartre challenges the idea that any father can love his child too much. (The real question, I suspect, is not how much but how wisely.) In Gustave's case, the father's disapproval over the failure in reading and his apparent withdrawal of love when the boy reached "the thankless age" of seven, was felt to be the result of his disgracing himself. The situation was made worse by the fact that Achille was installed as successor *after* Gustave's failure. As he grew older, he felt that some anomaly set him apart. (I might ask what adolescent has not, but in Flaubert's the feeling persisted.) Sartre writes,

> "I am not like the others"—Whatever may have been the meaning of that sentence when Gustave wrote it at twenty, it signifies on the primitive level [*archaîquement*]: Achille knew how to read at seven, and I at nine was incapable of it. [1:373]

Third, Sartre lists *inferiority*, closely associated with insufficiency but bearing directly on Gustave's relation to Achille. Since the first-born was the heir, the younger could see himself only as a poor copy, at best an understudy. Hence "the myth of condemnation."

Fourth, *submission* was the conduct chosen. Sartre argues that in this semifeudal family, Gustave accepted his brother's superior position as the external indication of intrinsic superiority. His own inferiority is both a verdict and a prophecy. He is doomed to prove that his being is flawed. "The worst is always sure," Flaubert liked to say. Sartre says that the words are "the recollection of a condemnation" (1:393). Revolt was useless because Gustave was convinced that his father's eyes could read his very soul.[18] He is afraid even to dream of revolt. And "submission, not being an act, remains a nightmare" (1:399).

Fifth, obedience sets limits; it forbids hate. But when consent and revolt are equally impossible, *resentment* appears. It is the effect of love denied, not of suppressed hatred, and it takes the form of pushing obedience to the limit. I may compare it to the attitude of a subordinate who continues to carry out to the letter an order which he knows to be working against the end his superior had in mind; the action is designed to show up the other as having been wrong. According to Sartre, Gustave liked to imagine himself living out his father's condemnation so fully that he would die and at last his father would be sorry. It is as if he said, "I flee from you by becoming against you what you wanted me to be" (1:48). Sartre says that resentment is lived as pathos, as passive activity, and as manipulation. This idea will be extremely important later, for Sartre holds that passive activity, a form of conduct in which the agent seems to himself not to be responsible for the results which he brings about, is the clue to Flaubert's nervous crisis in 1844 and his subsequent pattern of existence. For the present Sartre notes that in resentment Gustave begins to develop a more genuine sense of self as that which comes from within rather than from the Other. Selfness lodges itself like a worm in the alter ego that "they" gave to him (1:407). It is barely recognized. At this stage Flaubert's ego is "the blind spot in his reflexive look" (1:411).

Sixth, following close on resentment comes *envy*. Superficially envy might seem to be linked with desire for what is possessed by someone other than oneself. Sartre would not dispute this definition, but he distinguishes it very carefully from desire as such; he calls it, in fact, "the negative of desire." Gustave, he claims, never learned to desire spontaneously. He was not greatly tempted by specific examples of the goods of this world. What he desired was to be able to desire and to possess that which contented others who coveted it. In short, it was the satisfied desire that he envied in others. The envied person is the one who is contented with his being in the world, and the envious one calls him a fool for being so. Sartre argues that a basic anorexia in Flaubert was responsible for his feeling that he could never be satisfied. Partly from a rebound of pride and, later, partly under the influence of the romantics, he developed the idea that the greatness of a desire is measured by its insatisfaction. Desires which exalt the individual capable of feeling them are inexpressible because the objects that might satisfy them do not exist. This grandiose idea was merged with the petty malice that usually accompanies envy. Sartre claims that here we have the root of Flaubert's retreat into *le survol*, the overview or bird's-eye view. In imagination he could look down at the entire human species, scoff at its paltry goals and easy satisfactions, deride its unenlightened suffering, and feel that by detaching himself from all of it, he escaped his own denunciation. Meanwhile he was not above the desire to injure those who might otherwise be content. Sartre insists that along with the ideal of art for art's sake, the primary purpose of writing, for Flaubert, was always to demoralize.

Such, Sartre asks us to believe, were the effects of the paterfamilias on his second son. As with the mother, we will postpone the question of the verisimilitude of the portrait until we have examined Sartre's treatment of Flaubert's later life. For the moment let us simply note that as the result of his father's favoritism, Achille was the chosen successor of Achille-Cléophas; the second Caroline was the one Caroline senior had expected when Gustave was born. He arrived with no place prepared for him. At the age of seven he felt rejected by both parents.

Sartre suggests that if his mother had loved Gustave with a violent, possessive love, he might have developed an active aggressiveness instead of remaining a passive agent. Or if there had been open conflict between the two parents, he might have found it easier to solve his problems realistically. As it was, the mother limited herself to transmitting the orders given by her husband. Nevertheless a tension in attitudes did exist. Gustave, Sartre holds, encountered through his parents the conflicting claims of two ideologies. On his father's side there was an atomistic scientism, an atheistic rationalism. Not that Achille-Cléophas was a militant atheist; rather he was an "atheist within the church," one who had his children christened and who observed all the other ceremonies which were normal for the future bourgeois citizen, but one who enlivened the dinner table by scoffing at the priests and their teachings. The mother's nondogmatic Catholicism was vaguely deistic. Associated with it in Gustave's mind was the reality of the soul, a sense of the meaningful unity of all things, and the feeling that there were aspects of both the human being and outer reality that science could not grasp. We will find him vacillating between the two attitudes but without realizing that this is a matter of choosing one parent over the other.

The child torn between the conflicting religious commitments of his parents is a somewhat overfamiliar figure in novels and in real life, too. Unfortunately, Sartre seems to have erred in attributing this origin to Gustave Flaubert's ambivalent attitude to religious belief.

Bruneau and Levin have both pointed out that the evidence shows Madame Flaubert to have been a nonbeliever like her husband, and Sartre does not claim to have uncovered new documentary information.[19] If he drew from a real-life situation, I am afraid it was his own. He has given us a comparable description of his early life.

> When I was seven or eight years old, I lived along with my mother, who was a widow, between a Catholic grandmother and a Protesant grandfather. At table each one made fun of the other's religion. It was without malice—a family tradition. But a child's reasoning is straightforward. I concluded that neither of these persuasions had any value.[20]

Jean-Paul's grandfather was Protestant rather than atheistic; Sartre does not represent Caroline as fighting back against her husband. Oherwise the pictures are the same. Actually, there is reason to believe that the Flaubert family table was indeed the scene of noisy arguments, at least when the boys grew older, but we do not know the subjects of these debates.[21] It is not improbable that Gustave found his father's insistence on science as the sole access to truth an offense to his own poetic, half-mystical yearnings. We do know that he alternated between cynical derision of religious doctrines and nostalgic expressions of sympathy for simple souls able to believe. His attitude toward truth was ambivalent. In the tradition of his father he equated it with the kind of truth which could be established by science. To this truth he did not give full allegiance. What was the alternative? The imaginary, of course. But could one believe in it? Sartre maintains that "truth" is associated with praxis and knowledge; it has nothing to do with belief. Flaubert, in fact, neither lived nor judged in terms of truth but only of belief. This time the one responsible is his mother. Given his passive constitution and diminished sense of reality, "he escaped himself. Lack of power either to affirm or to deny reduced him to believing" (1:667). In *Being and Nothingness* Sartre showed how belief undermines itself. If someone asks if Peter is my friend and I say, "I believe so," suddenly I realize that "to believe is only to believe." It is not to know. Now Sartre comments further:

> The object of belief is given as an unstable being which can, at any moment, pass from real to illusory so that its reality is denounced, in its very presence, as potentially an illusion; inversely the illusion, for lack of being denied, always presents itself to his eyes as something which *could* be believed and which thus contains, to

some degree, however slight, a potential reality. Between the one and the other Gustave does not always have the means to establish a clear-cut distinction. [1:667]

This attitude, perhaps a natural one in a creative writer (though Sartre would never allow it in himself), seems to me more relevant to Flaubert's varying reactions to religious aspirations than the dubious assumption of a conflict between his parents. I may add that to presume such a cleavage would be to undermine the notion of the wholly submissive wife which Sartre has been at such pains to establish. Had Gustave perceived the necessity of choosing between his parents' commitments, this breach in the closed family structure might have had far different consequences.

Sartre claims that Gustave did not develop a genuine appetite for life. For that

he would have to have had another mother, another proto-history. . . . To love life, to wait confidently and hopefully each minute for the following minute, one must have been able to internalize the Other's love as a fundamental self-affirmation. [1:405]

Yet, although his youthful writing speaks often of suicide, Gustave did not kill himself. His heroes discover in themselves the "feeling for existence" (*sentiment de l'existence*). Sartre believes that its equivalent in Gustave was pride and the realization that to die would be to leave himself behind as a corpse, even more passively helpless in the hands of the unloving. Possible also it was because he began to discover a resistant core of self and an outlet for his resentment in the act of writing. Before leaving the account of Gustave's childhood, Sartre looks for evidence to be used retrospectively, information gleaned from the stories that Flaubert wrote in his early adolescence.

## THE EVIDENCE OF THE JUVENILIA

In my opinion Sartre's discussion of Flaubert's youthful writings does much to counteract the uneasiness elicited by his hypothetical reconstruction of the Golden Age, the Fall, and parental malediction, and the private emotions of Madame Flaubert. Some critics have attempted to downgrade the importance of this material because Gustave in many cases rewrote existing stories.[22] Yet, while there is a great deal of imitation of what he has read, even the least original works show that he has significantly changed emphases and interpretations, often details of plot. Moreover, there are themes which recur frequently enough so that the choice of the particular models is itself significant. It is Sartre's view that at this stage of his life Flaubert wrote for two reasons: "to understand himself and to avenge himself" (1:219). Both demanded that he must come to grips with his childhood. No short summary can do justice to Sartre's hundred and fifty pages of careful analysis, but I will try, by commenting briefly on his treatment of some of the most important examples, to show what seem to him to have been the dominant preoccupations of the young author.

*Quidquid Volueris,* as it stands, appears to be primarily an original story, though the rape scene was inspired by a tale concerning the violation and murder of a young girl by an orangutan. We have already considered this work in connection with what light it might throw on Gustave's "stupors," his difficulties with communication, and his *"bêtise."* That there is some measure of self-identification with Djalioh seems certain. In addition Sartre believes that we can see in the portrait of M. Paul Gustave's rancor against both his father and his brother. One thing is certain: to the point where it is a literary defect the author heaps abuse on the character of M. Paul. Next to Djalioh, "the monster of nature" was "M. Paul, that other monster or rather that marvel of civilization, who bore all its symbols, greatness of intellect, dryness of heart." "At college he was strong in mathematics. As for literature he had always found that stupid." He was incapable of love and planned to marry wholly out of expediency. He had no concern for Djalioh except insofar as the hybrid had enabled him to win a bet and prove a point. In contrast, the misfit, the ugly, brutelike Djalioh is all soul.

> He had lived a long time, a very long time, but not in thought; neither the cogitations nor the dreams of the scientist had occupied him for a minute in his whole life; but he had lived and grown with his soul, and he was already old in his heart. [p. 147][23]

Premature old age is a frequent theme in these adolescent writings. It is a constant in Flaubert's adult correspondence. Other passages seem more appropriate to the adolescent writer than to his character. Djalioh exclaims, "Why do I suffer so and feel so bored and hate myself?" (p. 160). The author comments, "Unhappiness is in the order of nature. Nature has given us the feeling for existence in order to preserve unhappiness longer" (p. 163). Here we already see Flaubert's ambivalent feeling for the heaviness of reality and its transience. "Oh! reality! a phantom heavy as a nightmare, and yet a brief duration only, like the mind" (p. 162). Flaubert's brief introduction to the story, which Sartre does not mention, strengthens the impression of morbidity in the young author. In place of the typical preface of his contemporaries or the ancient invocation of the Muses, he calls to his aid "memories of insomnia, the 'dreams of a poor madman,' the little demons that come to his room by night."

The identification of M. Paul with Gustave's father and brother is less certain. To the degree that both he and they represent the successful scientist before whom the ape-man feels inferior and resentful, Sartre is probably on solid ground. But it seems to me that the tension here is more general, between rational science and feeling soul rather than between persons. Sartre, in fact, believes that M. Paul is a composite figure, standing not only for the two older men in the Flaubert family but also for M. Schlésinger, the husband of the Elisa for whom Gustave had conceived an adolescent passion the previous summer. When Djalioh torments himself by imagining the sexual embraces of M. Paul and Adèle, we can easily see in him the fifteen-year-old boy, resentfully jealous with regard to a woman whom he could not expect to regard him seriously as a possible lover. We are told that Gustave first came to love Elisa when she was nursing her baby. Critics have commented on this fact as evidence that Flaubert idealized her as the untouchable mistress-mother. The violence with which Djalioh destroys the infant born of M. Paul and Adèle suggests an emotion quite different from that of tender identification with the baby at Elisa's breast. If Achille is present at all in the story, I suspect he is here. The brutality of the closing episode of *Quidquid Volueris* seems to testify to the sadomasochistic rage which Sartre feels seethed in Gustave as he attempted to cope with the sufferings induced by his protohistory. I think it could also be interpreted with more specific reference to Adèle as Elisa. Djalioh's rape of Adèle might simultaneously serve to satisfy Gustave's desire vicariously and yet seem to him a profanation punishable by death. Even with these qualifications, however, it is not unreasonable to see Djalioh's relation to M. Paul as reflecting that of Gustave to his father. M. Paul was responsible for bringing Djalioh into existence even if he did not beget him directly. By his decision to prove the scientific bet, he effectively created a monster with a soul. Sartre's point is that Gustave Flaubert, in mingled resentment and despair, resolved, "I will be that monster which you have made me—against you." That is what Djalioh did. Sartre goes so far as to suggest that to some degree Flaubert saw (or wanted to see) his father also in the orangutan; this would be to satisfy the wish to portray his mother as the victim rather than the willing partner of the resented father (1:212).

If the themes of paternal malediction and fraternal jealousy are not clearly primary in *Quidquid Volueris,* there is no question that they are dominant in *La Peste à Florence* (*The Plague at Florence*), written a year earlier (1836). Two brothers visit an old woman who foretells their future. To the older, François, she promises success in his projects but adds that he will finally be killed by the treachery of someone close to him. To Garcia she prophesies, "The cancer of envy and hate will gnaw your heart, the sword of murder will be in your hand, and you will find in the blood of your victim the expiation for the humiliation of your life" (p. 83). Drawing the obvious parallel between the Florentine family in the seventeenth century and the neofeudal Flaubert family, Sartre calls attention to the older son's steady rise to power and glory. Heir apparent and the obvious favorite of his father, he is honored by everyone. One day he is made a cardinal. At the ball given to celebrate François' appointment, Garcia, who has been given nothing but the shadow of glory reflected from his brother, is so filled with jealous rage that he can barely restrain himself from killing someone—*anyone* in order that he may spoil the festival and destroy the happiness of the celebrants. Instead he faints and is carried outside by one of the servants. Later he and François, on a hunt, are separated from the rest of the company. Garcia reminds François of the prophecy, describes the torments which years of humiliation and his own jealous hate have inflicted upon him. He draws his sword and kills his brother, then rejoins his hunting companions with blood still on his lace ruffs. On the following day the father summons Garcia to the room in which the dead François lies in state. He accuses his son of the murder, and Garcia falls at the feet of his brother. The father kills him, the Florentines are told that both sons died of the plague.

The themes of jealousy and resentment are too obvious to need comment. It is significant that Garcia never rebels against either his father or the social structure that places higher value on the first-born. François is his father's favorite because he is the older; as the older, he *is* superior, even in personal qualities. Flaubert does not, as he did in the case of Djalioh, point to an inner greatness on the part of the ill-prized. It is only in his sufferings that Garcia excels, and these are the effect as well as the cause of his hatred. Flaubert seems to imply that nature had assisted society in designing the older as the better. Sartre, of course, insists that the opposite is true—that society by its expectations and promises provides the scope for development of superior achievement and character. The idea that the brothers' relation is inevitable, even fated, is strengthened by the prophecy. Sartre quotes from Flaubert's correspondence to show that he regarded himself in his own life as simply living out the inevitable. At the end of this story the father has cursed and killed his son—justly, the tale seems to imply. For Gustave the malediction came first, like the sentence of the prophetess. Sartre notes a curious fact about the murder. It is not actually described. Instead Garcia has announced to François that Garcia is about to kill him. Then there follows a line of dots like those used in old-fashioned books to avoid an explicit description of sexual relations. After this we hear only that a scream rose up from amidst the foliage and flushed a nest of owls. Sartre points out that the author clearly would not or could not allow himself to work out the details. (I may add that this constitutes a serious flaw in the plot. Apparently there was no duel. Nothing explains how Garcia, after so long a verbal prologue, would be able to overpower his brother, who presumably would be armed too.) Sartre suggests two reasons for the lacuna. Gustave suppressed the description of the murder because it would have come too close to satisfying an inadmissible death-wish against Achille. And the violent act would have called for more than Gustave's passive constitution could have supported.

In a story midway in date between the two preceding, *Un parfum à sentir* (*A Perfume to Sense*), the heroine exemplifies still more obviously Gustave's feeling that the victim is both innocent and responsible. There is a foreword in which Flaubert says that no person is to blame for the tragic events that the story unfolds. He challenges the philosophers to suggest a remedy and concludes that they could find recourse only in Necessity, a sombre and mysterious divinity who laughs ferociously while watching men try to deny her existence while she crushes them in her hands like a giant juggling dried skulls. The tragic "necessity" stems from the natural physical ugliness of Marguerite, one of a group of traveling circus players. Despite her appearance she has married, before the narrative begins, and has three children. Her husband, Pedrillo, however, beats her and eventually carries on openly an affair with the beautiful Isabellada, another member of the troupe. When Marguerite reproaches him and violently proclaims her jealousy and hatred of Isabellada, Pedrillo literally throws her to the lions. She is rescued but badly lacerated. After she leaves the hospital, the people in the street make fun of her and call her "the mad woman" (*la folle*). Marguerite stops short, strikes her forehead, and with a wild laugh shouts, "Death." She rushes to the river and drowns herself. Her corpse is put up for sale for medical students who need a body for dissection.

Once again we see the central theme of jealousy on the part of the inferior individual in a pair between whom there is a great disparity. Sartre points to one of the minor, peripheral scenes as possibly referring directly to Gustave's traumatic reading lessons. Pedrillo urges on his unskilled and terrified son to walk a tightrope and follows his every movement with a threatening cudgel. The theme of the fall is present, too. In the midst of her grief, Marguerite is forced to perform a trick before the circus audience and falls from an extreme height. A net saves her from death, but she is mocked, disgraced, and blamed for ruining the performance. Here as in *Quidquid Volueris* the sufferer is humiliated even after death. Djalioh's skeleton was put in a museum, Marguerite's cadaver is examined by the medical students. Obviously this reflects Gustave's familiarity with the hospital dissection room. Sartre suggests something more. He argues that Flaubert had the *feeling*, not a formulated rational conviction, that in some way the body after death was dimly aware of what happened to it. The horror elicited by the fates of the ape-man and the ugly woman may be the negative counterparts, as it were, of Saint Anthony's desire to be matter.

Throughout the narrative Flaubert appears to be evoking our pity and yet doing everything possible to prevent us from viewing Marguerite as other than disgusting. Sartre points out that Flaubert, who in his youth was extraordinarily handsome, had a strong negative reaction to physical ugliness. Later, in the autobiographical *November*, he writes of his hero:

> Passionate for what is beautiful, he was repulsed by ugliness as by crime. There is in fact something terrible in a person's being ugly. At a distance he frightens you; close up he disgusts you; when he speaks, you suffer; if he weeps, his tears annoy you; you want to strike him when he laughs, and in silence his motionlessness seems to you the seat of all the vices and all the base instincts. [p. 457]

In this connection Sartre provides one of his interesting digressions—a phenomenological description of physical ugliness as many people react to it (1:308–11). He starts by pointing out the contradictory quality of the feeling that ugliness offends. Flaubert and the jeering crowd condemn Marguerite to death for "the sin of ugliness," as if she were ugly *in order to* bring distress to others. The ugliness is viewed as an affliction, as something which has come to the victim through no fault of her own—through some accident or by hazard of birth. At the same time the ugly person is obscurely felt to be blameworthy. Illogical as the attitude is, Sartre feels that it expresses a frequent and spontaneous reaction, which is based on a partial truth. We are accustomed always to see the total person in the body and to view the body as a totality, not as a collection of separate parts. If an attractive smile is juxtaposed with a red nose, it may temporarily make us forget the nose. And there is some truth in the statement that by the age of forty each person is responsible for the quality of his/her face. It is true also, Sartre adds, that "the feeling of being ugly makes one ugly." Still there are certain deformations of face and figure which cannot be accounted for by the psychology of the person who bears them. If there is an initial confusion between the aesthetic and the moral, if for many people we find that beauty reassures, and that ugliness appears to reveal the hideousness of the inner soul or that it seems to forecast misfortune for the one who sees it, then we must seek an explanation in the relation between the ugly person and the beholder. Sartre compares the ugly individual to one who is believed to cast the evil eye. Neither is thought to do injury deliberately. Still the maleficent effect is not taken to be merely the result of a material contagion as in the case of a disease, which though it can be transmitted by a human being remains external to the sufferer and can be got rid of. The one who is believed to cause bad luck may be wholly unaware of his power; the resulting injury may be the precise opposite of what he would wish. Yet somehow it is through him that the evil is made effective. The ugly woman, like the incarnator of the evil eye, cannot be said to be acting out of free will. She cannot rid herself of her ugliness, and she has no motive for causing injury. She represents rather the "will in bondage." The bad luck which has hit her seems to overflow on the others. She has interiorized misfortune; so long as she doesn't kill herself, she is held to be an accomplice of the evil power that has afflicted her. Her ugliness reveals "the intolerable truth of this world." It reminds us of our vulnerability to the accident that may befall us. For an onlooker who takes reminders as premonitory signs, the sight of an ugly or deformed person is prophetic of future catastrophe.

Sartre emphasizes that he has not attempted to give here a "true phenomenology of ugliness" but rather certain "intersubjective" reasons for "the reaction which it provokes in a very large number of people; the adolescent Gustave is one of them." Sartre points out that *Madame Bovary* is full of these premonitory signs that something worse is to come. I suppose that the maimed blind man would be one of them. For Gustave a hideously ugly man or woman would seem to announce to him his own evil destiny. In a footnote Sartre points out that, when a person is not simply encountered but is engaged as a practical agent in a collective enterprise, his or her ugliness seems hardly to be of any account. This is because "praxis has other criteria" (1:311). By implication Flaubert's overreaction to physical ugliness is probably to be allied with his passivity. He looks for external signs to tell him what will come to him.

There is a further point which should be noted in connection with *Un Parfum à sentir*. Sartre has remarked on the sadism or, in instances when there is some degree of self-identification, the sadomasochism that Flaubert shows toward all of his characters. In the case of Marguerite he seems almost to be on the side of her tormentors. To the extent that he identifies himself with her he does so because of his own self-dislike. Like Marguerite, he feels that he is guilty of some crime which he has not committed, that he has been made inferior, that he is "free to be unhappy" and by his presence to bring unhappiness to others. Who, Sartre asks, are these others? For Marguerite it is God (or Necessity), who made her ugly and forces her finally to sentence herself to drowning. Her death is an accusation against whoever or whatever made her what she was. In the view of her literary creator, the Other is easy to detect. It is not God the Father in Heaven, but the earthly father-god: "the Father who made Achille in his image and Gustave in the image of an ape-man or an ill-favored eyesore, rejected by everyone" (1:312). Once again we see "the monster you made me."

Before leaving the story, we should note the brief epilogue in which the author speaks to us directly of himself. Sartre believes that in these early works Gustave was both finding an outlet for his resentment and seeking to find out for himself who he was—revenge and self-discovery. Because of his dislike of his world, and of himself, he began to turn more and more toward the world of the imagination and seemed to himself to write under the spell of a directing inspiration. Hence the speed, the unrestrained flow of the words. All of the juvenilia are the result of feeling, not of that self-conscious creative construction which is so typical of the later Flaubert. Writing is, at least on the surface, a pure escape, like the earlier "stupors," though it may be also a part of a therapeutic device and a movement of personalization. Flaubert writes in the epilogue of *Un Parfum à sentir*,

> To write! Oh, to write is to grasp hold of the world, its prejudices, its virtues and to sum it all up in a book. It is to feel one's thought being born, growing, living, taking its place erect on its pedestal to remain there always. I have just finished this strange, bizarre, incomprehensible book.

We may assume that Gustave is telling us the truth when he calls the work strange and incomprehensible. He himself does not "know" the truths it has revealed though he "comprehends" them. Of this work, which in print takes up almost forty pages, he tells us that he wrote the first section in one day, five others in a week, and that he finished it in two days more. Then comes a typical feeling of fatigue and depression.

> I am now tired, exhausted, and I fall with lassitude on my sofa, without having the strength to thank you if you have read me.

Though Sartre has not commented on this particular passage, we may note that it is one more example of a point he has made: Flaubert's frequent juxtaposition of exultant rise and fall. This time the fall is not only an image of a return to prostrate passivity but its literal manifestation.

Even more briefly with regard to some of the other juvenile works, we may observe certain recurring motifs which Sartre finds in them. *Bibliomania* repeats the theme of jealousy. This time the rivalry is between a poor bookseller, Giacomo, and the well-to-do Baptisto, both of them fanatical collectors of rare books and manuscripts. As usual, the hero is the loser, Giacomo, prematurely aged, with white hair at thirty, whose jealous hatred finally leads him to steal a book from his rival, an act which earns him the death sentence. Sartre makes two particularly significant observations about this story. First, he notes that while we are given a full description of only a single scene in which Baptisto outbids Giacomo for a coveted volume, Flaubert stresses that this is but one of many similar occasions. Sartre reads in this a reference to oft-repeated occasions in the Flaubert household when the older Achille would be given a mark of preference, occasions relived in unhappy memories and anticipated with sure foreboding. A second point concerns Giacomo's obsessive love of the books that he collects. Flaubert tells us rather surprisingly that this book collector barely knew how to read. The intellectual contents of the books scarcely concerned him. Instead of reading them, he handled and caressed them.

> It was not at all the learning [*la science*] that he loved; it was its form and its expression; he loved a book because it was a book, he loved its odor, its form, its title. What he loved in a manuscript was its ancient illegible date, the bizarre and strange Gothic letters, the heavy gilt which filled its designs. [p. 98]

Sartre finds here both a specific recollection of the child Gustave and an anticipation of the adult Flaubert. He thinks that the love of books as physical objects, when even the human message they contain is ignored, expresses Flaubert's rejection of the human and preference for the nonhuman. Giacomo dreams of possessing a library so great that in its immense galleries one's sight would be lost in books. Whether one raised one's head or lowered it, looked to right or to left, one would be, as it were, immured in books. Envy and ambitious dreams of pride find their outlet in possessed material which is also a refuge.

The implied desire to escape from the human world into that of books suggests, of course, a preference for the nonhuman and for the nonreal. Its corollary is a misanthropy, which is manifest in almost all of these early works. It is most obvious in *Voyage en Enfer* (*Trip through Hell*), where Satan is guide for a tour of the universe and displays a world like that which Schopenhauer has described—one in which the amount of the world's suffering is equalled only by its wickedness. "This world is Hell." In *Agonies* also there is a sustained lament over the evils and unhappiness of human existence. "The worst is always sure," as Flaubert liked to say later. Some of Flaubert's critics would like to dismiss such utterances, attributing them to adolescent posing or temporary moods of depression. Yet we must recall not only Flaubert's constant complaints of ennui but also his statement that to hear of a new example of human baseness brought to him as much pleasure as a gift of money.[24] We will consider later the degree to which Flaubert's adult fiction reveals a deep misanthropy. There is no question that it is present in the juvenilia.

*Passion et Vertu* (*Passion and Virtue*), written just after *Quidquid Volueris*, tells the story of Mazza, a wife and mother who at age thirty takes a lover and is awakened to passion for the first time. The violence of her overwhelming desire begins to make the lover, Ernest, uncomfortable, and he is relieved to be able to write her that his business obliges him to go to Mexico. Mazza's hair turns white in a single night. Encumbered by her family, she is in despair at not being able to follow him. She frees herself by killing both husband and children, immediately after which she receives a letter from Ernest announcing his imminent marriage. Mazza writes a letter confessing the murders and kills herself. Sartre finds in the wholesale slaughter of husband and children, which Mazza carries out without a twinge of pity or regret, the culminating satisfaction of Gustave's resentment toward his family, noting however that he includes himself in the punishment—both as one of the children and in the person of Mazza herself. Sartre may be going a little too far, though one cannot deny that the sadomasochism is a strong ingredient. Another theme that makes its first appearance in this story recurs throughout Flaubert's adult correspondence and is present in *Madame Bovary*. Although Mazza kills her family in order to follow Ernest, she was never wholly satisfied when she was with him. Parting from him each time, she counterbalances the sense of letdown and insatisfaction by using imagination to stimulate desire to still greater frenzy. In this depiction of a passion which is never wholly satisfied, Flaubert was not attempting a study of either pathological frigidity or nymphomania. Mazza's superiority is shown by the fact that she cannot be satisfied with the ordinary level of physical satisfaction which suffices her mediocre husband and the cowardly Ernest. Her greatness is measured by her insatisfaction, her wanting more than is humanly possible. We will see later that Sartre finds in the statement, "I am too small for myself," the clue to Emma Bovary and to Flaubert's feelings about himself. To be "too small for oneself" means to have yearnings for levels of experience which the very structure of one's personality, one's habitual reactions prevent. Sartre thinks that in this feeling of being the cause of his own frustration, Flaubert is expressing an obscure comprehension of the restrictions of his own passive constitution. Years later in his relation with Louise Colet, Flaubert plays a role much closer to that of Ernest than that of Mazza. Yet it is with Mazza that the not quite sixteen-year-old Gustave would identify. This may be simple wish-fulfillment whereby the bored adolescent transposes his anorexia into a frenzy of passion. But Sartre suggests that a more subtle mechanism is at work. Gustave's lack of satisfaction with anything is transformed into a desire for the unattainable, for that which is beyond all human satisfactions. Thus Gustave-Mazza will be raised above the others, those ordinary beings who get what their petty wishes demand and find it sufficient. Gustave can simultaneously envy and despise the

Ernests and the Achilles of this world.

Two other incidents from the juvenilia should be mentioned. In *Un Secret de Philippe le Prudent Roi d'Espagne* the themes of jealousy and paternal malediction are both present but separated. The king of Spain, whose character has been warped by lifelong jealousy of his favored brother, pours out his malevolence on his innocent son Carlos. The child is kept sequestered in a room so designed that he can be constantly spied upon by his father and the Grand Inquisitor. The child senses that he is watched, judged, and alienated by being made an object for his father's look. Sartre relates the boy's feeling to that of Flaubert, whose father was described as having a look which pierced directly through one, discovering all lies, unmasking all secrets and deceptions. He believes that in Carlos as a young man, Gustave offers his own self-portrait. Carlos was physically attractive, his figure was that of a man of twenty. "But if you had seen his hollow cheeks, his blue eyes so sad and so melancholy, his forehead creased with wrinkles, you would have said: he is an old man" (quoted by Sartre, 1:324). Once again we have a hero old before his time because he "has suffered terrible and unheard-of griefs."

Finally *Agonies,* which is not a connected narrative but a *"cri de l'âme,"* relates a brief incident which may or may not be based on fact. The narrator reports that someone had directed him to consult a priest. He was received by a man with a crooked nose covered with pimples; scarcely was the conversation begun when the priest interrupted it to give his servant directions for tending to a large pot of potatoes. His visitor burst into laughter and left. Whose fault was it, he asks. Neither he nor the priest was to blame for the fact of the ugly nose and the suggestion of a too earthy appetite. "The fault is His Who makes crooked noses and potatoes" (p. 220). The episode is, of course, an anticipation of the more subtle scene in which Emma Bovary tries to speak to the village priest of her sufferings and finds him distracted by his unruly flock of schoolboys and with neither the time nor the sensitivity to perceive that she is suffering and seeking help. Taken by itself, the incident would be easy to dismiss as reflecting a much too finicky and somewhat snobbish attitude on the part of a proud adolescent looking for reasons to reject his religious training (Sartre constantly reminds us that Gustave Flaubert, however unhappy he may have been as younger son, never forgot his pride in being a Flaubert in the midst of non-Flauberts.) Quite rightly, I think, Sartre links with this incident a passage from a letter written by Flaubert at the age of twenty-eight when he made a visit in Jerusalem to the place of the Holy Sepulcher. His excited anti-cipations indicate that he clearly expected some especially moving experience if not a kind of revelation. Instead he experienced nothing at all save his own dryness of heart. In his travel notes he records, "It was one of the most bitter moments of my life." What exactly did he expect or want? Sartre believes that what he wished for was not overtly a religious experience in the usual sense of the term but rather an aesthetic-imaginary one; he hoped that somehow that half-mythical, half-historical, and holiest spot in Christendom might appear to him "as a beautiful, atemporal image, neither true nor false," that he might grasp the feeling of wholehearted devotion and mystery. This attitude is one of religiosity rather than of religion. As Sartre says, it is close to that "religion of aesthetes of which Châteaubriand, the agnostic, was the prophet, and Barrès, the unbeliever, was the last minister" (1:524). At the same time Sartre makes it clear that Flaubert's attitude is not quite that of a total atheist so firmly entrenched in his disbelief that his imagination can play with the beliefs of others as easily at Jerusalem as on Mount Olympus. As William James would put it, religion for Flaubert is not yet quite a dead option. The problem is that "he *does not believe enough.*" His skepticism will effectively prevent religiosity from turning into reli-gion. Yet hidden in its depths is the wistful, unacknowledged hope that some kind of discharge of the sacred would strike him like a thunderbolt and force him to believe. Hence the bitter sadness of this moment when he knows that he will never believe. In his notes written at Jerusalem, Flaubert wrote,

> This is the third day that we have been at Jerusalem. None of the emotions I anticipated has yet come to me: neither religious enthu-siasm, nor the excitement of my imagination, nor *hatred of priests*. . . . In front of everything that I see, I feel myself emptier than a drained cask. The truth is that this morning in Holy Sepulcher a dog would have been more moved than I. Whose fault, God of mercy? Theirs? Mine? Or Yours? Theirs, I believe, then mine, and above all Yours. [quoted, 1:523]

Sartre discusses one by one the three who are at fault. "They" are the clerics who make up the Church as an institution. The priest with the pimply nose and the well-intentioned but rather stupid and in-sensitive Abbé Bournisien (in *Madame Bovary*) represent "their" all too human fallibility. Sartre suggests that in part Flaubert's contempt for them stems from Achille-Cléophas' vociferous anticlericalism. In passages which inevitably remind one of Sartre's portrait of his grandfather in *The Words,* he imagines how the father who sent his son to attend Mass would undermine the Church's teachings. His attacks might take the form of criticism of the Church's political involvement with the monarchy. More often the rational scientist would identify all religious aspiration with literal belief in the teachings of the Bible—as if an inquiry concerning the existence of the soul were equivalent to asking about the details of Jonah's sojourn in the belly of the whale. Although Flaubert's choice of the imaginary world of art was in part motivated by his resistance to his father's scientism, he never questioned the validity of science as the best method for ascertaining the facts of the real world. Thus he embraced his father's skepticism concerning the teachings of Christianity. Achille-Cléophas was not solely responsible for Flaubert's inability to believe—any more than was the individual priest with the pimply nose. For Flaubert, Sartre says, the religious instinct manifested itself not in the hope of *knowing* but in the need to *believe.* But the yearning for the infinite cannot define the objects of its faith. Specific religions, says Sartre, are social imaginaries. "But—here we find again the generalization of the formula, 'I am too small for myself'—the imagination of the infinite by the finite can give rise to nothing other than childish and crude fables." If one tries to communicate a religious meaning, one must resort to images which are particular, human, and earthly.

> In trying, guided by instinct, to represent to us the Supernatural as an *object* of faith [imagination] blends nature and the Supernatural in anthropomorphic myths; the infinite is submerged and lost in a black stone or in an old man with a white beard. [1:580]

The basic fault that Flaubert finds in "them" is that they are satisfied to accept the finite as an answer to the quest for the infinite.

The fault is also "mine." Flaubert, Sartre says, believes that he lacks either the religious instinct itself or the capacity to respond to it. Why? Sartre claims that he wavers between two answers: "I am made this way" and "I make myself this way." He both envies and despises those who have the gift of easy faith. Sartre says that here is one more instance of others having been preferred to Gustave. At the same time Sartre feels that simultaneously to long for faith and to refuse it is in keeping with Flaubert's overall choice of unhappiness. As he expresses it, Flaubert, if given the chance, would have refused

Paradise or would have made a Hell out of it (1:559). Even his resentment would not push him to want to be saved while his father and brother were damned. This would make them more interesting! Thus we see two aspects in the fault which is "mine." On the one hand Flaubert holds himself guilty, like Marguerite, for having been made a crass individual who lacks the capacity for belief. It is this which causes his bitterness at the Holy Sepulcher, this which on one occasion leads him to sit for a while in a cathedral and imagine how his friends would laugh to see him.[25] Envy of the believer is transformed into sympathetic tenderness, almost empathy, when he describes the first communion of his niece Caroline, and in his description of Félicité's emotions on watching the first communion of her charge, Virginie, in *A Simple Heart*. Yet just at the moment when Flaubert feels most deprived, he effects a legerdemain whereby privation of the infinite is transformed into an infinite privation. If he sees himself as damned, then he recalls that the quality of a man is measured by his suffering (1:545–46). To an extent, Sartre claims, Flaubert identified himself with Satan. But there exists a secret hope that even if Satan has been justly cursed by God, still the Father might against all hope forgive his son and claim him.

Above all the fault is "Yours." God is at fault for having chosen servants so menial, for having made priests with gluttonous appetites and crooked, pimply noses. More than this, God is at fault for having created a world which itself is Hell.

> Creation is God's sin or His glaring error: if He believed He was making man in His image, so much the worse for us and for Him: the fragments of the mirror are microscopic and cannot reflect the immensity which is supposed to be reflected in it. If Being is suffering, Nothingness is better. [1:587]

This train of thought finds its culmination in Flaubert's suggestions that suicide, by effecting a nothingness of all creation, equals the original act whereby God made the world.[26] There is, of course, a suggestion of a certain idealism here comparable to Schopenhauer's claim that since the world is my idea, it is annihilated with my annihilation. Sartre, I believe, is correct in saying that with Flaubert the notion is less philosophical than aesthetic. By the time that Flaubert is ready to formulate his theory of art, both generally and for himself as an artist, he will anticipate, long before Valéry and Mallarmé, the claim that the universe is only a fault in the purity of

Nonbeing. It will be our concern in later chapters to show how Flaubert handled the stress of his neurosis in such a fashion that what might have assumed the form of a retreat from reality into madness became the artist's deliberate transformation of the real into the imaginary via the work of art.

One of the reviewers of *The Family Idiot* complained that Sartre takes from Flaubert's early writing only what fits his own theory so that the result is unconvincing.[27] I must disagree. Any reader of these stories will find numerous passages to match those specifically cited by Sartre. I myself find his interpretation quite in line with the overall thrust and tone. I cannot see that he has omitted anything which, if included in his account, would give us a radically different picture. Sartre does not discuss Flaubert's literary interests and developing artistic technique, but to do so would not be germane to his immediate purpose and would hardly affect his conclusions.[28] Obviously Gustave, in looking back on his childhood, finds that two different views are possible, depending perhaps on whether he is thinking of the earliest years, more imagined than remembered, or of those that came after he was seven. Sartre points out that Flaubert employs two striking and quite different images to express his sense of the meaning of his life as a child. One is best expressed in an unpublished passage from *Madame Bovary;* this is one of the places where Sartre believes that we legitimately apply the "Madame Bovary, c'est moi." Flaubert writes,

> Happy time of her youth when her heart was pure like the waters of the holy font and reflected like them only the arabesques of the stained glass with the tranquil elevation of celestial hopes. [1:332]

Is this image based on Gustave's memory of life before the Fall? Is it an imaginative reconstruction of what he would like his childhood to have been? It doesn't matter. What is important is that it reflects two things: Flaubert's recognition of the need for devotion, a belief and love addressed to some Seigneur, earthly or divine, and his longing to become one with surrounding nature, to be nothing but the pure reflection of beautiful and holy colors—a pure soul open to the totality and fulfilled by it. The second image is much more negative. Flaubert compares himself to a muddy pond which stinks when one stirs it up. This is in a letter to Louise Colet, one of the frequent passages in which Flaubert, not yet thirty, complains of feeling already old. Louise, he suggests, is the only one who can breathe some sort of new life into the cinders, can cause the lake of his heart to quiver. "But it is for the Ocean that the tempest is made. Ponds, when they are stirred up, give off only unhealthy odors" (1:185).

Though Sartre's description of the Father's Curse, the Fall, and expulsion from Paradise may be too sharply defined and too literary for us to believe that they correspond to Flaubert's life as he explicitly lived it, there is abundant testimony in the juvenilia to his feeling of his having suffered some sort of disillusioning and embittering experience. The second image would suggest a poisoning from within and may indeed refer, as Sartre suggests, to Gustave's repressed jealousy and resentment, even death wishes against both himself and others. There is also a sense of his having been wronged by factors over which he had no control, by life itself. The clearest expression of his feeling of having survived and of having been scarred by some sort of psychological crisis is the repetition of the idea of premature old age. Mazza's hair turns white in a single night; Djalioh, Giacomo, Carlos are young men who look old. Later in his life Flaubert referred even more explicitly to himself as having outlived his passions at an early age (probably, as we shall see, with specific reference to his nervous crisis). Why, when he was still in his teens, should he want to portray his young heroes as already old? Sartre suggests that the premature aging is related to Gustave's *ennui de vivre*. He connects the two in a long footnote which vividly demonstrates his peculiar blend of painstaking research and literary imagination. Sartre tracked down the thesis that Achille-Cléophas presented for his degree. In this the author commented on the fact that some patients seemed less able than others to survive operations, and he claimed that a certain psychic disposition, a form of ennui was responsible. (The French *ennui* includes a suggestion of world-weariness or lack of zest in living, along with the connotations of the English word "boredom.") In developing his thought he remarked that, while children know little of ennui, it is common among the old, a point on which he elaborates. Inspired by this passage, Sartre imagines a scene in which the doctor surprised his son yawning. The father would have said, "Are you bored? At your age! Children aren't bored, you have to be very old to be bored." The docile son would have concluded, "I am bored, *therefore* I am old" (1:184–85). This fascinating account of how a few words may have served to crystallize an attitude *could* be true. Sartre covers himself by noting that in any case old people are—or are popularly believed to be—subject to ennui. Be that as it may, the adult Flaubert did indeed link the two—ennui and a feeling of premature age because of suffering—and ascribed them both to himself. Sartre has attempted to show that in Gustave's childhood the pattern was already laid: in his constitution, thanks to his mother; in his own self-image, as the result of his relation with his father.

# CHAPTER TWO

## First Steps in the Spiral

### PERSONALIZATION AND STRESS

The first two volumes of *The Family Idiot* trace the history of Flaubert's individual psychological development; Sartre has divided his account into three sections. Up to this point our discussion has been limited primarily to material in part one, "The Constitution." Here he has analyzed the basic psychological structure, the foundation, so to speak, that underlies the development of Flaubert as a person. Sartre's negative judgment on all this is revealed by his referring to it as *"le mal"* (the injury). Discussion of the process itself is begun in part two, "Personalization"; it deals with the gradual building up of an orientation which will culminate in Flaubert's nervous crisis and his final choice of himself as a writer. Part three, "Elbenhon or the Last Spiral," analyzes the meaning and consequences of that choice. The second part, which we are about to consider, extends over a thousand pages. It is itself divided into three "books": 1, "What is Beauty if Not the Impossible"; 2, "School" (*Le Collège*); and 3, "The Preneurosis."

Up until now, Sartre says, we have been studying *le mal* but not *le stress*. He moves from one to the other in a paragraph worth quoting in full.

> Such is Gustave. Such they have constituted him. And of course, no determination is imposed upon a [human] existent which he does not surpass by his way of living it. In the small Flaubert, passive activity and coasting with the current [*vol à voile*] are his *way of living* the constituted passivity; resentment is his *way of living* the situation which has been assigned to him in the Flaubert family. In other words, the structures of this family are internalized in attitudes and reexternalized in practices by which the child makes

himself be what they have made of him. Inversely, we will find in him no conduct, however complex and elaborated it may appear, which is not originally the surpassing of an internalized determination. [1:653]

From this constant process of internalizing the external pressures (in attitudes) and then reexternalizing them (in activities in the external world) Sartre develops the notions of stress, the spiral, and personalization which are basic to his study. As a person encounters something new, the novel ingredient of his lived experience is not simply taken up and synthesized as in the Hegelian *Aufhebung*. We attempt to integrate the new into "the organic unity which we try to be so as to prevent it from injuring that unity and from remaining there like a worm in the fruit, rotting it from within" (1:653). Stating it more simply, we try to handle a new experience in such a way that it fits into our customary self-image and behavior without disruption and without planting the seeds of future conflict. Sartre says that the human being lives his life as a multiplicity of events, he is "haunted by a dream or a memory of synthetic unity." I think Sartre's meaning will be clearer if we recall that in his view consciousness exists as a process of a perpetual unification of past and present via a projection of itself into the future in the light of its basic orientation or "choice of being." Using terms favored in the *Critique,* Sartre now says that the very detotalization (that is, the person's encounter with that which until now has not been a part of his conscious experience) demands to be retotalized (that is, to be made part of the unity of this organic being). The new totalization is not a simple inventory—an adding onto—but an intentional, oriented enterprise of reunification. The present lived experience (*le vécu*) takes place as a process of effecting a new unity of all the subject's psychic life. Much of the time we are able to incorporate the new without endangering the form of the existing unity. What is novel does not necessarily appear as a threat to our basic orientation, particularly since our way of viewing the new will be determined by long-established forms of response. On occasion, however, an event cannot be accepted internally without our recognizing that it will not fit into our habitual pattern of unification. Sartre says that three responses are possible for us.

First, I may grasp the new possibilities with full awareness that they constitute a crisis and "make myself over" so as to receive them. In an extreme form this response is what Sartre calls a new "choice of being." We know it in the form of sudden conversions, of being "born again." Less dramatically, it may be recognized (at least retrospectively) as one of the turning points in a life.

Second, I may make myself believe that such a transformation has been effected when in reality it has not. Sartre calls this false belief *"une croyance pithiatique." "Pithiatique,"* a key term in *The Family Idiot*, is difficult to translate, and Sartre sometimes gives to it a meaning a bit different from its normal usage in psychiatric contexts. Robert's dictionary defines *pithiatique* as applicable to "a nonorganic trouble due to suggestion and curable by it." As Sartre employs the word, the suggestion may result from an imaginative interpretation of something in the environment (as, for example, an ugly sight may suggest an imminent disaster) or to autosuggestion. The result of the deceptive belief is that "the contradiction remains real and the assimilation is *imaginary*" (1:655). The consequences may or may not be heavily significant, depending on circumstances, but in any case that which makes up the unification, what we call the personality, will include some degree of unreality.

Third, I may permit the usual unification to continue without essential modification by the device of putting the new into parentheses, refusing to attach it to the ensemble of the lived (*le vécu*) and not allowing it to participate in any action of reexternalization of the conditioning. Sartre speaks here of a "false distraction" or an "imaginary forgetting." It is obviously akin to both Freudian repression and Sartrean bad faith. In order to sustain the seeming unity of the integrating movement, there must of necessity be some derealizing of the original relation to the external world. Most often the result is that the unassimilated element, by its simple presence, gives birth to antagonistic elements which ultimately force a modification of the organism's unity, having worse effects than the original factor that was denied assimilation. Sartre compares the process to the antibodies which invade the transplanted organ and cause the death of the organism they were supposed to defend.

I think that Sartre is pointing to processes familiar to all of us. Lest his terminology may make his intention a trifle obscure, I suggest some simple examples. When Saul of Tarsus, the persecutor of the Christians, was struck blind on the road to Damascus, when he was consequently cured and converted to Christianity, his decision to change his name to Paul was the outward signification of his new choice of being. The old unifying totalization was detotalized by effecting an entirely new unification. This is the first response Sartre suggests. But the psychological preparation for so cataclysmic a re-orientation must have taken a fairly long period of time. We may readily imagine that on occasion the sufferings of Saul's victims awakened his pity and that their self-confident faith evoked in him some degree of self-questioning. These momentary revelations he would have repressed, letting them exist like unrecognized enclaves in his field of consciousness. This is Sartre's third response. Finally, we may imagine that one of Paul's new converts, perhaps under an influence, family pressure, or mass hysteria, would have proclaimed himself a Christian, in all sincerity, but would think of his new persuasion as simply an intellectual belief which could be inserted into his existence without in any way modifying it. This is Sartre's second response. Obviously few confrontations with the new are so self-evidently critical or reactions so clear-cut, but I think the under-lying patterns remain the same.

Now we are ready for Sartre's definition of "stress."

> We shall give the name *stress* to the unity of the nonassimilable elements and of the global defense which the totalization develops against it inasmuch as the latter is infected to the same extent that it tries to neutralize the nonassimilable. [1:656]

Stress, for Sartre, includes both "characterological disturbances" (i.e., the affective patterns embedded in one's constitution by one's protohistory) and the attempt to deal with them along with the new experiences encountered. Stress is the ceaseless process of a totaliza-tion that is at once detotalized and retotalizing. As such we may call it also a personalization. In language reminiscent of that in *Being and Nothingness*, Sartre tells us that "the person" is never entirely made or constructed. We could even say that "the person" *is not*, inasmuch as at every instant he/she exists only as the surpassed result of all previous totalizing procedures by which we continually try to as-similate the nonassimilable. The greatest nonassimilable is first and foremost our childhood. It is disappointing that Sartre does not say why. I suppose it is because childhood is the period during which we developed, without knowing why, the very affective disposition that we now bring to bear in all our judgments. Or perhaps it is because we feel that somehow the answer to what we are is back there in an existence which is out of reach. Either view poses problems for an existentialist freedom, and we must return to this question later.

In defining stress Sartre associates it with neurosis. In speaking of personalization, however, he clearly is referring to what happens in any life. From one point of view the developing movement of the person is circular, for it retains the same center or cluster of centers—like a snowball. Yet insofar as the continued process of totalizing, detotalizing, and retotalizing introduces new significances and consequences and provides continual enrichment of the patterns in which the original centers are integrated, there is clearly a modification or change of direction which is inappropriate for the image of a circle with expanding circumference. Therefore Sartre prefers the analogy of the spiral.

> We may picture the circular movement as in a three-dimensional space, like a spiral with several centers, which does not cease to remove itself from them or to raise itself above them while executing an indefinite number of revolutions around its point of departure. [1:657]

Thus, while a reader of 1860 would not say that Gustave Flaubert is a frustrated and jealous younger brother, or one underloved, or a passive agent, the novelist has not ceased to be any one of these. They are all part of the self-objectification that has resulted in *Madame Bovary*. But Flaubert cannot be reduced to them, nor can he be said to be these in the same way that he was in 1837. There has been a series of transformations and even the fact of being or not being unassimilable may have changed for any of the given elements. In an important footnote, Sartre writes,

> Their meaning and their function have not ceased to vary since each revolution installs them in a richer ensemble, more differentiated and better integrated. It is in terms of the retotalization at a given conjuncture, at whatever level it is operative, that the constituting determinations are themselves determined as being or not being assimilable; and in the latter case that they are seen as having a role to play—real or imaginary according to whether the integration is actual or dreamed. [1:658]

In seeking to locate the secret "wound," *le mal* of Flaubert's childhood, Sartre has made use of material derived from the literary works written when Gustave was between thirteen and sixteen. The very act of writing shows him already at an elevated point in the spiral, from which vantage point he looks back at an earlier stage.

Tracing the first steps, Sartre brings us back again to that same critical year of seven. It was then that Gustave decided that he wanted to be a great actor.[1] This signifies the choice of the imaginary, the unreal, which we will find at each turn of the spiral. In almost the same terms Sartre raises the problem he grappled with in *The Words.* Gustave wanted to be a great actor. Jean-Paul wanted to be a famous writer. Children regularly have dreams of their future. To want to be a doctor or an explorer or an famous athelete is to dream of a reality attainable by praxis in the world. But in wanting to write or to act, the dream is "a dream of a future dream" (1:661). To have such a dream is to reverse the normal order of praxis by making the real into the means of attaining the unreal. No wonder, Sartre says, that families are disturbed at this opting out of the real world on the part of their offspring. Unhappiness is not enough by itself to insure the choice of the imaginary. Sartre has already shown us reasons for his belief that Gustave tended to confuse the categories of the real and the unreal. Gradually he allowed the unreal image to have priority over reality. Sartre does not mean that Gustave became autistic or that he retreated wholly into a fantasy world, but rather that his attitude toward himself and others was modeled on structures of the imagination, that he *acted* his being and had no sense of self except as the role he played was confirmed by others. In short, he made himself into an imaginary or make-believe child.

Analyzing Gustave's development from imaginary child to the artist of the imagination, Sartre points to three factors which resulted in his being affected with unreality from the start. Each one will correspond to one moment of temporalization, but the effects will be felt at every level of the totalizing spiral. They are: Gustave's relation to his mother, seen in the areas of action, language, and sexuality; his relation to his father, seen in the Other's look; his relation to his sister, seen in what Sartre calls the appearance of the gesture. We may note that the first two are the same ones that Sartre singled out as decisive in determining the constitution of Flaubert. For the third, Caroline has replaced Achille, and the influence now is positive rather than negative.

## Oedipus and the Phallic Mother

Sartre claims that Gustave sought to find his ego by coinciding with the self that others saw. It is not surprising that Sartre finds significance in Flaubert's references to mirrors. We recall Emma Bovary gazing into the looking-glass as she tries to seize the full implications of herself in the role, first of virtuous woman, and then of adulteress. Writing to Louise Colet, Flaubert consoles her for a failure by telling her that our only victories are those that we achieve in front of our mirror. He tries to cheer up Louis Bouilhet in a fit of depression by advising him to look in the glass and rearrange his hair. Admittedly, on the surface these last two examples seem to point to the mirror as a means of escape from the judgment of others. Particularly to Louise, Flaubert seems to say that she should be her own judge. Nevertheless Sartre argues that the direction to look into the mirror is revealing. In order to realize his independent consciousness (the for-itself), "Gustave chooses for an image of the *for itself* the object that manifests, in an illusory image, his *being-for-the-other*" (1:680–81 n.).

Sartre selects two of Flaubert's references to mirrors as the starting point for prolonged discussion of major themes in Flaubert's personalization. First he picks up Flaubert's remark that he could not shave before the looking glass without guffawing.[2] The obvious intent of this comment is to call attention to the absurdity of the universe and the futility of all human aspirations. In the face to be shaved, Flaubert sees already the future corpse, itself a mere collection of molecules. In the background Sartre finds the look and the laugh of Flaubert's scientific father. The son's laughter is to insure that he is on the side of the laughter and not its victim. In the next chapter we will see how the derisive laugh and the awareness of the Father's Look set the stage for a long series of developments as Flaubert lived through his adolescence and early manhood.

The second passage Sartre takes from *November,* the autobiographical novel that stands at the borderline between the juvenilia and the adult works. Here the young hero says, "I would like to be a woman so as to be able to admire myself, to stand nude...and to look at myself mirrored in the streams." Sartre writes, "The laugh has given way to admiration" (1:684). Flaubert himself is the object of both. In a long section called "The Mirror and the Fetish," Sartre discusses the quality of Flaubert's sexuality. This time it is the mother's influence which is paramount. Sartre attempts to show that Flaubert's sexuality is inextricably linked with a certain femininity in his personality, with onanism and fetishism, and with the old themes of passivity and the choice of the imaginary. To me, at least, the argument is persuasive and seems to fit what we know of Flaubert. While most of it is compatible with basic Freudian insights, it goes beyond what a traditional Freudian would be likely to say.

For the development of Flaubert's sexual attitudes, Sartre postulates two fundamental factors which might at first seem to be contradictory but which, by their mutual limitation, combine to give to

77

the sexuality its unique quality. One of these is Oedipal; the other is Flaubert's secret longing to be a girl. We have seen already that in Sartre's interpretation, Madame Flaubert greeted with disappointment the newborn son who usurped the place of the daughter she had hoped to have. If this was indeed the case, Sartre is probably right in claiming that the boy sensed the truth of the situation, if not at first then at least later when he watched his sister receiving a love and tenderness which had never been bestowed on him.[3] Sartre concludes that Gustave longed, and in imagination tried, to be the daughter his mother had wanted.

In the familiar facts of Flaubert's biography and in his novels there are numerous signs of a kind usually taken as indicative of an unresolved Oedipus complex: Elisa Schlessinger and the idealizations of her that appear in both versions of *A Sentimental Education,* Louise Colet, too—all of these women were older than their lovers and, except for Madame Renaud, mothers. Flaubert lived out most of his adult life in close dependency on his own mother. Even his preference for prostitutes and his refusal to marry might be interpreted as Oedipal. Sartre, however, is more interested in evidence coming from four short stories, written between ages fourteen and sixteen, and from a dream reported in *Memoirs of a Madman.* To this material he gives a psychoanalytical interpretation which is specifically connected with what Freud called the "family romance," a term Freud used referring to a variety of fantasies which are linked with the Oedipus complex. Most often these involve notions that either the child or his siblings are not really the offspring of either or both of its supposed parents. Laplanche and Pontalis say of them:

> Such phantasies are related to the Oedipal situation—they originate from the pressure exerted by the Oedipus complex. The precise motives for them are many and mixed; the desire to denigrate the parents from one angle while exalting them from another, notions of grandeur, attempts to circumvent the incest barrier, an expression of fraternal rivalry, etc.[4]

Sartre holds that Flaubert, in the stories and in the dream, was trying "to reconstruct the scandalous fact of coitus so as to render it more acceptable to him, to satisfy a fierce grudge which he nourished against his mother and in imagination to fulfill his sexual desires" (1:698). Each of the narratives treats the same double theme—the begetting and giving birth to children, the relations of mother and son.

In the first grim tale, *The Fiancée and the Tomb,* Annette, the chaste fiancée of Paul, is raped by Robert. Paul kills her ravisher but is wounded by Robert's guards. Dying, he tells Annette that, if she wishes to be united with him, she must secure both Robert's dagger and his head. She attempts to do so; but after she has mutilated the corpse with two blows of the sword, the weapon falls from her hand. Sartre comments, "This is because she is cowardly or, if you prefer, not virile enough to play her role of man to the end" (1:699). Annette is subsequently confronted by Satan in the form of Robert, whose seductions she firmly resists. Then, surprisingly, Paul's ghost appears and damns her to Hell, at which point the poor girl understandably dies of shock. The heroine of this grotesquerie stands for Flaubert's mother. Sartre writes of Flaubert-Oedipus,

> As we see, the rancor of the young lover is relentless. It is not enough for him to have killed the ignoble man who abused his fiancée; she will be purified in his eyes only if, become virile, she herself takes the sword (a phallic and social symbol of masculinity) in order to mutilate the corpse and take the dagger from it (another symbol). The mother is guilty of having allowed herself to be violated; let her rediscover her virility by castrating the man who rendered her a woman. [1:699]

What is expressed here is not sexual desire for the mother, and not precisely sexual jealousy either. Clearly, as Sartre points out, the only way for the child Gustave to find the thought of sexual relations between his parents bearable was to assume that these were thrust upon the mother against her will. At the same time she is culpable and must be punished. I think that taken by itself, this fourteen-year-old's story might at first thought seem to lend itself to Philip Slater's theory. Slater argues that the child commonly fears and distrusts his mother's sexuality, which he cannot understand but which, he feels, threatens the exclusive relation which he would like to maintain with her; consequently he would like to deprive her of her sex—or better yet have her give it up voluntarily.[5] Slater's view, however, could not account for the masculine role taken on by the mother. Sartre goes one step further than Slater. In the fantasy the mother rejects the satisfaction of her own feminine sexuality, but she does not cease to be a woman when she assumes the role of the man. Rather she becomes the phallic mother. We will see that this last notion becomes one of the keys in Sartre's explanation of Flaubert's adult sexual life.

A second story, *The Lady and the Hurdy-gurdy Player*, subtitled *The Mother and the Coffin*, more openly reproaches the mother and allows the son to satisfy his incestuous desires in all innocence. Henriette marries a wealthy duke and bears him a son seven months after their marriage. The child is really the son of a former lover, beloved but too poor for her to think of marrying him. (Here we have the familiar hero of the family romance, the boy whose supposed father is not the true parent.) In Flaubert's story, the poverty-stricken lover, as a result of the French Revolution, gains a fortune; the duke loses his. The mother discovers that her son has been taken away by "a hurdy-gurdy player," who is, of course, the true father. Sartre exclaims, "Behold the mother punished. Not enough. She is more and more degraded and at last forced by hunger to enter a brothel." When she is forty, a wealthy young man comes to the house and chooses her above all the others. Henriette "had never experienced so much pleasure as with him, never had kisses been so sweet, or words of tenderness so gentle and so well chosen." He pays her and leaves. Shortly thereafter the stranger is killed by vagrants. The mother recognizes her son in his corpse, goes mad, and throws herself beneath the wheels of his funeral coach. Oedipus, though punished, dies as innocently as he had lived. Sartre writes,

> Gustave triumphs. He avenges himself against his so-called father, Achille-Cléophas, dead, by sleeping with his widow; and he avenges himself on his mother, who neglected him in his infancy, by forcing her to find pleasure as she has never found it before and, since she refused him maternal love, defiling her with an incestuous love. [1:701]

Except for a possible reference to the specific denial of the mother's tenderness to the child Gustave, Sartre's interpretation of this tale is classically Freudian and might as such apply to any male.

*Madame d'Ecouy* repeats the theme of incest and once more punishes the mother for fulfilling herself sexually. This time, in a quite unbelievable sequel of erroneous assumptions, the adult son mistakenly makes love to his mother under the impression that he is with her maid, then kills his mother's lover in the belief that he is protecting her honor against slander. Sartre notes that chance has replaced psychological motivation but says that this emphasizes the fantastic and oneiric quality of the narrative. "Gustave is concerned with only one thing: to have sexual intercourse innocently with his guilty mother and to kill his father out of filial piety" (1:701–2).

In the last of the four stories, *Two Loves and Two Coffins*, the incest theme is missing, but a woman is slowly destroyed—punished,

Sartre says—for having been capable of loving her husband. She first loses him to another woman, then is poisoned by her. After her death Ernest, the wife's platonic friend, kills the criminal husband, saying, "You are the assassin. I am the executioner." It would appear that here Flaubert has identified himself with the sexless avenger. Ernest is like the son who loves exclusively and possessively, but not sexually. Sartre finds this last tale significantly similar to a more richly imaginative dream, a nightmare which Flaubert recorded from his student days in *Memoirs of a Madman*. It is worth quoting in full.

> It was in a green field decked with flowers along a riverside. I was with my mother walking close to the edge of the bank. She fell. I saw the water foam, circles spreading and suddenly disappearing. The water resumed its course and then I heard nothing any longer but the sound of the water which passed among the rushes and made the reeds bend low. Suddenly my mother called to me: "Help . . . Help! O my poor child, help me!" I leaned over to look, lying flat on my stomach on the grass. I saw nothing; the cries continued. An irresistible force held me to the ground, and I heard the cries: "I am drowning! I am drowning! Help me!" The water flowed on, flowed on, transparent. And that voice which I heard from the depths of the river overwhelmed me with despair and frenzy.[6]

Sartre views the mother's death by drowning and the son's failure to rescue her as both a Fall (stressing the sexual connotations of the word) and a death sentence. At first the two of them form a couple, and all is happiness. I presume that this would refer to infancy and early childhood as Flaubert would have liked it to be or perhaps as he had wishfully reconstructed it. When the mother slides into the river, it remains clear and transparent. "His mother has *become the river*. . . . The Fall represents here both her betrayal (she abandons her son and her authority and melts away into liquid docility) and the brutal revelation of her imposture and her punishment." She is not dead, Sartre goes on to say, since her voice remains; rather she is drowned in submission to the innumerable cares and concerns that separate her from her child. "She is lost, she is no longer the strong woman of my early childhood" (1:703). Suddenly the mother recognizes her powerlessness and begs her son for pardon and for rescue. Sartre sees in the son's failure both resentment and a confession of impotence. It is as if he were saying, "Where would I get the strength to rescue you? I am such as you have made me, inert and paralyzed." To jump into the river would in waking life have been a simple thing for Flaubert, who was, as Sartre reminds us, a good swimmer. In the dream situation he cannot move. For "it is to become a male and an agent; of that he is forever incapable." Caroline Flaubert reaps the harvest of her own transgression. Gustave's passivity is both her fault and her punishment. A traditional Freudian approach would emphasize the sexual significance of the river. Particularly if we posit an identification of mother and river, then the symbolism of the invitation to the son to plunge into it and his combined desire and inability to comply are self-evident. His resistance might be explained—in Freudian terms—as either the result of an inhibition too strong to give way even in dreams or of the castration complex. It is entirely possible that this signification is there as a subordinate meaning. But I think that Sartre's interpretation is richer and more convincing because it is more specific and more closely tied to Flaubert's individual situation. The dream reveals symbolically Flaubert's intuitive comprehension of his psychological reality. For Freud sexuality determines personality. For Sartre the quality of a person's sexual life depends on more basic structures. In *Being and Nothingness* he regarded sexuality as one more manifestation of an underlying choice of being. In *The Family Idiot* it is the product of one's constitution (childhood conditioning, especially the relation with the mother) and the gradual process of personalization. In the case of Flaubert, we may say that the maternal relation instilled in the child a fundamental passivity and condemned him to a sexual life which, to a significant extent, would be lived in the imaginary. Passivity and the imaginary resulted in a certain femininity, a tendency to onanism, a strong inclination to fetishism.

That there was a "feminine" side to Flaubert's personality is attested by contemporary comments. There was nothing whatsoever of the woman in his appearance. He was extraordinarily handsome in his youth but always large in build. As an adult he was more than six feet tall, loud-voiced and boisterous, awkward in his movements. Among the nicknames he like to attach to himself one of his favorites was "the Giant." On the other hand, Benjamin Bart cites Zola to the effect that some of Flaubert's many close women friends enjoyed him as a companion, but did not take him seriously as a man because he was a "feminine type," more like them.[7] Sartre reminds us that, when his physicians treated Flaubert like a nervous old woman, the novelist felt vaguely flattered. In a letter to George Sand, he suggests that he is "of both sexes"; to Madame Brainne, he declared, "Lesbos is my country. I have its refinements and its languors [*les délicatesses et les langueurs].*" Finally there is the fact that in *Madame Bovary* Flaubert chose to project himself (both satirically and with empathy) into a woman heroine. What must this Flaubert be, Sartre asked in *Search for a Method,* "in order to objectify himself in his work first as a mystic monk and then some years later as a resolute 'slightly masculine' woman?"[8]

A feminine quality in personality is not the same as a female sexuality. And what would we mean by speaking of feminine sexuality in a man? That he is a homosexual? This Sartre denies. If we are to understand this feminine side of Sartre's Flaubert, we must return to the hero of *November* who imagined himself to be a woman admiring her nude beauty in a looking glass. Sartre writes,

> Gustave would like to stand naked before his mirror. I have no doubt that he did so. From the time of his early childhood, face to face with his reflection, he played the role of a woman who undresses herself. [1:684]

Flaubert's preoccupation with his own image would be easy to understand in the light of Sartre's interpretation up to now. Gustave seeks a sense of self-identity in the *desirable object* which he is for the Other (1:686). If, as Sartre suggests, the usual outcome of the self-admiration and self-caressing was masturbation, that too fits. It is by realizing himself as the desired object—i.e., as both the subject and the object of desire—that Flaubert can best grasp the reality of his being as others see him. But why does this young boy before the mirror feel compelled to stretch imagination to the breaking point by seeing himself as a woman? And did he indeed do so? Sartre refers us to an entry in the *Intimate Notebook* (1840–41).

> There are days when one would like to be an athlete and others when one would like to be a woman. In the first case it is the muscle which quivers; in the second it is the flesh which yearns and flames.[9]

Sartre notes the disjunction. One cannot simultaneously be a Hercules working out with weights and a woman enjoying sexual pleasure. Sartre adds that Flaubert seems to associate sexual gratification with a certain passivity and specifically with what a woman would feel. Sexual enjoyment for Flaubert implies a consenting, expectant passivity, a swooning self-abandonment, and an expanding of flesh set aflame by caresses. Hence, Sartre argues, "If Gustave wants to be a woman, this is because his sexuality, partially feminine, requires a change of sex which would allow him a full development of his resources" (1:685). There is an evident connection between this feminine-passive reaction to sexual pleasure and the pantheistic ecstasies of Flaubert's boyhood. Another passage which Sartre cites from *November* makes this clear. Nature and the erotic are hardly separable. The hero longs to be smothered under roses, bruised and shattered by kisses; he yearns "to be the flower shaken by the wind, the bank moistened by the river, the earth made fertile by the sun." In all of these images, he is the passive object; furthermore, Sartre notes, that in each one the object in nature to which he compares himself is feminine in French (flower, bank, earth), while the active agents are masculine (wind, river, sun). What we have is "the *sexual* version of the pantheistic ecstasy" (1:685).

Gustave's wish that he might be a girl in order to win his mother's love (if Sartre is correct), his hero's imagining himself as the feminine partner to be moistened and fecundated by the male—all of this would ordinarily be interpreted by either psychotherapist or literary critic as pointing to overt or latent homosexuality. There is no incontrovertible evidence that Flaubert had sexual relations with any of the men with whom he maintained an intense friendship. Enid Starkie states, on the tenuous evidence of certain expressions in Flaubert's letters, that there was a homosexual attachment between him and Louis Bouilhet, but this seems highly unlikely.[10] No contemporary of Flaubert is known to have referred to him as being homosexual. Erotic relations in his fiction are without exception heterosexual. Of course this evidence is not conclusive, and the homosexual tendencies might have been present but repressed. Sartre rejects the idea that Flaubert was homosexual, partly on the basis of evidence from the correspondence and partly because he believes another explanation seems to fit better all that we know objectively of Flaubert as well as the picture Sartre himself has given of Gustave's childhood.

When Sartre, in *Search for a Method*, commented briefly on Flaubert's "femininity," he stated categorically that Flaubert was absolutely not "an invert." To document the pronouncement, he simply added a footnote to the effect that, while the letters to Louise Colet show him to be onanist and narcissistic, they boast of amorous exploits which Flaubert would not have dared to fabricate in writing to the only possible witness of them. This, of course, proves nothing, as Sartre surely knows. Male homosexuals are not necessarily or even usually impotent if they choose to have relations with women. In the biography Sartre is more cautious. He notes that Flaubert's attachments to his closest male friends (Alfred le Poittevin, Maxime Du Camp, Louis Bouilhet) were "homosexual but platonic" (1:682). He is willing to grant that under special circumstances Flaubert might be sexually aroused by males. He explains very carefully the reasons why, despite all this, he is unwilling to say that Flaubert *was* a homosexual. These come down to the fact that Sartre believes that what superficially appears to be homosexual in Flaubert is a secondary manifestation, and not primary.

Sartre's first objection to calling Flaubert homosexual is because of his *"parti pris* for nominalism, which forbids classifications." This is more than a laudable resistance to applying labels. In *Being and Nothingness,* as we have noted, Sartre insisted that, while all human relations are sexual, the particular quality of one's sexuality is a manifestation of one's basic choice of being; it does not determine the personality structures. Now he reaffirms his position and makes it more explicit.

> Sexuality is neither cause nor effect. It is a totalization, through sex, of the lived, which means that this totalization sums up and sexualizes all the structures which characterize a person. Moreover, inversely, every totalization of the lived, whatever its meaning may be, sums up and totalizes the sexual structures by going beyond them toward another end. [1:686n.]

Even if one were able to establish a certain hierarchy of human needs, Sartre goes on to say, the higher could not be reduced to the lower, and there is constantly a mutual influence of one upon the other in a circular pattern. For example, economic alienation may, and indeed must, at certain moments be lived as a sexual alienation. The complexity of any total human situation or human orientation is never the simple sum of its parts.

For Flaubert, Sartre holds that passivity and not homosexuality is more fundamental.

> Gustave needs to receive caresses more than to give them; he wants to be the game bird rather than the hunter. We know why. But this postulation of his passivity does not reach so far as to decide the sex of the aggressor. We must recognize rather that it is the aggression which counts and circumstances alone will decide the partner. [1:686–87]

To support this claim Sartre discusses some interesting material in letters which Flaubert wrote to Bouilhet from Egypt.

Flaubert comments with some slight surprise on the openness with which his Egyptian male acquaintances speak of their homosexual interests and relations. He remarks humorously, though possibly with a somewhat serious undertone, that, since he and du Camp are traveling for the sake of their education and with certain commissions from the government, they have concluded it is their duty to try this "mode of ejaculation."[11] He adds that such opportunities are usually provided at the baths. A later letter tells us of Flaubert's visit to one of these establishments. Submersion in the warm water he found "very voluptuous and tinged with a sweet melancholy." He enjoyed relaxing in quiet revery. He remarked that the bath attendants "handle you and turn you over like embalmers preparing you for the tomb." Sartre notes that in their hands Flaubert felt in himself the helplessness of the corpse; his passivity was internalized as voluptuousness. What of the projected sexual experiment? Flaubert reports to Bouilhet that the attendant, having finished washing, made a first gesture toward masturbation, calling out "baksheesh! baksheesh!" "He was a man about fifty years old, ignoble, disgusting." Flaubert pushed him away and laughed aloud. Sartre points out that the man's physical ugliness would explain Flaubert's total rejection, but he finds in the sequel of the story indication that Flaubert was sexually aroused all the same. A short time later, as he sat wrapped in towels and smoking a hookah, Flaubert inquired as to whether a handsome young man whom he had observed earlier was still around. Regrettably he was not. Or perhaps fortunately. Sartre finds it a bit suspicious that Flaubert did not try to send for him or to look for another handsome youth. To Sartre the significant and weak part of the tale is the absence of the one who might have brought the adventure to a conclusion. Evidently Louis Bouilhet was curious, too, for he asked whether anything happened after that. Sartre quotes the reply.

> Gustave, hitherto so prolix, replies to him briefly, "You ask whether I completed the work of the baths. Yes, and on a hefty young fellow, pock-marked, with an enormous white turban. It made me laugh, that's all. But I shall try again. For an experience to be done right, it must be repeated." After which he doesn't breathe another word on that subject. [1:688]

In close conjunction with the Egyptian experience Sartre quotes from an unfinished manuscript, *Pastiche,* written when Flaubert was eighteen, which reads like a parody of the work of the Marquis de Sade but at the same time reveals the more personal fantasies of its author. As the culmination of a night of sexual orgies, an oriental potentate calls for his young minions. He embraces and kisses the nude males, then has himself lifted up and carried in their arms (*se fait porter dans leurs bras*) (1:690).

Sartre's interpretation of the evidence in these documents may be summed up as follows: homosexual inclinations in Flaubert all point to an unacknowledged wish to be the passive partner. He is sexually excited by the voluptuousness of the bath and the feeling of being handled like an object in the hands of the masseur. Put off by the man's unattractive appearance, he thinks of the handsome young attendant he had seen earlier. But he does not seek him out; this would have been to assume the active male role, "to take." As for the later "confession" to Bouilhet, that is simply fake. The picturesque, literary details betray it as an invention. Either it was purely invented, or Flaubert was trying to hide the fact that for him the adventure was a fiasco. In a spirit of bravado Flaubert tells Bouilhet he will try again but does not make the attempt. Obviously the desire to be sexually fulfilled by a *man* is not primary. The passage from *Pastiche* is especially revealing. The role of the youths is active, but what precisely do they do? They lift up their master and carry him in their arms. The image suggests that of the child raised in the loving embrace of its parent. This, of course, is where Sartre has been leading us. Homosexuality is not a satisfactory solution for Flaubert. "His passivity requires his being reconstituted by the embrace of a mother-goddess" (1:703–4).

When Gustave imagined himself a girl admiring herself in the mirror, when he stood before the glass and caressed himself, his real desire is not to masturbate but to be masturbated. "Everything happened as if the child, frustrated by withheld caresses, tried miserably to incarnate the one who had the mandate to give them to him" (1:696). It was Flaubert's mother who remained the ultimate object of his sexual desire but not in the conventional pattern of Oedipus and Jocasta. Lacking all experience of reciprocal caresses, Flaubert did not develop the desire to assume the role of the father who takes the mother but maintained rather the need to be the object of her caresses. It was she who awakened him to the sense of his body as passive object. Under her hands, his flesh learned to crave a fulfillment in caresses which were never given; he was stimulated to long for what, at that time, he could neither understand nor express. Sartre writes,

> She had nothing of the man in her, the timid spouse of Achille-Cléophas. If the child endowed her with a secret masculinity, it was because of her imperious and cold efficiency. [1:696]

To the extent that his mother rendered Gustave passive, she became for him the agent. Together the two constituted a joyless androgynous couple.

> When he takes on the role of the woman before the mirror, and when he invokes a masculine partner, he cannot understand that in reality he demands to be possessed by his mother provided on the occasion with an imaginary phallus. [1:696]

As Sartre interprets, Gustave psychologically wanted to be the girl who would be tenderly loved by his mother; sexually he craved to be the object of caresses. We can see why the usual Oedipal and homosexual patterns do not quite fit Flaubert. Obviously, too, if there was to be sexual fulfillment, this would be possible only where relations were lived with a generous portion of the imaginary. Speaking of Flaubert as a young man, Sartre writes,

> He realizes obscurely that his mother is no longer the active half of the androgynous couple of which he is the passive half. She has been so, however, in illusion. Putting her imprint upon him, she has condemned him forever to have only an *imaginary* sexual life. An unreal woman in men's hands, he will be an unreal man in his relations with women. [1:703]

If the reader feels reluctant to put too much faith in Sartre's reconstructions of sexual musings before the mirror, he may be more impressed by what we know of Flaubert's liaison with Louise Colet. Slightly older than he, she was a woman of strong passions, "violent, possessive, vindictive." She is known to have stabbed an uncomplimentary critic, Alphonse Karr, with a butcher knife. Sartre cites contemporary evidence that she spoke of her sexuality in the same manner as was customary for men of that period. Although the liaison lasted for eight years, Flaubert saw her only for brief periods at rare intervals. He evidently reveled in being the object of her fierce passions and at the same time feared it. Sartre says,

> When he returned to her now and then at Paris or at Mantes, the long chastity to which he had reduced his mistress must have rendered her mad; she threw herself upon him. Violated! It was the fulfillment of his dream. [1:705]

The Goncourt brothers recorded in their journal that Flaubert once told how he had let Louise beat him while he fought against an almost compelling desire to kill her. Sartre finds that this episode epitomizes Flaubert's sexual life: the Norman giant submitting passively to her blows, refraining from holding her at a distance, as he could so easily have done, while an imaginary male murmurs within the depths of his heart, "I will kill you!"

The most persuasive piece of evidence for Sartre's theory comes from two letters to Louise. In the first of these Flaubert wrote, "Nature, believe me, was wrong in making you a woman; *you are on the side of the males.*" Toward the end of their affair, he said, even more significantly,

> I have always tried (but I seem to have failed) to make of you a sublime hermaphrodite. I want you to be a man above the waist, while below, you encumber and trouble me and engulf yourself with the female element. [1:706]

Admittedly, Flaubert's intention here was to endow Louise with a masculine mind, but the language betrays other levels of meaning. Sartre rightly finds it significant that although Louise at first appeared to Flaubert to be "on the side of the males," his claim to change her does not aim at removing her masculinity but as sublimating her femininity. Furthermore Louise as hermaphrodite would be male activity above, woman below. "Would not Gustave be the complementary hermaphrodite, a woman with a man's sex?" (1:706). Sartre suggests that Gustave, feeling himself to be the lost half of an androgynous being, dreams of a double hermaphrodite, each half "provided with a real sex and an imaginary sex." This would be, I suppose, a replica of the original mother-and-child relation as Sartre thinks Flaubert imagined it.

Sartre suggests that in Louise, Flaubert found the mistress of his adolescent dreams (as expressed especially in *November*). He longed to be loved with a love which would devour him and make him afraid, to have one of those terrible mistresses who make men their slaves. In a perceptive reading of *Passion and Virtue*, Sartre finds what may indeed be the clue to the essential sexual relations of the pair. There is a double and contradictory identification of the author with his characters. He is Mazza, the insatiable woman whose dormant desires are first awakened by the seductive Ernest and who then assumes the aggressive role until she frightens him off. But there is a degree of identification with the cowardly lover as well; in him

Flaubert could enjoy being the object desired by this devouring mistress. Sartre says, "Ernest puts the Ocean between him and the imperious Mazza; Gustave is content with a hundred kilometers" (1:707). Following Sartre, we are to imagine—or hypothesize—a complex interplay of real and imaginary in Flaubert's sexual engagement with Louise. His passivity and secret femininity are satisfied by her aggressive advances. Aroused by them he can then assume with her the role of dominant male. On the purely psychological level there was possibly more of play-acting in the second phase than in the first. Sartre sums up, "Gustave makes himself virile in order to feel himself female while penetrating his partner or, after coitus, under her caresses" (1:728).

Sartre suggests that there was always a large degree of onanism in Flaubert's sexuality. As an adult Flaubert refers nostalgically, gleefully, and without any evident sense of guilt to the school lavatories in which he carried on masturbatory practices.[12] The fact that he so readily and easily speaks of the matter would seem to indicate that he regarded masturbation as simply a natural procedure *faute de mieux*. Indeed, Sartre does not argue that Flaubert ever felt any guilt in this respect, and certainly his sex life was not lacking in partners—albeit the greater number of these were prostitutes. But Sartre makes two special claims in this connection, both of them pointing to the dominance of the imaginary. Referring once again to Flaubert caressing himself before the mirror, Sartre finds that the masturbation with which it presumably ended is different from the same practice in most men. If by an act of imagination Flaubert imagines himself to be a woman as desirable object, then he is not simply satisfying a need in the absence of a particular woman or even of Woman, represented by a composite of experiences or photographs. Rather Flaubert imagines that he is being masturbated. It is imagination "of the second degree," and it is possible only in solitude. Sartre suggests that this is one of the reasons why Flaubert rejected the offer of the Egyptian bath attendant. In *Being and Nothingness* and in *No Exit* Sartre wrote of the destructive power of the Third to destroy the efforts of a pair of lovers to set up some kind of complicity. For Flaubert, committed to the life of the imagination, Sartre states that even the second is an embarrassment. At best the partner serves as an analogue for the more significant relation which lives in Flaubert's imagination. Here we may find an additional explanation as to why he was content to love Louise mostly from a distance. Sartre finds it significant, too, that in *Memoirs of a Madman,* in which Flaubert wrote of his encounter with Elisa Schlessinger, the true revelation of his love for her comes to him at the point when a year later he visits the beach of Troubille and reconstructs the previous summer in his memory.

Sartre's final piece of evidence is a long passage which he cites from one of the unpublished sections of *Madame Bovary.* This throws light on still another aspect of Flaubert's sexuality—his fetishism. In real life it was Louise's bedroom slippers which he particularly cherished while separated from her. In the passage originally intended for the novel, Léon finds a glove which Emma has dropped. Lying in bed he holds it close to him.

> He smelled a faint perfume, something delicate, like faded violets. Then Léon half-closed his eyes; he glimpsed the glove on Emma's wrist, buttoned, taut, moving coquettishly in a thousand indeterminate functions. He breathed it in, kissed it; he thrust the four fingers of his right hand into it and slept with it beneath his mouth. [1:718]

We may observe, Sartre says, that Léon does not, as one might have expected, seek in the glove traces of Emma's past gestures. As he examines it and smells it, he seems to possess the whole body of Emma, as flesh. Emma is there "reduced to the inferior being of an instrument. It is Gustave's imaginary sadism which is satisfied; he reduces a living woman to the status of thing; she is *delivered to him.*" Sartre interprets Léon's response as a way of punishing Emma for his own weakness in wishing that he might surrender himself to her. But suddenly everything changes, Léon slips his own fingers into the glove and sleeps with it close to his lips. Obviously we have moved from the reaction of resentment to the satisfaction of erotic desire. The symbolism, Sartre thinks, works simultaneously on two levels. Léon's hand in the glove stands for Léon's penis. He penetrates and possesses Emma. But this is only secondary to an even more important meaning. Among the notes that Flaubert attached to his plans for this section, he wrote that the intention was to let the reader "understand that Léon aroused himself with the glove." Sartre feels that the "penetration" was only preliminary to the final voluptuous pleasure. The glove filled out with Léon's fingers "is the virile hand of Emma which masturbates him. . . . The fetish is a woman's hand and a phallus indistinguishably" (1:719). We are brought back to the phallic mother. We may note that Freud found evidence for the fact that often an individual may use the fetish as a substitute for the imagined maternal phallus.[13] Sartre quotes Mannoni in this connection. The neurotic says, "I know very well . . . but all the same. . . ." Here the fetishized object takes the place of the "all the same" and makes possible the bridge from reality to imaginary experience.

We can understand now the distinctive turn that Sartre gives to the Oedipal material and the problem of homosexuality. Like Freud, Sartre would say that Gustave's first sexual impulse was directed toward his mother and that this pattern dominated his adult sexual relations. To some degree all partners were surrogates for the mother.[14] So far one might rightly speak of an unresolved Oedipus complex. What is different from Freud's view is that while there may be resentment against the usurping father, any suppressed death-wish is not the result of the child's desire to assume the active role of the father. This is partially because the boy wishes he might have been the girl who was to have been and later became the object of the mother's tenderness, and partly due to the passivity induced by lack of maternal love. Consequently there develops a certain femininity but not a true homosexuality. A woman remains the object of Flaubert's central desire, but a woman who will caress him as a child so as to enable him subsequently to play the role of active adult male. The phallic mother fantasy is necessary if Flaubert is to rise to the feats of sexual prowess of which he boasted to Louise. Madame Colet was perhaps as well qualified for the role as anyone.

In Sartre's view Flaubert's sexuality is closely bound up with the hypothesis that his mother did indeed tend to her infant son dutifully but without real affection. Even if we accept Sartre's analysis of the adult man's reaction as valid, that does not by itself prove that the reconstruction of the early mother-child relation is correct. At most we can say that the hypothesis is reasonable and can be accepted as one possible explanation. At least this much I think we must grant to Sartre. Passivity and a certain tendency toward androgyny are essential ingredients of what we know of Flaubert's sexual life; yet they do not seem to add up to a clear-cut case of homosexuality induced by the Oedipus complex. The image of the phallic mother as an imaginative structure, of Flaubert's intimate sexual preference, makes sense so long as we do not make the mistake of supposing that it was there as something explicitly recognized—any more than the Oedipal implications would have been.

## THE SISTER AS MEDIATOR

> There are three children in the Flaubert family. The father favors
> the older boy, the mother favored in advance the younger girl.
> Gustave is not the favorite of anyone. In a few years, as we know,
> he will be jealous of Achille and will wish for his death. Is he going
> to be jealous of Caroline? [1:723]

There were three years between the second two. With regard to
Gustave's feelings at the very beginning, there can be no evidence.
Sartre suggests that at the age of three the child may have still felt
sufficiently secure in his father's love so as not to feel threatened by
the newcomer. The situation is more complex with regard to the
mother. Members of the family reported that from the start he
seemed to adore his baby sister. Sartre claims that this display of
affection must have been exaggerated to have elicited so much comment. It may have been partly to please the parents. Sartre suggests
another reason. Perhaps the small Gustave, realizing that the baby
was preferred, sought to disqualify that preference by loving the tiny
Caroline better than his mother could—and against her. It would
seem to me more natural to assume that the three-year-old child,
particularly if he was as passively dependent as Sartre has described
him, would tend to value what his mother valued and to imitate her
in emotional responses to the new arrival. Whatever the case may
have been, the decisive moment came when Gustave was seven. At
the time of the Fall and Second Weaning, the boy might very easily
have resented his sister, particularly when Madame Flaubert attempted to teach reading to the two of them together, resulting in
Gustave's social disgrace. That he did not become jealous Sartre attributes to two factors. First, she was a girl; within the Flaubert
family structure, this immediately marked her as inferior, not a rival.
Second, Gustave found in her a necessary means to fulfill a role he
had chosen for himself.

In introducing his discussion of the relations between Gustave and
Caroline, Sartre says, "If she were to give him the chance to love her
(I mean by that, with a strong affection, modest and true) he would
be saved" (1:722). To me, even keeping within the limits of Sartrean
premises, it seems that Caroline was indeed the means for her
brother's being saved—if by that we mean his finding a positive role
to play within the family structure and his achievement of the first
step toward becoming a creative writer. Sartre admits that there was

some satisfaction and an element of truth in the relationship, but his insistence that Caroline was one of the factors of derealization that led to Flaubert's choice of the imaginary over the real leads him to describe it chiefly in negative terms.

Flaubert's niece, the third Caroline, repeating what she must have learned from her grandmother, says that Gustave made of Caroline junior his pupil, telling her whatever he had learned, taking special delight in introducing her to his earliest literary efforts. Sartre remarks that the slow learner is not likely to have given his sister any real instruction. More probably he confided in her in order to make what he learned seem real. "Nothing of what happens to him is true until it is believed by another; Caroline, by listening to his statements, confers on them a truth" (1:726). If we accept Sartre's earlier claims that Gustave, the underloved, could not distinguish between belief and truth, that he held at best a precarious grip upon the real, then it would appear that already Caroline had contributed considerably to her brother s mental health. But beyond that, what was the relation between the two? Sartre suggests that originally Gustave liked to think that he offered her protection. In the years when she was scarcely more than an infant, the watchful eyes and restraining hand of the older boy may have been a genuine defense and help. By the time the two were able to talk with each other, it was obvious that Gustave as defender and sustainer was inefficacious. The parents were the true providers as well as ultimate authority. But there was one thing which the brother and he alone could offer. He could entertain and amuse her. In the gloomy surroundings of the hospital he could give to her the gift of laughter. He could imitate, take on ridiculous poses, play the buffoon and comedian to her utter delight. In short, he gave her the gift of himself, and she received it with joy and love. It seems that one might speak here of reciprocity, but Sartre will not. Psychologically, he says, Gustave was born of poverty, Caroline of abundance. Supported by her mother's love, Caroline developed a strong sense of herself as subject-agent, which Glaubert lacked. In her self-sufficiency she could enjoy and appreciate her brother's devotion, but she did not need him in order to realize her own being. Her enjoyment of his antics was real; his performance was in the imaginary.[15]

To the section discussing the relations of brother and sister Sartre has given the title " The Gesture of the Gift." The "gift" he interprets within the context of feudal relations. We have seen that, on Sartre's reading, Flaubert felt that his father as *le Seigneur* had refused the son's homage, thus depriving him of his status as recognized vassal. Sartre argues now that "the child remains a vassal since it is a fundamental intention of his personalization, but . . . he is metamorphosed into an imaginary vassal" (1:726). With Caroline he can persuade himself that the seigneur's generosity is not dead and that the perpetual chain from suzerain to lower suzerain can be maintained. Gustave, as rejected vassal, can nevertheless play the role of suzerain to Caroline as his vassal. In so doing he is the necessary intermediary by whom the gift is conveyed. Sartre claims that the role allows Flaubert to fulfill himself via a double identification: through Caroline he sees himself as recognized vassal; in bestowing the gift upon her, he identifies with Achille-Cléophas. At the same time, by his own generous bestowal he points the finger at his father as a bad master. Obviously such a game involves a large measure of derealization, and for several reasons it cannot satisfy Gustave's needs. In putting on an act before Caroline, he asks her to judge him as a performer. But she cannot play simultaneously the two incompatible roles of judge and recipient vassal. Furthermore, to the degree that he makes himself a spectacle before her as his public, he is dependent on her. In the decision to entertain her, Sartre says, Gustave came closer than ever before to genuine praxis. But inasmuch as Caroline responds to the personage he is portraying, not to the actor off stage, his sense of self is lost in the imaginary roles (1:735). Even the gaiety he assumes is play-acting, not the expression of a joy which comes from within. For Caroline the enjoyment is real and her brother is real, but there is a lack of reciprocity due to an imbalance. Gustave seeks to grasp his true being through Caroline's eyes, but she sees only a succession of images. Sartre says, "The fictive gift of the real becomes a gift of self and the latter is altogether a gift of nothing—a pure appearance of gift—and the sacrifice of the donor to nothingness (finally he becomes an appearance)" (1:734).

To my mind, Sartre's employment of the terms of feudal relations here is forced and unconvincing. In his earlier application of them to the relation between Flaubert and his father, I was willing to accept them as describing the essential quality of the son's attitudes and behavior, feelings which might well be accurately so described by an outsider while never seen in these precise terms by the subject himself. But the complexity of the double identification in the seigneur and vassal game with Caroline would seem to demand more of explicit knowledge and deliberate use of feudal relations than Sartre should ascribe to any child. Furthermore, if it were to work at all, it would involve even more of incompatibility and derealization than Sartre has indicated. The fact that Caroline is a girl might make it easier for Gustave to accept her without being threatened. But a girl cannot be a vassal. If he is to see her in this role, he must, by another act of imagination, see her as male. This is one place where I think that Sartre has allowed himself to employ too much of the novelist's technique; he appears to be more interested in sustaining his own symbol than in reconstructing the experience of Gustave Flaubert. There is no need for all this mystification. His purpose in this section is to show that the relations which evolved between brother and sister pushed Flaubert still closer to the choice of the imaginary over the real, which results finally in his becoming a writer, the author of *Madame Bovary*. This Sartre effectively demonstrates, and he might have done so without the strained comparison with feudal structures. Accepting Sartre's earlier portrait of relationships within the Flaubert family, we might say that in Caroline, Gustave was offered the opportunity for reciprocal love, for valorization, for the role of agent. He responds in terms of that passive activity which Sartre shows to be typical of Flaubert's life pattern. His "action" consists in setting himself up as an object to be admired—and laughed at—by the Other. He seeks his reality in the response of the Other. The pleasure that he must surely have taken in his sister's delighted acceptance of what he offered ( a point which Sartre ignores) must have encouraged him to seek to communicate by means of the imaginary. Companionship with his sister may have prevented him from becoming dangerously autistic. This is of course only a hypothesis, but it seems to me reasonable. I agree with Sartre's sensible suggestion that even with her mother's sustaining love Caroline might have found the hospital environment with dying patients and with corpses in the dissecting rooms too depressing without the comic antics of her older brother. The gift was of considerable value.

Sartre claims that Gustave played the role of intermediary between father-seigneur and sister-vassal, that he derived a limited satisfaction from it, but that the project ultimately failed because of its inherent contradictions. I myself see Caroline as the mediator in a more positive sense. It was through her that Gustave first found an incentive for action. Even though the activity he chose was the transformation of the real into the imaginary, it was purposeful; it sought to communicate. It was his first attempt to objectify himself by intentional acts. He was choosing rather than allowing himself to be chosen. Yet I do not wish to overemphasize the positive results. It is interesting that Flaubert never gave any important role to a sister in the early stories, possibly because she was an exception in his cynical view of the world and not one of the causes of his unhappiness. Still, the juvenile writings, as we have seen, express attitudes of jealous resentment, morbidity, despair, anything but the healthy imagination of a well-adjusted adolescent. Caroline did not prevent the later nervous crisis, but she may have been one of the influences that led him to make of it a beginning and not the end.

Sartre mentions two aspects of Flaubert's later development which he thinks derive from the childhood relation with Caroline. First, he sees it as the archetypal pattern for all or most of the relationships that Flaubert sustained with persons who, for reasons of age or sex or whatever, he considered to be inferior to himself. The example that Sartre chooses by way of illustration would seem to prove him right if it is indeed typical as he claims. At some length he discusses Flaubert's friendship with Edmond Laporte, in which Flaubert, Sartre says, assumed the role of seigneur and Laporte obligingly put on a show of being vassal. The terms seem to me more appropriate here than they were for Gustave and Caroline. Many things do indeed seem to suggest the repetition of the earlier pattern. On a trip which the two men took together, Flaubert entertained by playing the comic role of the Garçon. He bestowed presents on Laporte. In letters he signed himself "your Giant." And he accepted tokens of homage from Laporte. At times he seemed to invent useless errands for the man. More seriously, he accepted his friend's help—even financially. Finally there came a break. Laporte, who had already seriously damaged his business by signing a note for the worthless husband of Flaubert's niece, refused to put any more money into a hopeless situation. Caroline the third tried to persuade Flaubert that this was a betrayal. Sartre argues that Flaubert, who showed timid signs of wanting a reconciliation, could have understood the refusal. What put him off was a letter from Laporte in which the latter urged Flaubert to leave matters in Laporte's hands, saying that he and others would best arrange things. It was this that destroyed the myth of seigneur and vassal. Flaubert, Sartre argues, could neither give nor accept the relation for what it really was but must cloak it all with the imaginary.

Second, Sartre claims that the acting of roles to entertain his little sister contributed to furthering Flaubert's sense of alienation from his own ego. In the section called "He and I" (*Il et Moi*), Sartre returns to the problem of Flaubert's frustrated attempt to grasp the self that he is. The mirror for Flaubert represented the Other, whether by means of it he sought his father's laugh or his mother's hands. Still, the mirror was not wholly satisfactory inasmuch as the one looking into the glass effected too obviously the movements of the image. In Caroline, Gustave found an active mirror to reflect his image—one with the docility but not the inertia of the looking glass. With her he could hope to create the particular image that she would objectify and reflect back as being him.

> He makes himself an object before his sister in order that she may *objectivize him as subject* or, if you prefer, in order that she may *realize* him [i.e., make him real] as a generosity-object. [1:763]

The problem—as Sartre showed in *Being and Nothingness*—is that, though another person does indeed objectify that self which I am for him, I myself cannot grasp this self-for-others. Therefore, in attempting to find myself in that self which the Other sees, and in determining the self which he will see, I encounter a double failure. First, that self becomes what Sartre now calls an "unrealizable." Second, if that self is something deliberately created by me, it is "he" and not "I." It is like the "Hamlet," who is equally "he" for the actor Kean and for his audience. And of course, as Sartre reminds us, Hamlet is only an imaginary being, even for the spectators. He exists in the third person, never first and not second either. One may use "you" in speaking to Kean off stage, but not to Kean as Hamlet. Sartre acknowledges that Caroline used the second person singular in addressing Gustave, but he says that her appreciation was directed toward the "he" whom he enacted, not to the "you" of her brother. I question this and feel that she must on occasion have addressed her response to the boy who performed the various roles for her. But it is possible that Flaubert did not realize that. He may well have felt that he reached her only through the roles he played. Sartre suggests that Flaubert may not quite have realized whether he was playing another or himself. This was the period in which the "he" assumed absolute priority over the "I." Gustave Flaubert had definitely chosen the imaginary.

To support his view that Flaubert throughout his life tried to find his "I" in the "he" who appeared to others, Sartre cites several out of numerous examples from the correspondence in which Flaubert calls upon his friends to picture him as he is or as he has been or as he will be. Sartre points especially to a letter to Ernest Chevalier in which Flaubert seems to be asking his friend to establish objectively the reality of the grief that Flaubert felt, or believed he felt or should feel, at the death of Alfred le Poittevin (1:767–71). There is the added fact of Flaubert's well-known fondness for having others use special nicknames for him. He was almost childishly delighted when friends took up his identification with Saint Polycarp and celebrated with him on the saint's name day. Sartre suggests that in this kind of role-playing Gustave might have found a *modus vivendi* sufficient to sustain him, in which case we would never have heard of him. Instead he took the next step in the spiral—seeking to be an actor. Meanwhile he was going to school. Sartre claims that with his schoolmates Gustave played a more elaborate version of the game he enjoyed with Caroline.

# CHAPTER THREE

## The Schoolboy

### THE LOOK AND THE LAUGH

Flaubert entered the Collège Royal in 1831, was expelled from the school in 1839; he then studied at home and took his baccalaureate in 1840. Sartre says that during the decade preceding 1840 Gustave developed from an "imaginary child" playing private roles in the structured family to the near-adult who chose to objectify the imaginary in art. He progressed through the stages of actor, dramatist, and poet to conscious artist. The process of socialization at school and the cultivation of his intimate friendship with Alfred Le Poittevin resulted in his establishing the basic pattern for his future attitude to the bourgeois and his own relations to society. In the background of all of this activity we see the dominant relation with his father and the growing importance of Flaubert's involvement with language. Before considering the influence of the school directly, Sartre continues his exploration of Gustave's desire to be an actor. We should remember, however, that at this period he was attending classes and receiving formal instruction in the classics of French literature.

It was easy, almost inevitable, for the boy who entertained his sister with imitations and other comic actions to move on to the performance of scenes from plays. The vassal of Achille-Cléophas and seigneur of Caroline was happy to become the "vassal of Molière." The role of family idiot, Sartre suggests, was no more real than that of Harpagon. Gustave was scolded for exaggerated behavior and silly play-acting at the family table; he was praised for acting in costume on the stage of his father's billiard table. It was customary for him to play at what he believed; when he interpreted prefabricated roles, people believed in him. In all probability there was a gradual development. At first, most likely, Gustave simply imitated one of the familiar comic characters, perhaps doing one of the great scenes. Later Caroline performed with him, and occasionally Gustave's friend, Ernest Chevalier. Sartre says, quite reasonably, that even when the trio presented a play by Molière, for example, a certain amount of rewriting must have been necessary—to reduce the required number of actors, if for no other reason. Finally Gustave began writing his own plays, many or most of which may have been simply adaptations. In 1832, when he was ten years old, he wrote that he now had nearly thirty plays in his repertory.

When did Gustave begin to wish that he might *be* an actor and make himself famous? We do not know the exact date, though presumably it was sometime in the year or two preceding the accumulation of the impressive repertory in 1832. Sartre believes that he can fix the psychological moment. It was that instant at which Flaubert moved from nonreflective enjoyment of play-acting and began reflectively to see himself as one who might come to be defined as an actor. The moment of reflection would have been most naturally induced by a casual comment by one of the onlookers. Sartre imagines the carelessly spoken sentence: "You would make an excellent actor" (1:783). Admittedly, we have no evidence that this pronouncement was ever made, but it would be harder to believe that it was not, than that it was. We do know that the adult Flaubert acknowledged having such aspirations. At this point Sartre introduces a short essay on the power of words in molding our inner states. This time the words come from the Other; the result would have been the same if Gustave had spoken them himself.

"Words are devastating when they come to name that which was lived without being named." By means of the word, the reflective consciousness proposes for the activity of the nonreflective a signification which is "a mortgage on the future," an extension of itself which can be accepted on the reflective level only by a kind of vow. Sartre explains by elaborating an example which he had already cited and commented on briefly in *Being and Nothingness*. In Stendhal's *The Charterhouse of Parma*, Mosca, observing Fabrice and La Sanseverina, says of them, "If the word ''love' ever comes to be spoken between them, I am lost." The passage that follows shows Sartre at his best. Despite its length it seems to me worth quoting in its entirety.

> By this term [i.e., the word "love"] the collectivity affirms its right to look at the most purely subjective intimacy; it socializes the slightly foolish tenderness which the young aunt and her nephew feel for one another. It was indefinable, not because they were afraid to define it but because they simply did not care to give it an official standing, because they lived it day by day for the simple

pleasure of living it and because it was never more and never less than what it *appeared* to be when they were together, reaching beyond itself only by looks, smiles, and gestures which communicated it from each to the other, because it still avoided the vertigo of commitment. "Let the word love be pronounced," and it would be endowed with a past, a future, an objective essence, constituted by the historical evolution of customs, the common sense of worldly wisdom, endowed with a positive value and often with an anti-value, both bearing witness to the contradictions of the current ideology or of opposing ideologies. Its developments (it had none at first, it *existed*, nothing more) are foreseen, its end known in advance, whether mediocre or tragic; in short, it is a quasi object, a cultural product which must be internalized. Reflection is caught in the trap; it confirms the signification and, in order to preserve its signifying power, takes the signification to its own account. The change is radical. The emotion, the tenderness, even the sexual excitation were their own end. One smiled from happiness or from an impulse toward the other or because the other smiled and one wanted to feel this proffered smile on one's own lips. A shift in view: Love becomes the end. The tender emotion, the desire are means to maintain it in being; that is, to remain faithful to the vow. They are *proofs*, renewed promises, and, at the same time, nourishments for that abstract flame of love which is other, or others' love—which ceaselessly requires the combustible. For love is nothing but a vow extracted by society from each member of the couple with the complicity of the other, a vow which neither of the two can "betray" without denying his or her self. One will therefore nourish the vampire, one will be alienated in that infinite task for that final end—or ultimate mystification—fidelity to oneself. [1:783–84]

I think that Sartre has never better expressed the ambivalent movement by which the nonreflective consciousness finds itself transformed in the process of a reflection which objectifies it and brings it into the world of others. Before anything was spoken, the two persons employed language, for they were communicating. But *verbal* language, which always points outward toward the world, can be simultaneously a revealer and a betrayer. The word "love" falsifies the immediate experience by bringing to it an accretion of expectations which are not properly a part of it. At the same time it reveals possibilities for transcendence and further meanings which will not otherwise become evident. It is significant that in the case of Stendhal's man and woman, the word was never spoken, and the pair never realizes the potentialities of a full sexual relation. The purity of the present was protected at the expense of the future. This is one of the few places where Sartre, who is so often accused of being over-reflective, appears to be nostalgic for simple nonreflective existence. For Flaubert the fatal words were spoken—or we assume that they were. He will be an actor; that is, he will make himself an actor in the hope of finding some reality in his being. The make-believe will seek to find himself by passing from the painful intuition, "I am nothing but the roles which I play," to the proud cry, "I am a being whose real mission is to play roles" (1:785). He will *be* a "producer of images."

In analyzing Flaubert's expectations and the results of this new step in the spiral, Sartre includes fairly lengthy phenomenological descriptions of the actor and his function, of the laugh, and of the comic. These discussions are too thoroughly interwoven with the development of Flaubert's personalization for them to be considered as pure digressions, but they are likely to be of special interest to philosophers and psychologists who may not be particularly concerned with Flaubert. Let us examine these ideas of Sartre's by themselves before we look at Gustave in relation to them.

## The Actor as a Center of Derealization

Sartre approaches the subject of the actor indirectly by introducing a comparison and a new philosophical term which will be of primary importance throughout the rest of his books. The actor in his function resembles an art object—for example a statue of Venus. The statue is a "real and permanent center of derealization."

A statue is an imaginary woman. This Venus is not, has never been. But the marble exists as an *analogue* of the goddess. [1:785]

Sartre's interest in the function of the analogue dates back to *The Psychology of the Imagination* (1940). The analogue is the material object that serves to evoke the image of something which is nonexistent or absent. The paper photograph is the analogue of my friend. The impersonator with the straw hat, the cane, the peculiar gestures and accent is the analogue for Maurice Chevalier, who is being imitated. It is interesting to note that in the early work Sartre gave equivalent status to portrait and actor. In the present case of Venus, however, he is concerned with something other than the technique by which a consciousness cancels out what is present and real (the paper with its light and dark areas, the real comedian whose physical features may be quite unlike those of Chevalier) in order to intend the unreal image. Now his interest lies in examining more carefully the ontological status of the material object and of the impersonator as well as of the image. Let us return to the marble Venus.

Venus does not exist, but the marble does and so does (or did) the sculptor whose real tools and effort gave to the marble its unique shape. The statue is at the very least an example of worked-on matter (*matière œuvrée*). Its price, its fragility, and the care taken in packing it for shipping—all testify to its function as preserving the intention and meaning inscribed by the artist. And how, asks Sartre, are we to "distinguish the beauty, the purity of the material from this form which vampirizes it?" The statue is a "real and permanent center of derealization" in that it forces upon the public a particular act of imagination. If this marble has assumed "an individuated being" and has not remained an indistinguishable part of the stone slope of the mountain, this is because it has been given the function "of figuring a certain nonbeing." By virtue of our recognition of this nonbeing, the statue determines a specific "social imaginary." Consequently the entire object is "confirmed in its being."

> Society recognizes in it an ontological truth to the extent that the being of this object is considered a permanent incitement to make oneself unreal by derealizing this marble in Venus. The object is a support of the derealization, but the derealization gives it its necessity because the object is necessary in order that the derealization may take place. Here the imaginary is far from being a vague flight without contours; it has itself the force, the impenetrability and the limits of the piece of marble. [1:786]

In looking at the statue, if I am to see it even as a woman, I must necessarily enter into the imaginary, thus, as Sartre puts it, making myself unreal. If I am to see it as Venus, there is a still deeper involvement in the "social imaginary." I am reminded of a personal experience, but one open to anyone, which reinforces Sartre's point. On the slopes of Mount Pendeli, near Athens, one may see abandoned hunks of marble, broken drums which were intended to become parts of the columns of the Parthenon. I think that no person today could look at these fragments, which just missed becoming a part of history, without seeing in their very incompleteness the first beginnings of that figuration of nonbeing which puts us into the world of social imaginary. Here, of course, it is the signs of the human project that prevent us from seeing the marble as simply stone. Sartre goes on to point out that a reverse process is also taking place. Whenever one uses a material object, he said in *Search for a Method*, a kind of "transubstantiation" occurs. The thing becomes human to the exact extent that the person makes himself a thing.[1] When we look at the Venus, the same interaction takes place with regard to the material statue and the object of our imagination.

> Suddenly something of [the marble's] immutable consistency and of its radiant inertia passes into the Venus or the Pietà. The woman of stone is the ideal of being—the representation of for-itself which would be like the dream of the in-itself. Thus the sculptured stone, the mineral indispensable for the common derealization, possesses of course the *maximum of being* when we recall that within the social intersubjectivity, *being* is being-for-others when it is confirmed. [1:786]

Sartre goes on to say that "the being here is the practico-inert of the imaginary."

To write a full commentary on all of the implications of this concentrated passage would require a discussion of Sartre's entire philosophy. Inadequately but briefly, I may put its immediate import into more simple terms, noting its relation to both the ontology of *Being and Nothingness* and to the *Critique*. To speak of the marble woman as "the ideal of being" and as "the dream of the in-itself" is admittedly to confuse two levels of language—literary and evocative on the one hand, philosophical on the other, a procedure which Sartre has reproached himself for having done in *Being and Nothingness*.[2] Still we can see his meaning clearly enough in the metaphor. The statue has, as it were, fixed forever that "nothingness" or psychic withdrawal on the part of consciousness which allows it to go perpetually beyond the given, to transcend its immediate perception. It is as if nonconscious being attained to the transcending quality of consciousness while pinning down that transcendence, without ceasing to be itself. In this sense we might say that the statue represents symbolically the unattainable in-itself-for-itself, which every consciousness vainly tries to achieve, which—if it existed— would be an absoluteness of being accompanied by the awareness of freedom and psychic withdrawal. In the statue the For-itself has been transformed into In-itself while still maintaining the marks of its former avatar. This is to mention only two realms of Being. There is a third: being-for-others. For any particular for-itself or conscious person, objectification comes by means of the Other; it is he who transforms my acts, my gestures, my words and very expressions into things in the world, into "in-itselves," and these constitute my being-for-others. When it is looked at, the statue achieves, through its observer, a new being, the status of being-for-others. All of this, of course, is an extension of Sartre's thought in *Being and Nothingness*. In saying that the being of the statue is also the "practico-inert of the imaginary," Sartre employs the basic insights of the *Critique* to develop further his early ideas on the world of the image. In the real world all social relations, every individual, indeed all human activity, are carried on within the compass of the practico-inert, which gives them their reality. The practico-inert comprises the material universe as it has been subjected to human activity; it includes all established social structures, cultural patterns, language; in short, it *is* the objective environment of our lives. A consciousness exists in and by means of it as much as by its physical body. In what sense then can Sartre say that the being of the statue is the "practico-inert of the imaginary"? He means, I think, that without the worked-on material, the marble, in which the sculptor has inscribed a meaningful form, the viewer could not accomplish the particular imaginary act that invokes this Venus as goddess and as an ideal woman whose quality will, to be sure, be modified by each one who imagines her but who will also be to some extent the same for each one. Not only is the statue necessary for the imaginary act, but it forces the act upon us—just as the contours of the city in which we live or the television programs which we hear will modify the form of our individual projects. Shall we say then that the Venus is real or only that the statue has reality? This question will become of prime importance for us when we come to Flaubert's theory of art. For the moment let us simply note that in any case there is an interaction. The contours of the marble, its very material, influence the Venus whom it induces us to imagine. (Sartre here should be more satisfactory for critics who complained that in *The Psychology of the Imagination* he gave too little importance to the limitations imposed on the art object by the medium.) In turn, all that literary tradition and we as individuals have imagined about the goddess will influence what we see in the marble form. Venus herself is certainly a "social imaginary," but we may say that as such at least she has being. Our immediate concern, however, is the connection between the status of the art object and that of the actor.

"Kean is *recognized* by his public like the Venus de Milo" (1:787). At first thought the statement is surprising. One might have expected that the actor would be compared to the sculptor rather than to the statue. Of course Sartre has in mind the person who is performing on the stage, not the man off-duty who is having a drink at the bar. Still, it is the actor as producer of illusions who is meant, and this is what marks his resemblance to the statue. Sartre is aware of the difficulty. The statue is a simple example; with the actor the situation is more complex.

> What complicates things here is that the actor is not a piece of in-organic matter which has absorbed human work but a living, thinking man whose derealization each evening is an unpredict-able proportion of repetitions and invention. At worst he ap-proaches the automaton, at best he goes beyond acquired habits by "trying out" an effect. No matter. He resembles the statue in that he is a permanent, real, and recognized center of derealiza-tion. [1:786]

The actor's real person becomes the analogue that induces and en-ables the audience to leave the real for the imaginary and to see Hamlet or Harpagon. The actor is obviously real and recognized just as the statue is. His permanency as a center of derealization, unlike that of the statue, comes not from his material being but from the fact that the role is taken up again night after night. "Each evening he derealizes himself in order to involve five hundred persons in a collective derealization" (1:787). The audience comes to watch Ham-let in Kean as they enter the museum to look at Moses in the marble from the nearby mountain. We think of the actor as we think of "a real being which is the indispensable mediation between individual realities"; that is, between the individual members of the audience and "the unreal collective which is Hamlet" (1:788).

"The Hamlets pass, Hamlet remains." Hamlet, like Venus, is a social imaginary. The fact that for all practical purposes our Hamlet stems from the imagination of one man and not many, that he is a fictitious prince and not a goddess—none of this is essential or changes anything. Both imaginary beings have been subjected to a tradition of artistic interpretations. Each previous Hamlet, Sartre says, acts as a real center of derealization for the new actor. The dramatic role itself holds something of the intransigence of the practico-inert. The actor must in physical appearance measure up to it, or he will be "miscast." Sartre adds still another point of re-semblance to the work of art. The statue is a piece of merchandise; it has a price, can be bought and sold. The actor's power to create illusions is recognized by society. He is paid a salary, he may receive honors and knighthoods. The truly great may attain to almost the status of "a national property." Sometimes, Sartre says, young members of the actor's public may feel strangely disappointed when they see him off stage going quietly about his business outside the theater. Where is this quiet little person hiding the madness of Lear and the fury of Othello? They are nowhere, but they may be counted on to reappear when the actor on stage loses once again his real being for the sake of the imaginary. What is the being of the actor when he is not performing? Sartre suggests that his activity is still a show. "It is *his being* that he gives as a spectacle; he derealizes himself in the reality which he has won. Let us say that he fastens on to the truth which has come to him from outside." In other words, Kean away from the theater plays the role of the actor Kean. Sartre speculates as to whether perhaps the greatest actors were each at first a "stolen child."

> He is an imaginary who exhausted himself in playing roles so as to make himself recognized, one who has finally been recognized as a worker specializing in the imagination. His being has come to him by the socialization of his impotence to be. [1:790]

We may feel reluctant to accept this description as a final or complete portrait of the actor. We might argue, for example, that a person who felt particularly secure in his own being would be better equipped to develop the empathy necessary to imagine and represent the life of another than one who had no strong sense of self. I myself am a little uneasy as to the total appropriateness of the comparison of the actor with the work of art. From the point of view of the spectator, it may hold. Yet from the point of view of actor, it seems to me that the text of the play is the analogue and that the actor must first perform a task equivalent to that of the one who looks at the statue. When he is performing, the actor seems to me to be comparable to the sculptor. Still, I admit that the actor cannot watch himself act. From the perspective of a member of the audience, perhaps the analogy holds. The last touches of the portrait raise the uneasy feeling that Sartre may be guilty of a *petitio principi*. To call the successful actor a "stolen child" is to make us feel that we are not considering Kean or Jouvet or Olivier but solely the ten-year-old Gustave Flaubert on his father's billiard table.

Before returning to Flaubert himself, we should consider Sartre's phenomenological sketches of the laugh and of the comic. Sartre claims that Flaubert acted comedies only, not tragedies. This may or may not be correct; I rather suspect that it is.[3] In any case it is the comic roles which prepared the way for Flaubert's great participation in the performance of the Garçon during his later years at school.

## The Laugh, the Comic, and the Comedian

The laugh begins in panic but is very quickly accompanied by a feeling of superiority: As for me, I don't fall flat on my face when I am marching in a procession, and neither do my neighbors and all those who laugh with me. Me, I respect the sacred and don't risk compromising it by my naïveté, and that's the way with all the people in my set. Me, I know how to drink, I hold my liquor. Me, I'm not a cuckold, I belong, like all these others, to those truly human husbands whose wives will never deceive them. It is for this reason that the laugh, although it springs from fear, is accompanied by an intense pleasure, or at least by a gay excitement. Contagious and willingly accepted, it has come to me altogether *through the other* and has got its hold on my body; that means that it *has chosen me*, I have not produced it, I have submitted to it and I have stuck to it. It is the proof that I have all the qualities of a human being. [1:822–23]

For Sartre the laugh is a defense mechanism and can exist only within a collectivity. He does not insist that the explanation fits every variety of laughter, nor does he lay claim to total originality. He wishes "only to recall certain truths, acquired particularly since the study of Bergson and that of Jeanson," insofar as they are appropriate to the present study. As usual with Sartre, the synthesis is new even if the component ideas are not. Although there is great diversity in the origin and quality of the laughter we have known, Sartre holds that the laugh he is analyzing is "antique and primitive, as old as humanity," and he suggests that perhaps it may lie as the hidden "infrastructure" beneath all our laughter (1:811).

The laugh that Sartre describes is a laugh *at* someone. It is "a collective reaction . . . by which a group, when threatened with danger, disassociates itself from the person in whom the danger is embodied" (1:681). It is an attempt to remove the other from the group by treating the compromising person as a spectacle, his behavior as an event. In every collectivity, Sartre explains, all members hold in common a vague definition of "the human person." This derives from institutions, customs, and history. It "defines what these are by what they ought to be and what they ought to be by what they are" (1:811). When any member of the group, voluntarily or not, risks exposing this notion of the human as false or unreal, all of the other members feel that they are personally threatened. In serious cases the offender may be removed by execution, imprisonment, or exile. Often he can be tolerated by being made the butt of the group laugh. Take the example of the harmless drunkard. His volubility, his unstable carriage, his self-importance, and passionate protestations all serve to caricature normal human behavior. He thinks he is in command, but we the spectators know that he is at the mercy of the alcohol, which has precipitated the reactions which make him ridiculous. He reminds us that "the 'human person' does not resist being dissolved in a certain quantity of alcohol" (1:812). The spectators, since there is no obvious reason to beat up the drunkard or to drive him away, remain in a state of "passive activity." How to get rid of the displeasing sight without disturbing that passivity? It is no good simply to go away. "Behind the indignant backs, the ridicule of Humanity will continue. The laugh is the only appropriate response" (1:813). It announces that the intoxicated man is ridiculous but not dangerous.

The laugh spreads from person to person by contagion, as a yawn does. As an indirect communication, it serves as a signal, and Sartre believes that it must be one of the most ancient forms of human behavior. In a curious way it is almost mimetic. The spasmodic contractions of the laugh seem to reproduce physically the ridiculous, awkward, or grotesque, the "out of kilter" quality of the object at which the laugh is directed. The dialectical movement by which the group solves its problem with the laugh might be formulated like this: There is a contraction. The laughable drunkard is a human person, but he is not: he takes himself to be my fellowman, but I refuse all connection with him. By my laugh I internalize the contradiction. I decide that he is not my fellowman, another one like me, but a man who has become degraded. Now he can no longer threaten me by seeming to show me an unpleasant truth about myself, thus harming our species. "He is a subman who takes himself for a man, and I, human person by divine right, am witness to his grotesque and futile efforts to approach our condition" (1:814). In sum, we laugh at that which threatens the "spirit of seriousness," the overoptimistic and slightly grandiose image of itself which society has cherished.[4] Therefore "we laugh at the maladroit, at the unlucky, at cuckolds, at excrement." Scatology, Sartre says, gives rise to guffaws because generally, in bourgeois societies, bodily needs are thought to disparage the human character. We can also laugh at vice or failure or at any inclination or taste so long as it appears in the other person as a form of dehumanization. Sartre notes especially the case of "famous last words." In such jokes, the comic equivalent of the tragic Greek hubris, disaster strikes at the very moment when the speaker has just pronounced himself to be totally in control.

In another example Sartre shows more clearly the relation between the laugh and the "spirit of seriousness." A dignified magistrate, leading a procession, slips and falls on his ass. The crowd laughs, regardless of whether the official is generally despised or revered and even though later sober reflection may raise the question as to whether he is in pain or even seriously injured. Bergson was right in saying that we laugh because the fall shows us the mechanistic aspect of what we normally take as living and organic, but Sartre claims that Bergson has not "given us the social sense and the intention of this hilarity." If the mayor lies sprawled on his back, inanimate matter has triumphed over the human notion of sacred authority; it is a "sacrilege." The human order is threatened. Without the saving grace of the laugh, one might feel that the sacredness of power was suddenly unveiled as an empty illusion. But just as with the drunk, the unfortunate magistrate is disqualified by the laugh. The old fool thought that he possessed a portion of the charismatic power that society has in its power to bestow, but he was mistaken. "He never participated in the numinous." His fall proves it (1:818).

One might think that the laugh would result in undermining the serious attitude, the sanctity of human authority, and so on. Sartre admits that such a conclusion is logical and that it might well be reached as the result of a later, secondary reflection. But this is not its first or original intention. The ultimate seriousness of social beliefs is protected by making the poor unlucky man the butt of the community. At the same time there is no true group feeling in the laugh. Although laughter is a collective reaction, there is a sense in which each one laughs alone. This is because the protective device requires a temporary breaking of the intersubjectivity. Negative actions, such as lynching or banishing, reinforce the group's feeling of its own integration and are adopted exactly for that very reason. In contrast the exclusion of the laughable object from the intersubjectivity must be accompanied, Sartre believes, by a temporary suspension of all internal relation among the laughers. This is done in order that the scandalous object may cease to have the power to compromise the group in his own person. One laughs because one's neighbor laughs. There is a mutual conditioning, but it is an external linking, not an internal reciprocity. Sartre writes,

> Each member has made himself *mechanical,* thanks to all the others, and has replaced his Ego by an *alter ego* so as to consider the scandalous object as a machine; that is, from the point of view of the antithesis radicalized; in other words, of the mechanism. [1:817]

I find this passage rather unclear. I do not see that it is necessary to stress the machinelike qualities in oneself in order to see the characteristics of an automaton in the one who is laughed at. The suggestion that my usual ego is put into parentheses and replaced by an alter ego is reminiscent of Freud's explanation of the dynamics of the crowd in which each member has substituted the leader in place of his own ego ideal. But in speaking of the *alter ego* here, Sartre seems to mean that I put out of play all of my personal concerns and individualizing traits and sense of self except my awareness of being on the side of the laughers rather than the laughed-at. This laugh is, of course, nonreflective. Yet certainly some sense of solidarity must remain. On the other hand, we can see easily why the sense of common humanity cannot be too clearly in focus. It would preclude that total exclusion of the victim which the laugh is intended to accomplish. It might lead to pity, which is incompatible with the laugh that laughs *at* someone.

The laugh that Sartre has described is essentially conformist. A variant form of it is the "ignoble laugh," directed against someone who tries in vain to raise himself above the level of average humanity. In his failure he is revealed, not as a subman this time, but as one who falsely took himself seriously enough to try to rise "above himself"; that is, above the level of true "serious people." Laughable episodes come to us like a "happening," a sort of "theater in the street." "Serious people are amused momentarily and then they resume their gravity." It is, Sartre says, as if some divinity sent to us occasionally these spectacles of submen, travesties of our species, in order to divert us for a bit and to confirm us in the belief in our own value (1:824).

An obvious question arises: Can one laugh alone or at oneself? The two questions are not the same, of course. If I am alone and see, read of, or imagine the kind of sight which normally arouses the collective laugh, then I may seemingly laugh alone while implicitly invoking the presence of the collectivity. If, on the other hand, I should myself be the center of the ridiculous situation, I may think, "How they would laugh if they could see me now!" In this case my sense of the group's potential presence could give me a feeling of guilt, or it could mark the first signs of my real revolt against the values of my group. Another possibility is that I may laugh at myself. This may happen either when I am by myself or when I am in the midst of others. It may be genuine or assumed. If I perceive that I am about to become the butt of the social laugh, I may laugh quickly so as to seem to put myself with the laughers. This defense strategy has the effect of saying, "See, it was a momentary lapse, I am already safely back with you." But sometimes my laugh at myself is genuine. Sartre explains that in this instance I ally myself with a group and laugh at that remnant of rebellion in myself which resists integration, thus seeming to disassociate myself from it.

Since Sartre, while disclaiming any intention of explaining all kinds of laughter, nevertheless seems to feel that the defensive collective laugh is so basic and universal, I have found it interesting to consider two unplanned laughs which are recorded in interviews with him. In both of these the laugh is to some degree against him, and in each case he has joined in with the laughter. The first occasion was a *lapsus linguae*, which was preserved in a documentary film. Sartre is speaking of his reasons for never having joined the Communist party. He says that he would have been unwilling to recant anything which he had previously published and that one of the things which has meant most to him has been his free research.

*Sartre:* Descartes' "I am therefore I think," no, "I think therefore I am" has really been and is always my essential philosophical thought. [*Laughter*]
*Pouillon:* The slip is significant all the same.[5]

I suppose one could say that there is a lingering bit of the negative social laugh here. It is amusing to see a great philosopher make a mistake about something so simple that none of us would do it, a slight reminder that no mind is immune to error. But the real point of the laughter, I believe, lies in the fact that Sartre's involuntary statement reinforces the point in the surrounding context—that he could not bear to live without freely thinking. Possibly there is also the very slight suggestion that in the minds of his listeners, Sartre's value system tends to put thinking before living or that at least he has sometimes given that impression. If so, then the amusement comes from perceiving a self-revelation forced upon him. There is at least a hint here of the quality of the laugh that greeted the fall of the unfortunate official. It is to Sartre's credit that he joins in.

The second incident is an endearing one which comes at the end of the interview with Sartre on the occasion of his seventieth birthday. The interviewer asks whether Sartre has found life good. Sartre replies,

> On the whole, yes. I don't see what I could complain about. It has given me what I wanted and, at the same time, it has made me realize that it was not anything great. But what can you do? [*The interview ends in wild laughter provoked by the disillusioned tone of that last statement.*] You must keep the laugh. You will write down, *"Accompanied by laughter."* [6]

I think it is impossible to find anything hostile in this laugh. Yet what is so funny? And what does the laugh mean exactly? That it isn't enough to get what one wants? That, if Sartre's life has not been anything great, there is little hope for the rest of us? That no human life is truly happy? Perhaps a little of all of these and possibly, too, an intuition that we really don't know what we are talking about when we glibly speak of the "pursuit of happiness" and the like. I feel that it is a good laugh and one which forbids any of us to take ourselves too seriously. Yet it is a bit disquieting, too. There is nothing ignoble about it, but all the same it seems to remind us that we cannot go beyond ourselves. Perhaps, after all, Sartre's explanation fits here. His unpremeditated response is on the borderline between the comic and the tragic. The laughter of the persons present at the interview may, for a split second of time, represent a certain disassociation. *"You* may make that statement, but the rest of us find it preposterous." Sartre's laugh is a refusal to examine the disturbing insight. His wish to preserve the laughter amounts to a sign, "Handle with care!"

Sartre distinguishes between the ridiculous (or laughable) and the comic, and he makes some interesting observations concerning the close relationship and essential difference between the comic and the tragic. Risibility comes as an immediate, spontaneous reaction of the onlookers. The comic, like the tragic, is mediated, elaborated, it appears as a finished product. "The spontaneous laugh proclaims that *this* individual—who takes himself seriously—is only a subman. The laugh provoked by the comic claims to reveal to us that *every man* is a subman who takes himself seriously" (2:1440). In both the comic and the tragic, Sartre believes, the usual life categories of "real" and "possible" are suppressed in favor of the "necessary" and the "impossible." "The individual, never being necessary, is revealed as an impossibility or, if you prefer, his disappearance is a necessity" (2:1437). If it is taken literally, I do not think that this statement is true. With regard to the tragic hero Sartre adds only that the individual surmounts his death by dying. If instead of literal death we were to say that with the tragic the individual is in some way crushed or overcome by circumstances or by his own folly, and that his suffering may give him a certain grandeur, I suppose we might agree; the insight is hardly profound. In distinguishing between the two genres and in elaborating on at least one kind of comedy, Sartre is more satisfactory. The tragic hero, even if his death is inflicted on him by someone else, is always responsible. There is no chance in tragedy.[7] In a comic sequence the individual is totally at the mercy of chance.

> The human person first affirms himself as sovereign with the conviction that he acts upon the world and directs his life. Chance comes subsequently and denounces that illusion: the world is allergic to man, the *comic* testifies to us of the process of rejection. [2:1439]

Sartre's example is particularly apt—the sequence in a Chaplin film in which the hero is continually at the point where he is about to be killed and then just as unpredictably escapes. The underlying message is clear—we do not control our destinies. We are not at home in the world. In this passage there is a certain ambivalence as to whether the idea that the world is allergic to man should be viewed as belonging to the comic stance or as representing Sartre's own position. The matter will come up again in our discussion of the "practical joke" in connection with the Garçon.

The professional comedian, Sartre says, performs for society a certain cathartic function by enabling each member of the audience to experience the disassociation with one who embodies in exaggerated form those flaws that are encountered in everyday experience. But what about the comedian himself? "The laugh safeguards the serious, but as for the one whose profession is to make himself a laughable object, how could he be serious?" (1:826). It is not true, Sartre claims, that the public laughs only at the character assumed by the comedian and not at the man himself. He quotes Odette Laure, "If you are going to be a comic chanteuse, you can't like yourself very much" (1:827). And he refers to the common experience of comic actors who find themselves evoking smiles even when they are engaged in mundane pursuits off stage. As Sartre earlier referred to the actor as one who had been "a stolen child," so now he speculates as to the kind of person who is likely to become a comedian. "The future comic actor is the person who *is fixed* at the age of risibility" (1:827). Sartre reminds us of how we have all laughed benevolently and affectionately at a child's maladroit efforts to do things which are easy for adults. The laugh at the little subhuman is a kindly one, for we know that he is a human person "in the bud." The toddler takes pleasure in the adult's response, for he senses the protective love behind it. Normally as time goes by either, or both, of two things will happen. Either the stage is quickly passed over; the child develops both physical dexterity and a sense of himself, of his capacities and his limitations. Or else the child continues the awkwardness and discovers that the laugh has turned malevolent. This is the "second weaning." The family laughter now involves a degree of disassociation. "The parents show that they do not recognize themselves in their offspring, that they do not find in him *their blood*. A good beginning for the future comedian" (1:828). Of course, not all children become comedians. Special factors are necessary. Let us return to Gustave Flaubert.

## Flaubert as Child Actor

Somewhere between the ages of eight and twelve Gustave Flaubert decided that he wanted to be a famous actor. The dream of glory is commonplace in children. With Flaubert, Sartre believes it was inextricably linked with resentment and that it was colored by Gustave's relation with his father. "He wants glory in order to dazzle and to punish his father." By becoming famous as a comedian, a buffoon, he would be both "the pride and the shame of his family or, more exactly, would make his father's name illustrious by dishonoring it" (1:831). Glory, Sartre says, is a family relationship. As an adolescent Flaubert longed for it with unusual intensity. In a letter written in his early twenties he says, "Since the deaths of my father and sister, the desire for glory has left me" (1:795). Sartre discounts Caroline's part in this but takes the reference to Achille-Cléophas as being entirely sincere. I do not think that he is quite correct either in the generalization or with reference to Flaubert specifically. The full enjoyment of fame probably does require that there be some person or persons to attest to the distance traversed or to measure that between what one feels one simply "is" as compared with what one has accomplished. Few of us would be immune from deriving pleasure at having proved wrong those who had judged us as having little worth or talent. Even fewer would derive much satisfaction from recognition if there were nobody to share in the pleasure. If Gustave wanted to win his father's approval, thereby satisfying his own desire to be commended and to prove his father mistaken, there is no reason to feel that he did not also long to be able to share his happiness with Caroline. If we have accepted any of Sartre's portrait of the Flaubert family, however, we will agree that resentment and the desire for praise were probably intermingled. Sartre suggests that Flaubert's adult success as a comedian would have brought a certain punishment and shame upon the doctor in two ways—in addition to showing him the error of his early judgment. First, it was only after glory had been won and by the very greatest of actors that the stage was considered anything but a disgraceful career for the sons of the bourgeois. A comic actor would be doubly suspect since he would retain in his own person some of the character of the butt of the collective laugh. Second, Flaubert tended to regard unusual achievement as serving to indicate the inferiority of the average person. In a schoolboy composition, he rhetorically addresses Corneille, "Why were you born if not to humiliate the human race?" (1:800). The achievements of the great is our shame. This is, as Sartre notes, the precise opposite of the more prevalent attitude that in every individual achievement all humanity is honored. As Sartre wryly puts it,

> Armstrong has taken a giant step for mankind, and all women have circled the earth with Valentina. Future generations may reap the harvest of their accomplishment. But most people alive now might say in the style of Flaubert, "Man has taken four steps on the Moon, but *me*, I will never set foot there. [1:801]

Obviously Flaubert did not regard the performances on the billiard table as a training course for a future career. He must surely have derived much enjoyment from these activities, a point which Sartre tends to underemphasize in his generally gloomy picture of Flaubert's childhood. Sartre does recognize that the boy's success as an amateur actor compensated for his failures and greatly extended the scope of his imaginary play with Caroline. Sartre's primary interest, and our present concern, is the relation between Flaubert's repeated choice of the imaginary and the categories of the laugh, the actor, and the comic which we have just examined.

We recall that Flaubert once remarked that he could not shave before the mirror without breaking into a loud guffaw. Was he in truth laughing alone and at himself? Sartre believes that the laugh was insincere. He contrasts it with what Flaubert wrote to his friend Ernest, whom he suspected of taking himself too seriously and of being willing to enter comfortably into the career of the typical bourgeois. "Go look in your mirror and tell me if you don't have a great desire to laugh. So much the worse for you if you don't" (1:681). Here Flaubert is urging Ernest to disassociate himself from the serious men, whom Flaubert's group finds ridiculous, so as to find himself one with the freemasonry of the scoffing students. One collective is pitted against another. But we cannot explain Flaubert's own laugh in this way, nor can we say that he is laughing at those elements in him that resist integration into a collectivity. Sartre claims that Flaubert is invoking both the laugh and the look of his father. That clinical look of the scientific doctor which simultaneously analyzes and destroys, which pierces through all pretenses and dispels all aspirations to see in reality something more than the chance coming together of matter—it is this look which Gustave tries to adopt as his own. But what he laughs at is not himself but the human species; and by the laugh he accomplishes two things: He seems to put himself on the side of the laugher, thus disarming his father's look. And insofar as this kind of laugh is always an affirmation of superiority and a disassociation, he seems to rise above the object of his laugh. Since the object this time is the entire human race, the intended disassociation cannot be achieved except in imagination. But this is precisely the point. Gustave's laugh *is* imaginary, and that is why it is insincere. Sartre suggests that in all of Flaubert's attempts to play the clown he laughed in order to make himself laugh; that is, he hoped that by infecting others with hilarity, he might be moved to mirth himself.

As an actor Gustave wanted to attain a sense of self, of being, by identifying himself with the role that his audience saw. Obviously there was a trap. He knew that the others did not take him to be actually the character he portrayed, and he could not grasp their view of him as the performer behind the various roles. Still, he could gain some sense of reality in himself as "a real and permanent center of derealization"; at least it was his actions (even if imaginary actions) which for a time directed others' entrance into a particular realm of the imaginary. Gustave felt that he was real because he was seen, and it was he who determined what was seen. Because this much was real but at the same time was dependent upon the unreal, his sense of the borderline between real and imaginary became more blurred than ever. Increasingly it was in the imaginary that he seemed to exist.

Although Sartre stresses the father as the primary factor in Flaubert's brief career as actor, he points to a secondary relation with the mother, one which involves Flaubert's hidden femininity and his propensity to want to be a passive object for others. Sartre claims that the actor offers himself to the public as a woman offers herself to a male, hoping to be admired and accepted. The image is a bit offensive with its implied suggestion that prostitution is easily associated with woman and actor. Sartre does not help matters by going on to include sexual exhibitionism and masochism. He would have us believe that Flaubert, deprived of any loving response from the mother whose hands had unintentionally awakened his awareness of himself as a sexual object, now offered to the public for its admiring laughter his whole person in lieu of the ridiculous and rejected sexual organ (1:848). I confess that for me Sartre at this point has simply gone too far. If we are willing to grant that in all human relationships there is an element of sexuality, we may easily admit that there is an element of seduction in the actor's performance (though whether this should be thought of as masculine or feminine is open to question and may well depend on the peculiar quality of the actor or actress). To be fair, I am willing to grant that a tendency to exhibitionism is not inconsistent with masochism and that the actor's seeming ease at self-exposure may well have developed partly as the result of his desire to protect his everyday private self from the public eye. Sartre seems to me to be on much more solid ground when he says that Gustave's choice of comic roles may be linked with his earlier despair at having been designated "the family idiot." This would be one more example of his carrying obedience to the point where it turned back against the other. "I am only what you have made of me—humanity's buffoon" (1:844).

Sartre makes one other point regarding the ambivalence of Flaubert's choice of himself as comedian. He speaks of the "grandeur of the comic," with particular reference to the example of Don Quixote. This is a happy choice inasmuch as many critics have noted Cervantes' influence on Flaubert, who became acquainted with the adventures of the Knight of Sorrows when he was just learning to read. A complex character for Cervantes, Don Quixote, as Sartre points out, was a pure figure of fun for seventeenth-century readers. The romantics saw in him a comic hero who, even while his conduct remained ridiculous, disqualified the laughers and showed himself superior to them. By his devotion to an impossible ideal, by his stubborn clinging to an unreal image of what the life of the true knight should be, he revealed both the grandeur of the comic and the superiority of the imaginary over the real. Without claiming that Flaubert was deliberately modeling himself after the knight, Sartre argues persuasively that his attitude toward his own ridiculous antics as comic actor involved this same ambivalence.

Finally, Sartre finds in Flaubert's love of ridicule and willingness to entertain others by making himself a ridiculous character, a hidden attempt to injure. By caricaturing himself as ignominious, he will be at least sovereign in ignominy. By laughing first at himself, he seems to join the laughers. But beyond this self-protective behavior, there is something more, a sadism which accompanies the implicit masochism. "It is the deliberate choice to be a subman because of hatred of the human condition" (1:841). He will affect grand sentiments for the sake of ridiculing them. He makes himself a demonstration of the ignoble side of man.

> He raises a laugh at himself out of disgust with himself and with humanity. In his person he publicly destroys all human values in order to show both that he is unworthy of them and that they are unworthy of his immense and grotesque desire. [1:842]

Misanthropy is origin and goal. If Sartre is correct, Flaubert combines the attitudes of Don Quixote and of Cervantes. He hopes to redeem himself—at least in his own eyes—by rejecting the real in favor of an ennobling ideal which he knows to be unreal. He has chosen the impossible as his single possible (1:976–77).

Sartre has tried to show that the choice of the imaginary over the real was firmly asserted in Gustave's determination to be a great actor. Of course, there was never any real question of his becoming an actor once the childish games were over. Flaubert's correspondence makes no reference to any spoken prohibition or period of acute disappointment. But Sartre has found two allusions which may possibly imply a certain regret. To Ernest, when Gustave was eighteen, he wrote, "I could have made an excellent actor if I had been well directed." Later to Louise, "In the depths of my nature, whatever anyone may say, there is the showman [*saltimbanque*]. In my childhood and my youth I had an unrestrained love for the stage. Perhaps I would have been a great actor if heaven had had me born a poor man" (quoted, 1:872–73). The clue is in the last clause. For the sons in respectable middle-class families in nineteenth-century France the vocation of actor was as effectively barred as that of jurist was for the son of a worker. Dr. Flaubert might occasionally go to the theater, but he would not entertain actors at his table. Sartre surmises that this fact was effectively conveyed to Gustave by his father's attitude without a specific pronouncement ever being necessary. Had the doctor explicitly prohibited any such aspiration and voiced his disdain for the profession, Flaubert might, though it is unlikely, have found reason to revolt. As it was, the passive Gustave whom Sartre has portrayed for us would certainly never have rebelled against an attitude so strongly entrenched that its correctness was simply taken for granted.

It is possible that Gustave simply lost interest in the dramatic performances and turned to writing instead as he became more and more caught up in his life at school. Sartre does not think so and feels that the realization that his father had once and for all prevented his ever becoming a professional actor was a bitter traumatic experience for the boy.[8] This view is perhaps too extreme. Yet Sartre is correct, I think, in claiming that Flaubert continued to cherish a certain nostalgic longing to be associated with the theater, that his writing reveals the influence of concern with oral style, and that his delight in playing roles, such as that of Saint Polycarp, was a kind of compensation. At any rate the creator of dramatic personalities on stage was a forerunner of the writer of fiction. The first, Sartre tells us, made of himself a real center of derealization; the second created centers of derealization in written works of the imagination.

## SOCIALIZATION

Flaubert has left contradictory testimony regarding his life at the collège in Rouen. From his correspondence and from his 1870 preface to the posthumous edition of Bouilhet's *Dernières chansons* one would gather that he lived a life of romantic extravagance in close solidarity with his fellow students, a lively group, whom he praises in contrast with the unimaginative dullards of a later generation. "We were a pleiad of rum chaps who lived in a strange world, believe me. We alternated between madness and suicide." He says that some actually killed themselves, several out of boredom ruined themselves with debauch, and adds—"it was beautiful!" (quoted 2:1107).

These passages are in sharp contrast with those that appear in *Memoirs of a Madman*, written before Flaubert had left school, and in others of the early autobiographical works of fiction. Here we find neither solidarity nor admiration. For example,

> I was at school from the time I was ten, and I very early developed a profound aversion to people. That society of children is as cruel for its victims as the other small society, that of men. The same injustice of the crowd, the same egoism.[9]

As Sartre points out, both sets of passage are sweeping generalizations, allowing no exceptions, and they are mutually contradictory. Yet there is no reason to doubt that either is insincere. In part Sartre would explain their inconsistency by their date. Flaubert always had a tendency to idealize the past and to view his life as a process of deterioration. Both the positive and the negative aspects were originally part of the picture, but they were recorded at different periods. Sartre suggests that partly also the difference derives from locale. Flaubert's companions were his rivals in the classroom, his vassals in the schoolyard. It is possible also, I think, that the contrasting reactions reflect different stages in his career at school. After the initial days of timidity he learned to defend himself and even to take the initiative. Certainly he describes in himself two kinds of responses, which Sartre refers to respectively as "escapism" and "aggression." In *Memoirs of a Madman* Flaubert portrays himself in quick succession as victim and aggressor.

> I was found offensive in all my tastes: in class for my ideas, at recess for my inclinations for solitary unsociability.... Therefore I lived there alone and bored, plagued by my teachers, and jeered at by my companions. I had a scoffing, independent temperament, and my biting, cynical irony did not spare the caprice of a single boy any more than the tyranny of all. [p. 264]

Both reactions, as we might expect, Sartre relates to Gustave's sense of himself as the younger son in the Flaubert family. Let us consider, as Sartre does, first the classroom situation, then Gustave's relations with the other pupils outside of class.

## The Classroom

Sartre believes that because of Flaubert's father's position at the hospital (not to mention his mother's connections with the minor nobility), he probably entered school presuming that he would be considered superior. With regard to the family, however, he has everything to lose and nothing to gain. Achille has already won all the honors; the most that Gustave can hope to do is to imitate and equal him. Nothing will change his status as second son. If he should fail completely, he would confirm himself the "family idiot." He is caught between pride, which impels him to prove that he is a true Flaubert, worthy of his father's approval, and the resentful determination not to follow humbly in his brother's footsteps. He will not be a lesser Achille. Scholastically, the result was a compromise. His record was good but not brilliant. A year before he was to receive his baccalaureate, he got himself expelled as the result of a conflict with school authorities, studied by himself at home, and passed the final examination on the expected date but without distinction.

As in the case of Achille, Sartre refuses to give any weight to genetic factors, natural intelligence, specific talents, and the like. "The dunce and the prodigy are both monsters, two victims of the institutionalized family and institutionalized education" (2:1128). This is not to say that young Gustave was a puppet or a piece of malleable clay, rather that we can understand him only as a response from within to the pressures of two prestructured situations (family and school).

Obviously, Flaubert did not achieve his scholastic position as the result of a calculated deliberation. The compromise represents a weakness in decision rather than the success of a plan. Trapped between the refusal to emulate his brother and fear of total disgrace, he is, as it were, paralyzed and chooses neither alternative. Passively he accepts the conventional goals of high grades and prizes as well worth the effort. He works hard and *tries* to excel. At the same time he has secretly willed to lose. He will not be a "retread of Achille." This inner resolve undermines his conscious efforts.

> He works half-heartedly. His limbs grow heavy, his fingers at every moment seem about to let go of the pen; he has just begun to concentrate on his task, an image comes to him, he wants to grasp it, and suddenly it flits away. [2:1139]

The words on the page seem to resist him. Even with subjects in which he is interested and might excel, he only half-succeeds. In short, he is dominated by "the will to fail." Sartre speaks of a certain "somatization." It is as if Gustave's body understood and acted upon that which his mind refused to accept—the intuition that he must distinguish himself from Achille negatively, by not-being what Achille was. Since he is unwilling to accept the full consequences of this resolve, he works in constant conflict with himself.

Most psychologists would speak here of the unconscious blocking of consciously willed activity. In other contexts Sartre flatly declares that the will to fail is a form of bad faith. Here he is not so harsh. He insists, however, that the behavior patterns that constitute the failure conduct are intentional structures even though they are effective only so long as they are not known. Presumably Sartre means that Gustave possessed a certain comprehension of the fact that his secret will and his conscious efforts were at variance, but that he did not reflectively know and understand the precise meaning of his behavior. Sartre's introduction of the somatic level brings in an aspect of subsequent nonconscious development of a repressed decision which is quite different from anything found in *Being and Nothingness*. The problem will be especially important when we discuss the later nervous crisis. For the moment let us simply note that Sartre sees the will to fail as a form of passive activity. Gustave does not pursue a course of overt rebellion; instead he convinces himself that failure comes from the outside, from the Other, in spite of all he can do to win first place.

One might object that it is too much to speak of failure when Gustave Flaubert did ultimately win several school prizes. Still, these were during his later years at the lycée, and there must have been some bad moments near the beginning. Sartre thinks that Charles Bovary's first day at school, when he was the butt of laughter on the part of teacher and students alike, may reflect Gustave's feelings about himself.[10] I doubt that Flaubert felt very much identification with Charles. It is notable that he gives us nothing of Bovary's inner feelings, and the implication seems to be that he is too insensitive for the intense suffering on which Gustave tends to pride himself. But Sartre's claim that there is a certain complicity between teacher and pupils in their treatment of the graceless new arrival does seem to be reflected in Flaubert's statement that he was harassed by his teachers and ridiculed by his classmates.

In school Gustave entered a structured society. Sartre implies that, if that society had been different, Flaubert might have learned better ways of coping with the psychological pressures at home and might have overcome more of the limitations of his passive constitution. In fact, the school was a model of a serialized institution in all of its worst aspects. Here as in his discussion of the history of the school,

Sartre, quite evidently, is directing his remarks also at contemporary education and specifically at the events leading up to and following the French students' revolt in 1968. He introduces his discussion by quoting one of the graffiti from that later event. "Anybody who puts a grade on a paper is an asshole [*un con*]" (2:1121). The classroom, Sartre says, is the competitive society in miniature. Egalitarianism is the disguised ideological instrument of dehumanization and reification. Like their parents, the children have become the product of their product. The boy writes a paper and a grade is assigned to it, indicating its value—like a price tag. Only what happens is worse than that, for somehow it is the child himself who is assigned a value, his place in the line of applicants for both immediate distinction and later opportunities for advancement. Sartre remarks that in school, as later in the industrial market, each one is to some extent the victim of chance, which may remove him from a place already won. A new, brighter, or more effective student may join the class, another teacher may have different methods and expectations, etc. Worst of all, there is the absolute demand for specific, objective knowledge to be mastered; proof that one has digested it must be furnished by tests met in the standard fashion. Engrained in all this is the unavowed purpose of getting rid of the supernumerary. The classroom represents the first and consequential skirmish in the battle for survival.

One might object that Flaubert's later life shows him to be magnificently trained in history and in literature, his two chief concerns, and that he did not as an adult show any inclination to change things. At the time of the defeat of France by Prussia, he concluded that one explanation for it lay in the Germans' greater emphasis on scientific and practical training. But this remark was as much cynical as critical. To him the Latin culture, to which he attached supreme value, was about to be submerged in something close to cultural barbarism. At no time did he voice any objection to the French educational system as such. Yet he made one significant remark. Flaubert said of Gourgaud-Dugazon and Cheruel, the two instructors who took particular interest in him and encouraged him in his writing, that they barely acknowledged his gifts of imagination, which for them was a kind of emotional excess bordering on madness. It is possible that all that the teachers had done was to try to impose a little discipline on Gustave's exuberant style and uncritical handling of historical facts. Sartre prefers to see in this "bitter" remark evidence that there was no concern for the individualizing traits and needs of the pupils, that at most one might admire and help a gifted boy "outside the system" (2:1131). (I am reminded here of the frequent occasions I have heard professors remark that the most talented stuent in a class has received only a "B" or "C" because he/she was unwilling to modify his/her interests so as to meet the teacher's specific requirements.)

To sum up, Sartre finds that Gustave's undistinguished scholastic record at the Collège Royal[11] can be explained by three things: (1) His constituted passivity was not conducive to the formation of habits of analytic thought leading to precise, decisive judgments. His confusion between truth and belief did not render him adept at mathematics and sciences. He found it easier to "comprehend" the meanings of things, to think synthetically by imaginative processes rather than by strictly logical ones. (2) His "identity crisis" became more acute. He did not feel that the work which was expected of him was in any way "his" work. Within the system he seemed to be interchangeable with anybody else. Although not objecting to routine as such (his habits later at Croisset would belie any such assumption), he found it hard to accept restrictions and schedules which were adapted to the needs of everybody and nobody. A passage from the *Memoirs of a Madman*, which Sartre quotes, attests to this dislike of existence by the clock.

> This regularity, no doubt, is suited to the majority, but for the poor child who is nourished on poetry, on dreams . . . it is to suffocate him by dragging him into our atmostphere of materialism and common sense for which he has horror and disgust. [p. 269, quoted 2:1132]

"The imaginary child" is seen clearly in this passage. Sartre says of him, "He does his work badly because he no longer recognizes himself" (2:1134). (3) Finally, Gustave's achievement is undermined by the will to fail; that is, his refusal to ape his older brother.

As we have observed, Sartre speaks of two ways, one negative, the other positive, by which Flaubert attempted to cope with his situation at school—escapism and aggression. By escapism Sartre refers to the deep reveries that Flaubert deliberately induced. He quotes a particularly revealing sentence from the *Memoirs of a Madman*.

> I see myself still . . . thinking of what the child's imagination can dream of the most sublime, while the pedagogue makes fun of my Latin verses and my comrades look at me derisively and sneer. [p. 264, quoted 1:1179]

The self-protective, compensatory nature of the device is apparent. By retreating to daydreams Gustave can block out the painful reality. What is the content of these reveries? Sartre relates them to the earlier stupors, those half-trances into which the small Gustave retreated while his parents worried over his seeming stupidity. But there is a new and more specific content. At times Gustave finds compensation in dreaming vaguely of his future glory. (*November,* for example, records how the young hero imagined himself a great musician in spite of the fact that he had no particular talent or understanding of music and did not even greatly enjoy it.) Other reveries are openly sadistic. (There is an actual dream, a nightmare, in which Flaubert is first surrounded by cannibalistic savages [his classmates?] and then realizes uneasily that he has himself eaten human flesh.) Finally a particular pattern emerges which has lasting effects. Gustave, adopting his father's scientism, attempts to belittle all human endeavors by looking at them under the aspect of eternity. This is to assume an overview which amounts to considering life from the point of view of death. Sartre indicates the various stages of *le survol*. The evidence comes from the *Intimate Notebook,* which Flaubert began the year before he left school and did not finish until a year after graduation; but I see no reason to feel that the movement which Sartre describes is not the summation of the kind of thing which made up the content of the schoolboy's reveries. There are comparable, less extensive statements in other of the juvenile writings. Sartre calls the succession of images "an ascesis, not a reasoned argument [*raisonnement*]" (2:1181). It goes like this:

First stage: With indifference you look on at a dog fight or a children's squabble. Second stage: You climb to a high tower and from there watch with equal calm and detachment the struggles and infamous activities of petty human beings.[12] Third stage: Suddenly the point of view shifts. We are abandoned on our tower. There is a giant who looks down upon us from above and laughs at our complacency. Fourth stage: Sartre quotes directly from Flaubert. "Now you can compare Nature, God, infinite intelligence . . . to that man who is elevated a hundred feet, to that pyramid at a hundred thousand— after that, think of the wretchedness of our crimes and of our virtues, of our grandeurs and of our weaknesses" (quoted, 2:1182). Flaubert, Sartre says, identifies himself with the giant, who as intermediary both grasps the insignificance of humanity and transmits to others the insensible indifference and silence of God or nature. The giant, in relation to God, sits on an anthill, but he is superior to men because he comprehends the insignificance of the finite and the immense distance that separates it from the inapprehensible infinite. As Sartre expresses it, Flaubert wants to be a "bringer of ill tidings." By his infinite scorn of all human enterprises he tries to disqualify his own failures; in his misanthropy he attempts genocide. He is like Samson, willing to destroy everyone and everything along with himself. There is admittedly in this attitude something reminiscent of Camus' "Judge-penitent," Clamence, who nurtures his own need to feel superior by the knowledge that he has already discovered—and therefore partially transcends—the ignobility which he claims underlies all human conduct, even the most altruistic. Flaubert goes beyond this. Sartre finds at least two other consequences of assuming the point of view of the imaginary giant who looks down at our tower.

First, the dispassionate detachment of the overview (*le survol*) is only a disguise for extreme pessimism and misanthropy. Flaubert concludes that all human motives are tainted, all projects either unworthy or doomed, that suffering is the rule. He reverses the pronouncement of the ancient Megarians and Stoics that Being and the Good are one. "The ethical substance of the real is radical Evil."

> Since Evil is the law of being, every success is a crime. In defeat, on the other hand, no matter how ignominious, one finds the Good, humiliated, crushed, but still alive; the unrealized, the nonrealizable, the impossible ideal. [2:1176]

By a radical reversal, defeat becomes a triumph. Gustave satisfies both his Flaubert pride and his inner will to lose. We can see here, too, an echo of the despair that Sartre claims Flaubert discovered at the time of the Fall when he was seven years old and that will remain with him throughout his life—the *amari aliquid* that surges up amidst the flowers at the banquet.

Sartre refers to these reveries as marking a "new personalizing revolution" of the spiral. Henceforth Flaubert will seek to portray himself as the most disinherited and afflicted of humans. "Behold him the first of all men for the very reason that an exquisite, malign premeditation has made him the last of all" (2:1177). Sartre is well aware of the source of the promise that "the last shall be first." The Christian influence is there in Flaubert, but he has distorted the idea by putting it into a new context—that of the missing God, I suppose we might say. Sartre points out that the promise of the ultimate triumph of the humiliated is meaningful only within the context of Christianity as an institution. It is not God himself but the members of the Christian community who collectively act as mediator. By them the poor and lowly are explicitly pointed out as the special recipients of God's blessing. Without this spiritual framework, the sufferer testifies to nothing, is neither recognized nor rewarded. If Gustave is to view himself as the "last in the class and the first of the Elect," he can do so only by so total a retreat to the imaginary that it will border on madness. Indeed, Sartre claims that both now and in the months preceding the nervous crisis near Pont-l'Evêque, Flaubert was at once tempted and terrified by the idea of madness. In his scenario for *The Spiral*, the intention was to have his hero escape from his misery in a fantasy life which became proportionately more intense and ecstatic as his suffering increased; finally he would find his true happiness in an asylum. In reading Sartre's account one feels that this could have been Flaubert's own fate and that he recognized the possibility within himself.

One of the things that saved him may have been the very fact that he felt so little sense of an inner, separate self and habitually sought to discover himself in what he appeared to be for others. Sartre quotes a passage from the *Memoirs of a Madman*, which reveals both the autism and the acute awareness of others' judgments.

> Lost in these vague reveries, these dreams of the future, carried away by that adventurous thought . . . I stayed for whole hours, my head in my hands, looking at the floor of my study or watching a spider weaving its net on the master's desk. And when I came to, . . . they laughed at me, me the laziest of all, who would never have a positive idea, who would show no inclination for any profession, who would be useless in this world . . . who would never be good for anything—at most a clown, an animal showman or a maker of books. [pp. 266–67, quoted 2:1193–94]

This particular passage may seem to the average reader only the swan's recollections of its days as an ugly duckling. Sartre gives it a different interpretation. He thinks that Gustave, on a purely intellectual level, continued to believe that the others were right. He disdained the dreamer even while cherishing the dreams, recognized that imagination, because it was unreal, was inferior to the world of action. Even with literature itself Sartre feels that there was always an ambivalence in Flaubert's mind. He makes much of the fact that, while Flaubert generally viewed art as that which demands and justifies the sacrifice of all else, and while for most of his readers Flaubert personifies the ideal of art for art's sake, he has nevertheless expressed on more than one occasion the view that the literary artist is a bourgois who writes books in the country, much as a numismatist collects his coins. Flaubert seems to have retained in one part of himself a residual feeling that the creator of the imaginary is a poor copy of the person who performs irrevocable acts in the real world. For the schoolboy this was one more source of unhappiness, especially since at that time, and indeed later as well, he longed to write significant works but doubted that he was endowed with genius. Yet I think that at this early stage his ambivalent attitude toward indulgence in dreams may well have kept him from a much more serious alienation from reality.

We recall that the giant looking down at us on the tower is himself diminished from the point of view of God and nature. If he were actually *seen* by them, we would have an appeal to some sort of absolute being. But the Look of God is impersonal, nature is indifferent. In spite of his early ecstasies when Gustave felt that he all but dissolved in the presence of sun or sea, that he became "great as the world," Flaubert never found in all of this any fulfillment or justification for the human being. Sartre feels that there was little content to the stupors or pantheistic ecstasies beyond the apparent loss of self. Although Flaubert once remarked that he would have been a mystic if he had not been so rational, the truth is that he never held any belief in mysticism to be a positive avenue to truth. Much as he felt a nostalgic longing for a belief in God, he withheld his rational assent and refused to accept Pascal's wager. What is above the giant is nothing at all unless it is Flaubert's own perception of the futility and meaninglessness of things. The infinity is wholly negative. Thus Flaubert arrives at what Sarte calls a "cogito of Nothingness." "I am nothing; therefore I am" (2:1177). We see that all of the strands come together. In order to sustain his will to fail, Gustave must convince himself that he wants to succeed, to be the first. Yet he cherishes the hope that to be the last is one way to achieve being the first. From the superior vantage point of the one who sees the futility of the real and of all human endeavor, he chooses to create the unreal. This can be accomplished only by the annihilation of the real—at least in the imagination. It is in this context that we can understand why Flaubert claimed that the act of destruction equalled the act of creation. Satan, potentially at least, is the equal of God. If as the "bringer of ill tidings" Flaubert debases and ridicules himself, so much the better. This is the proof that by knowing where others are ignorant, he escapes the universal denunciation that he brings to bear on the human race as a whole. The last shall be first. The vanquished is the conqueror. The denouncer of the real is supreme in the realm of the imaginary.

Sartre points out that naturally this kind of escapism could not serve as adequate defense for Gustave at school. At some point he began to take the offensive. Unlike Charles Bovary, he fought back successfully. Sartre does not tell us where this boy with the passive constitution found the necessary strength. Perhaps it derived from his pride of family. At the period of the Garçon he is clearly one of the foremost spirits in a closely knit group of rebellious, though not revolutionary, adolescents. There is an obvious link between the misanthropic daydreams and the aggression. Behind the mordant, sarcastic comments which, by his own admission, he directed toward individuals, there was a more universal cynicism. We shall find it again in the creation of the Garçon.

### The Garçon

*The Role.* When Flaubert was in his midteens, he and his friends created the Garçon. This fictional personage was a role more than a character. The boys would take turns representing him. Some of the "acts" were so satisfying that they were repeated. On other occasions anyone who suddenly thought of a new angle might spontaneously start performing. For some of the more extreme exploits—for example, the "banquet of crap," there would be descriptive narration. The Garçon was the result of a spontaneous, continuous, group creation. Whether or not Flaubert planted the first seed we can never know. It seems probable that he was one of the original initiators; he was certainly one of the leaders in producing and sustaining the life of the Garçon. Sartre believes that he served as a kind of repository and ultimate authority, one who made the final decision as to what was or was not permissible and what would be in keeping with the character.

What exactly was the Garçon? The motive for his creation was, of course, to shock and scandalize, *épater le bourgeois*. It is far more difficult to pin down exactly what he represented, not because of the subtlety of the satire but because of a certain ambivalence in him.[13] The Garçon is both mocker and mocked. In his grossness, his open declaration of animal needs, in his excess, he is the antithesis of

131

bourgeois refinement. At the same time, in the intent of his creators, he *is* the bourgeois *par excellence*, not as the respectable citizen tries to see himself but as he is beneath his pretences. Even as the Garçon guffaws at the hypocrisy of polite society, he offers himself as its true portrait. Events fed into the hands of these adolescents. One can imagine their delight when the *censeur* of their school was caught in a brothel. Flaubert wrote,

> When I think of the Censeur's face, caught in the act . . . I can't believe it, I laugh, I eat it up, I chant, ah! ah! ah! ah! ah! and I let go with the laugh of Garçon. [*Corr.* 1:24–25]

Here Flaubert *is* the Garçon in his delight at this proof of iniquity in the guardian of morals. The difference between the unfortunate administrator and the Garçon is only that the latter does not pretend to be anything more than a lusty animal or "natural man."

Sartre sees a close connection between Flaubert as the Garçon and Flaubert as the giant. In his escapist dreams Gustave had imagined the giant as the "sombre caryatid of a heaven deaf and dumb to our dreams." When the "bringer of ill tidings" laughs at the news he bears, he becomes the Garçon. The link between the two is a "gigantism of scorn." We might say that the Garçon is the very incarnation of the laugh. Sartre, however, argues that in the Garçon we find not one laugh but two. These two quite different laughs are not easily compatible; there is a constant tension between them, and they correspond to two sides of Flaubert himself. Flaubert was, of course, the scholar or bookworm, the dreamer, the later hermit of Croisset. But there was also the vulgar, "loudmouth," the traveling salesman on a spree. This was the Flaubert who shocked the delicate sensibilities of the Goncourt brothers by his behavior at parties, who insisted on being the center of attention, who delighted in practical jokes not always in the best of taste. Sartre offers proof that this parallel between Flaubert and the Garçon is not his own invention. In 1866 Flaubert wrote of himself,

> There are two men in me. The one, you see, narrow-chested, bottom glued to the chair, the man made to be hunched over a table; the other, a traveling salesman, the genuine jollity of the traveling salesman away from home, and the taste for violent activities.

His niece described the Garçon as "a sort of modern Gargantua of Homeric exploits, in the skin of a traveling salesman" (2:1240).

In the beginning, Sartre says, the traveling salesman jeered at the bookworm. In the first laugh giant and traveling salesman are united. Since being is pure matter, let us scoff at all human efforts to rise above matter.

> Nothing is beautiful except what is gross, fat, and big. Long live matter, which is pure being! In the name of Being, I scorn, despise, and destroy all that is little—and particularly the human species. We have a negation of the negative in the name of absolute positivity. From this point of view what counts in the hyperbolic exuberance of the Garçon is less the egoistic satisfaction in being gigantic than the intoxication of reducing, of diminishing, of destroying. [2:1302]

Quickly the reflective thinker enters in to sober this cosmic hilarity. The second laugh is hypercosmic and glacial. It is the derisive voice of "Nothingness mocking Being." The giant is himself the object of scorn since Being is itself "comic when it is contemplated from the point of view of Nothingness." Sartre feels that already Flaubert has begun to affirm the superiority of the unreal over the real, of Nonbeing over Being, of eternal death over life, which becomes the preoccupation of poets in the last quarter of the nineteenth century. Flaubert, Sartre claims, would subscribe entirely to the lines addressed by Satan to the sun in Valéry's poem,

> You protect hearts from knowing
> That the universe is only a flaw
> In the purity of nonbeing. [quoted, 2:1301]

The two sides of the laugh that the Garçon incarnates may be related also to two aspects which Sartre distinguishes in the relationship between Flaubert and his associates in the game of mocking the bourgeois. As Flaubert gradually assumed the role of leader and director in producing the Garçon, he exhibited both the "generosity" of the feudal seigneur and the "sadism of the masochist." In this newest turn of the spiral we see a progression and further development of the structures established in Flaubert's play with his sister and in the child comedian. In taking on the role of the Garçon, Flaubert, as the seigneur, bestows the gift of his person. It is "a poisoned gift, but a gift all the same" (2:1228). Sartre says that in part the Garçon is a hyperbolic Flaubert, who mocked publicly what he cherished or wept over privately. He wanted to steal from others the laugh at him so as to create a community of laughers with himself as leader. To cover his own humiliating inadequacies, he enacts the

133

part of one who makes manifest "the original and infinite scandal of creation." In terms which certainly never were explicitly formulated by the Rouen schoolboys, Sartre claims that through the Garçon, Gustave Flaubert was raising the fundamentally embarrassing question:

> Why is there Being rather than Nothing? Why is this so-called Being only a determination of Nothing? Why is there Nothing rather than Being? Why is the Infinite only a pulverization of solitudes? . . . Why is there suffering rather than a calm, silent Nothingness? . . . In short, why does the Cosmos, infinite or finite, illusory or real, created or uncreated, remain wholly in the state of a scandalous cause? [2:1229]

On the face of it there is something preposterous in the veteran philosopher's attempt to turn this schoolboy prank into an ontological demonstration. If we are to find any truth at all in Sartre's claim, we must see it as an interpretation of meanings which escaped the perpetrators (including Gustave). For myself, I am willing to allow this much: insofar as the Garçon really was a projection of certain secret impulses in Gustave himself or—even more important— insofar as the Garçon represented an exaggeration of the grotesque person whom Gustave believed that others thought him to be, he was simultaneously offering himself up to be laughed at and disassociating himself from the figure he created. In Sartrean language, the seigneur offered his person in return for the homage of his vassals. By seeming to give himself as object, he asserted his right to be subject. Generosity to some degree binds the recipient, as Sartre constantly reminds us. The essential link between this self-ridicule and the cosmic laugh was the fact that Gustave never gave any hint that it was himself whom he portrayed in the Garçon. In fact, the self was a universalized self—that part of me which is Everyman. The Garçon as Homo sapiens does seem to throw into question all of human aspirations. By his passion this man-god makes us laugh at all of humankind. As Sartre puts it, Jesus came to save us, the Garçon came to destroy us (2:1268). By this time we are well beyond the gift of the seigneur and into what Sartre calls the "laugh which is the sadism of the masochist." Sartre speaks of the Garçon as a trap which Flaubert prepared for his friends, who unknowingly helped him set it up.

The effect of the game with the Garçon was to demoralize. Sartre defines "to demoralize" as "to ruin an existence by maneuvering it through fantasies" (2:1309); that is, to cause real, injurious effects by means of the unreal. Thus defined, "to demoralize" became the central purpose controlling Flaubert's relation to his own reading public, as we shall see in the discussion of *Madame Bovary*. It is Sartre's view that the basic structure of the process was already present in Flaubert's invention (or development) of the Garçon.

Sartre demonstrates the complexity and basic contradictions in the portrayal of the Garçon by a close analysis and extrapolating interpretation of one of the most successful acts the boys performed, which Flaubert himself described to the Goncourts (2:1258 ff.). Whenever the group passed by the Rouen cathedral, one of them, the "straight man," would say, "It is beautiful, this Gothic architecture, its uplifts the soul." To which the boy playing the part of the Garçon would reply, bellowing out, "Yes, it is beautiful . . . and Saint Bartholomew, too! And the Edict of Nantes and the Dragonnades—all that is beautiful, too!"[14] Who is being mocked here? asks Sartre. Obviously the Garçon is a boor, a man who, because of the excesses of some of its adherents, would condemn all of the Christian religion and the works of art it has inspired. His remark is comparable to some of the comments made by the atheist Homais (in *Madame Bovary*), and Sartre admits to there being a modicum of truth, albeit an oversimplification, in the Goncourts' statement that Homais is a reduced, final version of the Garçon.[15] But the first speaker is satirized as well. His trite remark is a succinct version of Flaubert's definition of "Gothic" in the *Dictionary of Accepted Ideas:* "Architectural style which inspires religious feeling to a greater degree than others." In short, the romantic aesthete is as much the butt of the joke as the philistine. Sartre reminds us that Flaubert himself said both that the Garçon was a caricature of the materialist philosopher Holbach, and that he showed up the humbug in materialism and romanticism alike. But against what are the exaggerations of the two attitudes played? Here lies the problem. For while we may ourselves assume a certain common-sense point of view as midpoint, no such position is ever presented by the Garçon and his interlocutors. Instead we are given a preview of the tragic outlook in *Madame Bovary;* there is offered no viable alternative to Emma's foolish romanticism and Homais' ugly realism. Flaubert presents us with an either/or, neither of which is acceptable.

Sartre extends his interpretation to bring it closer to Flaubert's personal attitudes and conflicts. He argues that in this particular instance the two speakers represent Flaubert's reflective response to his own initial impulse. In his *Intimate Notebook* he speaks of the feeling of exaltation that the incense and the flowers on the altar brought to him. At one time he entered a cathedral and immediately began to imagine how his companions would laugh if they could see him there. The Garçon's jeering response represents Gustave's internalization of this laugh, a laugh in which he himself defensively joins. The public self sneers at its own, secret feelings. Or, as Sartre puts it, the Garçon represents the reflective consciousness pronouncing judgment on the reflected consciousness. Sartre seems to me to be giving to the Garçon the original function of the "whipping boy," the lad who was educated along with the prince and punished for the latter's misconduct.

Sartre goes farther. Is the Garçon only mocking the first speaker? Or does he in truth find a certain beauty in the massacres and the bloody excesses committed in the name of religion? Once again stressing that the Garçon is often spokesman for Flaubert, rather than the object of his disdain, Sartre holds that in two ways the remark is approbatory. Flaubert, he reminds us, always maintained that religious convictions could not be sustained without fanaticism. The "mythologies" that make up the doctrines of the various religions are all pathetic, finite attempts to bring the infinite within human grasp. What saves them from being simply ridiculous is the fervor of their devotees.

> In this sense fanaticism and intolerance represent what is best in man. The martyr and the inquisitor are brothers; each one destroys the human species, in himself and in the other, in order that the kingdom of God may exist. Inquisitors would make excellent martyrs. Martyrs, when they survive, make the best inquisitors. [2:1260]

Sartre's second point is less kind to Flaubert. Pessimism, cynicism, misanthropy, if taken to excess, tend toward sadism and genocide. The adolescent Gustave placed Nero, Tamburlaine, and Genghis Khan among his favorite heroes. Later, disgust with his contemporaries led him to express the wish that he might invoke Attila to burn down Rouen and Paris in one great conflageration. Like other serious misanthropes, Flaubert took pleasure in hearing of new examples of human meanness and wickedness that provided fresh fuel for his indignation. Small wonder then that holy wars and religious persecution would seem to him the ultimate proof that his misanthropy was justified. Sartre writes,

Nero doesn't make us laugh; he kills for his pleasure. But when on both sides people pillage, torture, and kill in the name of the God of Justice and Love, the Garçon is in ecstasy. Man is revealed at last in the perfection of his nature: he is either a ridiculous torturer or a laughable victim. [2:1262–63]

Closely linked to the desire to annihilate the human species is the wish to make it appear wholly disgusting. The crowning point of the Garçon's career was an orgiastic banquet—the annual *Fête de la Merde,*a held at the *Hôtel des Farces* (the Crap Feast at the Hall of Farces). For this the boys' scatalogical imagination ran unrestrained. Orders were given for buckets of excrement and, curiously, for a dozen dildos, artificial phalluses made of wood.

In the coprophagy taken by itself, Sartre sees both a personal (Flaubertian) and a social symbolism.

Gustave's taste for scatological humor manifests his horror at the natural functions. From the moment that animals and plants are transformed in us and by us into that putrid matter, we are makers of shit. It doesn't matter what we do subsequently with our excrements. The most honest thing would be to re-eat them. Man would become what he is: a fecal cycle. [2:1316–17]

The Garçon's banquet of crap manifests the ultimate in Flaubert's attempt to demean the human race, reflecting his own self-disgust as well as a more general misanthropy. Sartre takes us one more step.

The first alimentary bolus is ingested, digested; from it is excreted what cannot be assimilated, and this, carefully reassembled, constitutes the second bolus. Surely there remain in it nutritive substances which a second digestion will be able to integrate. A third perhaps . . .? . . . The essential is not to lose anything.

We can anticipate where Sartre is going. In our avaricious and egoistic eagerness to harvest the last bit of profit from all of our activity we are figuratively crap-eaters. "Coprophagy is therefore *also* bourgeois utilitarianism." In the Garçon's holiday Flaubert jeers at all of the bourgeois traditions, including the yearly holidays. "The organizer of this high festival is the same person who wrote as a child to Ernest, 'You were right in saying that New Year's Day is stupid.'"

As one would expect, Sartre links the wooden phallus first of all with the notion of the phallic mother. He points out that there were no women at the Garçon's banquet. The imagined guests would be the group of schoolboys from the lycée at Rouen. Then why the dildos? Who could possibly use them, asks Sartre, except the pro-

137

stitutes frequented by the precocious youths. The fantasy of the phallic mother is at the root of this extravagant imagination, and Sartre does not hesitate to relate it specifically to Gustave Flaubert in whom the tendency was more pronounced.

> The matrix of these joyous inventions is fetishism, and the latter expresses his desire to let himself be taken, a feminine man by a virilized woman, a goddess mother, who would subject him to the rigidity of her imaginary phallus. A dozen dildos: a dozen men penetrated in turn by the same matron or by a dozen different ones. Nothing demonstrates better Flaubert's fetishism, nothing expresses more clearly the dreams of his passivity nor the fact that homosexuality is indirect and secondary. [2:1318]

Whether Gustave was himself the inventor of the fantasy of the Garçon's feast or whether he simply took particular delight in it, as is in any case suggested by his singling it out for comment to the Goncourts, Sartre believes that by means of it, he was imposing upon his companions the results of his own infantile fixations, which may or may not have corresponded in some cases to their own. The explicit fantasy of coprophagy and the implied suggestion of anal intercourse are naturally linked, Sartre argues. "Everything here is backwards: the woman takes the man, the anus becomes an entrance, excrement becomes nourishment" (2:1319).

Sartre sees still one other dimension, one less specifically connected with Flaubert's private sexuality. The wooden phalluses suggest a practical joke. The dream of the phallic mother is an empty one and Flaubert knows it; the longed-for phallus is not there. Whether in imagination it was to be worn by a woman or to rise provocatively beneath the clothing of a male, it is only wood. The dildo is a trap. The Garcon's laugh grows louder. It is all hysterically funny.

In Sartre's view, the Garçon himself ultimately partook of the nature of a practical joke, played by Flaubert with his friends as victims. To explain what he means, Sartre introduces a long discussion which, like comparable passages, is only superficially a digression. Actually it is an elaboration of the notion of demoralization, for the point of the practical joke (*la farce* or *la farce-attrape*) is to demoralize in the particular way in which Sartre claims that Flaubert used the Garçon to demoralize at the imaginary banquet.

*The Practical Joke.* The practical joke appears to be universal. It is perpetrated in the bosom of the loving family. Merchants have exploited it. I think, for example, of candies which are made to look like a collection of pebbles. Or one might choose an example from one of Sartre's own plays, the chocolates in gold wrappers that decorate Franz's uniform in *The Condemned of Altona*. According to Sartre, the underlying purpose of the joke is more defensive than sadistic; often, in fact, the victim is supposed to be the first to find it amusing.

> Its principle is simple. A small collectivity, in choosing a dupe to be fooled "for laughs," wants to exorcise the anguish of being-in-the-world. The latter, a specification of a fundamental anguish which is nothing other than our freedom, springs from an unsurpassable contradiction in our *praxis*. [2:1311–12]

The passage which follows is a colorful, even moving summation of Sartre's ideas on the alienated and mystified individual as he has expressed them throughout his career, in philosophical statements in *Being and Nothingness* and the *Critique*, as well as dramatically in *The Flies* and in *No Exit*. I move and act in a world which in some ultimate sense is strange, incomprehensible, and foreign to me. We all know that "appearances are deceiving," that "clothes do not make the man." Ordinarily absorbed in what I am doing, with no time to waste, I go about assuming that all things are what they seem. Indeed, Sartre might say, it is almost necessary and certainly reasonable for me to presume that this man in a blue-gray uniform is, indeed, the mailman and not an assassin, a visitor from outer space, or a long-lost relative returning to me. Although my senses have been known to deceive me, I cannot live without assuming that there is a broad area of daily life in which they can be safely trusted. Yet there remains in me a slight awareness of an ultimate unknowability in the things of which I am conscious. While the anguished awareness of this uncertainty is not present in every act, it exists as a part of "our global feeling of our insertion in the world." Sartre is not speaking here of an explicit doubt. An explicit and methodological doubt, like that of Descartes, he says, might actually offer reassurance. What is involved is rather an "estrangement," which corresponds to something real in our situation. Generally, it is covered over by custom or simply repressed, but it is there. This estrangement refers to my awareness of myself in relation to both the world of objects and the world of other people. It is through the world that I come to know myself. "I came to myself from horizons. The world is what separates me from myself and announces me to myself" (2:1312). Consequently, anything which is revealed in the world comes to me as "a disquieting threat or an even more suspect promise which is addressed to me in the depths of my existence." Sartre explains that he is not referring to explicit dangers—death, accidents, etc., but rather to the possibility that some abrupt transformation of some object in my environment may, by putting "my world" into question, reveal to me upsetting information as to what I am. The mood of these lines is close to that of Orestes (in *The Flies*) when he discovers that his freedom makes him an "exile from nature." Now Sartre moves on to the social dimension. It is through my daily work that I especially experience the "coefficient of adversity" in things. But here objects are no longer natural. Whatever material thing I encounter is overlaid with a host of human meanings. It is worked-on or processed matter (*matière œuvrée*), and it reflects the current means of production and all of the society that maintains these meanings. Not only the techniques I employ in dealing with the material world, but the very meaning of nature has been defined by others. "Thus the environment announces me as coming *also* to myself through others; that is to say, as alienation and destiny." From the time of his birth a person's relation to the world is lived in terms of those who immediately surround him and who themselves reflect the social structure.

> The text of the world is the meaning of the family context, itself conditioned by institutions; also we are "at ease" in the world only to the degree that we are "at ease" in our own family—and this "ease" in truth is only the least possible degree of being "ill at ease." [2:1312–13]

In view of this disquieting sense of not being wholly at home in a world which is thoroughly known and fully mine, any being which is shown to be only appearance, every appearance which reveals its underlying nonbeing may seem to proclaim that we, too, are only an appearance. Or it may reveal our "bedrock being" as ignominious or terrifying. When some supposedly familiar object suddenly becomes suspect, the whole world takes on a suspicious quality. All that we have taken for granted seems to be thrown into question. The monstrous suspicion arises that being is other than what it seems, and I no longer know who I am.

For most of us, I think, this kind of experience comes most often when, without our having time to reflect on it, we seem to have evidence that something is happening which we know to be impossible. I recall a pertinent experience of my own. Happening to get out of bed in the middle of the night, still half-asleep, I met in the dark hallway someone I "knew" was sleeping in a room some distance away. In the few seconds before common sense asserted itself, I was absolutely terrified. It was not a matter of thinking that there was an intruder in the house or that there was anything hostile in the presence of the other. It was the horrifying perception that this, my friend, was both here and over there. The disorientation was total, nothing of the normal world remained. I can remember no nightmare, nor can I imagine any hallucination more frightening.

The practical joke is perpetrated to evoke deliberately this kind of rupture in my normal relation with the world. Sartre uses the example of the person who offers to me what seems to be a cube of sugar but is in reality either a piece of marble or a celluloid cube. As I suddenly feel the "sugar" resistant to my bite or watch it float on top of my cup of tea, I am thrown off balance. I cannot believe my eyes. "I appear to myself as a stranger, my customs are disqualified, my past abolished, I am naked in a new present which is lost in an unknown future." Suddenly what I have always, in the back of my mind, suspected is true.

> My relation with being, with *my* being was only an appearance; the *true* relation is discovered. It is horrible; I come to myself, a terrifying monster—through a monstrous world. [2:1313]

One practical joke is not fatal. I would suggest that it might even be salutary. But Sartre may be right when he claims that a series of practical jokes played by the same persons against the same victim, and especially, I suspect, with a very young victim, might well induce in him "an artificial psychosis by forcing him to live his normal adaptation to the real as a permanent disadaptation" (2:1314).

We have been looking at the joke from the point of view of the victim. What does it satisfy in the joker? As with the crowd who laughed at the drunken man, there is a desolidarization. The dupe is mystified because he seems to witness an exception to the laws of nature. We in our superiority can laugh at his befuddlement because *we* know that it is only a seeming exception. The cube of "sugar" is not sugar, and it comfortably conforms to all the established criteria of the marble or celluloid we know it to be. Therefore for the laughers the absurd serves to reinforce our faith in the world's rationality and the enduring stability of natural laws. The victim's mystification can be explained away and so, by implication, can my own secret fears. "This instantaneous miniscandal appears therefore as a vaccine against the anguish of existing." Unfortunately, its effectiveness is of brief duration. Sartre holds that the practical joker is basically one of the anxious types.

Returning to the Garçon as an elaborate form of the practical joke, we find that Sartre makes no mention of its possible value as a vaccine. I think myself that its cathartic and therapeutic values were potentially considerable. For all of the boys the projection of their secret outrageous impulses onto the boorish Garçon must have served to relieve the repression demanded by puritanical social taboos. As for Gustave, in addition to the benefits of joining in a reciprocal "we" of camaraderie, he must have found in the Garçon a safety valve for his pent-up resentment. The entire experience seems to me to represent a repetition and intensification of his earlier play with Caroline, and I think that in both instances Sartre gives too little weight to the positive aspects. Instead he concentrates on the way in which Flaubert used the Garçon as a trap, a practical joke of which his comrades were unwittingly the dupes. In place of compromising the world by a false sugar cube, Flaubert presented to his friends a false world which they confused with the true one. The Garçon himself was the faked object, substituting for the marble or celluloid. I do not think that the parallel is immediately clear, but one can at least see why Sartre feels that the results were demoralizing. He argues that while the Garçon, on the surface, always responded to specific situations, involved himself in particular demonstrations or charges of stupidity, gross vulgarity, and cruelty, his words and actions were all in the name of certain unavowed but regulating principles: that "the worst is always sure," that being is ridiculous, that Creation is God's mistake, that any serious enterprise is futile, that romanticism is stupid, materialism is stupid, any noble venture is a disguise for what is base or else doomed, etc. The boy who slips into the skin of either the scoffing giant or the commercial traveler is forever tainted with its smell. He has exchanged a handful of eclectic, ill-assorted ideas for a total, cynical pessimism which spares nobody, including himself. If he suffers from the realization that the order which overarches even the giant is meaningless, impersonal, with no concern for the human, then any heroic attitude of despair is blasted by the giant's scornful derision of humankind.

If he plays the angel, the beast in him will laugh at his beautiful soul and at the nastiness which hypocritically produced his ecstasies. If he plays the beast, farting, pissing, shitting over everything, his ignominy provokes a laugh of desolidarity, at which he scoffs in turn by asking from *what point of view* these laughers can challenge him except from that of nothingness? The hilarity in this case expresses the radical condemnation of being and suggests a destructiveness which should be followed by a collective suicide. [2:1315]

Of course the Garçon is unreal, a mirage, Sartre says. But the point of view which those playing the Garçon adopted was a real point of view brought to bear upon the real world, even though the vision was distorted.

In summation we may say that the demoralization was accomplished as follows: First, the universal, cynical pessimism allowed for no exceptions, offered no alternatives, amounted to a genocidal denunciation of the entire human species. Momentarily, the attitude of lofty detachment, *le survol,* might bring a certain comfort by way of reinforcing one's own feeling of superiority in relation to those who had not yet discovered the pessimistic truth—a consolation akin to that of Camus' "judge-penitent" (as Sartre has recognized). But this transient exultation is blighted by the realization that it is only in imagination that one is with the giant. In reality one is among those whom the giant scorns. Flaubert identified himself not only with the Garçon who mocked the pretenses of the bourgeois, but with the Garçon who reveled in bestiality. The corollary to *le survol* is the perception that "I am too small for myself." Since the importance of this idea in later parts of Sartre's study of Flaubert can hardly be overemphasized, we should examine it a bit more closely.

In his early discussion of bad faith in *Being and Nothingness* Sartre made reference to the title of a play by Jean Sarment, *I Am Too Great for Myself (Je suis trop grand pour moi)*. Sartre's point was that the characters, in bad faith, used the notion expressed in the title as an excuse for their weaknesses and failures. Bad faith here involved the vacillation between facticity and transcendence, both of which together make up the human being. If I say, "I am too great for myself," I simultaneously affirm that I cannot help being the person I am objectively and that there is in me nevertheless a "real self" which is deserving of admiration and which I alone know. In other words, I *am* the self I aspire to be even though I *cannot be* it. In discussing the Garçon, Sartre tries to show that Flaubert has reversed Sarment's terms while keeping the same structure (2:1295–97). What an optimist Sarment is, Sartre declares. His basic message to us is summed up in the words, "You are worth more than your life!" In each of us the "I" is identified with the aspiring, ascending spirit. This "I," the essential person is held back by the weight of the terrestrial "me." Sarment gives us a secularized version of the Christian faith which holds that God judges our intentions. Indeed, Sartre holds that Sarment keeps the door open, that the ascent is always possible in principle, as is proved by my need to attempt it, and that someone or something there at the summit may someday extend a helping hand to draw me up. I do not personally read Sarment quite so optimistically. He seems to me rather to share the attitude of all comedy—the view that it is foolish to attempt to be more than we are and that what we are is, after all, not that bad, an attitude which might better be called comfortable resignation than optimism. Be that as it may, Sartre rejects any splitting of the ego into an "I" and a "me." I am responsible both for what I have been and for what I am projecting myself as being in the future. As Inez tells Garcin in *No Exit*, "You are your life and nothing more."

Flaubert's attitude, Sartre says, is the reverse of Sarment's in two ways. First, "Sarment saw in our vain postulation the sign of our grandeur. Flaubert, interpreting the Garçon, sees in it the mark of our stupidity." That part of Flaubert which adopts the attitude of the scientistic giant laughs equally at the notion that the world leaves room for a soul in man or for harmony and meaning in the universe. Second, the pronouns are reversed. For Flaubert the "I" is the worm of the earth, the "me" is at the summits. Both, of course, are imaginary; neither is the real Flaubert. But he sees himself as transfixed, condemned in advance by the mesmerizing regard of the Medusa-giant. It is as though he *is* the pygmy but occupied by the giant. The latter seems to him to be his reflecting—or reflexive—self, the "I," but it is not. It is an "alter ego" which has been internalized by Flaubert.

"I am too small for myself" is the way Sartre translates Flaubert's own statement, "I am a great man *manqué*." For himself Flaubert worried lest he might prove to have the creative imagination of a great writer without the "talent" to express himself in works of genius. Even his imagination, he feared, might be insufficiently concrete. I think we may fairly compare this sense of a lack in himself with his feeling about language. Words, he always maintained, cannot adequately express reality—neither the "taste of a plum pudding" nor the sense of an ecstatic dissolution in the whole of things which he apparently experienced as a child. Words are inadequate to fulfill their function, which is to communicate what is not words. Similarly the constitution—i.e., the mental and emotional capacity of

Gustave Flaubert, is lacking when it comes to realizing his infinite desires. And humanity, too, is too small for itself. Its aspirations go beyond the real and the possible; its achievements are inevitably a travesty of its aspirations. Reality is a marred photo of the world seen by the inner eye. Flaubert, Sartre recognizes, found an artistic solution to the problem of language in his concept of style. By means of it he was able to suggest meanings and feelings not resident in the words themselves as defined by dictionaries. What he wanted to express might be conveyed by what he did not say as well as by explicit statements—by connotations, by resonances and ambiguities, even by the "silences between the words." His defense against the giant's denunciation of reality was to create the unreal and to attach to it all of the value that reality lacked.

Sartre says that the practical joke, like comedy, reveals to its victim that "the world is allergic to man." This is also the final statement of the Garçon. To impose it upon his companions satisfied both Flaubert's sadism and his masochism, his misanthropy and his own self-disgust. The question, of course, is why the other students went along with the game. Even Flaubert himself could hardly have accepted so dismal a portrait of our world as literally true. That, says Sartre, is exactly the point: Flaubert was not working in categories of true and false. If pressed, he would probably have identified truth with the scientific truth of his father. As such he respected it but was not interested in pursuing it. Instead he thought in terms of the real versus the unreal.

> The real is not *true*, the unreal is not *false*. Then, one will ask, isn't the Garçon a *false* image of man? Doesn't he intend to deceive his comrades? Let us say that *for Gustave* this character is neither true nor false; he is unreal, that is all. [2:1327]

The other students, none of whom is likely to have been the same sort of make-believe child Sartre describes Flaubert as being, were not accustomed to dealing with images. Caught up in what was to them at first only a new game, they became infected with the overall view of the world it presupposed. And then, says Sartre, they accepted this as being true, according to the familiar criteria of truth and error. By itself this explanation seems weak. Would they have done so if there had not be something in them which wanted to believe that this picture of the human being as naturally corrupt in an amoral universe was a true description of things as they really are? No, Sartre replies. The Garçon did, indeed, fill a need for the students, but the relation between them and the imaginary personage was quite different from that sustained by Flaubert. To understand it we must examine certain events which took place at the school shortly before the entrance of Flaubert's class, events which both shaped the new students' world and reflected the history of the world outside.

Sartre concludes that in two ways the story of the Garçon anticipates later patterns in Flaubert's life. First, as we have seen, it represents a "demoralization," a demonstration of how the unreal may have real and injurious effects; demoralization plays the role of moral purpose in Flaubert's fiction. Second, the discrepancy between Flaubert's intention in the Garçon and the way in which the experience was lived by his comrades prefigures, according to Sartre, the misunderstanding that accompanied the publication of *Madame Bovary* and the public's acceptance of it as a realistic novel.

Insertion in History (1831–39)

During his years at school, Gustave Flaubert's personal history intermeshed with that of his companions and with the history of the Collège Royal; the latter reflected the political crisis in France. This was a relatively peaceful period for the country, coming in the wake of the July revolution of 1830 and the establishment in power of Louis-Philippe, the "bourgeois monarch." At the school they represent, in Sartre's view, a "collective retreat" following the failure of a student revolt in 1831, which took place a few months before Flaubert's first enrollment. This "psychodrama," as Sartre calls it, unfolds through various phases. Romanticism comes to fill the vacuum created by political disillusion and then is rejected in turn. The culmination is the Garçon. Where Flaubert sought to demoralize and destroy, he fulfilled a psychological need. The psychodrama ends in psychotherapy. Or we might say that we move from "psychodrama" as Sartre uses the word (that is, the history of the internal changes in attitude of a group) to "psychodrama" in the sense that it holds in American psychological circles (an impromptu acting-out, in which persons may play both themselves and others in an effort to understand and resolve their conflicts). The failed revolution, to which Sartre refers, took place in March. Headed by a pupil named Clouet, five or six of the boys refused to go to confession. Their own class supported them fully; the majority of the other students were sympathetic. Eggs were thrown at the vice-principal, rooms were occupied, the insurgents went on strike. After a day of negotiations, a bargain was struck. The strikers were pardoned, but the two ringleaders, who had been expelled, were not reinstated. The requirement of confession was not lifted. The school administrators shrewdly announced a short vacation, a bit in advance of the normal Easter recess.

Sartre claims that Clouet was an astute, youthful politician who deliberately used the dispute over the confession as provocation to initiate a political revolution. He points out that the event occurred soon after the departure of Lafayette, whose participation in the government had given the new monarchy some show of democratic liberalism. His removal had roused the indignation of even the apolitical Gustave. Louis-Philippe was looked upon as a traitor. Under his reactionary predecessor, Charles X, the Church had regained much of its ancient authority. Sartre claims that the action of Clouet and his friends was at once a defiance and a test to show whether the new regime had in fact changed things. He argues that the students expected their parents to support them and were surprised and disillusioned to find that the fathers sided with the authorities rather than with their sons. This assumption seems to me a bit surprising, since, as Sartre himself pointed out earlier, the typical bourgeois, while he might place himself in the tradition of Voltaire in conversation at the dinner table, would have his child baptized and confirmed—in short, brought up a Catholic. It is possible, however, that disillusionment at the discrepancy between their elders' democratic protestations and political conduct did play a part in the reaction of the students in the years following Clouet's abortive revolt. The bourgeois parents complained because all but the wealthiest were denied suffrage; what they feared most was revolution. The students had demonstrated once again that "a revolutionary order is possible and legitimate, whatever the kind of social unity envisioned, so long as it remains the living and intimate product of the group" (2:1343). In the eyes of their elders, popular power was the prelude to the ultimate anathema. In the defiant students the adult bourgeois saw not the champions and liberators of man, but the imminent return of the Terror. During the years leading to the revolution of 1789, the bourgeoisie had thought of itself as the universal class, as humanity. Now they began to realize that they were a particular class with their own special interests. They resented the nobility, but they were terrified of the proletariat, whom they chose to regard as the new barbarians. Inevitably, they began to make peace with their former, now weakened enemies, whose interests mostly coincided with their own. Sartre points out that the only hope for the children would have been an alliance with the workers, but nothing in their background or in the practical field of their immediate situation made this possible. As it was, the parents accused the children of assuming for themselves an authority for which they had no mandate. But the children believed they had been given a mandate by their parents. Sartre calls it a "dialogue of the deaf." It might be more accurate to say that there was no dialogue. In resentful silence each accused the other.

> The fathers accused their sons of betraying their family and their class; the sons reproached their fathers for forswearing themselves and, as a direct consequence, betraying their children. The sons were right, they had betrayed nobody, and their sires, in a few months, demoralized them forever. [2:1343]

It is apparent that Sartre has written this account with an eye on the French student revolution of 1968 and its aftermath, even though he makes no explicit comparison between the two periods. It may be interesting to note both certain obvious parallels and some sharp differences. On each occasion, if Sartre is correct, the revolt against educational administrators was a particular manifestation of a broader social discontent which had political implications. The students demanded the right to conduct their individual lives as they saw fit; they appealed in the name of principles to which their elders gave lip service, but which they had long forsaken in practice. Their parents, far from championing them, criticized school officials for being too lax in discipline. Refusing to acknowledge a revolutionary movement, they denounced anarchic violence and rowdyism. Failing to find a broader base for their activities, the rebels could not prolong their moment of triumph. In the years to come, a few might continue to work as radical leaders—within or outside the system. The generation of students that followed them was characterized by apathy and apoliticism. If the parallels seem slightly strained, the differences are striking. The dissident movement at Rouen was quelled in less than two days. The student demands were never explicitly formulated so as to include anything beyond their own immediate interest. One can see in it a collective movement for individual rights, but there is no sign of a true communal responsibility. It is certainly a generation conflict; it is in no way a class struggle. Nor was it—so far as we can tell—an expression of dissatisfaction with the educational cirriculum.[16] Someone may say that it is unfair to compare an isolated, brief act of defiance with a sustained grassroots movement which finally disrupted France as a whole, not to mention the worldwide upheavals of the sixties. I agree. Whatever may have been in the mind of Clouet himself, I think Sartre has read more into the incident than the evidence warrants. If the "collective retreat" had to be viewed solely as a response to Clouet's abortive effort, I myself would find it disproportionate. It would be particularly difficult to see how it would have had such a profound effect on Flaubert and his companions since they were not even present at the time the event occurred—though admittedly the older students would set the climate of opinion into which the newcomers would enter. If, however, we consider that the students at the Rouen lycée were reacting not only to the abortive revolt led by Clouet but to what was happening in France as a whole, then the notion of "a collective retreat" makes sense. Under Louis-Philippe the Great Bourgeoisie, as the true winners of the revolution of 1789 and the Napoleonic wars, no longer represented "the people" in the eyes of anyone. They were the Establishment, the military-industrial complex which for the most part worked hand-in-glove with the government. Flaubert's generation came after the dream of liberating humanity had been declared an illusion, giving way to the "self-evident truth" that each one could and should pursue his own best interest. Sartre calls the bourgeois self-entrenchment a counterrevolution against the proletariat. In this light it is even possible, though I should not press the point, that for some of the Rouen students, the Clouet affair may have held the same symbolic importance that it holds for Sartre. For myself I find that his analysis of the various stages of the psychodrama "feels right," even though what is said to have precipitated it seems insufficient by itself. As a description of the gradual depoliticizing of a generation moving from idealism to cynical acceptance, Sartre's account is disturbingly convincing; it fits all too well some aspects of the seventies, including the years immediately after Sartre's volume was published.

One of the confusing things about Sartre's discussion is the fact that he makes no adequate distinction between the students who witnessed the unsuccessful revolt and those who, like Flaubert, matriculated after it was all over. The description of the collective retreat implies that it was a communal reaction to the blighting of democratic hopes. But those who participated in the creation and performance of the Garçon were in Gustave's age group. As we read this account, we are asked to assume that all of these students—or at least the sensitive ones with whom Gustave associated—lived for nine years in the shadow of the events of March 1831. In addition, Sartre asks us to believe that Gustave found in all of it a quite different meaning than his companions did.

Sartre holds that there was some truth in Flaubert's later references to the cruelty of the boys to one another. "When the oppressor is or appears invincible, the oppressed kill one another" (2:1346).[17] Flaubert's own misanthropic tendencies made him see what were historically determined traits as if they represented a natural, universal hostility. At least two things he shared with the others. The first was a sense of his own passivity. Flaubert's was induced as the result of his family situation; the other boys had had passivity imposed upon them when the revolt failed. In the wake of the Clouet affair, they were in effect told, "Be quiet now. You can do politics when you grow up." The second point in common was a shared sense of resentment against both parental and school authorities, which created a sense of solidarity in the dormitory and at the playground in spite of the competitiveness that characterized the classroom. But there the resemblance ceased. Flaubert felt that his family connections made him superior to the others. He secretly felt that he was comparable to one of the sons of the nobility. The rest of the students saw themselves as sons of the bourgeois, a perception which in itself, according to Sartre, precipitated an identity crisis. Whereas the father reproached the rebel with betraying his class, the son was ashamed of belonging to it. He would have liked to declass himself. But first he must grasp a class consiousness which at present he did not have. Inevitably the question was posed: What does it mean for me to be a bourgeois? I, who am bourgeois, who am I?

To achieve a totally objective point of view on one's class-being Sartre holds to be as impossible as to grasp objectively the essence of one's subjective being as a free person. The bourgeois who sides with a radical workers' party remains a bourgeois turned revolutionary and keeps within himself some of his bourgeois-being as a kind of color-blindness. Sartre has ironically acknowledged this sort of limitation even in himself. As for the nineteenth-century bourgeois, Sartre sums him up neatly as a self-alienated person, one who lived by the guiding principle, "Act always in such a way that you sacrifice the man in you to the proprietor; that is, to the thing possessed" (2:1350). The entrenched bourgeoisie represented the triumph of a nonhuman order. Part of this, Sartre says, the boys at

Rouen could grasp. History had brought in certain changes. They could perceive the essential miserliness and narrowness of one bent on accumulation for its own sake when comfort and ease were just around the corner, when a sphere for nonproductive services was already opening up. Yet they were unable to detach themselves from the basic assumption that the desire for profit was a natural human trait, that highest value must be attached to the useful. But in the students' effort to attain a class consciousness, even if for the sake of repudiating their class, they needed something to contrast with the only thing they had ever known. At first they tried to pit provincial life against what they learned from their Parisian cousins of life in the capital. (In *Madame Bovary* Flaubert has recorded both his own early dreams of a glamorized Paris and his disgust with those who continued to hold them.) But the boys could not for very long identify "bourgeois" and "provincial." Presumably, though Sartre does not explicitly say so, they found that the cousins from Paris were bourgeois too. What they needed was access to a point of view which was not bourgeois, the "Look" of another class. Since the workers were cut off from them and—so far as the students were concerned—inarticulate, there remained only the class of the aristocrats. Those who still retained power and influence were viewed as collaborators with the bourgeoisie and might be despised; but there were the others, the romantics who expressed in literature their contempt for the middle class, their sense of estrangement from the average man, and their ideal of a humanity which no longer existed in this world. In short, without their knowing it, the boys "awaited romantic fiction." Sartre lists five stages which led to the final attainment of class consciousness: (1) The process began with "the passage to the imaginary," an identification with the romantic hero. (2) Then came disillusion, the result of what Sartre calls "the revenge of the Aristocrats." (3) The students' reaction to this was a double defiance which challenged both romantic and bourgeois. (4) They discovered the lifesaving device of the Garcon. (5) Finally came acceptance. The sons consented to recreate their fathers.

In describing the first stage, "the passage to the imaginary," Sartre includes a long discussion of reading. What he says shows the same ambivalence that we find in all of his writing on this subject, from *The Psychology of the Imagination* and *What Is Literature?* to *The Words*. On the one hand, the imaginary, the unreal, has real effects. The Rouen students changed as the result of their reading. We recall that the early Sartre, in pleading for an engaged literature, said that in writing, the author inevitably puts the real world into question, holds it up to the reader as if in a mirror and influences him either to accept things as they are or to change them. At the same time Sartre's old fear that literature is primarily an escape from the world and his disdain for people who prefer literature to life or would try to make life into literature remains as strong as ever. Reading, he tells us now, is a directed oneirism; it is related to autistic thought. It works with images, not with ideas. It is not a praxis and, unlike praxis, it is not allied with rational thought. Reading of romantic literature was spell-binding, not conducive to lucid reflection and thereby liberating. It paralyzed action rather than provoking it. Like any prolonged oneirism, it represented the triumph of the imaginary engagement over the free play of the imagination.

Sartre claims that when Clouet and his friends expressed their defiance in action, they were guided by faith in the perfectibility of humanity. For them the ideal had not been attained, but it was realizable. The disillusioned students abandoned the hope of realizing it. The unrealizable ideal, however, remained within them as "a fixed demand, as a remorse, as a bitter regret" (2:1373). Autism and dreams come naturally, Sartre reminds us, to those who feel themselves powerless. A person who believes that real action is possible has need of rational thought, for he must relate ends and means in a material world with its "coefficient of resistance." Those who can only imagine effective action are content with symbols.

Some novels may invite one simply to observe; the romantic novel, Sartre says, demands our complicity, our imaginary incarnation in the protagonist. He attributes this especially to the fact that the romantic hero seems to represent all of humanity. Therefore the movement from "he" to "I" is easier. At first thought one might be tempted to object that the extreme subjectivity of romantic writing makes it individualistic, not general. But what Sartre means is not that the romantic hero is an allegorical figure, but that in his intensity and bigness he represents the full development of human capacity—in the sense that we may say Faust is both a projection of Goethe and the author's vision of the heroic human as Goethe would like him to be, or that Werther is not only a self-portrait of the young author but the ultimate development of human passion.

In the reader's empathetic incarnation of the hero, Sartre says, it is as though the character enters into our heads, imposing upon us his feelings, thoughts, and way of looking at the world. In reality, of course, what happens is that, on the imaginary level, I choose to let myself become the character. So far there is nothing new here. Sartre, however, follows up this simple statement with a passage which seeks to explain the psychological process that effects the identification and that contrasts empathetic reading with autistic thought on the one hand and the free play of imagination that accompanies rational praxis, on the other. This discussion, which is couched in some of Sartre's densest and most difficult philosophical prose, is worth our attention and close examination. Once more Sartre both brings together ideas which have dominated his thought from the beginning and gives them a new turn. In his own terminology, he analyzes what takes place in the reader's "incarnation"in a Castilian noble, for example.

When I as reader read "he" or "him," the pronouns take on a new and complex meaning. Without quite ceasing to be held at a distance, they obscurely assume an implied equivalence to "I" and "me." This is because I *project my ego into the character.* As I read, "the avenging Castilian is both the object of an imaginary perception and the Ego, as a quasi object of reflection" (2:1376). The last sentence would be meaningless nonsense for traditional psychology. In a Sartrean context it is quite clear. For Sartre the personal ego, including both the "I" and the "me," is distinct from the original spontaneous consciousness. The ego is the purely ideal unity of all the psychic activity which I have been and will be. It is, in the psychic domain, what "the world" is in the empirical, perceptual environment. It comprises all of what I consider to be my "personality," which serves as the ground for the object of my immediate consciousness, but it can never be identified with consciousness. The ego, in short, is what I consider to be the "myself" which others know and which I can contemplate. It is not the unknowable and unpredictable awareness which at each moment chooses itself anew and which is identical with my freedom. The ego is a structure created *by* consciousness; it is not a structure *of* consciousness; it does not direct or determine consciousness. Therefore, since the ego is a quasi object on the horizon of the reading consciousness, I as reader am free to identify "my" ego with the ego of the Castilian hero.

Sartre reinforces his point by restating it in a sentence intended to clarify and to expand.

Or rather, the reading appears as an imaginary reflection in which the reflected-on would be the *lived* of the Castilian and in which, pushing the reflective dichotomy to the extreme, the imaginary re-

flection would make the Ego *its object* without the reflected consciousness being thereby deprived of its transparency. [2:1376]

In other words, when reading empathetically, I am not, of course,
reflecting on myself in the same way that I would in "thinking about
myself" when I am not reading. The reading consciousness is still implicitly aware of itself as reading, but this is the self-awareness of the
nonpersonalized consciousness, what Sartre calls the prereflective
consciousness, which is present in any conscious act. What the
reading consciousness directs itself on, what it "intends" is the
imaginary hero—the Castilian. But because it identifies its own ego
with the Castilian's ego, it simultaneously grasps this joint-ego as an
object while still allowing it to remain a transparent subjectivity.
This is possible because the "he" and the "I"—the active aspect of
the ego—have been present in the imaginary reflective act, as well as
the "him" and the "me" (i.e., the objectively lived experience).

Perhaps I may make Sartre's meaning clearer by comparing reading with daydreaming. I imagine myself reacting in an imaginary
situation. The "I," with its imagined emotions, is obviously a fantasy, but it remains the "I" of my ego. At the same time, while it is
the *object* of my consciousness, it is inextricably linked with it. In
fact, my free consciousness is what I imagine to be there responding
freely to the events I have invented. In reading, the "I" of my ego
and the "I" of the hero are merged, but I retain the feeling that
each is inextricably linked with a transparent consciousness. Since
the Castilian noble is objectified in my reading, I seem to grasp his
free consciousness—and my own. Of course, it is all an illusion because my reflection is on the imaginary level. This brings us to
another statement.

The Castilian is [the reader] himself appearing to himself at last as
the object which he is in the world, and at the same time the Castilian is his [the reader's] own subjectivity as it appears in *itself* to an
impartial, all-knowing observer. In short, it is the in-itself-for-
itself finally achieved. [2:1376]

I think that nobody acquainted with Sartre's early work can read
the concluding words of this passage without a gasp. The implications are breathtaking. For being-in-itself-for-itself, the missing
God, to be at last realized, even in illusion, is startling enough. For
the reading of literature, even romantic literature, to be identified
with this Great Mistake is even more so. (We must remember that the
books the schoolboys read were not trash from the lending library.

They read the fiction of Chateaubriand and Hugo, the poems of Byron, Vigny's *Chatterton*.) Yet Sartre is consistent after all. Being-in-itself-for-itself was defined by Sartre as equivalent to the Self-Cause of the scholastics, the goal for which "man sacrifices himself as man in order that God might exist"—a "useless passion" since God does not exist.[18] In more everyday terms, to act as if being-in-itself-for-itself were possible or had been achieved, to assume that one *is* being-in-itself-for-itself would be to assert that one is both free and guaranteed, that one is born with absolute rights or with a mandate while still freely working out one's destiny. In sum, it is to want to be full being while cherishing that lack of being that allows humans to stand off from nature and question it; it is to be a known and supported object while remaining a free subjectivity. It is in this last sense that Sartre declares that being-in-itself-for-itself is finally achieved in the imaginary "incarnation" realized in the schoolboys' reading of romantic literature. Sartre is not denouncing all empathetic reading, quite the contrary. Even while denouncing any ethical system erected on the premise that the missing God can be realized, he acknowledged that those activities that symbolically fulfill this need in us may be innocently and deeply satisfying. Bad faith comes in when we behave as if this self-contradictory goal were realized in reality, thus providing us with an escape from the anguished responsibilities of an unsupported freedom. In the case of the schoolboys at Rouen, their identification with the romantic hero was the first step toward their refusal to act and their final complacent acceptance of a social order they knew to be hypocritical and evil.

Sartre goes on to distinguish other aspects of this kind of reading. Once the "incarnation" is accomplished, the reader feels "deliciously free." Here Sartre provides a corollary, so to speak, of the propositions laid down in *The Psychology of the Imagination* and in *What Is Literature?* The reader is a creator of the book's imaginary world inasmuch as it is he who brings it to life by transforming the letters and the words into a meaningful whole. If he should toss the book aside, which he is free to do, the hero's life and world would return to being only black marks on white paper. But this creation is a re-creation, guided by the author. The reader's freedom commits itself to "a rigorous destiny." Sartre distinguishes reading from both action in the real world and pathological autism, putting it somewhere between the two. In contrast with active waking thought, both reading and autism involve a circumscribed, restricted imagination. In planning a course of action, in praxis, I continually dissociate myself from the real by the free play of imagination, for the active thought involved in carrying out a project could not function without imagination. In essence it is a cancelling-out of an existent situation for the sake of instituting changes to produce a future as yet still unreal. In autism, as in the nocturnal dream, I feel that I am forced to entertain the images that keep surging up as if beyond my control. And of reading, too, since I am committed to dream the Other's dream, we may say that it is "the triumph of the imaginary over the free play of imagination."

In a second respect, however, reading seems to be closer to reality than to autistic reveries; indeed, what is read may easily be confused with the perception of a real object. The lycée students fell into this error.

> Struck by the abyss which separates the poverty, the evanescence of mental images from the organization, the richness, the un-predictability, of the written imaginary (The duel on page 112 is a *fact* since one will find it again irrefutably the same each time the book is reopened at that page), they will be convinced that they have left their imagination and that to read is *in large measure to perceive*. [2:1377]

Obviously the readers do not think they literally see the duel, but the incident "leaps to their eyes like an event in the real world." The result is the strong feeling of certitude that "if the mental image is an unreal, the novelistic image is *on the side of* reality." Sartre speaks of this feeling as an error but says that it is inevitable. "One who does not commit it cannot be caught up in his reading." In what way is it an error? The story is not an account of what has actually taken place in real time and space. But it has a kind of objective existence which is different from that of the solitary daydream. The depicted event exists intersubjectively at least. It is, of course, "a real and permanent center of derealization" as the statue of Venus is. Only this time the confusion between the real center of derealization and the simple objective real comes about more easily because of two other aspects of the reading experience: the relation between "possibles" and "necessity."

Possibilities are an ever-present and essential ingredient of action in the real world. In pathological autism the will is in bondage. The imaginary engagement cannot be revoked—or the subject feels that it cannot be. Images come and go as if following some necessity of their own inner law. Just as in the nocturnal dream, "the possible" is suppressed. One cannot, in a nocturnal dream, deliberate over possibles, for "every conjecture is changed immediately into belief."[19] In reading there are two kinds of possibilities, both of which reinforce my sense of being closer to reality than to the dream. The first is the realization that I may, if I like, refuse to continue my creation of the imaginary world which the author has invited me to evoke. This is a real possible insofar as I can certainly close the book and not pick it up again. But—a point which Sartre does not make but would surely allow—I may find it impossible to prevent what I have already imagined from returning to my mind and having a real influence upon my future activity. If I continue to read, I experience the other kind of possibilities—the possibilities of the character. This is an illusion. First, the possibles are the character's, not mine, even though the identification of egos may seem to make them mine. Second, the outcome of these apparent possibles has all been fixed in advance. It is only when I have finished the book and moved from reading to revery that I can imagine that the character might have chosen differently.

Finally, Sartre says that reading and pathological autism are linked with each other and are distinct from praxis in that the former are marked by necessity and exclude contingency whereas chance, the unexpected, must always be taken into account in action on the real. In all praxis, I make a bet, as it were, that things will turn out as I plan. Contingency is an essential part of the structure of the existential project. Sartre, I think, would relate this contingency to two factors—the freedom of consciousness, which does not know what kind of consciousness will be present in the future, and the ever-present possibility that other people or the physical world itself will introduce a "counterfinality," will "steal my action from me." In autistic thought, whether it is pathological or the "guided oneirism" of reading, necessity seems to control everything. In reading, the necessity is twofold. First, events must develop as they have been fixed by the author—as rereading will confirm. Second, they will have been so linked that they seem to evolve by a chain of necessity. Here, Sartre claims, is the source of the students' error as they submerged themselves in the reading of romantic literature. Literary necessity appeared to them as the criterion of truth. "The error was inevitable—above all, for the reason that they needed to commit it" (2:1378).

Sartre summarizes his discussion by still another restatement, which both brings us back to the students and puts his own formulation in the perspective of the ontology laid down in the introduction to *Being and Nothingness.* In empathetic reading, Sartre says, there are "three levels of consciousness, linked together dialectically and conditioned by the form and content of the grapheme" (2:1379). Earlier he had said that in reading there is a hybrid consciousness, which is half-signifying and half-imagining (or image-making) (*mi-signifiante et mi-imageante*); that is, partly imagining the unreal and partly interpreting words as signs for information.[20] Now he adds to the complexity.

1. "On the surface the reader assumes a quasi-reflective consciousness of an imaginary Ego which, in the form of an Alter Ego, is presented as its *Fatum* and its necessity." In simple language, while seeming to be following the fate of the hero, I am—through imagination—identifying his fictitious ego with mine and assuming his character and fate as my own. Or, using the terminology of *Being and Nothingness*, consciousness is aware thetically *of* the character, with the joint-ego at the horizon of this awareness. He is not making himself an object as he would in introspection.

2. Just beneath the surface (*entre chair et cuir*) he is conscious of abandoning himself to produce the Other's (the author's) dream as *his* dream; in other words, of keeping himself continually in a certain suggestible state which is necessary for all directed oneirism. At this level, however, "what is given to intuition is not so much the consent to powerlessness as powerlessness itself recognized by the student as *his* powerlessness." This is a bit more difficult to fit into Sartre's earlier formulation. Certainly we cannot say that the reader is directly focusing on or intending his own passivity in the same way that he makes the hero his object. This would seem to throw him back to the level of full reflective consciousness. I would say that what we have here is a consciousness which *is* passive just as Sartre tells us that in fear there is a fear-consciousness (or fearful consciousness) and not a consciousness *of* fear. The difficulty arises, of course, from the fact that we are dealing with a quasi-reflective state and not true reflection. Possibly Sartre means by this that there can be a consciousness which holds itself midway between nonreflective and reflective—a vacillating or unstable structure, like that of bad faith, though here it is not a lie to oneself. On the other hand, I myself do not see why Sartre keeps this separate, second level which, in my opinion, might be thought of simply as an alternative or accompanying description of the third level. About the latter he does not leave us in doubt. "In depth (at the level of nonthetic consciousness) he is

reached as a freedom *which lends itself* and makes itself creative while letting itself be created." To read in this way is, as it were, to will to be spellbound.

After this half-digression on the way in which reading led the students at Rouen to think that something had actually happened to them and changed them, we may consider the rest of Sartre's descriptive analysis of the "collective retreat." Identification with a literary character would have had quite different consequences if the romantic writers had been portraying heroes who were revolutionaries with the faith that the human ideal might be realized. Instead the romantics depicted the ideal as impossible to achieve though worthy of being cherished. But it was no longer a faith in the perfectibility of humankind. It was individual and aristocratic.[21] As Sartre sees him, the romantic hero, because he and his ideal are too great for this world, is inevitably doomed. He makes of his *fatum* a free choice, suffers and endures. Passion has replaced reason as the highest value. In opposition to bourgeois miserliness and utilitarianism, he is generous and a pure consumer. What he extravagantly gives and spends is his own life. He is both Jesus and Antichrist.

> He is Jesus, returned to earth . . . to expiate a sin which he has not committed. He knows it, he knows in advance the stations of the cross, the detail of his sufferings. Born in exile, a mocked God, he *endures his provisional humanity* and lets himself be flagellated and murdered by the very ones he has come to save. The Passion, the proclaimed meaning of all Romantic life, is the consent to failure; it is sacred passivity. [2:1384–85]

The Antichrists are too great for this world. They (Sartre gives Melmoth as an example) suffer and are destroyed, but "they lose themselves in order to drag down the human race in their fall and to doom it more surely to Hell."

The idea of a triumph in defeat—if Sartre is correct—was familiar to Flaubert even before he read the romantic writers. His companions, Sartre says, "encountered it now when they needed it most." "The failure of revolt, the triumph of the established order, their impotence—these they discover to their amazement, are signs of their election" (2:1385). And again they made a natural error. In his own eyes the romantic hero failed; he was forced to agree with the world that the idea of man in his full perfection is impossible. But the young readers, subtly influenced by the author, declared otherwise; they knew that the hero was saved. And insofar as they identified with him, they, too, were saved in some mysterious sense. In-carnated in Thomas Chatterton, "the assassinated poet,"[22] they looked at their bourgeois society, at their families, at themselves with his eyes and with him despised it all as contemptible. Yet somehow they themselves escaped the judgment even as they helped to pronounce it. They might be of their father's flesh but not of his spirit. As Chirst was born of a human womb but remained God, so the sons saw themselves as "men born of bourgeois wombs."

Obviously so precarious a myth could not survive. Disillusion came in the form of what Sartre calls "the revenge of the Aristocrats" (2:1387). The destructive seeds lay partly in the romantic works themselves and partly in the boys' real situation. Sartre claims that the writers who most influenced them were aristocrats who lamented the lost privileges of their fallen nobility. Since their military leader-ship was no longer wanted, they all but literally made of their sword a pen. The enemy in this militant literature is the bourgeois, and gradually the youngsters realize that they are not exempt from the scornful judgment of these scions of noble blood. As Sartre expresses it, the attitude of a comte de Vigny amounted to a racism. In his play *Chatterton* he glorified the doomed poverty-stricken poet as the vic-tim of bourgeois society, but he was not interested in Flaubert and his friends. Byron's life was worthy of his hero's, but the adolescents at the Rouen lycée could not hope to go off to fight for Greek inde-pendence. Brought up short as if at the brink of a precipice, the spellbound reader suddenly realized that the author was born a noble and that this alone counted. As if blocked by an unreciprocated love, he realized that his incarnation was false—he belonged irrevo-cably with the despised bourgeois, the ordinary persons.

In addition to the problem of class, the students found it difficult to sustain the psychological burden of too close an identification with the doomed hero. Sartre has some interesting things to say apropos of a typical reader, Pagnerre, in relation to his hero Chatterton (2:1409 ff.). While reading Vigny's play, Pagnerre projects himself into Chatterton; after the book is closed Chatterton *is in Pagnerre.* Sartre is no longer speaking of an "incarnation" and literary identifi-cation. In truth I suspect he might be a bit embarrassed as to just where he does want to place Chatterton at this point. Sartre says of him, "without thereby becoming *real,* he loses the dimension of the imaginary." The image of Chatterton is there as the inaccessible

Other, who stands as what Pagnerre cannot be, whose presence serves both to direct and to judge Pagnerre. As image, he is of course unreal. Moreover, as a character in a book, he is, as Pagnerre knows, present to the other students now reading about him and absent to Pagnerre. He is being imagined and is giving rise to incarnations elsewhere. This very fact seems to give him some kind of objective being. He takes on the character of what Sartre calls a collective and defines as "a social object which deprives its being from the nonbeing, from the distance, from the noncommunication of the social agents who relate to it [s'y réfèrent]" (2:1409). In the *Critique*, Sartre used the word "collective" for such social realities as a bus schedule, the newspaper, television programs, public opinion polls, which seem to most of us very real indeed, even though the human relations they entail are those of the series (e.g., a ticket line) rather than personal confrontation. Small wonder, then, that he now concludes,

> It matters little after that whether he [Chatterton] is real or imaginary; his being comes to him from the fact that he infinitely overflows every consciousness even though he can exist only by means of it. [2:1409]

For Pagnerre while he is reading, the awareness that other readers are simultaneously incarnating themselves in Chatterton, similarly though with variations, adds to the richness of the experience. When his own reading is over, then Chatterton plays a role closely resembling that of the superego, except that in this case the "otherness" of the superego derives in part from the knowledge that other readers continually evoke for themselves the incarnation that Pagnerre had experienced earlier. It is interesting to compare Sartre's discussion of the imaginary object as a collective with Freud's analysis of human relations in the group with a charismatic leader. What happens there, Freud says, is that each member of the group substitutes the leader for his own ego-ideal. Thus the primary relation, an internal one, is between each individual and the leader, but the fact that every member cherishes the same ego-ideal establishes a secondary internal relation of all of them to one another.[23] In this context the ego-ideal for Freud is almost synonymous with the superego though the negative, judgmental aspects of the latter are played down. Sartre's imaginary object as a "collective" works within a strikingly similar, though not identical structure. Each one of the readers allows himself to be influenced by the same imaginary character—on whom his creator has bestowed a certain objective existence though Sartre does not call him real. For each of the adolescents this image serves as superego. The readers are thus united by a secondary bond as with Freud. But there are two differences. Because Chatterton as an equivalent to the leader is only imaginary, he cannot by himself initiate action. And because the reading is a solitary or, at least, an individual act, the bond remains that of the series. Nothing comes to effect the group-in-fusion, whereas Freud's leader may very well incite the group to collective action.

Returning to Pagnerre and Chatterton, Sartre points out once more the way in which the imaginary can poison the real; this time he goes on to show how, by a further development, the real may finally enter in to erode the effects of the imaginary. In unpublished passages from *Madame Bovary* Flaubert described the way in which students would return from weekends in their bourgeois homes and talk about the parties and other activities they had enjoyed in an environment far removed from the world of their feverish midnight reading. The romantic heroes, Sartre says, are there in their heads to remind them that if they are at home in this world, then they belong with the contemptible bourgeois who destroyed Chatterton. There is another problem. Most of Flaubert's friends have not in their inmost depths opted for death and despair. "The 'being-to-die- [*l'être-pour-mourir*], so loudly proclaimed, is only a borrowed being, an occasional, peripheral response to the difficulties of adolescence" (2:1413). They are really for life and happiness. Moreover, some of them genuinely love their parents. At close quarters it is hard for the boys to see their own fathers and mothers as deserving the vituperation poured over them by the aristocratic writers. And if the son, not being born a noble, cannot escape his class in any case . . . Suddenly, Sartre says, Chatterton appears to be an enemy. Pagnerre feels that he has been damned from birth but that the sentence is unjust. Of course, the bourgeois parents would be glad to welcome back the prodigal, to say to him in effect, Abandon the hope of being a superman, Give up the ideal of a perfect humanity. "You are the worthy son of your father; and you have no other task in this life than to resign yourself humbly to being, like him, only a bourgeois" (2:1418). But the students are not yet willing to enter into this "monstrous alliance." First they will fight on two fronts at once, defying both the romantics and their bourgeois parents. Sartre outlines four rapidly traversed stages in this new phase.

The first is pure rage. "Turning the Romantics' own weapons

against them, they devalorize being in favor of Nothingness"
(2:1418). They declare that Chatterton and Vigny and they themselves are all equally pursuing the impossible. The romantics have
not fulfilled the ideal of humanity. By a kind of reverse ontological
proof, they conclude that nothing is beautiful and good except that
which does not exist. "Humanity," which had been still realizable
for Clouet, had become in turn aristocratic and impossible. Now it
was hateful. Here is the first appearance of a genocidal misanthropy.
Not having the luxury of an *acte gratuit,* they opt for pure gratuity.
Sartre gives examples of fantastic and extravagant behavior, pure
play-acting by those who could no longer hope to feel identified with
their heroes but imitated their mannerisms. Insofar as they could,
they disengaged themselves from the real world. They are not interested in it. But "they cannot hide from themselves the fact that this is
the alibi of a cad. They are absorbed in playing at being what they
know they are not in order to avoid seeing what they truly are"
(2:1432). If reality is impossible, one solution is suicide. The rest of
the students were shocked and sobered when two of the boys actually killed themselves. Sartre writes, "These decided *for that generation of bourgeois children,* born around 1820, that life was not livable.
And I acknowledge that they were right" (2:1434).

Sartre recognizes, however, that to leave life is to escape from it,
not to triumph over it. Anticipating his later discussion of Flaubert's
nervous crisis, he says that Flaubert, too, died symbolically to life in
order that he might escape the real in literature. Sainthood was the
last avatar of the collegiate community. But the majority of the students were shocked out of their bad faith. They could no longer play
at suicide after the real deaths of their companions. They conclude
that the Sancho Panza in them is their real self. They welcome the
revelation of their own ignobility. The laugh has replaced the dream.
Were they laughing at the world or at their failed suicide?

> Both. Let us say that their failure revealed their imposture. Their
> being-in-the-world-to-die was a comedy. They are in it *to live in it.*
> This disgrace renders them *comic* in their own eyes. [2:1437]

It is in this context that Sartre discusses the close connection between
the comic and the tragic that we considered earlier. In both of them
the human being is seen to be at the mercy of the nonhuman in a
world which is "allergic to man" (2:1439). The laugh elicited by the
comic reveals that "every man is a subman who takes himself seriously." Their grandparents mistakenly assumed that the bourgeoisie

was a universal class. The grandsons identify it with the human species. They decide that even the nobles are only bourgeois who don't know that they are. "Atomism, determinism, mechanism— *there* is the real." Faced with the declaration of the two suicides— "Life is impossible, therefore I die"—the students conclude that man is tragic, but they are submen, defined by their ignoble appetite for life. The choice is to kill oneself or to laugh at everything, first and foremost at oneself. Finally they laugh even at the two suicides— "those two imbeciles who somehow or other killed themselves *by mistake*" (2:1441). This hilarity Sartre calls the "*Ersatz* of a suicide in this sense, that the adolescents refuse to take seriously their own seriousness or even the despair from which it resulted and from which any hope might be reborn" (2:1443). They want the cathartic laugh to save them by dissociating them from the human species which they mock. Again Sartre compares them with Camus' "judge-penitent."

The end of the psychodrama is self-acceptance. At this point (about 1837) the students have baptized themselves "*les Blasés.*" Out of the encounter between Flaubert and *les Blasés* was born the Garçon. Flaubert sought to demoralize his companions, but they were already demoralized. Instead, he gave them exactly what they needed for reassurance. "Thinking to kill them, he fulfills them" (2:1445). Flaubert's pride in family and his childhood fantasies had predisposed him to feel that he was not one of the same bourgeois species as his schoolmates. His reading in the romantics confirmed this sense that in some important way he was one of the nobility, by blood and in spirit if not by title. Pagnerre wanted to flee his real class; Flaubert wanted to claim what he believed to be his (2:1444–45). In offering to his friends a caricature of himself and his own inner conflicts, he aimed at playing the seigneur, asserting his own superiority, and blasting their aspirations with the glacial cosmic laugh. What happened instead was that the adolescents saw in the Garçon a projection and externalization of their own contradictions. The cosmic laugh reassured them. Uneasily fearful that the scorn they felt for their fellowman might be justly directed only against their own particular sector of humanity, they were liberated by Flaubert's insistence that the contemptible object was the entire human species. To reject everything, Sartre reminds us, is to accept everything. Although neither Flaubert nor his friends realized it, misanthropy is a sign of complicity with the established order. To conclude that there is no noble cause is tantamount to supporting the evils of the status quo. The game with the Garçon delayed the moment when the sons would consent to step into their fathers' footsteps, but it insured that finally they would do so. Gustave wanted to catch these realists in a trap set by the imaginary. But what counts for them is that their own laugh is finally real.

"The laugh becomes an alibi" (2:1460). Sartre contrasts Clouet's revolt with the incident that precipitated Flaubert's expulsion from school. Motivated by dislike of a newly appointed and poorly qualified teacher, the students created a rumpus in the classroom. The instructor imposed a penalty on the whole class. When Flaubert and certain of the others refused to carry out the assignment, he and two of the other ringleaders were expelled.

> In 1831 Clouet fought against the Church; in December 1839 the philosophy students wanted to have the skin of a poor devil who didn't have enough diplomas to merit their respect and who didn't appear to them worthy to teach the sons of the Rouen bourgoisie. [2:1461–62]

Certainly there is no sign of political engagement in the action. Flaubert did not boast of his part in it; neither did he show any signs of shame at being ignominiously dismissed. Sartre hints that he may have been pleased to be out of the school and in a sense worked to arrange it.

> He persists in his dislike of the collège, arranges at registration in 1838 to return to the status of day student, and succeeds in getting himself kicked out at the beginning of the school year 1839–40. [2:1456]

What should we conclude with regard to Gustave's relations with the other students? Did the Garçon put him where he wanted to be? Obviously he was accepted by his peers and perhaps even recognized as a leader. Was he finally happy? Sartre's answer is carefully qualified. On the positive side he says, "If this misanthrope ever experienced a deep and warm feeling for a community of Equals," it was during those last four years at the lycée, not at the dinner parties with the great and famous who honored him later (2:1455–56). Sartre goes so far as to conclude that "The value of the Garçon is that he enables the young people to love each other" (2:1450). This is because the production of the Garçon was in effect a psychotherapeutic drama. Since the boys acted for one another, there was no public which might challenge the truth of the message.

Everyone participated, all contributing material for the central character, taking turns at incarnating him; nobody was wholly spectator or actor. There was no fixed audience for the group as a whole. The Garçon was a collective. Each one of the players anonymously contributed his bit to the common ego of the character, thereby getting rid of his own repressions. Sartre grants that this common project displayed some of the characteristics of the group-in-fusion. No one individual was object or other to the rest. In spite of the pessimistic misanthropy which the group adopted as its way of viewing the human species, their collaborative creation brought to them the joy that stems from genuine human relations. Yet Sartre insists that the cathartic psychodrama had not put an end to their demoralization. It was at best a reprieve. At worst it was a device which, like any total cynicism, would serve as an excuse for participating in what they decreed could not be helped. The laugh enabled them to feel that they were superior to their parents but did not motivate them to change either their own lives or the social structure.

As for Gustave Flaubert, Sartre feels that his very real satisfaction and sense of community were shadowed over by certain problems (2:1451 ff.). In allowing the Garçon to become a collective creation, he gave up his position as author but probably found adequate compensation in being allowed to take his turn at playing the leading role and knowing that his original idea continued to be at the source of the group activity. But he, too, had to submit to the collective surveillance. He could inspire and animate but not command. He remained seigneur only in his own imagination. His triumphs were only outside the classroom; he was not the first in scholastic achievement. Again his success stemmed from the imaginary, which intensified his own sense of unreality. Finally, Gustave was integrated in the group, but Sartre asks, "Did he love his comrades?" Sartre's answer is that probably Flaubert himself hardly knew and that he did not really understand his own situation. He wavered between the view that the other boys were simply narrowminded bourgeois like their fathers and the belief that they were the sublime perpetrators of scornful extravagance. He gloried in being accepted by them, but he cherished his sense of being different, an exile among them. He confusedly felt that as seigneur he was within the group and that as the demoralizer he was outside. The inconsistency of his later appraisal of those days reflects his own confusion. Yet some of his comrades remained his closest friends in later life. Sartre points out that in Flaubert's often boisterous and dubious behavior in the Paris clubs and salons, he continued to try to evoke the unruly freemasonry of the "black chivalry" of the Garçon.

## FROM ACTOR TO ARTIST

Reading, play-acting, and the Garçon were not the only things that absorbed Gustave's attention during the eight and a half years that he attended school. During this period he began to work seriously at writing, and he became involved in his first intense friendship, with Alfred le Poittevin. We have considered the Garçon as a natural extension of Gustave's fun with Caroline and his performances in the billiard room. Sartre believes Gustave's participation in enacting the role was a surrogate for acting on the stage, and this may be correct. But the Garçon was hardly a true fulfillment for one who aimed at becoming a great actor. The Garçon must have made his appearance somewhere between 1835 and 1837. It is Sartre's hypothesis that it was in 1836 that Gustave decided to be a writer. Further explanation is needed. This time Sartre does not speculate on the probability that some adult told him he "would make a fine writer," though it seems to me likely that encouragement from his teachers may have had something to do with it. But it is probable, too, as Sartre says, that Flaubert's discovery that he *was* a writer (in the sense that he could write and enjoyed it) was inseparably linked with the resolution (Sartre speaks of a "vow") that he would make writing his vocation. Sartre gives two explanations as to why this resolve became a life-long determinant, one linked with Gustave's disappointment at realizing he could never be an actor and the other the natural outcome of Flaubert's constitution and family situation.

Sartre treats Dr. Flaubert's tacit prohibition against an acting career for his son as a major factor in Gustave's life. Infelicitously, he says that the "frustrated career" was a "castration." I find this unfortunate for two reasons. First, the effectiveness of the term is blunted by Sartre's overuse of it. On page 875 he says that it was Gustave's mother who, by developing in him a basic "passive activity," prevented him from ever displaying a truly "virile aggression," thus in effect castrating him. Now on page 900 he writes, "The original castration has been twice repeated: there was the Fall, then the frustrated vocation." Evidently the frustrated career is the third castration, a bit too much for one man's life. Perhaps this is mere quibbling, an objection to phraseology rather than to basic argument. What bothers me much more is Sartre's insistence on putting Gustave's realization that he cannot hope to be an actor on the same level as the original and decisive relation with either parent. When Flaubert said, "I could have been a great actor if I had been born poor," he expressed a valid sociological insight. But while Flaubert was always fascinated with the theater and deeply disappointed at the failure of his play, *The Candidate,* there is no evidence that he would willingly have renounced writing for the sake of being an *actor.* Rather than feeling that literature was a *pis-aller* for the disappointed actor, we might view acting and even play-writing as an Ingres' violin for the novelist. Many children want unrealistically to be actors—as they want to be explorers and cowboys. What was different in Flaubert's case was that the youthful author's experience with his own dramatic productions influenced his distinctive qualities as a writer. What Sartre says in this connection is entirely valid and fits in with other aspects of his personality as well. I cannot agree with Sartre when he attributes Flaubert's ambivalent attitude toward his vocation to his belief (acknowledged or suppressed) that it was second-best to acting. That he frequently doubted his own talent as a writer is explicable on other grounds. As we observed earlier, Sartre points out that Flaubert wavered between two views of literature: an ideal worth every sacrifice or a mere hobby like any other. In other contexts Sartre attributes this vacillation to Flaubert's ambivalent feelings with respect to the imaginary; it is another form of the old conflict between the two ideologies. In revolt against his father's scientism, he placed all value with artistic creation; yet the conviction stayed with him that truth and reality were on his father's side. In depressed moods, the artist seemed simply one who played with the unreal. Surely Flaubert would not have viewed the actor any differently.

In the section called "From Actor to Author," despite his over-insistence on the negative aspects, Sartre presents an interesting account of how things probably developed. A natural question one might ask is why Flaubert would expect his father to be any more willing for him to become a writer than an actor. Sartre's response to this is that Dr. Flaubert would respect and honor *great* writers, but would doubt that his son would be one. This is a natural reaction and one which I suspect is the real reason behind most parents' reluctance to see their child go into the arts. But this was a judgment Flaubert could fight against—not openly, but with his customary passive activity.

The first steps toward writing were all ancillary to play production in the billiard room. Abridgement and consequent rewriting were imperative for an acting company of two, occasionally reinforced by a third or fourth. It became easier to write new plays which gradually became less imitative. Sartre guesses that Flaubert may have been particularly influenced by Molière, who had a hand in all aspects of the theater and who, as a comedian, would have appealed especially to Gustave. When he finally turned to prose fiction, traces of the oral style remained. Other critics, too, have commented on this as well as on Flaubert's tendency to construct his novels in blocks, leading toward the big scene.

In the chapter called "Scripta Manent" Sartre writes more positively and, to my mind, much more convincingly on the reasons leading to Gustave's choice of himself as a writer. Sartre asks a double question: In what way is writing as such a satisfaction? And what particular desires were satisfied in Gustave's early stories? (1:935). The answer to the first is simple but not adequate unless it is linked with the second. What is written endures (scripta manent). But why did Gustave Flaubert seek this kind of permanence? What did he hope to find? Sartre recognizes the importance of what Freud called "the family romance." We have seen traces of it in Flaubert's early fiction. But to point out that many, if not all of us, tend to imagine fictional origins for ourselves is but to raise another question. Why does only an occasional person go on to become a writer of fiction?[24] It is in trying to answer this for Flaubert that Sartre is at his best. The Family Idiot as a whole attempts to show how Flaubert became the author of Madame Bovary, "Scripta Manent" is the chapter in which we see best why he turned to literature; and here we glimpse the origin of some of his basic traits as a writer. The chief reasons given by Sartre are these:

First, Flaubert wrote to assuage his resentment. Sartre reminds us of a brief outline for a story never written which Flaubert made years later, after the publication of Madame Bovary. In this story of a married couple the woman is married to a man she detests but is constrained to remain with him by her love of luxury. Flaubert says of her, "She gets her revenge by monologue." Assuming that Flaubert meant a silent, internal monologue, Sartre feels that the portrait applies precisely to Gustave's situation as a child and adolescent. The inner diatribe, the perfect outlet for resentment, "tends toward fiction" (1:944). In a manner reminiscent of the compensatory dreams of Thurber's Walter Mitty, a resentful person may work out in imagination a chain of events which serves to raise the victim to the triumph his true worth demands, bring the resented tormentor or rival to a fall, and culminates in a denunciatory diatribe. If kept within day-dreams, the narrative and denunciatory speech will be filled with inconsistencies and repetitions. The process of objectifying it as fiction smoothes it out and gives it coherence. In addition there may be a move from first to third person which allows the author to imagine and describe feelings of both parties as well as the reaction of neutral witnesses. Gustave *satisfied* his resentment in his early fiction, he did not simply express it. Sartre points out that if literature were only an articulation of the inner monologue, we would find diatribes against the father and brother. Instead we have adapted and presented original stories. Obviously resentment by itself is not enough to make the writer. But at this level we can see it as one of the ingredients. Gustave achieved a species of catharsis by externalizing and transforming his unhappiness into creative activity rather than by the endless brooding of melancholy introspection.

He wrote also in an effort to find himself, but Sartre interprets this in a way peculiarly appropriate to Flaubert. Introspection for Flaubert was not for the purpose of affirming the truth of what he himself really felt and believed in contrast with the role assigned to him by others. It was rather an escape from the real and an attempt to put himself in an imaginary world. As Sartre expresses it, it was "to lay claim to his anomaly and transform it into a mystery" (1:911). He once wrote, "I am so difficult to know that I myself do not know myself." Flaubert, Sartre says, *comprehended* himself better than almost anyone else, but he did not *know* himself, or make any serious effort to do so (1:948). In another sense, to find himself, for Flaubert, meant to personalize himself, to give himself the feelings or desires he yearned for but did not yet feel. The hero of *November* wrote an imaginary love letter so that he might feel that he was in love. The adult Flaubert said, "I write to give myself pleasure and to read myself." Consistent with Flaubert's sense that his self was bestowed upon him from the outside, through others, he can see himself in his own self-projections only when he can adapt toward them the point of view of the Other, reading what has already been set down.

"Unreal desires were satisfied on the level of the isolated word; real desires, expressed by the monologue, were satisfied by the written fiction" (1:945). What Sartre calls real desires were precisely those that Gustave would not allow himself to recognize. In writing *The Plague at Florence* he did not admit to himself that the hero was a disguised form of Gustave, who murdered Achille and was condemned to death by Achille-Cléophas. Yet the unacknowledged identification is there, so strong that we can all but see it struggling with the opposing inhibition in the awkwardly handled murder scene. The "unreal desires" were the vague longings for passion and luxury, power, and intensities of experience which formed the content of Gustave's waking dreams. Sartre perceptively calls these "the desire for desire." The autobiographical *November* is particularly rich in examples. The hero yearns to be a great musician although he has no real appreciation for music. What is desired is not only fame but the state of being consumed with the passion for music. More obvious are the overt sexual cravings. In an effort to evoke at least an imaginary experience, he repeats aloud to himself the words, "woman," "mistress," "adultery." The word, Sartre says, serves as an analogue for the imagined experience. If Flaubert writes it down, the materialization is complete. It functions for him as a real and permanent center of derealization—like the statue of Venus.

This point is extremely important for Sartre. In the first place it reinforces his earlier claim that Gustave as a child thought of words and of language generally as something material and external to him rather than as the flexible tools by which specific and reciprocal communication is carried on. More important, it is a clue to Flaubert's sense of style and of the function of words in literature as contrasted with their use in science or practical activity. Words were never for him signs to be effaced before the signified. Paradoxically, he valued their materiality and their connotations rather than their denotative meanings. Thus they could be used to convey the inarticulable, to express what cannot be said (*l'indisable*).

The materiality of words is linked with both their sound and the evocative patterns of the orthographical fragments that compose them. In *November* Flaubert writes,

> Oh, India, India above all! White mountains filled with pagodas and idols. . . . If only I could perish while rounding the Cape, die of cholera in Calcutta, of pestilence in Constantinople!
> [Oh! L'Inde! L'Inde! surtout! Des montagnes blanches, remplies de pagodes et d'idoles. . . . Puissé-je périr en doublant le Cap, mourir du choléra à Calcutta ou de la peste à Constantinople. 1:926.]

The repetition of India is like an incantation. But Sartre comments particularly on the last sentence. To speak of dying while rounding the Cape or in Calcutta or in Constantinople is not to play up the wonders of those particular places as in the popular utterance, "To see Naples and die!" It expresses a romantic longing for death, no matter where, so long as it is far removed from the dull reality of the places one knows. But the choice of cities is not accidental. The pattern of sound—the *ko* and *ka* sounds of *choléra à Calcutta*, reinforced by *le Cap* and *Constantinople*, the *st* that unites *peste* and *Constantinople*—casts over the whole a poetic coloring and sense of fitness and inner harmony quite at variance with either real suicide at home or the kind of death actually associated with cholera or the plague. The auditory is uppermost here, and we know that Flaubert was hypersensitive to the oral effects of his prose. Sartre refers to this particular example, with its vowel scheme (o-é-a-a-u-a), as being like a symphony in A major. But he insists that even visually a comparable effect is produced. Going further, Sartre comments on the phrase from Mallarmé's poem, "Brise Marine,"

> perdus sans mâts, sans mâts
> [lost without masts, without masts]

With the cross stroke, the *t* is raised above the other letters like the mast above the ship; the letters are massed around it: there is the hull, the bridge. Some people (I am one of them) apprehend in that white letter, the vowel *a*—crushed under its circumflex accent as if under a low, cloudy sky—the collapsed sail. [1:930][25]

I confess that Sartre seems to me here to be invoking private personal resonances which few other readers would share. His observations of the connotative echoes in syllabic fragments of words seem to me more persuasive.

When I read the word "Florence," he says, even though the context clearly indicates the city, I awaken echoes of woman and flower (*flor* as in floral, *fleur* in French). Or more elaborately (in an example impossible to translate), the "Château d'Amboise" is heard by us as more than a simple name or proper noun; it carries overtones of *framboise* (raspberry), *boisé* (wooded), *boiserie* (wooden panelling), *ambrosie* (ambrosia), Ambroise (Ambrose).[26] Sartre calls these letter clusters "passive syntheses" since they are material qualifications, not imposed by the mind. They do not alter the signification of the dominant "Amboise." Often they are scarcely perceived, ineffectual as when one states simply, "I have a telegram from Amboise." But if they are used in a literary setting where the intention is to provoke the imagination, then they speak to us forcefully even if they are not the focus of our primary intention. The evocative vocable is "in the grapheme" and works its effects either for the eye or for the ear.[27]

It is this dual aspect of words—their objective materiality and their power to evoke meanings beyond their denotation—that allowed them to function for Gustave Flaubert as analogues. The repetition of a word served him as an autohypnosis, a technique to plunge him into revery. When he used written words to express the crystallized product of his imagining, they continued to express more than even their creator realized. To write was to rid himself of his repressions (1:954). It was also a form of materializing himself, satisfying symbolically the ancient wish "to become matter." Paradoxically, words both made experience real for Flaubert and furnished him with the means of escaping the real.

Sartre claims that it was Flaubert's gradual recognition that a book was a *real* center of *derealization* that transformed him from a mute poet to a writer of literature. Flaubert, at least with regard to himself, identified poetry with the inarticulable, with those ecstatic, pantheistic experiences described in *Quidquid Volueris* and elaborated in the first version of *The Temptation of Saint Anthony*. One of the Saint's temptations is an inclination toward what can only be called a material cosmic consciousness. Sartre distinguishes two moments in the development. There is first a fascination with a particular existent— say, a drop of water—so absorbing that finally one seems to become one with it (an experience remarkably like that of Roquentin and the chestnut tree root in Sartre's *Nausea*); then there is the leap to the universal, the feeling that the All is present in the drop of water or that the drop and oneself are inextricably united with the Whole. Sartre says that the first moment is real whereas the second requires an act of imagination and that Flaubert himself distinguished between them.

> Thus we must distinguish between the ecstatic experience of the totalized and the task of the retotalizer. Gustave makes the distinction *himself:* he calls the latter *poetry* and the former literature (or Art). [1:973]

Sartre quotes from Flaubert, "It was necessary to redescend from these sublime regions toward words . . . and how to render in words that harmony which rises up in the heart of the poet?" Flaubert confronted this problem when he was fourteen. He had described the act of writing as a way "to get a grip on the world and to sum it up in a book."[28] Sartre contends that somewhere in that same year (1836) he realized that this was a mistake; at that point the conversion from poet to writer took place. The imaginative creation, being unreal, could not grasp and sum up the real world. Yet one may find that the highest *value* belongs not to the real but to the imaginary world. "The justification of the Unreal is Beauty, which is in the Kantian sense of the term, the Ideal of the Imagination. It is not given in the ekstasis; it might be given to him who would know how to render the ecstatic totalization in words" (1:974). It would be some years before Flaubert would wholly renounce the lyric style that seemed to flow from poetic inspiration and turn to the notion of the artist as meticulous craftsman, but the first step had been taken.

Sartre predictably links Gustave's "conversion" to his relation with his father. The underlying motivation for creating an imaginary world which is organically and harmoniously unified is a reaction against the father's mechanistic scientism. Gustave's resentment, his self-disgust and misanthropy, are responsible for a certain nihilistic tinge in his first outline of aesthetic theory. If he wants through literature to get a grip on the world, says Sartre, it is in order that he may annihilate it. On one level he hopes, by a countercreation, to make himself the (imaginary) equal of God and thus to give to himself an absolute Being. But in a deeper sense, the literary work appeared to him as "the most elevated form of suicide" (1:967). Disclaiming any idea that he is attributing Mallarmé's complex view of literature as suicide to the young Gustave, Sartre nevertheless insists that the connection between art and death is present. He points out that at this period Flaubert entertained notions of suicide (at least theoretically). Like Schopenhauer (whom he had not yet read), he felt that by self-destruction, he would destroy the world of which he was witness. In this way the act of suicide equaled the act of original creation. Theoretically, I can acknowledge a certain validity in this feeling, illogical as it is. I find it harder to accept Sartre's claim that for the fifteen-year-old Gustave the creation of literature and suicide held any equivalence. What Sartre goes on to write seems to me to apply only to the later Flaubert. Sartre writes,

> Detached consciousness [*conscience de survol*], imaginary master of word-images: *this and nothing more*. This is to die. The author denies *real* needs (or satisfies them perfunctorily); he abstains from *living his life*. [1:967–68]

In later years Flaubert did indeed think that the writer must to some degree deny himself as person in order to realize the artist, must renounce real passions so as to free himself for inventing imaginary ones. He arrived at this view after the crisis of 1844, by Sartre's own account, but Sartre believes that an obscure presentiment of it was present already in the adolescent. Saint Anthony's greatest temptation came not from Being but from Nothingness, not from the desire to participate in any of the world's sensual pleasures or vertiginous heights of fame and power, but from the wish to be lost in nonconscious nature. Sartre makes the observation that the greatest temptation for anyone is to become completely *Other*; that is, to choose momentarily as one's values all the antivalues of one's accustomed system (1:1072). The most extreme of such choices would be to opt for Nothingness over Being. Suicide is a possibility which one can recognize and resist. The real peril comes when Nothingness is identified with Beauty (1:1074). In Sartre's view, this step is made easy by the fact that beauty is ontologically linked with Nonbeing, an idea which Sartre presented in *Being and Nothingness* and has never abandoned. It derives, of course, from his fundamental principle that all sense of form is the achievement of the ordering for-itself, which imposes itself as a point of view on nonsignifying being-in-itself. In the same way Sartre had argued that the symphony, as an aesthetic object, exists only when the consciousness of the composer or of the listener organizes its sounds and silences in a temporal whole.[29]

"What is Beauty if not the impossible?" asked Flaubert. And Sartre adds that Flaubert, like Don Quixote, "chose impossibility as his unique possible." Beauty is impossible "since it is the imaginary totalization of the world by language and since language by its very nature is incapable of fulfilling its function" (2:976–77). The man who chooses despite all to pursue it bears witness to the impossibility of being man. Sartre points out that all of the heroes of Flaubert's juvenilia are submen or robots, incomplete or defeated. Gustave's will to fail and to find grandeur in the very defeat is at least to find his own truth, a kind of Being at last. Sartre says that at this stage— indeed throughout his lifetime—Flaubert's attitude toward himself as writer fluctuated between bitter pride and despair. He shared with Baudelaire the view that "the work of art is the sole relic of a long shipwreck in which the artist is lost, body and goods" (1:977). But even this pessimism, which at least nourished his pride, Gustave could not long sustain. The truly great writers—Homer and Shakespeare—were there to reproach him. He could neither call them failures nor hope to equal them.

"Gustave the imaginary made himself Gustave the writer" (1:977). Sartre dates the conversion at 1836, the year in which he wrote his original stories. According to Sartre there was one more necessary stage before Flaubert clarified in his own mind the role of the writer in society and completed the change "from Poet to Artist." In 1837 he became an intimate friend of Alfred Le Poittevin, five years his senior. Sartre claims that Gustave was profoundly influenced by Alfred, both directly and in reaction against him. A hundred and twenty-five pages are devoted to their relation.

Sartre's novelistic tendencies are most attractively and convincingly displayed as he gives us an analytic-synthetic account in miniature of Alfred's character, a dramatic portrayal of the rise and fall of "the frustrated friendship," and an evaluative summation of the permanent effect of the relation on Flaubert. This chapter, called "From Poet to Artist," might stand as a separate essay worth reading for itself. The greater part of it is not essential to my purpose here; I will summarize briefly what seems to me most relevant.

Alfred Le Poittevin was a brilliant, self-confident, cynical young man with literary aspirations. He was Gustave's new seigneur, and he influenced the younger boy more than the later Flaubert was willing to admit. Flaubert's first openly autobiographical works, *Agonies* and *Memories of a Madman*, are dedicated to Alfred. The dedication to the latter concludes with the words, "Adieu, think of me and for me." Their parents were friends, their acquaintance seemed fated, but it was not until they were respectively fifteen and twenty that they became close to each other. Sartre holds that the age difference may have been partly responsible for the history of the friendship. In the beginning Alfred sought an audience, and Gustave was content to listen, to learn, to be impressed. As time made the discrepancy less important, Alfred continued to want receptivity where Gustave sought reciprocity. It is Sartre's view that a coldness began to develop on Alfred's side even before Gustave became impatient and disillusioned. Sartre grants that there *may* have been sexual relations between them but doubts that there were and feels that at any rate they did not last very long. Rather surprisingly, in the light of his earlier comments on Flaubert and homosexuality, he speculates that Gustave was attracted to Alfred to the extent of being sexually disturbed (*troublé*) and that resentment at Alfred's failure to reciprocate played a part in the ultimate quality of the friendship and its conclusion.

Sartre guesses that unlike Gustave, Alfred was loved by his mother. As a result he had an Oedipus complex, jealously resented having to share her with anyone else, developed a deep dislike of women, and resorted to prostitutes—excessively and brutally. (One begins to wonder just what course of conduct a mother *can* adopt without injuring her child!) As an adolescent Alfred was charac-

terized by anorexia and the desire for ataraxia. These negative qualities led him first to adopt a nihilism which appealed to Gustave. His
guiding principle was *vivre sans vivre,* an extreme equivalent to the
detached overview cultivated by Flaubert. Meanwhile he displayed a
considerable talent in poems and stories which expressed his
nihilism and a philosophical mishmash of Eastern and Pythagorean
ideas, closer to atheism than to genuine mysticism. To Flaubert's
dismay, Alfred's Byronic despair proved to be only a mask. Flaubert
was angry when Alfred began to speak of the necessity of molding
his writing to suit public taste. As Alfred began to lose interest in
writing, Gustave suspected that he was simply lazy. Nihilism became a cynical and feverish *carpe diem.* Finally the constant *à quoi bon*
("what's the use") turned toward conformity. If there is no point to
anything, why resist? Why not settle down to a conventional marriage and a bourgeois existence? Which is what Alfred did. Toward
the end, Sartre feels, Gustave loved him without illusions. When
Alfred died in 1848, Flaubert himself washed the dead body and
wrapped it in the winding sheet. Sadly he spoke of death as a liberation for Alfred. Sartre suspects that it was secretly a release for
Flaubert, and he makes some unkind remarks to the effect that to
handle the helpless corpse perhaps gave to him a satisfying sense of
superiority.

   Alfred's nihilistic cynicism undoubtedly reinforced Flaubert's own
pessimism and tendency to retreat from the real world. The most
important influence Sartre links with the economic circumstances of
the two. Neither knew what it was to be *un homme du besoin,* a man
whose life was determined by need. The Flaubert household was a
family *du nécessaire;* they had all they required for comfort. The
household of the elder Le Poittevin was one *du superflu.* They were
accustomed to the superfluous, to luxury. Husband and wife were
united in what Sartre calls a "conjugal marriage." The beautiful
Madame Le Poittevin was important within the family and at social
gatherings. Her life was relatively independent. But for all that, she
was, Sartre claims, chiefly an adornment for her husband to display,
a luxury. And since she had no career, did no real work, she was a
beautiful superfluity. Loving his mother, resenting his father, Alfred
rejected all notion of utilitarianism. He refused to be useful and
deliberately squandered himself. It may have been partly in
Alfred's company that Flaubert developed a longing for luxury.
Sartre points out that one of his letters expressed the wish that he
were wealthy enough so that he might give of the superfluous to

those who had the necessary—hardly the ideal of the social reformer. He wished in vain that he might live like "the superfluous man"[30] (Sartre intends the double force of the pun). He was prevented from doing so, not only by his practical circumstances but because his family conditioning had instilled in him a strong sense of the "work ethic." Partly under Alfred's influence and partly in rebellion against him, Gustave worked out a compromise. As a writer, he would work indefatigably to produce, but what he would create would be works of pure gratuity, things of beauty but of no utility. The artist replaced the poet. Alfred had taught him to refuse all human ends but had left him with the feeling that he was not an end in himself. Therefore he resolved to make himself a means for a nonhuman end, the creation of the unreal. Alfred had aimed at ataraxia as simply desirable; Gustave felt the need to justify it, to make noninvolvement the categorical imperative for the artist. Gradually he began to speak less of inspiration and more of hard work. He became more self-critical and began to worry lest his power of imagination be inadequate.

> Alfred expends a part of the paternal profit and his own life *for nothing*. Gustave, *with no profit for anybody*, will expend his strength and his life in producing at great cost splendid futilities [*inanités*]. . . . Literature is an artisan's craft, writing is likened to a physical effort: one works with chisel strokes in the marble of language. And what is the result? An object which is its own end as Alfred claims to be his. [1:1089]

Alfred's influence did not turn Gustave into an epigone. It changed him into himself (1:1045). Sartre believes that Gustave had longed to become like Alfred, a man of taste, at ease with luxury, *un homme du superflu*, but he felt hopelessly inferior. Now he says in effect that the works he creates will be like a reproduction of Alfred. "I cannot *be* you, but I can engender you, ungrateful lover!" The hidden sense of sexual resentment is present, too, Sartre thinks.

> This perhaps explains Flaubert's insistence on presenting artistic invention under the image of erection. The rejected lover takes his revenge by making himself the begetter of his beloved. Writing is Gustave's virility. [1:1089][31]

Sartre concludes finally that after Alfred's death, Flaubert does more than engender Alfred; he incorporates him, trying to be at once both Alfred and Gustave. This conclusion is a little overnovelistic. (The entire chapter has the makings of a novella if it isn't quite one as it stands.) Yet metaphorically it seems to describe Gustave Flaubert as he was after being subjected to Alfred's influence. He once wrote that the work of art should be "cold like Boileau and unruly [*échevelé*] like Shakespeare." Sartre translates this into: "Cold like Alfred, unruly like Gustave. Dry heat. Frozen by language" (1:1092). The unique blend of classicism and romanticism that Flaubert perfected and that holds him forever remote from simple naturalism may well derive in large part from his early encounter with Alfred.

Within a year after the two became friends rather than acquaintances, Flaubert began to speak of "art" and its demands. At this stage of the spiral he had seriously chosen himself as "a worker in the imaginary." There still remained the task of reconciling this choice with the expectations his father held for him. Characteristically, there was never an open confrontation. One wonders whether Gustave ever acknowledged even to himself that he was engaged in mortal conflict with his father. Openly conforming, he waged the battle by means of his usual passive activity. The climax was the nervous attack that occurred near Pont-l'Evêque in January 1844. Gustave both lost and won.

In his notes for the fourth volume, Sartre refers to his own discussion in "Scripta Manent" (1:922–26) of Flaubert's use of words as mediators. In Flaubert's treatment of the word *maîtresse*, he says, we can see all of *Madame Bovary*. The application to *Madame Bovary* will be reserved until we discuss Sartre's criticism of the novel, and indeed Sartre did not mention Emma Bovary in the passage to which he refers. His discussion does, however, sum up and illuminate in marvelous fashion many of the major ideas he has introduced, and I think that a brief summation of it is an appropriate conclusion to our survey of Sartre's portrait of Flaubert from his birth to the end of his school days at the lycée.

Sartre begins with a long series of quotations from *November*, of which I will repeat only a few lines.

> Certain words bowled me over, *woman* and *mistress* [*maîtresse*] especially . . . a *Mistress* was for me a satanic being; the magic of the noun alone threw me into long ecstasies.

It was for their mistresses that kings won and ruined provinces; for them . . .

> gold was wrought, marble was chiseled, the world was remade.

Closely associated with *mistress* is

> one word which seems the most beautiful of words: *adultery*. An
> exquisite sweetness hovers obscurely over it. It is fragrant with a
> strange magic. Every story told, every book read, every gesture
> made is an eternal commentary upon it for the young man's heart;
> he wantonly steeps himself in it, he finds here a supreme poetry
> mingled of malediction and voluptuousness.

Autohypnosis is evident here, but the choice of *mistress* (along
with the related *adultery*) holds a special significance for our understanding of Flaubert which includes but goes beyond what would
have been true of most young men of his period and class. Sartre
notes that the word "mistress" changed its meaning over the
centuries—in French as in English. In literature before the eighteenth
century it referred simply to the beloved woman, neither implying
nor excluding the existence of sexual relations. It was sometimes
synonymous with fiancée. Then it took on the connotation of a
woman who took a lover outside of marriage. Flaubert would have
heard it spoken only in the second sense, but it would have retained
its earlier connotations from literature. Consequently the two
meanings interpenetrated. Even before he "knew how women were
made," the word "referred to a mysterious beyond," "something of
which he had no clear concept but which he could dimly apprehend," "a beyond of kisses and caresses." At the same time she
was "a woman damned." Gustave accepted all the connotations of
the family tabu arising from bourgeois prudery: *Mistresses*, "forbidden loves, lost and venal creatures who ruined households"; "Evil,
wholly naked, in its satanic splendor." Still there remained in the
word something of "the platonic beloved, the radiant fiancée of long
ago." It was a typically Flaubert reaction, Sartre says.

> He begins with obedience to bourgeois standards. He is not the
> one, certainly, whom we will see breaking lances to defend women
> who live an irregular life; they are demons, bent on destroying the
> respectable man, the father of a family. After which, precisely for
> the crimes which are imputed to "mistresses," he throws himself
> into loving them. [2:924–25]

Are they venal? But what magnificent useless expense they have
incurred! By means of it they bring "the whole world to the abyss of
the incredible reign they hold over the powerful. *Mistress, luxury,*
and *gold* are drawn together and form a constellation of re-
splendence" (2:925). We see here the association of illicit love and

luxury that plays so prominent a part in *Madame Bovary*. Flaubert goes on to say of the splendidly wicked woman that she will sit "on the throne, far from the crowd whose execration and idol she is." Sartre comments, "A beautiful revenge for the cursed son: the infamous crowd which has made her suffer so greatly cannot restrain itself from idolizing the favorite whom it execrates." Sartre adds still a third connotation which he finds peculiarly appropriate to Flaubert. "A mistress has slaves over whom she holds the right of life and death." Here the reference is to the poets of earlier centuries who claimed to live or die by the will of the cruel mistress. Sartre imagines how this would appeal to Gustave's passivity and his masochism.

> Elevated above men by a goddess' favor, he will use his power to ruin them and, by the same stroke, will throw himself at the feet of the triumphant demon. What joys he promises himself! [1:926]

Though Sartre does not explicitly say so, presumably there is a reference here to Flaubert's confused sexuality and his ambivalent feelings toward his mother.

All of this mélange (or something like it) surged up in Flaubert's imagination when he repeated the word "mistress" aloud. Why then did he need to write? Because, Sartre tells us, he wanted to materialize his revery and to push imagination to the limit. The vocables by themselves, repeated in his head without hearers, bore too little resemblance to images to serve as satisfactory analogues. Unless the revery was objectified in some way it remained too subjective and too evanescent. We are brought back again to *scripta manent* and the "worker in the imaginary."

# CHAPTER FOUR

## The Turning Point

One evening in January '44, Achille and Gustave were returning from Deauville where they had been to see the site of the new country house. It was pitch dark, Gustave himself was driving the cabriolet. Suddenly, in the vicinity of Pont-l'Evêque, a wagon passed to the right of the carriage; Gustave dropped the reins and fell thunderstruck at his brother's feet. Seeing his corpselike immobility, Achille believed him to be dead or dying. In the distance the lights of a house were seen. The elder son carried the younger there and urgently took care of him. Gustave remained for a few minutes in this cataleptic state; he did, however, retain his full consciousness. When he opened his eyes, did he have convulsions or not? It is difficult to know. In any case his brother took him to Rouen the same night. [2:1771]

With this concise summary Sartre describes the event which, with its aftermath, is the focal point of part three, "Elbenhon or the Last Spiral,"[1] comprising more than three hundred and fifty pages. For all Flaubert scholars and for Flaubert himself it marked a turning point. In Sartre's view it was the moment of choice, the point at which Flaubert fixed once and for all the essential patterns of his personality. Objectively, it put an end to any plans for a career in law; for some months he was an invalid, later the recluse at Croisset. (Attacks recurred frequently during the first few days after the initial one and fairly often for six months; after that they became increasingly rare and disappeared entirely after ten years.) His "malady" did not prevent Flaubert from taking a journey to remote points in Egypt and the Near East. Either in spite of it or because of it he wrote the works that made him famous. And exactly *there* is the question. Or rather there are two related questions: What, medically, was the cause of what Flaubert referred to as his "nervous crisis"? Was it epilepsy or hysteria? And more important: Was the attack an accident, like small pox or scarlet fever? Or was it the culmination of psychosomatic processes with an intentional structure? Epilepsy would suggest the former, hysteria the latter.

Critics have disagreed as to which is the more likely diagnosis. Dr. Flaubert at first thought the cause was some sort of cerebral congestion, like apoplexy. In the months following the first attack, he felt that it must have been something else and admitted the possibility of a form of epilepsy. Among Flaubert biographers, some (Dumesnil and Spencer, for example) believed that descriptions of the attack by Flaubert and others do not fit epilepsy. Steegmuller, while granting that it might possibly have been epilepsy, concluded that it was in any case atypical. Benjamin Bart confidently declared that it must certainly have been epilepsy, and Brombert, perhaps influenced by Bart, agrees that it "very probably" was. Bart gathered evidence from all relevant documents and submitted them to Dr. Arthur Ecker, a clinical professor of neurological surgery at the Upstate Medical Center in Syracuse, New York. Dr. Ecker diagnosed the malady as temporal lobe epilepsy. Bart thinks we can be "reasonably sure" that this diagnosis is correct and tries to match details of Flaubert's affliction with descriptions of this form of epilepsy in medical studies. He remarks that temporal lobe epilepsy had not yet been recognized in the nineteenth century, a point that does not clinch the argument. It is true that if the physicians had known of it and if Flaubert's symptoms had matched, they might have settled the matter once and for all. It is also nearly certain, as Sartre points out, that they would not have probed for information and asked the questions which doctors today would need to have answered in order to arrive at any decision. Spencer has pointed out that until 1888 hysteria was believed to occur only in women. (Notations of Flaubert's doctor in fact compared him to hysterical women and treated him accordingly.) Charcot and Janet had not yet written about hysteria as a specific mental affliction. Dr. Flaubert would not have known what symptoms to look for. Spencer, not insisting that hysteria is certainly the answer, finds it a more reasonable hypothesis than epilepsy and agrees with another modern physician, Dr. D. Russell Dains, reader in clinical psychology at Cambridge, that the data at our disposal will remain forever too uncertain and scanty, the witnesses' accounts too unreliable, for any final decision.[2]

Sartre, while not referring specifically to the technical arguments advanced on either side, and while recognizing that certainty is not possible, is convinced in his own mind that it was hysteria and that only this hypothesis makes sense in the total picture. The name of the malady would be unimportant except for one thing: if we hold that it was epilepsy, then the "crisis" is not significantly related to Flaubert's psychological development up to the point of its first appearance and is only externally related to what follows. It would become one of the fateful accidents in a life, and we would find it difficult to accept Sartre's view of the crisis as in any sense a choice. Bart in fact speaks of the affliction in exactly this way, regarding it as a wholly negative obstacle against which Flaubert fought heroically but for which he was in no way responsible. He even halfway agrees with Du Camp, who said that the attacks had impaired Flaubert's creative abilities. While not accepting Du Camp's snide implications that Flaubert was a mediocre writer who might have been a great one if he had not contracted the illness, Bart takes an equally negative view of Flaubert's change of writing style and ascribes it to physiological causes.

> It is possible that some earlier brain damage caused both the epilepsy and the loss of rapid creative facility with words, especially as neither showed any increase with the passing of time. The impairment of abstract thinking . . . is the essential behavioral impairment which results from brain damage. [pp. 95–96]

I know of no other critic who looks so disparagingly at Flaubert's move "from poet to artist." In this passage Bart, it seems to me, suggests that the hypothesis of epilepsy does not cover all of the facts (Flaubert did not recover his ease and rapidity in writing after the attacks had ceased) and feels impelled to offer a conjecture as to still another physiological cause. Yet bent as he is on seeing in the nervous affliction only a purely physical thing which happened to Flaubert, Bart notes that Gustave "had always been preparing for disaster" and that his will played a curious part in it all. He could not voluntarily induce the attacks, but "he learned with time to dispel these epileptic hallucinations by will power, or so he felt." This same uneasiness is revealed by other biographers who have adopted the hypothesis of epilepsy less confidently than Bart. Most stress the suspicious convenience of the ailment's appearing just when it did. Starkie, for example, after referring to "epilepsy or some other nervous ailment," remarks, "psychologists might think that his illness was a subconscious attempt to escape from the life which he thought was destroying him, taking away all his joy in living, and which was bound, in the long run, to kill him artistically. It was an unconscious bid for escape."[3] She adds that Flaubert might never have become the great artist he was if his nervous disorders had not allowed him to retreat from the usual demands of life. Steegmuller even more strongly stresses the positive results of the crisis. "His illness was a godsend" (p. 15). Flaubert, he argues, had a will to become a writer "which was protesting increasingly against being denied." His attack near Pont-l'Evêque "solved the problem of his law career" (p. 34). None of this, of course, would preclude the position that epilepsy came as a fortunate accident, a blessing in disguise. And until Sartre, the proponents of "hysteria" had never attempted to study the origins and development of the neurotic symptoms. Dumesnil, Sartre complains, treats hysteria no differently from any other external accident which might have befallen the young man. I do not intend here to attempt presumptuously to prove, even theoretically, that one of the two diagnoses must be accepted as the correct one. I would argue only that the evidence does not warrant our summarily dismissing Sartre's psychological explanation as unsound in the light of a demonstrated physiological cause. The case has simply not been proved. Whether even epilepsy might be the result of psychosomatic factors, I would not pretend to know. The one new medical point which Sartre offers is the statement that "it is admitted today that certain forms of epilepsy have their origin in hysteria" (2:1786). This, for my part, I find important. What matters most, however, is that Sartre has for the first time attempted to outline and to document the external pressures and internal responses that psychosomatically precipitated and sustained the nervous attacks, and he has shown them to be integrally related to other aspects of Flaubert's psychic life. If Sartre's account is convincing, there is no reason to be greatly concerned with the medical label. Sartre here introduces a much more complex concept of the interdependency of psyche and body than one would gather from *Being and Nothingness* or indeed from any of his earlier work. At times the "somatization" of which he speaks comes perilously close to the "unconscious motivation" which he had always rejected. Yet he consistently insists that Flaubert's conduct—his will to fail—was "intentional though not deliberate," a controlling pattern "comprehended" by him though not "known." Sartre's discussion of the psychosomatic aspect is original; it is not in line with traditional psychology, but it is consistent with his own existential psychoanalysis as this was foreshadowed in *The Emotions* and formally outlined in *Being and Nothingness*.

Sartre views the crisis of Pont-l'Evêque as both a conclusion and a beginning. As a conclusion, it is a negative response to an urgency, the culmination of experiences during the seven years leading up to it, a period which Sartre calls "the preneurosis." As a beginning, it represents "a positive strategy," a life plan which remains with Flaubert until his death.

## THE PRENEUROSIS

Sartre points out that between 1838 and 1844 Flaubert suffered from a series of minor ailments, almost certainly psychosomatic in origin. His father failed to see them as forming a pattern, but he must have been disturbed. Sartre reminds us that the lapse of time between Flaubert's achievement of the baccalaureate in August 1840 and his enrollment as a law student in November 1841 is abnormally long. The father would not have allowed his son to remain idle for so long, Sartre thinks, if he had not been uneasy about Gustave's health. Sartre divides the preneurosis into two periods. Between 1837 and 1840 Gustave was struggling with "literary disappointments" and was vaguely concerned about the problem of eventually having to choose a profession. From 1840 until 1844 the question of a career was increasingly pressing; by 1842 the conflict between the son's choice of art and the father's expectations became acute, all the more so because it was never openly acknowledged.

Sartre's term, "literary diappointments," may be a bit misleading. While Flaubert was still at the lycée, his work appeared in a school literary journal which he himself helped to establish. Until *Madame Bovary* he never submitted anything elsewhere for publication. There is no evidence that he received unfavorable criticism from even his closest friends until Bouilhet and Du Camp condemned the first version of *The Temptation of Saint Anthony* in 1849. When Sartre speaks of "literary disappointments," he refers to two things: first, to Gustave's self-doubts about his literary ability and his dissatisfaction with what he had written; second, to his abortive attempts to find or to fix a personal self by means of his writing. Much of what Sartre says here is an elaboration of ideas he has already presented in "Scripta Manent"; what is new derives partly from Gustave's sense of urgency, facing the necessity of choosing a profession, and partly from Sartre's very interesting examination of the works Gustave produced in these years.

At this early stage, Sartre says, Gustave had worked out in his own mind a reconciliation between his inclinations to literature and his father's utilitarianism. In the Flaubert family father and sons are all expected to work, but the labor of the artist is harder and calls for more self-sacrifice than the vocation of a physician. Therefore Gustave "will in good conscience apply to his extrahuman activity the family norms, the ethics of that class which he denies without being able to contest its virtues" (2:1596). But his dilemma is this: The father's command is addressed to the "younger son"; the aesthetic imperative is addressed to Gustave personally. In the name of the the latter, he might challenge the former. But how can he be sure that he has the vocation? The book still to be written can never justify the confidence that one is truly a writer. As for completed works, Sartre quotes abundantly from the *Correspondence* and the *Intimate Notebook* to show Gustave's discouragement. Until his *November* in 1842, he was never wholly satisfied with any of these writings of his late adolescence. In addition to those things that would disturb any young writer still unsure of himself, Sartre singles out two anxieties peculiar to Flaubert and essentially linked with his ultimate achievement as a writer. He worried as to whether or not he had creative taste, not ordinary critical sense but that something more which goes to make up the true "poetic palate." Sartre claims that in this vaguely expressed notion Flaubert was groping to express an idea which sets him and Baudelaire apart as the first modern writers. "Taste," Sartre says, "is historically conditioned"—not just particular tastes but the concept itself. Until the mid-nineteenth century taste was something recognized and shared by authors and their public. For classicism it was expressed in specific formulations. A writer might dare to challenge the rules, but he did so in the hope of enlarging the expectation of what was acceptable. It was a conscious risk, for he wrote to please. The public was present and was consulted, so to speak, at the author's desk. But Flaubert, like Baudelaire, rejected all complicity with the public, which he despised. He wrote neither for the bourgeois nor for the aristocracy, certainly not for the workers. In theory, at least, he wrote for nobody. If he wrote for himself, it was to satisfy himself as an artist concerned solely for the demands of impersonal art. Only those critical principles are valid, he believed, which are relevant to the particular work itself and the nonpersonal intention behind it. "Art for art's sake," of course, but there is a problem. How can the artist be sure—impersonally—that he has succeeded? Only God could judge, but God was as silent for Flaubert as He has been for Sartre.

The other difficulty, which we have touched on before, was that

Flaubert was undergoing a painful transition with regard to his own aims in writing. When he was still "the poet," Gustave realized that words could not express the ecstatic content of his retreats from the real, but there were two compensations: first, there was the wholly private world of the *"hébétudes,"* in which he could be satisfied with simple feeling and afford a proud disdain of mere words. Second, when he did put words on paper, writing was still an escape from the real. He wrote uncritically and unrestrainedly under the influence of enthusiastic inspiration. He was little concerned about questions of realistic probability; to write convincingly was to invoke all his powers of rhetoric. Lyric passion passed for aesthetic intention. When he began to conceive of himself as an artist, everything changed. As Sartre puts it, his task now was "to devalorize the real by realizing the imaginary" (2:1488). But this demanded both a totalizing grasp of reality and a deliberate construction of the imaginary; it required decisions and a self-criticism difficult for a passive agent. Gustave found to his chagrin that it was not only the feelings of ecstatic flights which could not be expressed in words. Precise verbal equivalents are as nonexistent for conveying the "flavor of plum pudding" as for communicating cosmic consciousness. Sartre believes that it was at this early period that Flaubert was arriving at the discovery he expressed in the last sentence of *Intimate Notebook* (1840–41): "Art is nothing but this strange translation of thought by form." Retrospectively, we may say that this is the moment at which the artist was born, but it is unlikely that the young Gustave experienced it immediately as a liberation. Its first manifestation was his finding that now it was difficult to do what he had always found easy. His feeling, I think, must have resembled that of a person who arrives at a plateau in learning a new skill, when the old techniques are employed less well and the ability to use new ones not yet manifest. Flaubert felt that he had lost something irrecoverable; yet he sensed obscurely that he was in a state of transition. In February 1839 he wrote to Ernest Chevalier,

> Formerly I thought, I meditated, I wrote, I got down on paper somehow or other the animation I had in my heart; now I don't think any more, I don't meditate any more. I write less. Maybe poetry has withdrawn out of boredom and left me. Poor angel, then you will never return! And yet I feel confusedly something agitating inside me; I am now in a transitional period and I am curious to see what will result from it, how I will come out of it. *I am moulting* (in the intellectual sense); will I be henceforth bald or

superb? I am in doubt. We shall see. My thoughts are confused, I can't do any work of imagination; everything I produce is dry, labored, forced, painfully extracted. [*Corr.* 1:41–42]

Meanwhile he attempted to find himself, both as artist and person, in a series of literary works which Sartre refers to as "internal and external totalizations." In these Flaubert alternated between subjective autobiographical writing (*Agonies, Memoirs of a Madman*) and objective philosophical pieces (*Journey through Hell* [later incorporated in *Death Agonies* in the form of a philosophical parable], *Song of Death*, and *Smahr*). The latter are all variations on the scornful laugh of the giant, adding a new theme, the impossibility of grasping truth. Satan displays the wickedness and the suffering of the world, the futility of human existence. In every instance he is triumphant save in *Smahr*, when he yields the field to Yuk, the god who personifies all that is grotesque, ridiculous, and disgusting.

Sartre claims that the alternation between the personal first-person narrator and the return to the point of view of the infinite represented Flaubert's vacillation between a sincere attempt to learn to know himself and a refusal of self-knowledge. The *Intimate Notebook* (1840–41) Sartre finds especially rich in examples of self-comprehension as contrasted with self-knowledge. It is a collection of reflections and illustrative anecdotes, not quite a diary, not quite a confessional. I think one is inevitably reminded of Montaigne but the differences are more profound than the superficial resemblances. Both authors express their personal likes and dislikes, their amazed fascination at the complex of traits that makes them what they are. But where Montaigne is delighted with the unpredictability and diversity of the "incomparable monster" he has come to know and understand, Flaubert is frustrated and bewildered. He discovers in himself a jealousy of the rich and the great and he records—but not in the same passage—that he takes delight in tracking down examples of their looseness and pettiness. Sartre comments particularly on a significant reference to an encounter with a man (unnamed but evidently Flaubert's brother-in-law Hamard) who displayed great depths of grief over the loss of someone close to him. "That man humiliated me. It was because he was filled with feeling and I was empty of it. . . . He is pathetically stupid, but I recall how I hated myself and found myself despicable at that moment."[4] Sartre feels that this episode represents one of those instants at which Flaubert experienced a self-revelation which went beyond the particular occasion, one which illuminated his own inner dryness and incapacity to feel for others. "He took it for the expression of his intimate reality, of his concrete relations with the various members of his family" (2:1550). Yet this passage illustrates also Sartre's other point—that Flaubert refused to allow these "self-comprehensions" to become "self-knowledge" and that the technique he employed was to transform immediately any self-perception into a generalization about the human character. In the present instance, for example, he disarms the personal insight by introducing it with a general question, "Why is it that when we do not hold the same feelings as the people we are with, we feel ourselves awkward and embarrassed?" In the same way, he confesses to secret sadistic and immoral desires but concludes immediately that this is the case with everyone and makes no attempt to examine the content of his own particular impulses. Finally, Sartre claims, Flaubert translates his refusal to know himself into the conclusion that it is impossible to know oneself. The conclusion of *Smahr*, that truth is unattainable for man, that the grotesque kills truth, is a univeralization of the same conclusion. Sartre believes that these metaphysical parables represent Flaubert's refuge in the overview (*le survol*), the universal despair that seemed to raise him above his own particular unhappiness. It was also, Sartre maintains, a recourse of pride when Gustave wanted to reject the masochistic unheroic self he saw in the autobiographic writing.

Even in the latter Sartre finds Flaubert hovering between an "I" which is personal and an "I" which is purely abstract. This is particularly true in *Memoirs of a Madman* (1838). There Flaubert recounts the story of his boyhood encounter with Elisa Schlésinger, his first experience of romantic love and jealousy, but the narrative is set in the context of melancholic reflections on life and a despair which curiously seem to precede the experience said to have caused them. Sartre points out that the story presents the experiences of a very young man from the point of view of a white-haired old one looking back over years long gone. Here a bit more is involved than the usual effort to be detached. Flaubert, Sartre says, tries to see his life solely in terms of a past and an unreal distant future in order to avoid having to confront the real and imminent future which filled him with fear.

It is time to consider now the growing pressure of that future. Sartre states that about two years before Flaubert was to receive the baccalaureate he simultaneously felt that he had lost his imagination, did in fact lose his illusion of belonging to the nobility, and discovered his "bourgeois-being." In the role of the Garçon he had denounced the bourgeois and thereby convinced himself that he was detached from his class. What brought his bourgeois-being home to him now was the realization that he was expected to choose a profession. A bourgeois son is defined by the particular careers open to him and the necessity to commit himself to one of them. Sartre points out that the option to rebel against one's intellectual parents by becoming a carpenter is open to twentieth-century adolescents but was unthinkable for bourgeois sons in the middle 1800s. If Flaubert's rebellious reveries led him to declass himself, he dreamed of such bizarre things as becoming a beggar in Italy or a ferryman on the Ganges. Not being born, like Alfred, in the family of a wealthy industrialist, he had no alternative but to train for one of the respectable professions. His father, as he gradually gave up any hope that Gustave's health or scholastic record would allow him to follow in his brother's footsteps, found that the most obvious second choice was law. While there is no evidence that Gustave would have preferred any other profession, he never looked on the law as offering to him anything but the dreariest of futures. The imaginative boy who could picture himself winning laurels as an actor or musician never dreamed of winning fame as a great lawyer or politician. Instead he saw himself condemned to being a notary in a small provincial town. It was a death-in-life. Worst of all it was—according to Sartre—the final and most terrible manifestation of the paternal curse. He was to be openly consigned to an inferior position, classified once and for all as a mediocrity in a situation where dull respectability would deny even the suggestion of an ennobling defeat. He could not accept it; with his habitual passivity he could not openly revolt against it. His inner doubts as to his own talent—Flaubert never laid claim to genius—reinforced his sense of helplessness. It is probable that no protest was uttered to his parents. To his friends he first wrote that he would refuse to study law, then declared that he would study but never practice it. In a spirit of bravado he expressed the wish that he might some day use his skill, as the Garçon had done, for the sole purpose of defending the flagrantly guilty. In November 1841 he enrolled at Paris for the course in law. At the same time he initiated a strategy based on the pattern of his childhood response to the father's unjust malediction: by obedience he would bring himself to the death that the curse implied. His passive activity took the form of an inner resistance which led to the crisis at Pont-l'Evêque, which Flaubert always regarded as the death of the person he had been.

The established facts are simple. Flaubert failed his first examinations when he presented himself in August 1842. He passed them in December. He failed the second set in August of the following year and again in December. If the nervous crisis had not occurred, he would have had to try again. Sartre tells us that we should look upon this series of failures as something abnormal, something which needs an explanation. Gustave's friend, Ernest Chevalier, completed the course without a single setback and was immediately launched on a brilliant career. One might argue that he *wanted* to succeed and made every possible effort. True, but the nonchalant Alfred Le Poittevin, that serious practitioner of *carpe diem*, secured his diploma with equal ease. What then was wrong with Gustave?

Flaubert's critics have recognized that the failure at law was inevitable. His heart was not in it. He was "temperamentally unsuited." The wonder is that he stuck it out for so long. Until Sartre nobody had commented more than superficially on the quality and inner structure of those years. Sartre views this period as one of genuine conflict and anguish. The will to fail was present from the start and finally prevailed, but this does not mean that Flaubert simply and consistently "wanted" to fail. The question of whether he would finally pursue a career in law and the problem of passing his examinations were not the same even though the one obviously required the other. Sartre argues persuasively that Flaubert was torn between two basic attitudes, two "axioms" (2:1709). On one level he accepted the family's belief that "he who can do the most can do the least." The future artist should certainly be able to master the mundane matter of the Code. If Gustave's less gifted friend Ernest had succeeded by sweating it out, he himself should surely be able to loaf for some months and then pass with flying colors. At the same time, more deeply and more profoundly, he believed that the greatest *cannot* do the least. The eagle does not win in the footrace. Failure may be a sign of election. From this point of view successful completion of the law course would remove all excuse for his not becoming a provincial notary and would seem to demonstrate that this humble position was what his nature destined for him. The only solution was to show himself incapable of achieving the task assigned. The second attitude might easily become simple rationalization, and indeed Flaubert at times used it as a balm for his wounded pride, particularly in his rather breezy letters to Ernest after the first failure. His "stupidity before the law" he projected into the law itself. He could not learn it because there was nothing there to learn. It was the stupidity of the Code itself that was slowly "cretinizing" him.

All the same he believed in both of these contradictory "axioms," and each one was there to undermine the other. Where no resolution is possible, any attempted compromise is a failure. Sartre claims that in vacillating between them, Flaubert mostly allowed the second to dominate during the early months when the examinations were still remote. As they came closer, he realized that his father would never accept the excuse of failure due to superiority, and his anguish became more acute. But both attitudes were constantly present even when one was subordinate; each distilled its venom into the other whether Flaubert was making an honest attempt to study or proudly disdaining to get down to work until the last moment.

How seriously did he work at preparing himself? After enrolling in November, he declared that he would not open his books until April or May and would then make a gargantuan effort, studying fifteen hours a day. Actually he set to work about two months before that. Sartre suggests that this may have been because of discouragement with *November*, which he began that winter and then laid aside unfinished. The idea of fifteen hours of study daily was quickly abandoned. Flaubert professed to be seeking consolation in dissipation. There were some episodes with prostitutes. He drank a bit more than was good for him, but Sartre believes that his claims of excessive debauchery were exaggerated. I am inclined to agree, especially for the first year, during most of which Flaubert lived not at Paris but with his family. In truth Flaubert himself recognized that *carpe diem* was for him no solution. Sartre quotes a passage from *Intimate Notebook* saying the secret of being happy is to know how to enjoy life's pleasures. "In order to be happy, you must be so already" (quoted, 2:1535).

But if Gustave spent an adequate amount of time on his books and if he really tried, why did he fail? Sartre has offered a partial explanation in indicating Flaubert's ambivalent attitude toward success and failure. The strategy of first disdaining study and then frantically trying to make up for lost time may have satisfied his contradictory needs, but it was hardly designed to insure success. Still, it *might* have worked. Sartre believes that the quantity of work Flaubert put in was adequate but that its quality was deficient. What was required was primarily memorization, and we know that Flaubert had an unusually fine memory. Why did the will to fail ultimately prevail over the pride that would have carried him through?

Sartre is concerned to show that "the passive agent, though

alienated, remains free" (2:1689). Facing the Code, Flaubert experiences the same sort of helplessness that he once felt before the alphabet. He understands nothing and can retain nothing of what he reads. He who had boasted of working fifteen hours at a stretch cannot concentrate for a single hour. His passivity had made open revolt inconceivable; when he tries to obey his father he finds that he cannot. He would like to succeed and then say no, but the Code resists him like a physical force. Until now obedience may have been disagreeable, but it was always possible. What has changed?

What has happened, Sartre says, is that Flaubert, at the moment he begins to study, is called upon to be an agent. Up until now others (in this case his father) seemed to control his destiny. At present he himself must make the effort necessary to realize it. Although he may seek to console himself by imagining a future declaration of disobedience, nothing in his past or present gives him realistic hope that he will find the strength to carry it out. There is much to be gained by failing. In any case he must act; he does act, but the only form of action he finds open to him is passive activity.

> This type of activity is . . . the opposite of methodical praxis. The latter holds its ends at a distance, defines them and thereby determines a field of possibilities among which to *choose* the most economical means. There is a double decision since the objective is *posited* and one chooses the instruments which will allow it to be attained. Passive activity attains its ends only so that they may be kept hidden from the agent; that is, so as to have lived them obscurely as the internal structures of passivity. [2:1688–89]

The passive agent is convinced that he is borne along by events outside and not by his own autonomous will. This does not mean that he does not act. As with any agent he must internalize his situation and respond to it. If he "coasts with the current," it is he who allows himself to do so and thus secretly directs his course, but he will persuade himself that he is submitting to the inevitable. If he wants to alter the direction, "his way of acting is to trick himself so as to influence the course of things by means of the Other's will." In either case he will hold himself not responsible, by virtue of a certain "premeditated innocence." Sartre describes the internal process as follows:

> His spontaneity unifies the succession of experiences by giving them the quality of imposed realities. And of course these passive syntheses are penetrated with intentions which come from Gus-

tave himself, but these intentions can modify the course of the lived only on condition of not being *recognized* [*se reconnaître*]; that is, of disguising their real end and their significance. [2:1688]

Is this an appeal to the unconscious? Sartre does not think so. It may contain an element of bad faith. Sartre believes that Flaubert realized, without admitting it openly to himself, that his real fault lay in having carried his passivity too far. To this extent we may say that he lied to himself in order to avoid the responsibility of seeming to make a choice. But passive activity is not the same as unconscious motivation. Flaubert had never developed a sufficiently clear concept of self to provide himself with the necessary instruments for suddenly putting himself on the level of lucid praxis. We may recall his statement to Ernest, that he felt some sort of agitation surging up obscurely within him. Even with respect to his own inner reactions, he shows himself curiously passive. In a situation where another adolescent might experience the torment of indecision and uncertainty, Gustave waits to see what will happen. Some psychologists might view his difficulties with the study of law as the result of the conflict between the conscious will to succeed and the unconscious wish to fail. Sartre points out that the notion of a conscious will posed a particular problem for Flaubert. He was not accustomed to recognize in himself any personal will. Furthermore the situation was complicated by the fact that his formulated decision—that he would provisionally obey his father—was to will submission to a heteronomous will. Therefore to will was to will the will of another and not his own will. The recourse of the passive agent is to posit ends as imaginary possibilities which the force of events might bring to pass. It was accompanied in Flaubert by a kind of ethics of passivity. He associated energetic, deliberate action with superficiality, contrasting it with authentic passion. And in his own case passion was indeed associated with his deeper inclinations rather than action.

Meanwhile he has to do something despite himself. Once he has opened his books, he is "in the works." Suddenly obedience is transformed into praxis, innocence into culpability, heteronomy into autonomy (2:1699). If he continues to obey, he is inescapably making himself a bourgeois. He knows this, but he cannot see any way out except to endure. Therefore he acts, he studies, but his secret resolve transforms each of his acts into a mere gesture. "He *will play the role of the student*." He will sit for long hours at his desk in order to persuade, not others, but himself that he is truly working. Sartre compares him to Pascal falling on his knees in the hope that he may believe (2:1702). Indeed, Flaubert was sincere insofar as he hoped that somehow this ritualistic act would magically accomplish the task for him, but he withheld all of the inner assistance that would have made it possible. He read the Code, Sartre suggests, in the way that one proofreads; that is, he read it passively, paying attention to the literal details but without any attempt to synthesize the material into a meaningful structure. As a result he found it mere gibberish. Perhaps someone else might have found it interesting from the point of view of its historical development, but he himself refused to take that approach. His cynicism might have found satisfaction in detecting inconsistencies and injustice in the law. But, as Sartre points out, the Code reflected the interests of property owners; Flaubert's dislike of the bourgeoisie did not extend to the institution of private property. He was never a social reformer. In any case the self-imposed hardship of subjecting himself to a painful boredom which he did nothing to relieve reflects a pattern of conduct entirely consistent with what Sartre has shown us of Flaubert. His passivity exacted obedience, but this did not preclude resentment. He would do as he was told, but he would persist in regarding the assignment as an unjust sentence. The more he suffered, the more certainly he seemed to himself an innocent victim. If his efforts were clearly futile, if even the most assiduous devotion to his books proved to be of no avail, then nobody could blame him. His wretchedness attested to the sincerity of his attempt. Of course he blamed the law and not the frame of mind with which he approached it. In the same way he declared that the boring stupidity of the lectures he attended so enraged him that he could not listen to them. Sartre suggests that he put himself in a state of fury *in order that* he might not find himself interested in or at least understand what he heard (2:1705). Similarly, his heavy drinking may have been not only an escape but a means of making failure more probable. To sum up, Flaubert's behavior at this point was obviously not a deliberate deception. It was not entirely the manifestation of a hidden will to fail. It was a painful compromise between conflicting fears where success and failure were both intolerable.

> The positive motivations lead him to play a role, hoping that he will be caught up in the game; the negative motivations have the effect of making these attempts perfectly futile. [2:1705]

Sartre feels that the compromise Flaubert worked out might be called a project of "limited failure." Meanwhile, subterraneously, this growing awareness of failure as a real possibility and of the positive gains it would bring (despite the shame and humiliation) was evoking a more serious temptation—the thought that he might be engulfed in a much more radical failure. Outlined dimly on the horizon was thought that his destiny might include more than failed examinations, perhaps even the judgment that he was incapable of leading a normal life (2:1710). This masked future Flaubert could not yet face or even acknowledge as possible. But Sartre believes that we can find it in *November*, which, ironically, postponed the fatality and gave to Flaubert the self-confidence and psychic energy that enabled him to pass the examinations on his second attempt in December.

Flaubert wrote in a letter to Louise,

> If you have paid close attention to *November*, you should have detected a host of *inarticulable* [*indisable*] things which perhaps explain what I am. But that period is past, this work was the end of my youth. What remains from it is very little but stands firmly fixed. [*Corr.* 1:410]

This novel was the only one of the early works which the adult Flaubert was willing for his friends to read. His contemporaries and later critics have mostly agreed that it displays in embryo many of the characteristics that distinguish his later fiction. Some would unabashedly rank it with the novels of his maturity. It reads curiously like the work of a young romantic who is at the verge of renouncing romanticism. Its debt to a variety of romantic authors is obvious in imagery and in overall style as well as in content. Yet though it is derivative in detail, the final product is an original work of art, one which is autobiographical even when the author tries to be the most objective. The book is divided into three parts. The first is written in the form of an introspective, plotless journal, lyrical, melancholy, reflective, a bit morbid—the portrayal of an adolescent with vague aspirations for fame, fortune, and adventure, inclined to seek mystic fulfillment in nature, indulging in a virgin's voluptuous dreams of sexuality. The second part relates the hero's first sexual experience—with a prostitute. It includes a long first-person narrative by her. In many ways she anticipates Emma Bovary. The episode has been generally recognized as based on Flaubert's meeting with Eulalie Foucaud, his own first significant erotic experience; Bruneau suggests that it may reflect also Flaubert's encounters with prostitutes in Paris.[5] At the same time Marie, like Emma, represents Flaubert himself in the passionate pursuit of an unattainable kind of love, a thirst for the infinite. The hero, who shares in the futile quest, shows us the cynical side of Flaubert as well in his acknowledgment of his disappointment: "So Love was no more than that! So Woman was no more than that!" The third part breaks abruptly in two. It begins with a return to the style of the opening section. Now the hero tells of his continued unhappiness and disillusion, his sense of premature age, the bitter sweetness of his impossible dreams. After an abrupt stop, a third-person narrator takes over. He is a friend of the hero, now dead, and holds in his hands the manuscript we have just read. He tells us of the hero's last days, his retreat from life, his near suicide, his final death without any organic cause but "by the force of thought alone."

It may be interesting to compare Sartre's discussion of *November* with the critical comment of Jean Bruneau, who has written the fullest and most thoughtful treatment of the novel that I have found. Sartre, who has read Bruneau and quotes from him, would not question any of his views on the book's literary ancestry, its anticipation of later Flaubert novels, or its artistic merit. I think that Sartre, though he does not explicitly say so, would agree with Bruneau's statement that "*November* recounts the failure of sensuality as, two years earlier, *Memoirs of a Madman* had recounted the failure of love" (p. 319). Both men accept almost the same time-frame for the writing of the book: Flaubert began it in the winter of 1840–41, put it aside and returned to it at intervals, and finished it in October 1842. Significantly, Bruneau, while acknowledging that there is no absolute proof, suggests that Flaubert may have written the beginning of the third part (i.e., first-person narrative) in the early part of 1842 and the concluding third-person account in the summer and autumn. Sartre states confidently that Flaubert did not touch the work between late February and the examinations in August and that it was after his failure that he wrote the conclusion. Bruneau and Sartre are alike in feeling that the sudden appearance of the second narrator is of primary importance and signifies an abrupt change in point of view on the part of the author as well as in the structure of the work itself. Both would relate this change to developments in Flaubert's personal life. But here there is divergence.

Bruneau expresses uncertainty as to whether or not this change from the hero to his friend was in Flaubert's mind from the beginning. He regards it as a common romantic device which the author used for purely aesthetic reasons. Like Marie's long narrative, it allows a more impersonal psychological portrayal to accompany the autobiographical. Bruneau writes,

> The hero is seen first by himself, then analyzed and judged by one of his friends. Here again we can see how Flaubert got out of pure subjectivity. [p. 329]

Bruneau makes two observations on the death of the hero who never completed his manuscript. On the last page of the novel Flaubert wrote,

> Finally last December he died, but slowly, little by little, by the force of thought alone without any organ having been diseased, as one dies from sorrow, which would appear difficult to people who have suffered greatly but which we must put up with in a novel for love of the marvelous.[6]

This sentence, to Bruneau, reveals Flaubert's sure sense of himself as a writer, aware that he is "leaving reality for ideal or literary truth." A similar sense of "aesthetic necessity" led Flaubert to provide a psychological explanation for the transition from first to third person. Flaubert wrote,

> It must be that feelings have too few words at their service; otherwise the book would have been finished in the first person. No doubt our man found nothing more to say. He found himself at a point where one doesn't write anymore and where one carries on in thought. So much the worse for the reader! [p. 456]

Again Bruneau stresses that the reason is aesthetic. After the hero's marvelous and pathetic dreams of escape, the author deems it best to leave him there at the height of his poetic flight. Yet there is a need of a change of tone if the narrative is to be brought to a satisfactory conclusion. Suicide would have been "too positive, too violent an act for his hero" (p. 328). The second narrator provides the more objective tone and can serve as a witness to report the "death by thought."

Bruneau's second observation ties in the hero's demise and the shift in narrative with Flaubert's personal development. He makes three points. First, just as the hero of *November* denounces some of the writers he used to love and finds that even the best of them no longer give him pleasure, so Flaubert "bade farewell to the historical, philosophical, and autobiographical romanticism of his youth" (p. 341). Second, although the third part of *November* (surely Bruneau means to refer to the *second half* of the third part) seems to be written by a new pen, Flaubert does not yet see his way clear to a new path in literature; the death of the old is not yet accompanied by an artistic rebirth. "The hero of *November* has not been able to find his way in the domain of the art. He dies from the author's indecision" (p. 340). Finally, Bruneau, in positive terms, portrays Flaubert as sensing that he is in between two stages. After his experience with Eulalie Foucaud, new acquaintances at Trouville, and a year in Paris, he has discovered the world and the "other." "On the threshold of this new existence, which he so far has only glimpsed, he questions, he hesitates, he is silent" (p. 341).

I do not think that Sartre would take exception to Bruneau's critical judgment of the aesthetic qualities of *November*. Bruneau's idea that the hero's death signifies the end of Flaubert's romantic phase corresponds to Sartre's belief that Flaubert was already moving from the poet who dreamed of another world to the artist who created one. But to Sartre *November* reflects far more than an artistic crisis; it is Flaubert the person who symbolically dies and is judged. The concluding narrative is not only in a style as if from another pen. It is written by another man—or so Flaubert wanted to believe.

In two ways Sartre links *November* with the crisis on the road near Pont-l'Evêque: the novel anticipated the experience as if Flaubert lived it proleptically. And by writing of it, Flaubert succeeded in postponing the crisis for a little over two years. Sartre is convinced that the introduction of the second narrator was not in the original plan. He argues that the opening of the novel and the meeting with Marie suggest a plan similar to that of the *Memoirs of a Madman*. There is nothing to suggest that Flaubert felt the need of an outside observer. Even if we were to assume that he did, Sarte claims, he has not been true to the models which are said to have influenced him. In those the frame was firmly established by introducing the witness at the beginning as well as at the end. The objective narrator may explain how he happened to have the manuscript, or he may sketch his impressions of the hero who has written what is to follow. There is almost always something which will serve to introduce and, so to speak, protect the extreme subjectivity of the first-person account. We find nothing in the beginning of *November* to suggest that the second narrator will appear. The confessional outpourings are not even put in the form of a diary or "letter to the world." In the first part the hero states that he was "born with the desire to death," and he describes the temptation that comes to him one day to throw himself down from the attic window. But his manuscript does not end with a resolution to kill himself. A long period of later life is described by the second narrator, one which includes but extends beyond a second suicide attempt. In *November,* unlike the models, the external witness is not there simply to describe the death that could not be self-described. He judges but he is not really detached. I think Sartre is right here. Usually this kind of objective narrator is careful to describe exactly how he came to know of the hero's life and inner feelings. Flaubert's narrator is more like an omniscient author. He describes, as if from within, the hero's abortive attempt to kill himself. He passes judgment as if he were in the secret recesses of the hero's self. He is, Sartre says, a double of Gustave. But of which Gustave, since the hero himself is a self-portrait? The second narrator is the disgraced student who went to join his family at Trouville after failing the examination. He is presented to us as superior to the first narrator, and yet there are indications that despite the dead hero's shortcomings—or because of them—both the second narrator and the author himself find the dead man better than all the rest. The concluding narrator's dryness of tone, the absence in him of all emotion and imagination, these lead the reader to wonder on what basis this physician-detective may claim to be superior to the man he is dissecting. In this first effort by Flaubert to "translate thought by form," he has left us with all those inarticulable ambivalences that words by themselves cannot convey (2:1718).

Sartre takes almost literally the explanation that the hero-Flaubert stopped because he had nothing more to say. But where Bruneau feels that this represents the impasse of the romantic writer, Sartre views it as the failure of Flaubert's effort to understand himself. The young writer wanted to discover and to reveal himself, but he found he could only recount his dreams. Since he had chosen the imaginary, his was only "a fictive ego." Even in the first two parts of the novel when Flaubert reveals his personal tastes and reveries, he seeks to universalize. (This is a point which Bruneau also makes, but he interprets it so as to show that the portrait is simultaneously of an individual and of a generation stamped with romanticism.) Sartre claims that here as always Flaubert universalized just when the attempts at self-knowledge became too painful. In Sartre's view Flaubert stopped writing the novel in February partly because he was uncomfortable with the figure he saw portrayed there and partly because he was incapable of advancing any further in the effort to reveal a self he could not grasp. Later he picked it up again, resolving to finish it, at exactly the moment when he realized "he *could no longer* speak of himself in the first person" (2:1717). This was not because he recognized at the start that he had changed and wrote to record the fact. It is more probable that it was the process of writing which made it possible for him to achieve another view of himself.[7]

Sartre believes that Gustave's realization that he had failed, plus his awareness of the conflicting feelings he had about success and failure, precipitated in him an almost intolerable depression and that the near suicide at the end of the novel reflects a real experience. Flaubert had always felt that the worst was sure. Now the real "worst" had happened. He had always imagined death. Once he had confronted suicide as a real possibility and rejected it, a self-confrontation was unavoidable. Gustave asked himself two questions:

> What am I to do, what is to become of me, if I can no longer either live or die? And *why* did I *wish* to kill myself? The two questions receive a single reply. First I must know myself. I have both the need and the means since *I do not recognize myself*. At this moment of life when I appear to myself as *another,* I must observe myself and judge myself as *another.* [2:1723]

The second narrator, Sartre says, resembles a doctor or a detective seeking to track down and judge the person who wrote the earlier pages. He is not detached; he is a bit sinister, he is anguished. But he is also healthy, not neurotic, and he is resolute. He is, Sartre suggests, Flaubert passing judgment on Gustave. The young author of the conclusion of *November* is determined both to finish the novel and to pass his law examination the next time round in December. Accomplishing the first enabled him to achieve the second.

Sartre claims that Flaubert first introduced impersonalism in his writing in the effort to know himself as he appeared to others. He halted the process of derealization, put the imaginary itself into question, and sought to find "behind the eagle's flight, the little true fact." For the first time, instead of trying to find in himself universal man, he looked on himself as a particular anomaly altogether different from all others. His judgment was severe. Self-knowledge began with self-dislike. Gustave was a lazy, idle dreamer without any goal. He was prone to false emotion. He was perhaps too much the poet to succeed in literature. What he wrote was exaggeration and amphigory. Under inspection "the Flaubert son, the imaginary child with infinite aspirations, is *in reality* a wash-out [*un raté*]" (2:1724). Self-denunciation as radical as this can easily lead to suicide, and Flaubert apparently came close to it. Fortunately, the detachment that makes it possible to denounce what one has been is at the same time a transcendence. In the process of writing the last past of *November*, Flaubert found that he was recording *now* what he *was then*. By so doing he turned a real failure into an artistic triumph.

Sartre says that by writing *November* Flaubert staved off his nervous crisis for two years. At the same time Sartre claims that the narrative prefigures the events of late January 1844. He reconciles these seemingly inconsistent statements by a thorough inquiry into the meaning behind the hero's "death by thought." This leads to an interesting, original, and important discussion of auto-suggestion (*pithiatisme*) and "somatization" (the psychosomatic). If we accept the view that the second narrator is Flaubert himself in a new aspect, then it is obvious that he stands in the same relation to the first narrator that the retired invalid in the early months of 1844 held with regard to the student he had been. Flaubert often referred to the crisis as a kind of death. It was as though his life had been cut in two. He thought of his second self as prematurely aged, as a man whose passional nature was dead. He was like a survivor of a disaster, a man to whom the worst had already happened and who could not be expected to live like normal people. This kind of dissociation is frequent in neurotics. Sartre tells us that an imaginary anticipation of a mental crisis is not rare either. This is correct—although with most persons it is more likely to be foreshadowed in dreams. Sartre offers a bold hypothesis: The "death by thought" prefigures the onset of mental illness and represents Flaubert's fear of what his own body might do to him; what he secretly feared was imbecility.

To support his claim, Sartre refers us to the second narrator's description of the hero's behavior in the months preceding his death (2:1731 ff.). "Worn out by boredom, a terrible habit, and finding even a certain pleasure in the brutishness [*abrutissement*] which is its consequence, he was like people who watch themselves die."[8] He no longer washed or shaved or combed his hair and rarely changed his clothes. Inside the house he gave himself no fresh air. He disregarded the most elementary rules for protecting his health. In all of this, which Sartre believes is a reflection of Gustave's own conduct during his depressed period, there was an imitation of the apathy of a person who is about to die; that is of one who cuts himself off from the future. It is a device to escape from a particular future which is feared or hated, but it holds within it the will to embrace a radical final escape; it is not merely a present distraction. For those who are actually dying, the body "prophesies" that there will be no future. Sartre argues that Gustave intermittently believed that his own body had displayed signs indicating that horrors he had imagined might be realized for him in an actual, intolerable destiny. What he feared was not death but some form of mental deterioration and degradation. Sartre points to three things as possible evidence. The first, I think, we must regard as hypothesis only. Sartre connects the present extreme apathy with Gustave's childhood stupors (*hébétudes*). They, too, had rendered him inactive, immobile, and seemed to remove him from ordinary life. To the objection that if the *hébétudes* are indeed comparable, they are nothing new, Sartre responds, "Precisely. It is their meaning which has changed. At first they were evasions; later he saw in them proof of his genius. Now they are premonitions; they signify to him his future dementia" (2:1733). One may hesitate to accept this point as evidence. There is no proof that Flaubert himself felt that there was any connection between his present wretched apathy and the childhood trances. On the other hand, I am inclined to think that his recollections of his early stupors might indeed be a source of uneasiness to him. He must have known that the adults of the family looked with disapproval on these trancelike retreats which on at least one occasion so absorbed him that he actually fell off his chair. They were taken as not quite "normal." And, as Sartre asks in the present occasion, what—to Gustave's own mind—precipitated them? They did not appear to come as the result of an act of will. Nobody sent them to him. The body seemed to produce them. At present, too, the body seemed to contribute to his unhappy state. Insomnia and nightmares alternately disturbed his nights. He arose in the morning more fatigued than when he went to bed. His organism prolonged his apathy. Sartre reminds us that in nervous troubles there is always a reciprocal reaction. "The peculiar property of nerves is that their pains move in two directions. One submits to them, and one makes them. These organs often impose on us only what we have first imposed on them" (2:1733). Sartre suggests that Gustave feared lest the brutish apathy might be imposed upon him as a definitive state.

Sartre's second point seems to me stronger. Flaubert confessed in a letter to Louise that one time when he was standing before a shop in Paris, the idea of castrating himself got hold of him "with an imperious intensity, at a time when I remained for two whole years without seeing a woman" (*Corr.* 3:76–77). Flaubert does not say whether the sexual abstinence preceded or followed the castration temptation, but he dates the experience in the year 1841, which would put it just before the writing of *November*. Flaubert spoke on other occasions of his voluntary sexual abstinence at that period. Sartre feels that he protested a bit too loudly and that he was covering up a temporary impotence or sexual anorexia. If this is true, and I see no reason to doubt it, Flaubert might well have been frightened to see the body seem to respond by fulfilling his involuntary desire. Strangely, Sartre overlooked an earlier sentence in the same letter, one which seems to me to give considerable support to his theory. Flaubert refers to Balzac's *Louis Lambert*, which he had just finished.

> It hit me like a bolt of lightning. It is the story of a man who goes mad by dint of thinking of intangible things. That fastened on to me with a thousand hooks.

Louis Lambert did indeed castrate himself at the end of the book, and this would be enough to remind Flaubert of his own strong impulse. But obviously he was even more affected by the hero's being driven mad as the result of his own thoughts. This brings us to Sartre's third and, to my mind, most convincing piece of evidence.

In his *Correspondence* Flaubert refers to his having delighted, during his late student years, in doing imitations of odd characters. His favorite act was the impersonation of an epileptic. Sartre quotes the important passage.

> My father finally forbade me to imitate certain people (he was persuaded that I must suffer considerably in it, which was true although I denied it), among others an epileptic beggar whom I met one day on the beach. He had told me his story; he had first been a journalist, etc. It was superb. It is certain that when I rendered this comic fellow, I was in his skin. You couldn't have seen anything more hideous than me at that moment. Can you understand the satisfaction I got out of it? I'm sure you can't. [*Corr.* 1:362]

In this letter lies the clue to Flaubert's discovery of his autosuggestibility and his fear of what his body might do. Whether or not the unfortunate man had really at one time been a journalist, he represented for Flaubert a person who had fallen from above to the level of subman. But why did Gustave feel such strong pleasure in portraying him? Flaubert does not explain, and perhaps he did not know. He may have felt uneasy about it. We recall that the hero of *November* confessed to a certain enjoyment of his abject state—or more accurately, the judgmental second narrator ascribed this pleasure to him. Flaubert's delight in imitating the epileptic was linked with his sense of becoming like him, of being "inside his skin." Sartre says that in the act Flaubert "played himself as an epileptic," and I think this is a fair way to express it. What then was the attraction? In part, Sartre says, it was because it satisfied both his masochism and his sadism, as though he simultaneously embraced his humiliation and said to his parents, "See what you have made of me." More important, as he remembered the act later, it symbolized one way of escape from his present impasse, a solution which both tempted and terrified him. To feel himself "inside the skin" of the epileptic was to evade all demands by showing himself incapable of responding to them. In the unfortunate man, Flaubert grasped his own dilemma.

> In order not to go into law, he would have to succumb to some sort of mental affliction but, by the same stroke, he would lose the recourse of looking down on his good friends, and he would have to submit in impotent rage to the weight of their just pity. [2:1734]

Sartre suggests that Gustave may have felt it increasingly difficult to pull himself out of the role he was playing. This we do not know. What is certain is that both he and his father were afraid that the act was injurious to Gustave. Implied is the fear that so empathetic an imitation of madness might result in some kind of loss of mental balance. In support of Sartre, I find it significant that the passage regarding his imitation follows Flaubert's confession that he had written a letter to Eulalie Foucaud which expressed a tenderness which he felt only while he was writing.

> When I was writing to her, with that faculty I have for being moved by my pen, I took my subject seriously, but *only while I was writing*. Many things which leave me cold either when I see them or when others speak of them fill me with enthusiasm, excite me, hurt me if I myself speak of them and especially if I write of them. There you have one of the effects of my nature as a clown.

In short, as Sartre says, Flaubert had discovered his own auto-suggestibility (2:1736).

One may object that autosuggestion is not the same as somatization. This is true, but the two are closely related. The tie is particularly strong in a personality characterized by passivity. Sartre writes,

> Passive activity, constituted by my first relations with the Other, is always supported by the organism's *active passivity*. It is at the point where the two meet that the phenomena of autosuggestion arise. [2:1742]

The body, while it cannot be said to carry on intentional activity for its own purpose, is not inert any more than the still burning cigarette tossed into a pile of dry leaves by a careless smoker.

It is Sartre's contention that Gustave—as in the instance of the castration impulse and period of sexual abstinence—was aware of "the body's incredible docility" and was frightened by it. As Sartre reads the concluding paragraph of *November*, it reveals on the part of the author "an intuition which makes him uneasy" (2:1748). The disclaimer, that the marvelous must be tolerated in a novel, Sartre thinks is inappropriate for the end of a book which is a thinly disguised autobiography and psychologically realistic. The words, he claims, are insincere and perhaps written for self-reassurance. If Flaubert did not believe, he at least feared that one might in very truth "die of thought." Or that one might become mad if one imagined that one might and if one found pleasure in playing the role of the madman.

In discussing the experience that he supposes Flaubert to have had with the temptation to castrate himself and the temporary impotence that was its consequence, Sartre's analysis of the process includes these steps: a wish is acknowledged, but it is not a wholehearted desire. It is not what one fully wants; rather, it is posited as a possibility which exerts a certain attraction. "But the body does not know the possible." It is like a devoted but stupid servant who takes his master's impulsive request too literally and carries it out to his detriment. Sartre imagines Flaubert aghast at his body's compliance with the temptation he had decisively resisted. He wonders what he is to believe.

> Must we see in the body an obscure and confused thought which overreaches us and harms us because it takes our desires literally and, for lack of understanding them, caricatures them? Or, on the contrary, is it from the organic materiality that we learn our true wishes in their radical form? If the first hypothesis disquiets him, the second terrifies him. [2:1740]

As a passive agent, Flaubert always felt that he was coasting with the current, letting himself be borne along by external forces. Now there comes a new fear. From within himself there comes an enemy power. Thought is not the simple representation of possibilities. It puts into play certain corporal mediations which constitute an act with consequences. "He knows that the organism, taking charge of the negative idea, makes of it an inert material negation." Suddenly "the force of thought is not, cannot be the force of the thinker" (2:1749). The thinker cannot, by a willed fiat, bend the body to his deliberate will, but the body's active passivity can translate a suggestion into a reality without the knowledge of the suggestible person. In autosuggestion, Sartre says, "thought has two faces."

> It is lived consciously as passive activity because it is realized as active passivity in the very functions of life; and inversely, the conscious effort *to believe in it*—that is, to make of it a vital determination of the person—accelerates its organic realization. [2:1749]

Sartre adds that although he has said this happens to the person *à l'insu* (without his knowledge), "this is an *insu* which is not ignorant of itself, an intentional *insu* which is *played* as the necessary condition of the process." In short, we are not dealing with an unconscious but with the structure of autosuggestion and somatization in a passive agent. A thought, without ever being brought out and acted upon, becomes a law of the organic life.

In all of this Sartre assumes that Flaubert believed that his body behaved in this way and might determine for him a future which he looked upon with horror. If the only evidence were the hero's "death by thought" in *November*, it would be flimsy indeed. Sartre's other two points—Flaubert's recognition of his own autosuggestibility as he described it in the letter to Louise, and his experience apropos of the castration impulse—seem to me to add considerable weight to his argument. When later we examine Flaubert's own attitude toward his illness in 1844, I think we will find more evidence that his fear was inextricably linked with an intentional hidden strategy. He never believed that his illness was simply an accident which came from external causes, and he definitely viewed it as the consequence of the reciprocal influence of bodily and psychic processes.

Two points which Sartre does not stress seem to me important. First, Flaubert and his contemporaries were uncertain in their minds as to whether mental illness was physical in origin or the result of psychic experiences. They felt that even extreme emotions and temperament stemmed from the physical nature of the brain, and yet Dr. Flaubert worried lest his son's mimetic portrayal of epilepsy might damage him. This attitude might well result in Gustave's attempt to read in his body both the result of his thought and the prophecy of a later mental state. We should remember that in the mid-nineteenth century the real nature of epilepsy was not understood. It was looked upon as an affliction akin to insanity and mental retardation—at once a disaster and a disgrace. Second, I am surprised that Sartre has not made more of the significance of Flaubert's pleasure in imitating the epileptic and the fact that epilepsy appeared later to his physicians as a possible explanation of his illness but not as a cause they could fix on with certainty. We have noted Sartre's reminder that certain cases exhibiting epileptic symptoms have their origin in hysteria. This fact, together with Flaubert's earlier fascination with the epileptic whom he imitated, seems to me to lend support to the hypothesis that the nervous attack at Pont-l'Evêque was indeed hysteria and that the fall represented for Flaubert the same combination of escape and humiliation that had so strangely satisfied and frightened him when he played the role of epileptic years earlier.

The conviction that in *November* he had finally written something which could stand up to his matured critical sense increased Flaubert's overall self-confidence. Sartre declares that the completed book signified "the neurosis rejected." Gustave determined to resist the escape by means of failure and all that it might entail. He actually passed the examinations a few weeks later in December. Returning to Paris after the holiday visit with his parents, he enjoyed a brief period of calm and relative happiness. He called on friends whom he had met at Trouville the previous summer. He savored Parisian life and found it good—except that he cursed his poverty. He began work on the first *Sentimental Education,* which he laid aside in order to prepare for the next set of examinations. But of course nothing was solved. Paradoxically, the literary success that gave him self-assurance must have made the idea of a career in law still more repugnant, and he still felt himself incapable of an overt refusal. The psychosomatic ailments had reappeared even before the December examinations. When at about the first of June he began to prepare for the next set, the old story was repeated. He maintained himself in a state alternating between apathy and nightmare. After the first failure in August he made no attempt whatsoever. He did nothing. Even before he presented himself, again unsuccessfully, in December 1843, his letters were filled with hints that his heart and his rightful place were at home in Rouen. It was a tribunal but also a refuge (2:1765). The temptation of a more radical failure was becoming more insistent.

In concluding this part of his discussion, Sartre says, "We can divine Flaubert's intention when we reread *The Metamorphosis"*

(2:1753). Without quite claiming that Kafka's story was influenced by his knowledge of Flaubert, Sartre says that he has not made the comparison by chance. Kafka loved the French novelist and often quoted from him. Both men had disturbed relations with their fathers.

> In Kafka's novella remorse and resentment are inseparable. And finally, what does he describe? The *crisis*. That which he fears but of which he will never be the victim—immunized against it by the tuberculosis from which he died—that is exactly what Flaubert manages for himself.

Whether or not there really is so close a resemblance between two authors, I think Sartre's use of Kafka's symbol for Flaubert is illuminating and richly suggestive. Changed into a gigantic and horrid insect, Gregor henceforth escaped and gradually forgot his hated existence as a traveling salesman, but his shame and unhappiness remained.

> That horrible beast who dies of shame and who plunges his family into disgrace, guilty, punished, innocent victim of his family [*des siens*], that beast repulsive in every aspect—he is an excellent symbol of the dreadful unknown which he is preparing to become *by means of the crisis*. Something is going to happen to him, something terrible—death, old age, it doesn't matter what it is called. The essential thing is that he will be *other*. Other and degraded.... A being awaits him which he must become, who will not be he and who will say: myself.... With horror Gustave sees approaching the moment and the place of his metamorphosis into vermin. He is the more sure of his final tumble in that the fall has already begun.

In this vague premonition, "an unbearable truth" is clear. "The young man will not escape his family's demands without being made forever incapable of fulfilling them. In other words, the exit is not into Heaven but into Hell. He must plunge downward; he will plunge" (2:1753).

## THE CRISIS

Sartre's analytical description of Flaubert's attack near Pont-l'Evêque is to me the most fascinating section of *The Family Idiot*, the most imaginative and the most persuasive. It portrays a double reality—the objective event and the symbolic meaning of the experience as it was lived in depth by the sufferer. Some critics will inevitably ask whether this imaginary reconstruction of an interior experience is legitimate for a biography or should be restricted to fiction. This time I feel that the question is less appropriate than it might be, for example, with respect to the relations between the infant Gustave and his mother. Sartre is not imagining facts, not even by way of interpretive hypothesis, nor is his method here that of the novelist. In writing a novel, an author might attempt to convey the multilevel quality of the experience either by the use of juxtaposed images or by some form of stream of consciousness. Sartre does neither. Step by step he analyzes each factor, showing the significance he believes it held for Flaubert, frequently explaining the philosophical or psychological grounds for the interpretation. One is free to claim that Sartre's Flaubert is not the "real Flaubert" or that one prefers the "Flaubert" of other more traditional biographers. I think one cannot rightly argue that this presentation of the Pont-l'Evêque crisis is inappropriate to Sartre's Flaubert. I myself would go beyond that. I think that the interpretation provided here is so well supported by what Flaubert wrote in his letters that this part of the book is the most effective in making the reader feel that Sartre's Flaubert is close to that real man whom we can never know directly.

After the Christmas holidays in 1843 Flaubert returned to Paris. For a few days he simply vegetated. His despair seemed to paralyze him. Then he received a letter from his sister, asking him to call on Hamard. The latter's engagement to Caroline had not yet been announced, but it was understood by the family that the two would probably marry. Sartre finds in this visit to Hamard the precipitating cause of what followed (2:1779–82). Two factors were involved. First, Flaubert probably felt jealous. In any case, his own exclusive relation with Caroline was broken. In Sartre's terms, the only person who served as vassal to Gustave had betrayed him. He now came first to nobody and was disgraced in the eyes of his own seigneur-father. Second, this was the encounter of "a half-mad man with one already mad." We have noted Flaubert's earlier uneasiness before Hamard's great suffering at the death of his mother. Now the wretched man was experiencing uncontrollable grief over his dying brother. Flaubert professed "horror" at the sight of such pain. (Hamard later lost his reason completely after Caroline's death.) Sartre suggests that on the one hand Flaubert was again disturbed at this stupid fellow's ability to feel more deeply than he could. In addition, Sartre believes, the encounter with one who was totally unbalanced by his suffering, may have nudged Flaubert on to letting go of his own rational control. Both points seem to me relevant. Flaubert may well have felt that his own inner unhappiness was greater than Hamard's even though it was not grief in response to one of the recognized causes for mourning. Neurosis is often precipitated by the unstable witness of it in another. We may recall Shakespeare's subtle insight in allowing King Lear to let go the reins of rational control at the moment when he encounters the apparently total insanity of Edgar.[9] Sartre feels that it was at this point that Flaubert's choice was made. All that was needed was the appropriate setting and a "sign" from outside.

Flaubert himself arranged for the setting by asking for permission to come home for a few days to recover from the traumatic effects of the call on Hamard. Sartre refers to the journey from Paris to Rouen as a flight, which of course it was. Back with his law books Flaubert had realized once more the impossibility of either obedience or the refusal to obey.

> There is no solution. He knows it but he knows also that *there will be one*. His flight does not resolve anything. It is a magical conduct; one turns one's back on danger in order that it may be annihilated. [2:1812]

In this simple passage Sartre is invoking ideas from an early work of his own. What he says there is significantly relevant to his understanding of Flaubert's final resolution of his dilemma and may justify a short digression on our part.

In *The Emotions* (1939) Sartre argued that emotional behavior is purposeful. As contrasted with rational procedure, it is ineffective and may be said to resemble magical practice. By means of the body a person alters his relation to his situation when he cannot alter the objective situation itself. Sartre recalls now his earlier example: a person suddenly confronting a wild animal in his path may faint. He cannot annihilate the beast, but by a modification of his body he removes himself. I am surprised that Sartre did not pick up another of his earlier examples, one which seems to me to shed even more illumination on Flaubert's flight and later fall. Sartre imagines himself, or someone else, engaged in an intellectual debate. Seeing himself about to be defeated, he gets angry, calls his opponent names, declares it impossible to carry on the discussion in these terms, etc. Obviously this conduct is ineffective in terms of the problem as originally presented. But it does indeed transform the situation from what it was (one in which victory was impossible and defeat unbearable) into one in which a different and inferior kind of solution is possible. At Paris Flaubert could see no acceptable way out. His emotional flight temporarily annihilates the conflict by postponing its resolution. By leaving he doesn't need to decide anything right now. But what is more important in this context is the event toward which he is running. The nervous crisis is emotional behavior, too, and it transforms Flaubert's situation in the same way as in Sartre's illustration. Instead of having to choose between obedience and refusal, neither of which any longer seems possible to him, he puts himself on a level where the command is no longer appropriate. In more than one sense he accomplishes this by annihilating himself. His attitude afterward seems to include the same kind of mingled relief and shame (but in more intense form) that the debater must have felt on his way home.

We may return now to Flaubert's trip from Paris to Rouen. No doubt he told himself that he was leaving for only "two or three days," but Sartre feels that he dimly saw some kind of disaster outlined on the horizon. "He is running toward *something*," and "this is the *lived meaning* of every turn of the wheel, every step of the horses" (2:1812). Sartre suggests that the trip itself may have intensified Gustave's sense of unreality. When one's surroundings are not inserted into any kind of meaningful praxis, when one's being is suspended, any object one sees appears as a meaningless, useless apparition. Eventually one of them may take on the nature of a sign from the outside as to what is going to happen to one. By their air of unreality, objects come to assume an imaginary significance. This is exactly what happened a day or so later when Gustave accompanied his brother Achille to inspect the estate at Deauville where the father was planning to establish a family residence. Sartre suggests that this spot may have symbolized for a moment the future that Gustave would like to have—a retreat to family property without the family tensions he had known at l'Hôtel Dieu. The drive back was another matter. Rouen was just one stage. Beyond that the road led to Paris. "The return to Rouen will be lived as a Calvary" (2:1821).

Gustave was driving. Ordinarily, perhaps, he liked to drive for sport as he loved to swim. This time, Sartre claims, he must have felt that he was guiding himself toward what he hated, what everything in him wanted to flee. As driver he was doing actively what all of his passive inclinations opposed. In this sense, says Sartre, "To drive the horse, to work at the Code is all one" (2:1823). He is obediently going to his own destruction. By driving, Sartre says, he took refuge in the role of active agent so that the concentration needed might distract him from attention to the signs of bodily resistance. Thus he could "run innocently toward death" (2:1826). The journey through the pitch-black night symbolizes his own "nocturnal life." He attempts to resist the night, to find a way through it. The external blackness seems a reflection of what is within.

> The obscurity announces the absurdity of every enterprise, the crushing of projects by the nonhuman order of causes and effects; it reflects to him the dumb desire of his constituted passivity, by revealing that *praxis* is on principle impossible, that there are only agitations and gestures. [2:1827–28]

At this moment "the meaning of the practical field is abolition." Passively, Flaubert awaits a sign in order that something may happen to him. With fear or desire? Perhaps both.

But there must be a witness. Achille was there. Sartre thinks that Achille was perhaps the most essential factor and served as a catalyst. Of course the father is the true designated spectator, but his presence might have inhibited his son and prevented—or postponed—the dramatic denouement. For Gustave the doctor was still the dreaded being "whose surgical look pierces through the most secret lies or, rather, reduces the belief of autosuggestion to being nothing but a lie" (2:1829). Gustave did not fear Achille, though he may have despised and secretly hated him. Furthermore, as elder son and heir, Achille represented the paternal authority and would be the most trusted witness. To fall helpless at his brother's feet was the utmost humiliation. It was the strongest temptation to Gustave's masochism and the surest proof to himself that he could not have willed so abhorrent a solution. It represented in the most dramatic form that absolute Fall to subhumanity, that radical failure which alone could release him from his intolerable conflict.

> This is indeed the worst: to realize and proclaim his radical inferiority before the enemy brother to whom he believed himself so superior, to recognize that the father's choice was just, to confirm it by showing himself a subman and, finally, to put himself into the hands of Achille, to be dependent on his good will, on his medical knowledge, on his diagnostic and therapeutic abilities. . . . Here was the washout [*le raté*] believing he could compensate for his shortcomings by imagination. And behold, in him imagination confesses that it was only a symptom of failure; that is of his malady. As for Achille, he never imagined anything, in him inventive ability served only to diagnose. [2:1831]

In his distress Gustave seemed to be Garcia calling on François to save him.

Sartre claims that the practical field is a medium through which an active agent makes known to himself who he is; that is, I "carve out my being in the world" by my actions, by the things which I do to my surrounding environment. I "leave my mark." The passive agent, too, finds himself indicated by the structures in the practico-inert, but he does not recognize that these have been inscribed by himself. It is something out there which will announce to me through my body what I am about to become. In order to upset the present equilibrium and precipitate a decisive change, there must be something to serve as a *fiat*, like the match applied to the explosive.[10] That which pulled the trigger, creating the instant that cut Flaubert's life in two, was the sudden appearance of a wagon on the right of the cabriolet. Flaubert at once fell prostrate on the floor. There is no reason to believe that he was afraid of an accident. He never recorded any significant reaction to the wagon as such. Apparently he did not feel any fear. Rather the sudden emergence of an object out of the black night, perhaps the sight of the wagon's light served as a sign that the tension was breaking, that something must happen. It was as though he "annihilated himself *on command*" (2:1839). The fall was a "consent." He did not faint into unconsciousness. This was not a case of responding to fear by separating himself from the object that inspired it. He lay in a catatonic state. Although he was unable to speak, he did not at any point lose consciousness; neither was he fully aware of his surroundings. The lanterns on the vehicles, the lights from a nearby farmhouse may or may not have served as external stimuli which his consciousness translated into its own terms. He remained for a short time (perhaps ten minutes) purely within the realm of the imaginary. In describing the experience Flaubert referred to three things which seemed to be happening. First he was aware of flashing lights and of rapid images which came and went, bursting in his head "like fireworks." Second, he refers to "terrible pains." Third, he experienced a dissociation between "soul" and body which he expressed in two different images. He spoke of feeling his soul escape while all of his physical forces cried out to hold it back. He felt that he was dying. But on one occasion he said that his soul seemed to pull back on itself, "like a porcupine which injured itself with its own quills" (*Corr.* 2:51; 3:270).

To the section in which Sartre discusses these two images, Sartre, liking the wordplay, gives the title "Neurosis and Necrosis" (*Névrose et nécrose*). He claims that in all of Flaubert's references to the crisis—both in his descriptions of what he experienced and in his attitude toward the event, "death and madness are two inseparable aspects of the affliction" (2:1841). The image of the soul withdrawing expresses Flaubert's belief that he was dying. The corpselike, cataleptic state was a direct imitation of death. The hysterical paralysis which rendered him incapable of speech as of motion reinforced the likeness to death. The other image, the soul turning in on itself like a porcupine jabbing itself with its own quills, seems to Sartre to suggest madness. The soul takes the initiative in breaking with the external world and infects itself with hysterical belief. Flaubert in one letter says specifically that the fantastic images that came to him after he fell were accompanied by the awareness that he was becoming mad (*Corr.* 2:51). Sartre adds his own interpretation of both the images and the "terrible pains." He emphasizes the fact that Flaubert always looked on the "hemorrhage of images" as involuntary but hallucinatory; that is, he never took them as having any reality outside his own psyche. Flaubert lived these disconnected images as the "dissociation of his own person" (2:1843). Sartre points out that in cases of shock and a subsequent feeling of detachment from the world, although there may seem to be a much more intense inner mental awareness, actually there is a deceleration of ideational activity. It is as if analysis and synthesis give way to "a syncretism of interpenetration" (2:1844). The usual synthetic unity and selectivity of thought is absent with the result that there is a state of confusion, a "whirlpool of images." Flaubert did not take these hallucinatory fantasies as external realities, but he believed, Sartre argues, that they were leading him to future madness in which he would not be able to escape these spontaneous eruptions into his psyche. Here one is inevitably reminded of Sartre's own experience with mescaline-induced halucinations and his belief that they presaged insanity. Obviously it appears natural to him that Flaubert might have had the same reaction, and Flaubert's statements appear to confirm this hypothesis.[11]

The "terrible pains" of which Flaubert complained Sartre believes to have been a translation of psychic agony into physical. "The agony of consciousness is transformed into consciousness of agony" (2:1849). This does not mean that Flaubert did not feel a bodily suffering, but Sartre holds it to be the effect of autosuggestion. The terror of sinking into madness becomes a physical suffering. At this point Flaubert has done for himself what Sartre claims he accomplished for the hero of *November*. He "has translated the psychosomatic into terms of pure *soma*" (2:1744). His pain fulfills his need to feel that his body has taken over, that he is no longer responsible for what has happened. His physical suffering reassures him that he is not pretending or willing but only submitting.

The attack came as a Fall, both literally and figuratively. Flaubert might after all have simply slumped in his seat. Instead he dramatically falls prostrate on the floor. Verticality, a fascination with the extremes of high and low, Sartre finds to be a constant theme in Flaubert's early writing. We may recall, for example, the play of levels in Flaubert's fable of the people on the plain, the observer on the tower, the overtowering giant, and the impersonal sky of nature above. The Garçon, too, alternated between scornful giant and groveling subman. Sartre claims that for Flaubert a standing position symbolized the acceptance of the human condition and its responsibilities (2:1857). Rejection of it, the refusal of a role too difficult to play, might take the form of the imaginary, desituating overview (*le survol*) or descent to the subman. The fall in the cabriolet obviously symbolizes the latter. We might even say that it extends to the nonhuman. To Sartre the catatonic state carries also the suggestion of mineralization, realizing the old dream to become matter—only this time without the implied suggestion of pantheism or expansion. It is rather a contraction as if Flaubert had been transformed into one of the stone figures reclining on a tomb. Yet we must not forget that the fall had a positive aspect as well. It was more than an escape from demands Flaubert felt he could not meet. It was also a release which allowed him to pursue what he felt was natural for him. Sartre takes this as indicating more than the possibility of becoming a writer rather than a notary. If standing signified activity, the fall is the "revelation of his true nature which is, according to him, absolute inertia" (2:1858). The body is the mediator. Sartre would not deny that the "malady," viewed objectively, is neurotic and pathological. Yet with reference to what Flaubert really is, Sartre feels that we cannot say that the attack is an "abnormal reaction." It is rather the abrupt manifestation, the lived stunning illumination of the absolute "truth of Flaubert." The Fall is the epiphany of "triumphant passivity." Sartre adds, "The proof of this is that shortly afterward Gustave will state proudly that he must live *according to his nature*" (2:1859).

Taken by itself the Fall was more symbolic than efficacious in solving Gustave's problems. In his own mind it was an irreversible event. But if he recovered, he would have to continue his preparations for a career. In fact he seems even to have gone back to Paris briefly, though one doubts that either he or his family believed he could stay for very long. Somehow it was necessary to insure, in the minds of his father and other members of his family, that there could be no return to his former life. Sartre calls this unacknowledged resolution "the hysterical engagement." With diminishing frequency the attacks recurred. They resembled the first one to the point of seeming to relive it except for two things: There were convulsions but not catalepsy, and they were presaged by a kind of "aura." Years later Flaubert described this to Taine.

> First an indefinite anxiety, a vague malaise, a feeling of painful expectancy, *as happens before poetic inspiration,* when one feels that "something is going to happen" (a state which can be compared only to that of a man screwing [*fouteur*], feeling the sperm rising and the discharge which is getting ready). [*Corr.,* Supp. 2:94]

I find it significant that Flaubert uses the images of creativity rather than of distress, a point which seems to support Sartre's claim that these attacks served to confirm the irreversibility of Flaubert's secret refusal and retreat.

In the first days of his illness Flaubert's attitude was strangely calm, almost content. Everyone commented on his docility. The reaction, Sartre says, was that of one who feels that the die has been cast, the worst is over. Now he was free to realize the positive values of the situation for which he had paid so high a price. Sartre discusses in detail the practical and psychological benefits derived and perhaps intentionally aimed at during the years of the preneurosis. We may divide them into three groups: (1) those which were basically regressive, which satisfied needs deriving from his childhood; (2) those which served to settle the conflict between Flaubert and his father; and (3) those which resolved the issue between his destiny as a bourgeois and his resolution to be an artist.

First, the regressive or neurotic satisfactions: like Kafka's Gregor, Gustave lived in retreat like a monster in the bosom of his family. A source of shame and disgrace, he was nevertheless cared for by his own. Sartre claims that his forced dependence on his family satisfied psychological needs, neurotic but real. Not only did he escape responsibility; his family's concern reassured him that he was loved. In the hands of his physician father, he could feel that he was tended, cared for like a newborn baby (2:1862–66). It was also a form of vengeance against Achille. By his energetic intelligence the older son had proved himself his father's heir and successor, but he was obliged to leave home and establish a family of his own. The younger son, weak and helpless, was established at the heart of the family sanctuary and made the center of their concern (2:1876). A second satisfaction involved a symbolic change of sex. Sons must go out into the world. Daughters may stay by the family hearth. Gustave might now enjoy the "feminine condition." His secret dream of femininity was fulfilled as he prepared to settle down for the rest of his life as Caroline would have been expected to do if she had not married (2:1675). Finally, the new life was a sequestration, a retreat in the full regressive sense of the word. It represented a refusal to live his life as an adventure. The house became his "carapace." He rejected historical and vectorial time for cyclic—the eternal recurrence of domestic and seasonal rituals. More than ever Flaubert tried to assume the point of view of death on life; only this time it was as though he had survived his own death to give himself the right to speak as if from beyond the tomb. He was convinced that nothing more would ever happen to him, that he himself would never change. There is something almost laughable in all of this for us who know what his future actually held: his travels to Asia and Africa, his stormy liaison with Louise, his books and the fame they brought to him, his acceptance in courtly circles under the Second Empire, and his experiences with the disastrous fall of that empire and the Prussian invasion. But this does not alter the fact that it seemed to him in 1844 that his passional life was over, that he no longer desired anything more than imaginary activity. Nor is Sartre alone among critics in feeling that essentially the inner Flaubert did not subsequently change. Whatever the circumstances, whichever of his books we read, the same Flaubert is our center of reference.

In the conflict between Flaubert and his father, the doctor played both a real and an imaginary role. Sartre distinguishes between them by saying he was at once Achille-Cléophas and Moses. Achille-Cléophas could order his son to return to his books in Paris; he might be outwitted. Moses had pronounced the malediction, either he or Flaubert must die. Sartre says that Flaubert's "malady" was, among other things, the "ritual murder of the father" (2:1882 ff.). Naturally the symbolic meanings refer primarily to Moses, but the line cannot be drawn too sharply. Sartre claims that the Fall represents the old theme of self-punishment linked with revenge that we have observed in Flaubert's early fiction. It is intended in part to awaken the Father's remorse when it is too late. Primarily it simultaneously challenges the authority of the paterfamilias and kills Moses. In defiance the son says to the father, "See what you have made of me! But you, too, are a marionette who cannot control the result of your acts. You have made me such that I *cannot* obey you." The "ritual murder" destroys Moses in three ways. First, says Sartre, it feminizes him. The physician father must bestow on his sick, "newborn," son the intimate cares normally rendered by mother or nurse. The genitor is transformed into a genitrix (2:1866). Sartre believes that while this satisfied Gustave's need for tenderness, he was aware that it involved also a subtle ridicule. I am unable to go along with this view myself. The change of role seems to me to be not from masculine to feminine but from the revered doctor of others to parent caring for his child. This would be to replace Moses with Achille-Cléophas. Second, Sartre claims that Flaubert sought to ridicule his father as a doctor. He seems to have felt that he understood more of the cause and nature of his affliction than his father did (a point to which we shall return later). Then there was the affair of the burned hand. On one occasion Dr. Flaubert accidentally burned his son's hand with boiling water—so badly that it was permanently scarred. Gustave never openly blamed his father. The burning occurred at the time of one of the nervous attacks and apparently resulted from the doctor's distressed alarm; this proof of concern must in itself have been gratifying to Gustave, a partial consolation for the pain. But Sartre quotes from the correspondence to show that Flaubert saw in the burned hand a symbol. He wrote to Louise,

> My burned hand[12] with the skin wrinkled like a mummy's is more insensitive than my other one to cold and heat. My soul is the same; it has passed through fire. Is it surprising that it isn't warmed again by the sun? Consider it a weakness in me. [*Corr.* 2:12]

Sartre thinks that for Flaubert the scarred hand "symbolizes his father's medical incompetence and, more profoundly, is the indelible brand of the paternal malediction" (2:1886). His explanation to Louise means that "one arrives at indifference only after having suffered the most agonizing punishments." Sartre argues that the importance of the symbol is reinforced by a passage in an earlier letter to Louise. Here again the context is Flaubert's claim that he is incapable of feeling passionately, that he has, as it were, a "callus on his heart." Once more he suggests that this is because he has been scarred by burning. Laboriously he introduces a reference to

Herodotus' description of how the Numidians burned the skin on top of their children's skulls to make them less sensitive to the heat of the sun. "Imagine that I was raised in Numidia" (*Corr.* 1:277). I think Sartre is certainly right in claiming that Flaubert felt that the scarred hand symbolized his sufferings and their culmination in the Fall which marked a close to one phase of his existence. Whether he saw in it the sign of Dr. Flaubert's ineptitude as a physician is debatable; it is certainly possible.

The ritual murder of the father logically demands his replacement by the son. There was no way this could be accomplished even symbolically while Achille-Cléophas was still alive though it is possible that Gustave's presence in the house held an implicit promise to him of future replacement. Sartre believes that, when the father died two years later, in January 1846, Gustave did indeed feel himself to be "the *paterfamilias* in flesh and blood" (2:1898). Achille's succession to his father's position as director of the hospital was not automatic. To insure it, certain visits had to be made, contracts set up, a round of diplomatic maneuvers. Convention would not allow the candidate himself to do these things. It was the younger son who, in a burst of unexpected activity, managed it all. How difficult it was, whether there was actually any serious opposition, we cannot know. Gustave himself declared proudly that he had got Achille's position for him. At any rate he was acting as the head of the family on behalf of one of its members. The feeling of having replaced his father may have been intensified when he and his mother went to live at the country estate of Croisset. Achille did not take his family to live in the apartment at the Hôtel Dieu.

The continuation of the nervous attacks settled once and for all the question of a career in law. Here Flaubert won a decisive victory over his father. Yet Sartre points out a glaring irony in this achievement. In Flaubert's own mind to be an artist was also to refuse to be a bourgeois. Sartre goes so far as to say that rejection of the bourgeois condition was one of the reasons for becoming a worker in the imaginary. By rejecting a professional career and living on income from investments made by someone else, Flaubert seemed to receive as a gift what they wanted him to work for. In his eyes this may have likened him to one of the nobility; in actuality it was the moment of establishing himself as irretrievably bourgeois. Flaubert claimed that the artist must be willing to sacrifice everything for art. At the same time he must be free from all distractions and these included worries over money. Sartre translates this contradiction: "It is required of the candidate that he renounce *desires;* in exchange he has the right to demand the satisfaction of his *needs"* (2:1912). Years later, when it appeared that the financial machinations of his niece's husband might result in the loss of Croisset and its rents, Flaubert complained bitterly. "In my life I have sacrificed everything for the freedom of my intelligence! And it is taken away from me *by this reverse of fortune"* (quoted, 2:1911). In short, Flaubert had made a kind of bargain, taken a calculated risk. The fall at Pont-l'Evêque was *"against* Destiny and *for* Art" (2:1914). What he risked was idiocy. What he was willing to pay was the death of his active, passionate life. What he had to gain was the position of a *rentier* with leisure to live the life of the mind. With a certain cynicism Sartre writes that the great man *manqué* first came to judge himself a misfired bourgeois (*un raté*) and finally transformed himself into a landed proprietor (*propriétaire foncier*) (2:1878). In his very flight from his class, Flaubert showed that he belonged to it.

It is Sartre's view that the plan to live on inherited income was part of Gustave's unacknowledged strategy from the time that the will to radical failure was secretly embraced. Anticipating that someone will raise objections to his ascribing economic motives to Flaubert at this early period of his life, Sartre attempts to answer them. He points out first that we have evidence in Gustave's early writings that he dreamed of a life made easy by inherited wealth. This strikes me as true but unconvincing as an argument. In such daydreams Gustave imagined himself the inheritor of a large fortune, but so, I suspect, have more than half of the world's children. Another reference by Sartre may be more significant.

> As early as 1839 did he not calculate the income which his father would leave him, and did he not see himself living on them at Naples where life is less expensive than at Paris, *without doing anything?* [2:1881]

I think Sartre must be referring to a passage from a letter to Chevalier, dated December 31, 1841, in which Flaubert acknowledges the wish that, when he is of age, he might "clear out and go to live very well with an income of four thousand francs in Sicily or Naples, where I shall live as if at Paris on twenty" (*Corr.* 1:93). We do not know that this was actually based on a realistic calculation of what his inheritance would be. His knowledge that such an existence was possible for him is an important element in the picture. I think Sartre is on firm ground in arguing that if his father had not had the means to support him, Gustave would probably not have accepted the status of invalid so easily, if at all. His "stress" is conditioned by both his family's economic situation and his own attitude that earned money is vulgar and inherited wealth to be welcomed.

It is in no way astonishing if by a downfall which includes within it commitment to sequestration, he determines to live in advance his condition as legatee. [2:1881]

The daydream of going to live in Naples when he came of age obviously ignored one important obstacle. Achille Cléophas was hardly likely to hand over Gustave's inheritance prematurely. For two years the invalid lived quietly at home, and the attacks persisted. Then in January 1846 Dr. Flaubert died. Almost immediately Gustave began to recover. Sartre speaks of this two-year period (1844–46) as one of "active waiting" (2:1914). He does not mean, of course, that Flaubert had reason to expect that his father would die soon or that the son ever acknowledged to himself any wish for that death. Yet after the event he wrote that he had so often in anguish feared and anticipated his father's death that he hardly felt surprise when it came prematurely. Sartre interprets the anticipatory foreboding as a disguised wish. Gustave, he says, was a "passive parricide."

The most convincing parricides—in dream—are those passive agents who long for the annihilation of the obstacle because they are incapable of either bypassing it or moving it. [2:1895]

This is strong language and may be offensive to some of Flaubert's admirers. But we must remember that Sartre is not saying that this is Flaubert's only feeling toward his father or that he was unashamedly longing to be rid of him. Objectively, his father's death was the only means by which he could be independent and live the kind of life he wanted. We would be unrealistic to assume that Gustave never consciously realized this fact, nor is there any reason to suppose that when he acknowledged the advantage his father's death would bring to him, he did not quickly feel ashamed and repress the thought.

We have seen that, according to Sartre, the illness following the attack near Pont-l'Evêque restored Gustave to his family, saved him from having to train for a profession, settled his quarrel with his father, and allowed him to wait quietly for the opportunity to commit himself wholly to being an artist. Should we look upon all this as the unexpectedly happy result of a physical accident, or is it, as Sartre claims, the consequence of an organized secret strategy? To attempt to answer this question, we must consider Flaubert's response to the crisis and his later attitude toward this stage in his life.

## THE AFTERMATH

### The Self-diagnosis

In 1874, depressed and ill with flu, Flaubert wrote to George Sand,

> What you tell me of your dear little ones has touched me in the depths of my soul. Why did I never have that? Yet I was born with all the tender affections. But one does not make one's destiny, one submits to it. I was a coward in my youth, *I am afraid* of life. [*Corr.* 7:122]

Earlier, in 1857 when he was starting *Salammbô*, he complained to Mlle de Chantepie of the tortures he underwent when writing.

> How happy are those who do not dream of the impossible! One believes oneself wise because one has renounced active passions. What vanity! It is easier to become a millionaire and live in Venetian palaces filled with masterpieces than to write one good page and be satisfied with oneself. [*Corr.* 4:230–31]

In the same letter he says, after a reference to his passionate youth,

> I have taken pleasure in fighting my senses and in torturing my heart. I have rejected the human raptures which were offered to me. Relentlessly against myself, with my two hands, two hands full of force and pride, I uprooted the man. From that tree with verdant foliage I wanted to make an utterly bare column so that I might place there on high, as if on an altar, some kind of celestial flame. . . . That is why at thirty-six I find myself so empty and sometimes so fatigued.

The two letters not only reflect two different attitudes of Flaubert with respect to his youth. They may be taken to refer respectively to the negative aspect of the crisis as an escape and to its positive structure as a strategy. They show us why we may regard the affliction as both a conclusion and a beginning. If we look at them carefully, we may see why Sartre maintains that the neurotic project and the artistic project are inextricably united and condition each other. Along with other comparable remarks by Flaubert they enable us to understand Sartre's summary statement:

Flaubert never ceased to consider his neurosis as the most highly significant fact of his life. This "death and transfiguration,"—far from seeing in it an accident, he does not distinguish it from his own person. It is *he* inasmuch as he has become what he was. He never thought, as Dumesnil believes, that he adjusted or would adjust to his affliction but, quite the contrary, that his affliction was in itself an adaptation. In short, he took it for a *response,* for a solution. [2:1809–10]

In the letter to George Sand, Flaubert shows himself the true passive agent. One submits to one's destiny, something or somebody has made him what he is. At the same time, he judges himself objectively and seems to be acknowledging some responsibility. He *was* a coward in his youth. He *is* afraid of life. It would perhaps be going too far to say that Flaubert has in mind the whole pattern of failure and fall. He may be referring to no more than his embrace of quietism and deliberate refusal of emotional involvement. Yet there is an implicit confession that when he was young, he handled things badly and that his entire life has been needlessly infected with the desire to retreat from potentially enriching engagements. From this point of view the Fall was a negative response to an intolerable situation. The neurotic project was a life-saving device, a desperate solution *faute de mieux.*

The second letter unequivocally testifies to the strategy of an artistic project. In Flaubert's eyes the origin of the artist's endeavor is the dream of the impossible which leads him to create the imaginary. The striking image he uses to represent his thought vividly expresses both his feeling that art is something sacred to which the artist should be willing to sacrifice himself and the sense in which he believed his own life to have been such a sacrifice. Particularly in the light of the remark about George Sand's children, I think we are justified in seeing sexual overtones in the metaphor. The branch which becomes a bare standing column is obviously a phallic symbol of creativity. For his living passions and the normal family he might have had, Flaubert has substituted devotion to artistic production. Sartre sees in the image the distillation of all that led to and resulted from the crisis.

It is all here: the ruthlessness against himself or rather against the human condition, the effort to deny his needs, pushed to hysterical impotence, the refusal of passions and of human ends, the attempt to transform life into inorganic matter, eternal and smooth, conserving from the original tree only verticality—in short, the delirious choice of inhumanity even at the cost of a fall below the human. [2:2096]

Flaubert's most specific statements concerning the meaning that the crisis held for him are in two letters to Louise. In the first he explains that he is incapable of a total, consuming passion and that he is "not made for enjoying." About the crisis itself, he writes,

Before knowing you I was calm, I had become so. I was entering a manly period of moral health. My youth had passed. The nervous illness [*la maladie de nerfs*] which lasted for two years was the conclusion, the closing, the logical result. In order to have had what I had, it was necessary that something must first have happened in a rather tragic way in the box of my brain. Then everything was reestablished. I had seen clearly into things, and into myself, which is more rare. I proceeded with the correctness of a particular system made for a special case. . . . I was never more tranquil. [*Corr.* 1:229–30; *L'Idiot* 2:1798]

Later in the same month, he wrote,

I have had two quite distinct existences. External events were the symbol of the end of the first and the birth of the second. All that is mathematical. My active, passionate life, full of sudden reversals and multiple sensations ended at twenty-two. At that time I suddenly made great progess and something else came about. [*Corr.* 1:277–78; *L'Idiot* 2:1799]

These passages seem to me to lend strong support to Sartre's claim that Flaubert did not regard his affliction as a nonsignifying accident and that the neurosis and the aesthetic project were intertwined. The evidence does not justify our concluding (nor would Sartre so conclude) that Flaubert actually recognized the development as one intended by him, but he quite obviously regards it as an important positive event in his life. What is most important for Sartre's thesis is that in Flaubert's attempt to explain just how the illness was a logical culmination, he resorts to hypotheses involving autosuggestion and somatization. He gives on various occasions two explanations, different but not incompatible.

The first explanation is that "a long suffering wore him out, disordering his nervous system" (2:1800). Sartre quotes three short sentences from the *Correspondence*.

Think how much I must have suffered so that . . . I succumbed to a nervous illness which lasted two years. [*Corr.* 1:309]

[I fell] ill from studying law and being bored. [*Corr.* 2:461].

At twenty-one I just missed death from a nervous illness brought on by a series of irritations and troubles, by dint of sleeplessness and anger. [*Corr.* 4:169]

In these statements Flaubert seems to lay the blame primarily on the suffering he endured while being forced to study law against all his inclinations, but there are vague references to other troubles which, Sartre thinks, include his fear of lacking genius, of being "too small for himself." The second passage quoted occurs in a letter in which Flaubert objects to Musset's claim that poetry depends on the artist's personal emotion. Flaubert declares that poetry is not a weakness of the mind, but that nervous susceptibilities and excessive feelings are. He explains first by a reference to himself and then by the example of certain musical children. He says that if he had had a more robust brain, he would not have fallen ill from study and boredom. He would have profited instead of being injured. "Distress [*chagrin*] instead of staying in my skull, ran down into my limbs and contracted them in convulsions. It was a *deviation*." Sartre insists—rightly, I am sure—that Flaubert did not mean that if his brain had been stronger, he would have been able to pass his exams and succeed at law. Rather, he is saying that he woud have been able to take his pain not as a source of inspiration but as an instrument for effecting the aesthetic distance necessary for great art. It is only by standing aloof from passions that one can adequately create them in the imaginary. Flaubert's example makes this clear and again stresses the idea of somatization. There are some children, he says, who are so affected by music that it makes them ill. Their nerves are over-irritated. "You won't find any future Mozarts there. The *vocation* has been displaced, the idea has passed into the flesh where it remains sterile, and the flesh is impaired. The result is neither genius nor health." Sartre comments at length on this passage. Obviously Flaubert sees himself in these children who will never be Mozarts. His too great sensibility stole from him part of his powers. His suggestibility "deprived him of genius by substituting for it a somatization" (2:1807). Flaubert seems to say that in hypersensitive constitutions an idea expresses itself in a bodily reaction before it can be subjected to aesthetic creation. By juxtaposing his example with reference to his illness in 1844, he suggests that his body had accomplished in its own unsatisfactory fashion what ought to have been effected by an artistic transformation.

Flaubert's second explanation makes his illness the direct outcome of his own unbridled imagination and intense eagerness to sound all extremes of human experience, especially "madness and lust." He feels that these explorations will prevent him from becoming either an insane person or a marquis de Sade. "But I have been burnt by it. My nervous illness was the dregs of these little intellectual games" (*Corr.* 3:270).[13] He goes on to describe how during each of his attacks it was as though he suffered a hemorrhage of nervous stimulations with images exploding "like fireworks." Flaubert, Sartre says, appears to feel that his earlier excessive use of imagination (as in his imitation of the epileptic beggar) served as a sort of inoculation against serious mental alienation but that it may have induced the illness of 1844 (2:1801). If true, this might account in part for his strange tranquility. He always assumed that after the first attack, his condition would not become more serious.

Sartre points out that this second explanation also makes use of autosuggestion and somatization. As late as 1847 Flaubert wrote to Louise that she need not be anxious about his health since he was convinced that it would hold up for a long time. "But I shall live as I live now always suffering from nerves, that transmission point between soul and body, which I have perhaps wanted to make too many things pass through" (*Corr.* 2:72–73). In the sentences that follow this passage, Sartre points out, there is a curious inconsistency. Flaubert begins by accenting his will. He says that he taught his nature to leave him at peace and offers as evidence that at fifteen he ate only two meals a week for a month and that in his early twenties he remained chaste for two and a half years. But then he adds that the strange thing is that this abstinence did not result from resolution and deliberate persistence. "It happens, I don't know why, apparently because it must happen. [*Cela se fait je ne sais pourquoi, apparemment parce qu'il faut que ça se fasse.*]" Sartre regards this last statement, which amounts almost to a correction of what preceded, as profoundly revealing, pointing to a deep inner organization of the lived.

> Flaubert's will is a superficial inclination which would have no consequence if the body did not spontaneously take it in charge. He is sick, he says, from having made *too many* things pass by the nerves; but immediately he corrects himself; in fact it is the nerves which on their own have transmitted too many things to the organism. Because what happened had necessarily to happen, Flaubert divines behind the strange plasticity of his body a secret intention. Not only does he recognize his auto suggestibility, but

228

also he surmises that it is constituted, oriented toward an end. [2:1808]

If Sartre is correct, Flaubert believed that in some way his body turned the things imagined into a kind of reality. The explosion of images, the fireworks do not, of course, resemble the earlier imagined desires and wild daydreams. "This is because the body, docilely, stupidly, set out by itself to produce the fantastic; that is, a hemorrhage of the imagistic faculty of the brain" [2:1808].

Sartre feels that the two explanations, rather than contradicting, complement each other. The first explains causally, the second interprets in terms of finality. While neither is phrased in scientific terms, Sartre by implication accepts them as a correct view of what actually happened. "In the two conceptions . . . the young man shows himself perfectly conscious of the psychosomatic character of his ailment" (2:1809).

One might ask, of course, whether there is any reason to accept the patient's own judgment on the nature of his illness. Sartre anticipates this objection; in responding to it, he makes some interesting remarks about his own method in writing the biography. It would never be appropriate, he says to accept the patient's self-diagnosis if we knew the person only from the outside. A special code or hermeneutic would be necessary in order to decipher the message. But with Flaubert we have the code. "We have never treated him from the outside as a pure object of conceptual knowledge. Everything which we have known of him, he has lived and said." The controlling purpose of these volumes has been "to hold fast always at the level where the internalization of the external is transformed into the externalization of the internal" (2:1787). Now, Sartre feels, he has the right and the means to "read" Flaubert as a person, to find in his own interpretation of his illness the necessary clues for Sartre's interpretation, which goes beyond Flaubert's but without contradicting it.

Naturally, the patient's testimony is not all that Sartre uses to support his claim that the "hysterical engagement" was a positive strategy. He refers to Gustave's behavior in the early days of his illness and, much more important, to the circumstances of his recovery. Back at his father's home, Gustave apparently felt no sense of shame once the dreaded event had happened. He did not complain of the illness itself. He wrote to Alfred in May that he was really rather well now that he had "consented to be ill forever." (Sartre believes that the consent was itself the illness [2:1794].) But before the end of February Gustave began to complain of "the stupid regimen" his father had ordered. The tone implies that he felt it was unrelated to the true nature of his illness. Sartre notes that Flaubert had been reading some of his father's books on nervous afflictions and was beginning to doubt the doctor's diagnosis. At any rate he sought to make a connection with an earlier experience in Paris. He recalled waking up with an extraordinary lassitude with no apparent cause which lasted for a week. Now he wondered whether he might have had one of his attacks during the night. Sartre thinks this is unlikely (I agree) but says that the speculation marks a transition in Gustave—a movement from astonishment at what had happened to the fatalistic feeling that it had happened inevitably to the declaration that it had already happened earlier.

For two years the attacks recurred frequently. They were so closely repetitive of the first one that they seemed to be almost an imitation. Gustave even seemed to be seeing the lanterns and the carriages once again. It was ten years before the attacks ceased entirely, but we have seen that Flaubert himself spoke of the illness as lasting for two years. This was because at that time the attacks began to come at greatly diminished intervals. In his own mind the cure began in early 1846, shortly after his father's death. Neither Flaubert nor Sartre ever believed that it was coincidence.

Just fifteen days after his father's burial Flaubert wrote that the death, plus anxiety for Caroline, fatally ill after giving birth to a daughter, and the pressure of insuring Achille's appointment as director of the hospital had horribly shaken his nerves. But he adds, "Perhaps I am cured; this seems to me perhaps the effect of something like getting rid of a wart by burning" (quoted, 2:1797). It was indeed the beginning of a rapid improvement. Sartre disagrees in only one respect. "The death of Achille-Cléophas did not cure him, it made him decide to cure himself." Years later Flaubert described to Mlle de Chantepie how he healed himself by a combination of science and will (2:1797 ff.). He tried to understand what was happening inside him and he used his imagination to cope with the hallucinatory aspects. "I played with madness and the fantastic like Mithridates with his poison." There may possibly be an implied reference to the connection between the present involuntary images and the earlier reveries and impersonations. The important point is that he believed firmly that he did cure himself, and he came to this decision only after his father died.

Sartre states flatly, "On January 15, 1846 Gustave had the good luck of his lifetime: he became his father's orphan" (2:1895). That Flaubert "very consciously" felt the death to be a liberation, even though sadness may have been present too, is proved, in Sartre's view, by three things (2:1895 ff.): first, there is the fact of the cure. At the end of seven months, Flaubert declared, a bit prematurely, that this had been accomplished. Second, within six months, he had resumed his sexual activity by allowing himself to become involved with Louise Colet. Third, soon after Caroline's death he declared joyfully, "At last! At last! I am going to work!" His confidence in his ability to manage his own affairs is indicated by his statement in April to Maxime du Camp that if his mother, too, should die, he would go to live somewhere in Italy. He might well have wondered whether Madame Flaubert could survive the shock of two deaths in two months. Should we read here also an unacknowledged wish? Sartre suspects this. I rather doubt it myself, but one can't help observing that the move to Italy corresponds to Flaubert's dream during the period of the preneurosis. Sartre portrays Flaubert as one who suffers a neurotic's ability to feel no real concern for others. I think he overstates the case. Once again I think we should remind ourselves that feelings of deliverance and relief are not incompatible with genuine sorrow. Even if we accept Sartre's thesis of Gustave's illness as a positive strategy in the conflict with his father, there is no reason why we should doubt his sincerity when he expressed his sense of outrage and revolt at the "injustice" of Caroline's death. His outcry follows a significant statement:

> In placing my life above the common sphere, by withdrawing from ambitions and vulgar vanities *in order that something more solid might exist*, I had believed that I would achieve, if not happiness, at least repose. A mistake! There is always in us the man, with all his affections [*entrailles*] and the powerful attachments which link him to humanity. Nobody can escape pain. I know something about it. [*Corr.* 1:200; my italics]

Sartre does not comment on this passage. I think it tends to underscore still more firmly Flaubert's resolve that the Fall was to mark his entry into the realm of art. It shows also that it is easier to dream of the death of the emotions than to uproot them entirely.

## The Artist-hero

When Flaubert fell ill, he had on his hands the unfinished manuscript of the first *Sentimental Education*, which he had worked on in

Paris between February and June 1843 and briefly at Rouen in September and October. He resumed his writing of it in early May 1844 and finished it the following January. The initial delay is explained by his preparations for the examinations with the consequent failure, depression, and illness. Sartre thinks that between January and May in 1844 Flaubert may have been afraid to show himself well enough to write for fear that his father would accuse him of faking or else find in his efforts evidence that he was well enough to return to his study of law. Be that as it may, we must share Sartre's marveling admiration at Flaubert's ability to complete the book during seven months of severe illness, not even a true convalescence. Sartre said of *November* that it represented "the neurosis rejected" whereas the crisis near Pont-l'Evêque was "the neurosis accepted." Perhaps we might speak of the first *Sentimental Education* as "the neurosis distilled." As in *November,* there is a marked shift in intention, and this time I think no critic would deny that it is linked with the dramatic change in Flaubert's own life. While it is possible that he may from the outset have intended to polarize his two heroes, there is nothing whatsoever to suggest that the author's interest and sympathy would shift suddenly from one to the other; nor is there for either Henri or Jules any real explanation of the profound change that occurred in them. The greater part of the book was probably written after Flaubert's illness, though the change in the narrator's attitude is first evident only three chapters before the end. The story of Henri, the law student who runs off to America with a married woman, obviously reflects both Flaubert's experiences in Paris and the imagined outcome of his love for Elisa Schlésinger. Their gradual disillusion and boredom with each other reflect Flaubert's long entrenched cynicism toward all human aspirations. That Henri, after his return to France, should contentedly resume his studies and rapidly become the quintessence of the successful, conformist bourgeois is not foreshadowed. Possibly it represents what Flaubert imagined might have happened to him if he had passed his examinations. Or perhaps Henri bears some resemblance to Ernest Chevalier, whose development (except for the romance) proved to be much the same. The transformation is announced rather than explained. Either Flaubert felt unable to handle the internal process of character change or was simply not interested in it. From our point of view the themes of Parisian life and frustrated romantic love have been so much more adequately treated in the second *Sentimental Education* and *Madame Bovary* that the story of Henri by itself would hardly hold our inter-

est. The case is far different for Jules. It is he who personifies
Flaubert's newly developed aesthetic creed. It is Jules who becomes a
great artist only after and by means of a break in his life which
symbolizes the death of the passions and a rebirth.

Sartre does not offer a critique of the novel as a whole, nor is his
interpretation of Jules sharply at variance with that of most other
critics. He is chiefly concerned with the link between Jules' aesthetic
and Flaubert's, particularly as character and author view the relation
between reality and artistic creation, between the life of the artist
and the works he imagines. (We will return to this subject later.)
Sartre makes an important point with regard to the parallel between
Flaubert's crisis and the evening that marks the turning point in
Jules' development. Jules at first, Sartre says, was "a pale remake" of
the hero of *November*, definitely a man "who is too small for himself." Flaubert seems to have held him in contempt. His passions are
commonplace; he is "a poet without much talent." The author seems
to delight in humiliating him undramatically. As Sartre says rather
sarcastically, "Jules *works*. Imagine that! He took a job in order *to
earn his living*" (2:1925). His one unfortunate love affair is almost a
travesty of Henri's liaison with Madame Renaud. He loves a small-
time actress who leaves him, and he cures himself by talking of her
with her successful lover. Then suddenly in chapter 26, Jules' humili-
ations seem to be the mark of "an election." His "falls" have a certain
profundity. Sartre thinks that in this chapter Flaubert symbolically
describes the crisis of Pont-l'Evêque. He does not present any directly equivalent event. In fact, as Sartre observes, Jules' thought,
before his strange experiences, is well on the road to the conclusions
he reaches afterward. We may note also that he already feels so
estranged from his past that it seems to belong to another person. It
is possible that Jules represents here the reflections of Flaubert just
before the Fall, though certainly Jules' evening is not meant to be the
precise counterpart of that day and night in January.

The chapter depicts two significant experiences which seem, on
the surface at least, to be in sharp contrast with one another. Inexplicably Sartre does not discuss the first one although some of
Jules' reflections leading up to it he regards as significantly linked
with Flaubert's aesthetic theory. Jules is wandering through the
countryside in haunts of his childhood. Even as he feels estranged
from his past, he seems (in memory) to relive it in all its richness, its
innocent glory and its wretched unhappiness. He recognizes that all
of it was necessary to bring him where he is now, a point at which

"every feeling had been transmuted into an idea" (p. 244).[14] It occurs to him that if he is to attain truth through art, then all of his past suffering was necessary. He could no more deny a phase of his own existence than the historian could ignore at whim one of the periods in history. Everything he had experienced "had perhaps happened for unknown ends, with a fixed and constant purpose, unperceived but real" (p. 245). Suddenly he realizes that even this wretched past might be made to reveal beauty and harmony; if one synthesized it and reduced it to absolute principles, it might be linked harmoniously with the pattern of the whole.

> The entire world appeared to him, reproducing the infinite and reflecting the face of God. Art drew all these lines, sang all these sounds, sculptured all these forms, grasped their respective proportions, and by unknown paths led them to that beauty more beautiful than beauty itself since it reached up to that ideal from which beauty was derived. [p. 246]

This intellectual vision is accompanied by or followed by (it is not quite clear which) a kind of pantheistic ecstasy. Jules awakens with a feeling of freshness. He hardly knows what has been happening or how long he has been there. He has to make an effort "to return to the reality from which he had escaped" (p. 246). In this scene I find—under Sartre's influence—two familiar themes. It recalls Gustave's childhood ecstasies in which he seemed to melt and become one with unified nature. The truth of this revelation is an aesthetic promise: it is the artist alone who can distill the unity and beauty which the external world otherwise will not reveal.

Jules' awakening is followed, without transition, by a much-discussed scene with a dog. The animal that suddenly runs up to him is singularly ugly and pathetic—dirty, mangy, half-starved, lame in one leg, and persistent in its unwelcome attentions. Jules does everything possible to get rid of it, even throws a stone at it, but the dog will not leave. Soon he begins to wonder if it is his old spaniel Fox, whom he had raised and finally given to the faithless Lucinde. Recalling his former delight in Fox, he feels "an infinite compassion for this inferior being that looked at him with so much love" (p. 248). He starts to pet it but is repelled by its ugliness and decides that after all it is not Fox. He leaves. The dog follows him, barking constantly. Jules tries to find some meaning in the furious sounds, but they are all alike in their monotony; he cannot discern anything that communicates. Then it seems that the dog is leading him toward a bridge. Jules remembers that once he was tempted to commit suicide there. Now he wonders if perhaps Lucinde herself lies dead in the water. But there is nobody and nothing. In a moment of silence he and the dog stare at each other. "The man trembled beneath the look of the beast in which he believed he saw a soul, and the beast trembled at the look of the man in whom perhaps he saw a God" (p. 252). Jules kicks the dog with fear and hatred, but he feels that it is following him as he goes home. Behind his locked door, he tries to discover the meaning of all he had felt in relation to the beast. He was positive that he had not been dreaming. But in this adventure

> there was something so intimate, so profound, so clear that at the same time it was necessary to recognize a reality of another kind, one as real as the everyday reality although seemingly inconsistent with it. Now all that was tangible and sensible in existence disappeared in his thought as secondary and useless, as an illusion that is only its superficial surface. [p. 254]

Both fearing and longing to see if the animal was still there, Jules finally opened the door and saw the dog still lying by the threshold. At this point the chapter stops. The next one begins with the sentence, "That was his last day of pathos [*le pathétique*]; henceforth he was cured of superstitious fears and was no longer afraid of meeting mangy dogs running about the countryside" (p. 255). It is as though the true crisis took place between the two chapters. "We can imagine anything," writes Sartre, "except that, seeing the beast, he calmly shut the door and went back upstairs to bed" (2:1929). Between evening and morning the definitive rupture with *le pathétique* was effected, but we are not present to see how it happened. The whole episode, in Sartre's view, "is the covering event which reveals and at the same time masks the true event of Pont-l'Evêque." This chapter "describes *symbolically* Jules' break with his past; that is, the instant in which the convert in fear and trembling sees his life totalized in all its ugliness, is tempted to hold on to it again, then flees it, and escapes it by sequestration." Thus in Sartre's view the dog represents to Jules-Flaubert both the temptation of *le pathétique* and his wretched past as it now appeared to him to have been (2:1927). Sartre finds it striking that Flaubert, while passing over the moment of conversion in silence, managed to give it an air of the supernatural or surreal, almost the sacred. He accomplished this by the mention of another reality, preceding the abrupt break in which something apocalyptic must be presumed to have happened. Like one who undergoes a religious conversion, Jules feels the quotidian reality fall away to be replaced by a greater reality which contradicts it.

> We can therefore confidently assert that—*at least* during that summer and autumn following his attack—Flaubert considered this as an authentic *conversion* in the metaphysical, if not the religious, sense of the term. [2:1929]

In my opinion Sartre is correct in assuming that the break between the two chapters echoes the harrowing but liberating rupture in Flaubert's own life. Yet there are certain difficulties—or gaps—in Sartre's reading which seem to me to derive from two factors: first, he ignores Jules' moment of pantheistic ecstasy; second, he does not explain why ideas are attributed to Jules before the night of mystery which logically should have come to him afterward.[15] Since the dog episode has been studied intensively both by critics preceding Sartre and by those who had his book in mind, it may be worth our while to compare his interpretation with those of others. Bruneau, in *Les Débuts littéraires de Gustave Flaubert (1831–1845)*, which Sartre had read, summed up the most important existing critical views, accepted what seemed sound to him, and offered an interpretation of his own which, while different from Sartre's, is not wholly incompatible with it.[16] Bruneau, while recognizing that the effect of the crisis at Pont-l'Evêque is present throughout the last chapters, does not associate (any more than other early critics) the specific event with this particular episode. He argues, in fact, that the details and setting of Jules' meeting with the dog are so unusually carefully worked out and clear that they may well derive from a real event in Flaubert's life not unlike Jules' experience.[17] As for its symbolic meaning, he concludes that the episode represents "a last attack of the ailment [*le mal*] from which Jules suffered for so long." This ailment, he states, is "the refusal of reality." Bruneau believes that although the mangy dog at first seems to contrast everyday reality with the pantheistic ecstasy that immediately preceded, the "lesson" that it brings complements and reinforces the vision of unified nature. Jules finally concludes that the encounter with the dog (his past) points to another reality, one incompatible with the world of our mundane senses. By demonstrating to the artist that he cannot deny his past, it, too, points to "the *unitary* character of life; there are no privileged experiences, everything is harmoniously ordered by the same laws.... Flaubert's great philosophical discovery [is] pantheism, which in his earlier works was limited to ecstasies in nature" (p. 429). After his last day of *le pathétique* Jules realizes that by viewing his past objectively without denying it, he may see in it "its impersonal character and infinite grandeur." Finally, Bruneau concludes, this scene is "the first clear example" in Flaubert's work of "the ironic acceptance of existence" (p. 429).

Neither Bruneau's interpretation nor that of any of the other scholars whom he mentions attaches much significance to the break between chapters. They anticipate Sartre's view that Flaubert's attitude toward his own life and his aesthetic creed are intertwined; the crisis symbolized is both psychological and artistic. All assume that the rupture with the past has already taken place, the problem is how to relate it to the present in a new way. It is as though they see both parts of the chapter as expressing Flaubert's struggles in the weeks after Pont-l'Evêque with no reference to the crisis itself.

Of critics since *The Family Idiot* was published, the one who has most directly challenged Sartre with respect to the episode in question is Neil Hertz in his article, "Flaubert's Conversion."[18]

Hertz points out that both Jules and Flaubert felt the need to see their lives in terms of a distinct "before" and "after."

> There is no doubt that [Sartre] is in touch with one of Flaubert's intentions when he places Jules' conversion at the end of chapter 26 and sees in it a representation of Pont-l'Evêque, for Flaubert himself has a stake in imagining Jules' life in these reassuring terms. [pp. 11–12]

But while he agrees with Sartre on this fundamental point, he has two important objections to Sartre's approach—the first specifically related to Sartre's discussion of this chapter, and the second illustrated here but extending to *The Family Idiot* as a whole. Hertz first points to Sartre's inconsistency, mentioned earlier, in quoting several passages from the first pages of the chapter to define Jules' attitude as it was crystallized after the night of his meeting with the dog; i.e., after his conversion. Hertz is right to object, and I do not think that Sartre's observation that at the beginning of the chapter Jules was already well advanced on the path of conversion is an adequate explanation. Hertz explains the confusion in terms which Sartre ought to be willing to accept.

> Chapter 26 makes sense when it is seen to be organized around two distinct time-schemes, one (Jules') moving forward to a "conversion" at the end of the chapter, the other (Flaubert's) looking backward to a "conversion" that had already taken place in Janu-

ary '44. Sometimes the two rhythms seem to be consonant, sometimes not, and out of this play there emerges a telling uncertainty.
[p. 10]

Hertz seems to me to have found the clue. It accounts for the reader's
uneasy feeling that Jules has already arrived at the conclusions to
which his subsequent experiences are to lead him. Hertz's intention,
however, was not simply to clarify what Sartre had left unclear,
though, in fact, he has, I believe, given us reason to find Sartre's
procedure more acceptable. Hertz's hypothesis as to what the dog
episode symbolized for both Jules and Flaubert sets him apart from
Sartre as decisively as it separates him from the pre-Sartrean critics.

Hertz does not see the dog as primarily a symbol of the past and not
quite as a symbol of ordinary reality either. He stresses that the dog
comes on the scene at the moment when Jules, after the ecstatic
"moment of plenitude and totalization, reawakens to a sense of self."

> Jules' consciousness, like Flaubert's, is both the scene of this vision
> and a supplementary and disturbing element within that scene.
> And, significantly, Flaubert's scene immediately darkens.

The dog, Hertz argues, is a "projected creature of the self." He is in
violent contrast to the ecstatic totalization. His barks are meaningless
repetitions, he serves to evoke in Jules only morbid imagining, recollections of unhappiness and thoughts of suicide. Hertz holds that
Jules' reaction is that of a person who confronts the discrepancy
between "an imagining self and whatever it seeks to totalize." When
Jules-Flaubert attempts to see the intervening night as marking a
clear before and after, this is a defense mechanism to hide the fact
that in reality there never was any decisive moment of conversion in
which a life was totalized in the sense of fixing its basic choice and
meaning. The episode with the dog would indicate that the artist's
resolution cannot extend to the man's view of himself. "Flaubert's
relation to Jules—that is, to an imagined self—is as shifty, as open to
dislocating fantasy, as is Jules' to the dog" (p. 12). Hertz wants to
show that Sartre is wrong in seeing the crisis at Pont-l'Evêque as "the
moment in which a life totalizes itself and realizes the destiny it
carries within itself" (2:1799). He is evidently skeptical with regard to
the basic supposition underlying Sartre's book—that it is possible to
find a fundamental meaning and unity in a life; that if we know all
that can be known about it, we will not find on our hands only "a
collection of 'heterogeneous and irreducible layers of meaning.'"
Hertz hints that Sartre's eagerness to prove this point was one of the

reasons leading him to write a biography of Flaubert rather than of someone else; he would have us believe that Sartre, Flaubert, and even Jules are deceived in their hope for the totalizing critical event and that the episode with the dog suggests that Flaubert realized the fact. To my mind Hertz's interpretation of the episode is too strained to be convincing. It fails to account for Jules' feeling that the encounter had put him in touch with another reality. Its motivation—to show that there was not one conversion, but a series of failed totalizations—is at least as much *parti-pris* as Sartre's desire to point up the climactic nature of what happened at Pont-l'Evêque.

Two other post-Sartrean critics have commented on the meaning of the dog. Marie Diamond regards the episode as an unsuccessful attempt by Flaubert to bridge the gap between "the acceptance of one's past and a pantheistic aesthetics."[19] Although she does not deny the possiblity that the night of Pont-l'Evêque may be in the background, she is concerned primarily with the novel itself, not with its autobiographical implications. She accepts Sartre's idea that "the appearance of the dog is a *totalization* of the past," but insists that as such it was accepted by Jules only on the unconscious level.

> Without the episode of the dog Jules' new aesthetics would be based only on his desire that art should provide a magnificent synthesis between himself and the world. Flaubert rightly felt that such a radical change of direction needed some extraordinary validation, some convincing emotional base. [p. 88]

Diamond's complaint is that "the dog is after the fact" and the leap from the personal to the aesthetic illogical. The break between the chapters represents a contradiction between two attitudes rather than a progression. Still under the influence of romanticism, Jules accepts the experience with the dog emotionally at the end of chapter 26 and totally rejects it in the opening sentence of chapter 27.

Finally, Jonathan Culler [20] would like to contrast his reading with all of the preceding by taking the story of the dog quite literally. He reminds us that the first of the interpreters was Jules himself, who tried in vain to detect a whole series of messages and meanings in the dog's behavior only to realize finally that the creature cannot be reduced to any set of verbalized meanings.

> The moment of supreme "Romantic synthesis" which takes one beyond the *pathétique* grants a sense of another reality to be grasped in the excess of the concrete itself and not statable except as an absence dialectically created by this presence. [p. 66]

Jules was frightened by his inability to place the dog. But once he had confronted the fear itself (by opening the door to look at the dog), he was no longer afraid. As for the rest of the night:

> To have left the moment of crisis a blank is both a powerful representation and a suggestion that we need not try to formulate what happens there, that whatever versions we might invent would only falsify by particularizing. [p. 63]

By way of concluding this rapid survey of critical approaches to the puzzling episode, I will say that I myself can find no persuasive reason either to abandon the earlier idea that the dog symbolizes Jules' past or to reject the autobiographical connections that Sartre would attach to it. I think that the three post-Sartrean critics have contributed insights which may fill out and enrich Sartre's rather sketchy interpretation of chapter 26 and the concluding silence as a symbolization of Flaubert's crisis, and which may tighten the connection between the personal experience and the aesthetic theory. Hertz's hypothesis of the two time-schemes is helpful. So is Diamond's insistence that insights such as Jules experienced in the first part of the chapter must be reinforced, implemented as it were, if they are to become living guides to thought. I see nothing strange in assuming that Jules might have arrived intellectually at the convictions attributed to him in the opening pages of chapter 26 (before the conversion) without being able fearlessly to integrate them into his life and plans for the future. If the ideas are to be incarnated in the lived, there must be, as Diamond says, some kind of decisive experience to "realize" the conversion. (I use the word, as Sartre does, in the double sense of understanding and making real.) Almost certainly Flaubert himself, long before the crisis, had resolved to achieve through the imaginary the sense of unity evoked in his childhood ecstatic stupors. What changed after his crisis was his attitude toward the requisite relation between art and the artist's private existence—just as with Jules.

Culler's argument, that the dog resists all of Jules' attempts to assign a meaning to him, seems to me important, too, though not quite for the reasons Culler gives. (Hertz, we recall, also emphasizes the *unintelligibility* of the dog's barking.) While I have no wish to offer still another interpretation, I suggest that we might reinforce and strengthen Sartre's view, which seems to me essentially correct, by giving greater emphasis in two small points: first, Flaubert's feeling of special empathy with animals; second, the fact that Jules finally *leaves* the dog outside. The pantheistic experience was only a vision of what imagination would like to make of reality, a form of nonbeing unrelated to the daily life of Jules-Flaubert. The dog represents the pathetic failure (*le raté*), the unhappy dreamer who had foolishly tried to find meaning and beauty in real life, who aspired to a realm beyond ordinary reality but could only fall to the subhuman. His efforts are nonsignifying (Hertz and Culler). In shutting the door on his past self, Jules-Flaubert declares that the future will be unlike the past. He will no longer seek in vain for fulfillment of his passions; he will not look for the infinite in tawdry reality. The past can no longer threaten him, for he has cut himself off from it. The other reality is to be captured in art, to be created by the imagination, not discovered in living. The artist has replaced the man, who "dies" on this night just as Gustave seemed to himself to have "died" near Pont-l'Evêque.[21]

This does not mean either that Jules *is* Flaubert without reservations or that we should see in him only a portrait of the ideal artist. His aesthetic theory, of course, is Flaubert's own, and Jules' "impersonalism" includes what Flaubert believed to be the proper relation of the artist to his material and to his own life. In these respects we might indeed think of him as an idealized portrait of "the artist." But Sartre points out that in two ways Jules is specifically related to the Gustave who survived the night of Pont-l'Evêque. First, he represents the "positive aspect" of the attack. Jules no longer suffers because he has succeeded in uprooting all passions in himself. For his art it is enough that he observe them in others or in his earlier self. Similarly, Sartre claims, Flaubert believed that he no longer suffered. The belief in a "petrified heart" was obviously not supported by reality. No matter how decisive the break with the past, it would at least, Sartre says, have to be accompanied by a period of mourning. The only way Flaubert could persuade himself that he did not suffer was to put himself into "a state of hysterical distraction," a form of self-deception with regard to his natural feelings. In short, he derealized them by living as if his life were imaginary, which is precisely what Jules does, achieving a sense of inner glory despite the sadness of his life. To the degree that he was successful, this effort, accompanied by the genuine relief derived from the feeling that the die was cast, that "the worst had already happened," enabled Flaubert at last even to love his life, at least as it had been in the past, because it had brought him to his present summit. The Fall had brought him to the point of feeling that he had finally achieved the detached overview toward which he had always aspired in his imagination. In one important respect Jules is not like Flaubert. Jules is so content with his imaginary creations that he has no interest in seeing his works published or his plays performed. Sartre makes the interesting observation that his retreat into dream is so complete that one wonders why, logically, he should not have been content to dream that he wrote. In fact Flaubert assigned first such a conclusion to a character in *The Spiral,* a painter who follows the lead of the imaginary to the point of finally going insane. Sartre suggests that aesthetically this conclusion would have been appropriate to Jules. He offers two reasons as to why Flaubert did not use it. First, at this particular period he was afraid. The nervous crisis was dangerously close to mental illness. He felt he had risked madness as well as coming close to physical death. He might well have feared the autosuggestion inherent in assigning the extreme of pathological retreat from reality to Jules. Even more important, Sartre feels that the happy ending, in which Jules is recognized as a great artist, is expressing the secret hope which during these years was at the heart of Flaubert's project. Sartre sums this up in one of his own favorite expressions, representing a notion he has employed in many contexts—particularly in *The Condemned of Altona* and in his study of Genet: "Loser Wins" (*Qui perd gagne*).

Like Jules, Flaubert was not overconcerned with being published or at least in no great hurry to be recognized. As an adolescent he liked to imagine himself publishing nothing until he was fifty and then bringing out his "complete works" all at once. As a mature writer he continued to despise his public, in theory at least, and was never anxious for general popularity, provided his work won his own approval and that of a few persons whose judgment he respected. But at the time of the first *Sentimental Education,* he was not yet able to respond to the question he posed to himself. "Am I called to be a great writer?" It is for this reason that Flaubert announces so firmly that Jules' history of sufferings has made him what he is—a great artist. For a long time Flaubert had believed that suffering and self-sacrifice were necessary conditions for genius. Now he wants to assure himself that they are also sufficient, that when one has lost everything, one will find that one can write. In other words, he seeks desperately to find in Pont-l'Evêque a meaning which is also a promise: "To die to the world *is* to be reborn an artist" (2:1996). Sartre speaks of Flaubert's "conversion to optimisim."

There is still more in the strategy behind "Loser Wins." Referring to the passage in which Jules concludes that perhaps everything in his past had been leading toward some fixed, unperceived goal, Sartre writes,

> When I reread this passage I cannot help recalling the Kierkegaardian "repetition." At the moment of conversion Flaubert consents to lose everything and, precisely for that reason, all is abundantly returned to him. [2:1930]

What is returned is not only the past in a form which is now acceptable, but the future. Succumbing to the crisis was a form of self-abandon, but the true meaning of this kind of giving-up is not despair. Rather, Sartre says, it is a cry for help. It asks someone else to take charge of one's life. At this moment all of the themes Sartre finds present at Pont-l'Evêque come together. We have noted how Flaubert was asking to be received back into the family house as the beloved child, His hope was that he might reenter forever "the age of gold." His self-abandon carried with it the plea that suffering is recognized as merit, and he wanted to be consoled. It was as though he cried out, "Father, I am sick, take me in your arms and comfort me" (2:2084). The appeal was addressed to Achille-Cléophas, but included in it was an implied "identification of the Father with God which used to guarantee his personal identity" (2:2083). Sartre argues that even though intellectually Flaubert remained agnostic, he lived with an implicit "theodicy of failure." It is, I suppose, another form of the belief that "he who can do the most cannot do the least." Sartre remarks that Flaubert, like Baudelaire, sometimes viewed art as accomplishing the work of Satan (the *Flowers of Evil*); its intent was to injure by demoralizing. But on the horizon was the half-formulated notion of the artist who, even in his role of *poète maudit* (the poet under a curse), served as the annointed of a good God to accomplish His hidden purpose. Sartre wryly points out that numerous theologians have tried to vindicate God by arguing that the evils He sends to us are the conditions of greater goods. Flaubert went one step further.

> As if Art, an exquisite crime, born from despair, were charged with perpetuating our unhappiness. As if God said to the Artist, "You will be born and will die in despair, cursed. You will persist in denying My existence, and I will not undeceive you. You will have My invisible assistance only in order that you may produce works which will the better dishearten your species. Your merit in

243

My eyes will be twofold since your unhappiness will be extreme and since you will infect others with it. Such is the will of the infinite love that I bear for you" [2:2087]

Sartre would not claim that Flaubert ever went quite this far in explicit formulation, but he insists that such was the underlying truth of his attitude in 1844 and for the rest of his life. We shall see that it received its final formulation in "The Legend of Saint Julian the Hospitaler," written in 1875–76 at a time when Flaubert felt he had lost everything, just four years before his death.

Thus the Fall at Pont-l'Evêque, literally and symbolically, freed Gustave from his father's plans for his career and restored him to his father's love; it was meant to show that he merited the gift of genius from a God his writing would continue to deny. It killed (or Flaubert believed it did) all passions in him save one—to realize himself as an artist. It was the last turn of the spiral.

# PART TWO

*The Writer in Situation*

# The Objective Mind

If volumes 1 and 2 of *The Family Idiot* are unconventional biography, most the first two-thirds of volume 3 seems scarcely to be biography at all. There is a brilliant survey of the French literary tradition in the eighteenth and early nineteenth centuries and its influence on the new writers of the mid-nineteenth century. Sartre analyzes the change in the concept of humanity and humanism and the particular *Weltanschauung* of the French reading public in the wake of the abortive revolution of 1848. Yet these more than four hundred pages do not constitute a digression, nor are they the kind of thing that would be appropriate only to a book called "Flaubert and His Time." In at least three ways all this is essential to Sartre's purpose:

First, he wants to show how it happened that Flaubert's readers, while they misunderstood his intention in *Madame Bovary*, found that the book "spoke to their condition."

Second, Sartre claims that Flaubert made himself what he was as the result of two lines of conditioning. The first two volumes have traced the development of his personal neurosis in terms of his response to the pressures of the family situation and career expectations. Now Sartre wants to show that the objective situation of literature and Flaubert's personal problems are related. In order to understand this reciprocity Sartre proposes first to define for the mid-century what he calls the "objective mind" and the "objective neurosis." We shall see what at this period are the demands and the contradictions of literature, what questions it poses to the post-romantics, and why only a neurotic response is possible.

Then, returning to Flaubert we will attempt to determine *to what extent* and *how* the insoluble problems of Art are at the source of

> his troubles; in other words, how the latter—in spite of the seeming contradictions—can be at one and the same time a neurotic response to a subjective malaise and to the objective malaise of literature. [3:40–41]

Sartre is not claiming that the literature Flaubert had read was responsible for his personal neurosis, but rather that the solution he had gradually worked out for his own dilemma rendered him peculiarly suited to respond to this moment of crisis in the history of literature and the changing role of the artist in society. Flaubert was one of the first to recognize and to welcome a new phenomenon in cultural history—the divorce between the writer and his public. If he had written a subjective, confessional self-portrait, his book might or might not have been published; it would almost certainly have been ignored—as were the works of de Sade for nearly a century and a half. Fortunately—or, as Sartre would prefer to phrase it, as the inevitable consequence of political events in France—*Madame Bovary,* because it appeared to be an impersonal, objective work, was received as a faithful report of life as it really is. This was due to the fact that the public for its part was living with an "objective neurosis." What they found in Flaubert's novel coincided with a view of humanity which assuaged their own hidden guilt and hatred.

Finally, both for his immediate followers and for a later generation who better understood what he had tried to do, Flaubert's novels altered the course of the history of literature. Here, if anywhere, we see the evidence for Sartre's claim that by his internalization of what society has made of him, the "singular universal" gives a new form to his sector of the social order.

Sartre's discussion of the objective mind combines and develops further implications of ideas laid down in the *Critique* and in the early set of essays, *What Is Literature?* The objective mind comes close to being simply the equivalent of the cultural heritage, but Sartre seeks to clarify what we mean by that vague notion and to explain something of our interaction with this inheritance at any present moment. Warning us not to retain any of its Hegelian idealist associations, Sartre defines the term as follows:

> The objective mind—in a specific society at a given period—is none other than Culture as practico-inert. [3:44]

The origin of culture lies in the first work performed on nature in an act which both adapts to nature and transforms it. "The tool becomes for the worker, by the use which he makes of it, an *organ of percep-*

*tion:* it reveals the world and man in the world" (3:45). Even on the most primitive level, the use of common tools by members of a group results in a shared nonverbal comprehension of the human being's relation to the natural environment and the relations of persons to one another. Any cultural object comes to us accompanied by a hypothetical imperative. This is obvious in the case of a package bearing written directions for opening it. Whether instructions are printed or oral or must be reconstructed by trial and error, any utilizable object says in effect that it must be handled in a particular way if it is not to be broken or rendered useless. The objective mind represents culture as the collection of imperatives which have been handed down to a particular society (3:48). For Sartre, materiality and implied imperative are essential to the objective mind at any level. The early Sartrean ontology assigned to the For-itself the introduction of meaning into being. This view Sartre has never retracted, but in the *Critique* he states that it is not consciousness which fixes and perpetuates meanings. "Matter alone *sets* meanings. It retains them in itself like inscriptions and gives to them their true efficacy" (p. 245). Praxis objectifies human intentions in worked-on matter [*matière œuvrée* or *travaillée*], which becomes the "motive force of history."

> It is simultaneously the social memory of a collectivity, its transcendent, yet internal unity, the made totality of all dispersed activities, the fixed threat of the future, the synthetic relation of otherness which unites all persons. [p. 250]

It is this inscribed or worked-on matter that constitutes the total environment in which we live—physically and socially: its organized space, means of production, institutions, its "social facts," and codified patterns of behavior, in short the practico-inert. This material reality is a resistance to our projects, a limit to our knowledge, and our only possible instrumentality for living (p. 247). In the *Critique* Sartre was interested especially in those social structures of the practico-inert that result in our alienation by deviating our action or stealing it from us. In discussing the objective mind he refers specifically to what has been written. The original act of the worker in transforming the environment included a practical knowledge and the relating of means and end. Theory is born from reflection and requires language. But "language is matter." Once an idea has been verbalized, it takes on some of the material inertia of a thing. "Written words are stones." Sartre states, "I call these irreducible passivities *as a whole* the Objective mind" (p. 47). In this section of *The*

*Family Idiot* Sartre's primary concern is with that sector of the objective mind which we call literature. It stands before us as "the elaborated unity of ideologies, cosmogonies, ethical-aesthetic and confessional systems as it is manifested as the structuring of a discourse" (p. 48).

> This explosive compound of values, truths, ideologies, myths and mystifications, which are mutually opposed inasmuch as they emanate from different classes and—within classes—from different social strata, nevertheless offers itself as a multifarious and contradictory comprehension of our species as a product of its history, of the present conjuncture, and of the future which it prepares for itself "on the basis of prior conditions." It has been confined in writing, it has become "tinned thought." [3:49]

Sartre's metaphor of ideas preserved like fruit in a jar implies that the product has been transformed in the process. Indeed, this is his point. Living thought is petrified and dead as it rests on the library shelves. The reader who revivifies it out of the signs on the printed page in a "guided re-creation" inevitably modifies its meaning by what he brings to it from his own psychological and sociological orientation. So much Sartre had said in *What Is Literature?* Here he adds another factor, making the original duality of writer and reader into a triune relation. The addition is the presence of the objective mind, which as an implicit totality serves as background for my reading of a particular book. This happens in two ways. First, any book refers explicitly or implicitly to the body of written knowledge that precedes and surrounds it. This is most obvious, I suppose, when there are overt references to the Bible or ancient myths or to other cultural artifacts. It is equally true when a given state of scientific achievement or social attitude is presupposed. Similarly, in reading a work of fiction, I bring to it a set of expectations and ready keys to interpretation which are derived from my acquaintance with other literature. Second, I read with the awareness that others have read and will read what I am reading. An older work comes to me already encrusted with external judgments. Even if I open a book of which—as a reviewer, for example—I have heard nothing, I know that others may get something out of it which I do not, will find interpretations which I have not found or which challenge mine, and these other readings will in turn be influenced by experience with other areas of the objective mind. Thus no reading is ever complete; the ramifications are infinite. The book is a collective, a "preserved object," a thing, which elicits subjective responses everywhere, but my relations with these other readers (save in those instances where reading is a group activity) is that of the series. Instead of uniting us, the book reveals to each one the impossibility of surmounting his own limited situation so as to grasp the totality. Sartre writes, "the Objective Mind reveals to us our finitude and compels us to regard it as a fault" (3:55). The book continues to offer me more than I can understand, more that I ought to understand. Referring to that part of culture which has been committed to writing, Sartre concludes, "the Objective Mind of a period is both the sum of the works published at a given date and the multiplicity of the totalizations effected by the contemporary readers" (3:57). Obviously, it will be filled with contradictions and opposing imperatives which every reader must somehow synthesize in his own total view of the world. Thus "the Objective Mind tells us, contradictorily but imperatively, who we are; in other words, what we have to do" (3:58).

Young persons who have chosen to become writers themselves form a special group of readers. Usually the would-be writer begins by trying to put new content into old forms. Nobody reinvents literature; he or she enters into it. If, as Sartre claims, an individual turns to writing because of some inward sense of disadaptation, he will quickly find himself at odds with established procedures. When he reads with the intention of writing, the reading is prospective (3:59). He seeks in earlier works not only helpful techniques but the sense of the public for whom he should write, the nature of aesthetic demands, the function of the writer and his position vis-à-vis society. He forms out of existing literature (*la littérature faite*) his concept of what literature should be—the literature to-be-written (*la littérature à faire*), just as any appraisal of the existing state of things suggests to us the compelling demands of a future dimly glimpsed.

The already written literature offers contradictory demands. That in itself is difficult enough. Worse than that, the collective imperatives of the objective mind may present as a command a "You ought" to which the young writer's society replies "You cannot." When this occurs, the only possible response is a neurotic solution and recourse to the unreal. Such, Sartre believes, was the situation of Flaubert's generation. To establish this point, he analyzes two sets of authors who still exerted a demand upon the budding writer in the 1840s. Together they offered contradictory definitions of literature and of the proper role of the artist; neither proposed a view which was compatible with the social situation in which the would-be writer found himself. Sartre has analyzed these contradictions as they were confronted by a person growing to maturity (1830–48) under Louis Philippe and writing during the Second Empire (1852–70).

## CHAPTER FIVE

# The Literary Tradition (La Littérature Faite)

## THE GRANDFATHERS

Sartre claims that for Flaubert's generation the French writers of the seventeenth century, *le grand siècle,* were "dead gods" or, like the shadowy figure of Ouranos behind the Olympians, they existed and were granted a position of honor, but were no longer consulted (3:67). One had studied Racine and the others at school; one rarely reread them. In the objective mind two groups of authors still lived—"the grandfathers," those of the eighteenth century, and the "elder brothers," the romantics; the second, of course, were in many ways radically opposed to the first. Sartre observes that the imperatives derived from one group frequently interfered with those of the other.

From the eighteenth century there seemed to come the imperative, "Be that writer which we were" (3:68). Sartre admits that we can hardly create a model which would fit perfectly all of this varied group of strong individuals, even if we were to exclude such partially aberrant writers as de Sade and Laclos, but he believes that in a rough sort of way we may adequately grasp the nature of the influence they exerted on the "apprentice writer" of 1850.

His models appear to be primarily Voltaire, Rousseau, and the other Encyclopedists. Sartre's critical summation is Marxist in the sense that he considers both works and author from the point of view of class interest and ideology; he is concerned also with the aesthetic—the question of style and especially the writers' concept of the function of art—and he is interested in the relation between literature and science.

Sartre says of literature in the eighteenth century that it was "negative, concrete, practical"; it fought on all sides to establish and preserve its own autonomy. In calling it negative, he has two things in mind. First, the literature was negative in that the eighteenth century adopted the critical, analytic, rational approach of contemporary science. "Science is none other than Reason itself, constitutive and constituted, not even its product but its movement. Therefore one cannot imagine the slightest opposition between it and literature" (3:68). The crack that would later split the "two cultures" was still invisible—Voltaire found it easy to present Newtonian theory to his French readers; the Philosophes produced the *Encyclopedia*. In fiction and in philosophical essays, the writers of the period sought to present the universal principles that defined and governed humanity.

> Human nature, invariable and universal, restored to the bosom of Nature: there you have the *subject* of that literature which wants to be philosophical. [3:69]

Yet these so-called Philosophes, according to Sartre, were invoking "a false synthesis." As a vestige of their childhood faith, they *believed in* nature and human nature, just as they *believed in* "natural law," which they derived from the Romans. But this vaunted unity of nature and of man-in-nature could not for long hide the discrepancy that existed between itself and the science that supposedly supported it. Under the cloak of deism, reductionist analyses of both natural phenomena and human behavior revealed an atomistic universe and showed man himself to be nothing more than "a ballet of molecules, governed externally by laws of association" (3:69).

Reason was also a negative weapon in the social sphere. "Natural law" was used as a criterion against which to measure existing inequities. Humankind was represented as naturally good but corrupted by the evils of society. Most important of all, the universal man whom the Philosophes professed to study was man as the bourgeois conceived him to be. Forging a class concept, though it was not recognized as such, this group of authors, most of whom came from bourgeois families, took itself as a universal class, identifying it with humankind. Thus in the name of impersonal universality they attacked the institutions and practices of the dominant nobility in the interests of the rising bourgeois. To the adolescent of 1840 their books issued as an imperative the demand to treat as its subject the totality of man and the world, but behind it was glimpsed a "mechanistic materialism," a corrosive acid which dissolved claims to special privileges for either particular man or mankind.

In explaining how eighteenth-century literature was "concrete," Sartre links social demands with the development of style. Since

Church and state effectively forebade direct attacks on the structure of society, writers limited themselves to denouncing them indirectly through their consequences. Pamphlets, concerned with specific issues, tracked down particular facts, carefully traced the past course of events. Literature tended to become "the critical and detailed chronicle [*récit*] of the human adventure." Its vocabulary was enlarged and, as it were, secularized. Its sacred imperative to the next century commanded: Extend literature to the domain of everyday banality without thereby violating the rules prescribed by good taste (3:72).

That this literature was "practical" follows almost as a corollary to the preceding. The social responsibility of the writer was taken for granted and constantly put into action. He put his life in danger. His specific pleas were creating, unwittingly, the fundamentals of a new ideology. "The imperative this time can be summed up as follows: Write always in such a way that your work is an act" (3:72).

Finally, eighteenth-century writers demanded the autonomy of literature. Sartre carefully points out that the authors, who frequently had their books proscribed and who occasionally found themselves in the Bastille, laid claim to the right of free thought, not as citizens but as writers. They sought to assure for *literature* "the right to fulfill its function, which is to reveal to men the pure thought of universal man regarding himself and the world" (3:72). As Sartre analyzes it, this fight for autonomy was less radical politically and more consequential in the history of literature than the Philosophes could ever have imagined. In claiming (and to some degree achieving) a right for themselves which was denied to other sectors of society, they sowed the first seeds of divorce between the writer and his public. Moreover, though in fact they contested the structures and values of their society, their plea for freedom of expression was based on a definition of literature which seemed to remove it from the daily fracas.

> Literature lays claim to its permanent autonomy inasmuch as it takes itself for Beauty, put in the service of Truth, and inasmuch as, for it, there is Truth only in the unchanging universality of the concept. [3:73][1]

Such a view of literature would appear to demand a position of noncommitment, and indeed, the writers of this period firmly believed that they held themselves aloof from all parties and factions, serving only the truth of humanity. They were mistaken, of course. Sartre argues that while they looked on themselves as spokesmen for the human race, the class that supported them regarded them as its spokesmen. To their grandchildren, the autonomy of literature was a major imperative, but for this later generation it meant the necessity of total noncommitment to anything save art itself.

The social position of the writer reflected and perhaps in turn intensified the contradiction in this literature which proclaimed itself only human, yet served the interests of the rising class. If successful, he associated freely with the nobility, even with monarchs. He ate at their tables at a time when, as Sartre points out, musicians were still served in the kitchen. Was he a traitor to his class? Sartre defends him against such a charge. Class conflicts were not clearly defined. Furthermore, his association with the aristocracy was quite in the interests of the well-to-do bourgeois, who did not want to abolish existing structures but rather to improve their own position within them. They would be content to strengthen the monarchy against some of the more powerful nobility if only the monarch would recognize them as honored and influential supporters. As for the writer, his conviction that he was writing about and for all mankind allowed him to separate the person from the office in his patron. He could love the man as a friend while deploring the injustice committed in his name. Moreover, his own reading public was split. It included the bourgeois and the already committed or persuadable aristocrats to whom he could openly address appeals for correcting injustice. But his books were read also by reactionaries, whom the writer wished to demoralize by pointing out the inadequacies of their views and the hopelessness of their feeble defense. The patrons could not always be relied upon to support the intrepid author. When they did retain him in their company, he provided good publicity. These writers, according to Sartre, were often conscious of the irony involved in their being rewarded for their denunciations of privilege by entertainment at the homes of the privileged. They were not aware that their strength and truth derived from the class from which they had sprung.

Such was this sector of the objective mind as it offered itself to the apprentice writer in the 1840s. What was his response? Ambivalence, first of all. His parents revered the eighteenth-century writers, whose excellence was officially attested. But if, as Sartre claims, one's first impulse to write stems from some sense of disadaptation, parental approval would not predispose the adolescent to make his elders' favorites his own. Even under the best of circumstances their books came to him with an air of *déjà vu* and *déjà lu*. A good writer, since he is not an imitator, will necessarily be writing to some extent against those who preceded him. So much might be said of any period. But Sartre argues that Flaubert's generation confronted "the grand-fathers" under unique circumstances. The republican sentiments of the bourgeois families were sympathetic to the older libertarian thinking. But so much had happened in the preceding century—the Revolution, the Napoleonic Wars, the uneasy restoration of first one and then another Bourbon monarchy—that no real sense of continuity remained. The apprentice writer reinterpreted the declared goals of the earlier literature even and especially when he was most attracted by them. The grandson did not recognize any more than his ancestor the falsehood imbedded in the identification of "human" and "bourgeois." Moreover, the significance of this identification was profoundly altered now that the bourgeoisie was firmly entrenched as the dominant class even if not yet formally the ruling class. Sartre shows how this change is reflected in the young writer's response to each one of the imperatives and the concept of the writer's position as these had been laid down by the prerevolutionary writers.

The ambivalence of the apprentice writer confronting the literature of the preceding century was perhaps most manifest with regard to what Sartre called its negativity; that is, its reliance on analytic, scientific reason as a critical weapon. In the hands of the Philosophes reason was a penetrating tool by which to attack the mystification inherent in arguments for special privilege or the power of the Church or the divine right of kings. Now it had become the familiar tool of the triumphant middle class, whose ideology the new writer wished to challenge. The inherited imperative demanded that reason be employed to make comprehensible the totality of man in the world, but the new science seemed to deny the possibility of any such totality. For their agnostic parents Voltaire's near-atheism was a liberation. The sons, despite being brought up nominally as Catholics, had mostly lost their faith but felt a nostalgic longing for its possibility. They blamed Voltaire for being right (3:84). This ambivalence extended to science itself. The cleavage between it and literature was now too great for a writer any longer to pass easily from one to the other, and there was felt to be a certain opposition between the two. Yet the new writers, while they might reject the conclusions of science, felt impelled to adopt its method. Unwilling to reject the notion that their task was to reveal the truth of man, yet convinced that truth was revealed by scientific rationality, their first recourse was the attempt to attain "a new rigor by a scientific use of pure imagination." They were victims, Sartre says, of the myth of "empiricism," which holds that the accumulation of observations in experience may serve as an adequate substitute for scientific experiments. Once he had raised the question of the relation between literature and truth, the apprentice found himself confronting three unacceptable solutions. (1) He might hold himself to be a specialist in human nature, whose only scientific tool was accumulated observations. But this was to rely on a false conception, for scientific truth is not attainable by passive accumulation. (2) He might try to discover objective laws of the imagination and let himself be guided by them. But this idea is clearly contradictory with the fact that art demands the totally free play of the imagination—without restrictive rules. (3) He could declare openly that the realm reserved for literature was the territory of the irrational, but this solution precluded any further claim to objective truth.

What appealed most strongly was the earlier writer's insistence on the autonomy of literature, but their descendants so altered the concept as to make it almost unrecognizable. In their defense they might have argued that they merely took what was said literally and extended it to its logical conclusion. The autonomy of literature had been justified by the author's claim to be committed to no faction or cause but solely to humanity and to truth, served by beauty. Since, as we have seen, humanity was implicitly identified with the bourgeois class, literature at that time could consistently be linked with social activism. For the writer of 1840 autonomy meant freedom from commitment to any ideology or class, including above all that class in which the writers were born. The ideal was to be without roots anywhere—a desituation which was nontemporal and extrahuman. Obviously so complete a detachment is impossible, but one way by which a writer might deceive himself into thinking he could attain it was by refusing to deal with any specific social issue. The eighteenth-century writer claimed that literature must serve all humanity. A hundred years later, in the name of this same autonomy, writers refused to serve anybody or anything. They declared that the work of authors such as Alexandre Dumas père or Eugène Sue, which either reflected the positive ideology of current society or pandered to its desire for sheer entertainment, was simply not literature. But what role was left for literature? For whom was one to write if the universal class was the despised bourgeoisie? Sartre says that for the first time in history the serious writer found himself with no public.

Sartre had listed two other characteristics of eighteenth-century literature: it was "concrete," and it was "practical." As concrete, it extended the imperative to extend the sphere of language to include all of reality but within the limits of taste. The appeal to good taste was possible since both writers and readers shared the tradition set by classicism. For their grandsons no such common tradition existed. There were languages, Sartre says, but no common language. For the most part, the taste of their bourgeois parents seemed to their sons to be either prudery or vulgarity; in short it was bad taste. The beauty of a work could no longer be judged by any standard save the laws of its own creation.

What Sartre does with regard to the practicality of the older literature is most surprising. Obviously, the new generation would not take to heart the engagement to serve its own class. Might it not have heeded its commitment to correct injustice and liberate all of humankind—specifically the new proletariat? But that would have demanded a dialectical reason which had not yet emerged. Flaubert and his friends did not read Hegel. Moreover, the specific immediacy of the "practical" works of the preceding century militated against their effectiveness in rousing the young writers to continue the battle for human rights. Whether successful or not, they had dealt with issues which by now had long been settled for better or for worse. The books took on the quality of the practico-inert. They were like things. They had brought their authors fame. But the message they now spoke was no longer "serve humanity" but "Win glory as we did." As for those literary works that smacked less of the pamphleteer, some of them—such as Voltaire's plays—were recognized to be simply poor. Voltaire's *Candide* seemed to urge retreat rather than activism. Rousseau's *Confessions* appealed because of the very neurotic traits from which its author had tried to free himself by writing.

Out of all this, Sartre tells us, a divorce came about between the writer and his public. Literature ceased to be a dual enterprise between author and reader. The book was no longer regarded as a communication but as a thing in itself addressed to no one and—ideally—separated even from its creator. The primary cause, of course, was that the apprentice confronted the demand for autonomy in literature at the very moment that he discovered that his natural public and his own place by birth were bourgeois. This entailed two corollaries.

First, the young author felt that it was imperative that he declass himself, and he believed that the position of the writer in the *ancien régime* gave him precedent. But he totally misunderstood what this position had been, and he took the effect for the cause. This was partly the fault of his predecessor. When his books won him the privilege of associating with the nobility, he thought (falsely, Sartre insists) that he had indeed been accepted as one of them. But the fact that acceptance did not make him truly one "of the blood," plus his loyalty to the interests of the class from which he came, led him to proclaim himself a member of no class save that of the human race. The second generation after him committed two errors in judging his situation. First, they failed to take into account that the free mingling with the upper class and the consequent possibility of claiming to be above all class distinctions came as the *reward* of the successful writer. In the 1840s it appeared that *déclassement* was the *necessary condition* for being a writer. Second, they did not realize that a true *déclassement* was impossible for them. On a practical basis even the semblance of being lifted out of one's class was no longer possible. To be honored for one's books now was to receive recognition from a government serving the interests of the bourgeoisie. It was to serve and to collaborate with one's class. The alternative was to speak, as Flaubert did, of the artists as forming a new nobility, the aristocrats *"du Bon Dieu."* But aside from the problem that, given God's nonexistence, such membership could be only self-bestowed, God's aristocrats could not thereby escape their class of origin. One can serve the interests of another class, out of either altruism or self-interest. In a society where class distinctions are a fact of life, it is impossible not to be affiliated somewhere. Sartre compares the writer who aimed at total detachment to Kant's dove, which wished it might fly freely without the resistance of the air (3:114). While this would be impossible in any historical period known to us, Sartre claims that the belief in the possibility of total *déclassement* led the writer of the mid-nineteenth century into a particularly glaring and painful contradiction. A century earlier an author who believed that he served all humanity was quite willing to accept payment for his service. When autonomy was later translated into the refusal to serve any interests but those of art, then to make one's pen a tool for one's livelihood was viewed as a betrayal. Still the writer must live, which meant that he must be financially independent. Whatever means was available to him—a secondary job, a state pension or sinecure, inherited rents and dividends—was in flagrant contradiction to his proclaimed autonomy. Sartre sums it up neatly.

> He can write on *everything* and in total independence (with no need to please his bourgeois public or even to publish at all) *on condition that* his thought—inasmuch as it more or less clearly expresses his position—be penetrated with bourgeois ideology. [3:105]

Ideally, he must find himself in the position which Flaubert secured for himself after the painful but fortunate tragedy of his Fall and his father's death.

Rejection of all social commitment and the refusal to write for his only real public—the bourgeois class—gradually resulted in a totally new aesthetic. To be sure, one could write for other writers, but even this was secondary. The work must itself be autonomous, addressed to no one and, insofar as possible, with no reference to the personal qualities of the person who wrote it. Language began to be viewed as independent of those who spoke it. It was "in itself and by itself. Not for the other" (3:100). Sartre illustrates his point by a reference to one of his own contemporary poets, who has taken to an extreme the view that words should "be loved for themselves more than for their meaning."

> Francis Ponge one day will show us a monkey—after our species has disappeared in some disaster—hunched over a book which he examines with his fingers without discovering how to use it. This alarmist hypothesis is never excluded in the minds of 1840: humanity is a mortal species. [3:100]

Sartre adds that in the eyes of Flaubert and his followers, so long as the apes kept the books in hothouses of the proper temperature, nothing would detract from the eternal life of the literary masterpiece. The carefully inscribed phrases would still, like a flower, breathe forth their beauty "on the desert air." By a strange reversal, freedom to serve humanity had become a rejection of the human.

## THE OLDER BROTHERS

The eighteenth-century writers occupied only one area in the sector of the objective mind that Sartre is analyzing. Their influence was intensified and in some cases blocked and deviated by a group of writers closer in time—by the highly subjective and openly partisan romantics. In many respects their values and goals were in direct opposition to those of the Philosophes.

Chronologically, the romantics might better be called uncles than brothers. But Sartre is right in suggesting that for the apprentice writer of the 1840s they seemed to stand as a buffer between him and his father. His association with them was entirely different from his acquaintance with the Philosophes. The latter resided on the shelves of the paternal library; the romantics were read alone at night in his bedroom or by a forbidden candle in the school dormitory. Parents and children might on occasion join in admiration of a work by Hugo, but for the most part, the romantics spoke neither for nor to the older generation of the bourgeoisie. The father might invoke the authority of Voltaire to support an argument at the family dinner table. He was not likely to quote the verses of Lamartine. The world of the romantics seemed to promise an escape and a liberation from the utilitarian environment in which the apprentice writer had lived his childhood. He reveled in the illusion that they expressed his own personal revolt against his surroundings.

While Sartre is concerned primarily with the French romantics (he mentions by name Hugo, Lamartine, de Vigny, Musset), he makes reference also to a few of the foreign writers who were read and admired by Flaubert and his friends—especially Goethe and Byron. And we have seen that the adolescents cherished the image of Chatterton and of Keats, perhaps more for their tragic lives than for their poetry. Sartre sets the beginning of true romanticism in France at about 1815, when Louis XVIII replaced Napoleon. As forerunner of the movement, Chateaubriand set forth the basic themes. Himself a proponent of the monarchy, Chateaubriand, in *The Genius of Christianity* expressed his aristocratic inclinations in a religious aestheticism.

> Passing lightly over questions of dogma and the real existence of the Almighty, he showed in the Christian aspiration toward the Infinite the source of the most beautiful movements of art and literature. For the first time negativity, losing its practical power of continuous corrosion, was made Negation. Beauty, born from insatisfaction, contested the real as a whole and testified to the Christian impulse toward the other world and the hidden God. Other defensive themes were energized. History reconsidered was opposed to analytic Reason; compact, indissoluble, by its regained temporality it legitimized, if not all the privileges, at least the prin-

ciple of the monarchy. The heart's reasons, restored by the beauty of style, were felicitously opposed to those of Reason. [3:107–8]

This passage combines the two themes around which Sartre develops his critical sketch of romanticism: its opposition to scientific rationality and its commitment to the nobility as opposed to the bourgeois.

Whereas the eighteenth-century writer demanded autonomy in order that he might be free to speak the whole truth (*dire tout*), the romantic laid claim to the power to express the whole (*dire le tout*). As Sartre put it, the romantic identified analytic reason with the Revolution and scorned both. Deliberately choosing the irrational, he claimed to find in reality an organicism, the presence of which he did not try to demonstrate by argument but to "prove by beauty" (3:115). This included both the natural and the human worlds, and it was based on a notion borrowed from medieval Catholicism: "that the world is an organic totality which manifests itself wholly in each of its parts." In this way it was possible both to accept a social hierarchy and to praise the excellence of the lowest class, so long as its members exemplified the particular virtues to which they were born. The romantic was doubly drawn toward assigning a higher value to the imaginary than to the real. Rejecting the scientific approach to nature, he preferred to feel at one with its heart rather than to understand its component operations. (I recall here Faust's rejection of even the vision of the great Chain of Being in favor of emotional communion with the Earth Spirit.) In addition there was a discrepancy between his ideal concept of the true nobility as he liked to imagine it might have been in the days of its power and the living nobles who had managed to regain some of their lost estates and prestige. The romantics liked to think of themselves as born at a time of disorder with a special mandate to restore a lost harmony. In France, Sartre claims, most of them were blood relatives of the dispossessed aristocrats. Some wrote in exile. Even Hugo was royalist on his mother's side. Sartre argues that what they wrote was openly a class literature—aristocratic, proroyalist, and antibourgeois. At times the notion of inherited nobility might be extended so as to include, somewhat sentimentally, the "natural nobility" discovered in certain members of the proletariat, those other victims of the bourgeoisie. The war against the dominant middle class was bitter and relentless. The romantics would have liked, Sartre says, to blast them out of existence by the works directed against them. Picking up Flaubert's witticism: "I call bourgeois whoever thinks meanly [*bassement*],"

Sartre claims that Hugo might have said, "I call aristocrat whoever thinks nobly" (3:122). Their belief that the world was naturally good led the romantics to claim a theoretical belief in the potential goodness of humanity, but this was almost forgotten in the individualistic emphasis on the distinction between the rare quality of a few noble souls and the vulgar rapacity of the majority of humankind. The typical romantic hero was lonely, isolated from normal human society; he nourished a predilection for lost causes. Self-sacrifice for an impossible ideal tended, at least in the mind of the writer, to pass into a love of failure seen as inevitable and magnificent.

Sartre finds a certain ambivalence in the Romantic's attitude toward the role of the writer. On the one hand literature became for the dispossessed nobleman a substitute for the military service he was formerly expected to offer to his sovereign. Writing was not a trade but the natural activity of a gentleman. When he does not fight, he sings (3:110). He regarded his work as a service freely offered. Although he distinguished writing from other occupations, he did not disdain payment for what he produced. At the same time, his sense of himself as the loyal supporter of an ideal harmonious order led him to regard his work as a gift; it did not serve any existing party or ideology. Literature was not intended to be useful, nor was it believed to be the product of conscious labor. Instead it welled up by a kind of divine inspiration. The romantics might proclaim themselves unbelievers, but their faith in a unified, organic whole demanded something to support it. When they wrote, Sartre claims, they relied on that creator in whom they could not believe. As Keats proclaimed, we do not need to distinguish between beauty and truth. Sartre concludes that for the romantics their deity "served to guarantee the beauty of their works as that of Descartes guaranteed truth" (3:127).

The imperative laid down by the romantics was self-contradictory. It bade the apprentice writer to continue to create beauty, but forbade him to do so since he was not born a member of the gifted elite. Or, as Sartre phrases it, the aristocratic writer, "beneath the positive idea of syntheic totality (i.e., of creation) hides two negations: The one, compensated—the victory-in-defeat of the nobility; the other unchanging and absolute—the radical condemnation of the bourgeois" (3:133–34).

If these writers were so exclusive and so hostile toward the class that read them, how did they exert so great an influence? Sartre replies that it was because they appealed to the less-well-integrated members of the middle class. The most intelligent and most numerous of their readers were women and adolescents. Both groups enjoyed a certain "suppleness of thought," the women because they were victims as well as accomplices of the society that oppressed them, the young because they were still learning about the world and not yet caught up in the business of earning a living. Among the men were a number of petty bourgeois whose interests were more intellectual than those of the wealthy industrialists and who resented the fact that the franchise was denied them and given only to those who could meet certain financial requirements. Then, too, the apprentice writer received and reinterpreted the romantic imperative to suit his own situation. To the closed circle of blood, he opposed the notion of "God's aristocrats." In the name of beauty, they aimed at portraying the world as it might have been if God had endowed it with a humanity worthy of it. For the first time, Sartre states, the imaginary "ceases to be a means of attaining the true and becomes, *against truth* the fundamental objective of literary art." As a result, "the autonomy of literature came dangerously close to being the autonomy of the imaginary" (3:129–30). The sons of the bourgeois accepted the romantics' attack upon their class but transformed it into a general misanthropy. The shift was accomplished easily since one of the things they had accepted from their own parents was the conviction that human nature is bad. Thus from the romantics they derived the idea of the gratuity of art, the antiscientific, deliberate confusion of beauty and truth, the value attached to insatisfaction, and the rejection of their own class. Of these some would evidently tend to reinforce the heritage from the writers of the previous century, others were in direct contradiction. To the objective mind in the mid-forties, Sartre believes, no rational solution was possible.

Before we look at his analysis of what he calls "the neurotic response" of Flaubert's generation of writers, we should ask whether we can accept Sartre's descriptive survey of this century and a half of literary history. Personally, I find Sartre's summation both brilliant and perverse. Clearly he is overselective. Among the influences on an aspiring writer of novels, one would expect to find some mention of the individual novelists who immediately preceded him—Constant, Stendhal, and his own older contemporary, Balzac. The discussion of the Philosophes is quite persuasive, but there were other writers in the eighteenth century who were radically different from them. Sartre does not mention the somewhat precious, graceful, and artificial Marivaux, probably because he considers him to be unworthy of notice and because Marivaux was no longer respected in the succeeding century. That is fair enough, I suppose; still, his popularity with his contemporaries was considerable. Sartre recognizes that de Sade and Laclos must be viewed as aberrant. Both were aristocrats; neither shared the Philosophes' faith in the natural goodness of human nature. Sartre inexplicably dismisses Laclos' eroticism as "superficial and well-bred" (*de bonne compagnie*) (3:83n.). Actually, there he may have given up too much. It might be argued that *Les Liaisons dangereuses* has applied quite pitilessly the weapon of negative reason and that the book helped to undermine social pretenses—despite the final conventional distributions of punishments to the evildoers. It is with Rousseau that Sartre begins to get into trouble. He admits that the *Confessions* stands apart as a highly subjective and neurotic work—though he argues that Rousseau, in contrast to nineteenth-century writers, wrote in order to rid himself of his unhealthy preoccupations rather than to make introspection an end in itself. What Sartre omits entirely is the profound influence of Rousseau on romanticism, especially in England. The fact is that, with the exception of Byron, Sartre's description fits none of the leading British romantics except in the emphasis on individual feeling, a half-mystic view of unified nature, and the devotion to the ideal of beauty. They were not aristocrats but strongly sympathetic to democratic ideals. Robert Burns represents the opposite of almost everything which Sartre said. Wordsworth hailed the birth of liberty in the French Revolution and mourned its eclipse with the advent of Napoleon. Shelley, the son of well-to-do but not noble parents, wrote socialistic political tracts. Keats, whose life and works seem almost to personify the romantic *poète maudit*, was the son of a liveryman. In Germany Goethe comes closest to fitting into the picture; even with him there is a problem. Faust rejected science, but his author wrote a scientific treatise on the nature of light and color.

Sartre might perhaps reply that, despite his occasional mention of English or German poets, he was concerned primarily with the essential qualities of romanticism in France. Here he is on much sounder ground. Hugo came more and more to glorify the common man, and he was forced into exile under Napoleon III. But if we consider only his earlier activity (his support of the relatives of Napoleon I and the son of Louis Philippe) and his literary works before 1844, what Sartre says of the romantic writers seems to apply to him. Still, one may feel that the influence of Rousseau has been

266

underestimated and reactionary political leanings overemphasized. Lamartine, for example, was of aristocratic origin and clung to a vaguely pantheistic Catholicism. His glorification of a peasant family in *Graziella* is hardly a plea for social reform. Yet his commitment to democratic politics brought him to the point where he was briefly head of the provisional government after the 1848 revolution; he was even the unsuccessful rival of Bonaparte for the presidency.

Sartre's essay in literary history is clearly incomplete, one-sided, even misleading. Is it of any value? One can see that it is perverse. If I have added that it is brilliant, this is not simply because of its verbal pyrotechnics. One may feel (I do, myself) that whatever the reality behind the fact, this is the way in which the literary tradition appealed to Flaubert. We know, for example, that it was the poetic and exotic aspects of Hugo's work that attracted him, and that he deplored rather than commended the political engagement that led to Hugo's exile. There is at no period of Flaubert's life any evidence that he was interested in the socialistic ideas of Rousseau himself or of the British poets influenced by him. Sartre's use of Marxist analysis in relating the social position of the writer to his concept of his own role as artist and his aesthetics strikes me as being especially fruitful. And while Sartre is not the first to trace the twisted and sometimes surprising patterns of influence exerted by one literary generation upon another, his discussion of how the objective mind is formed and modified is strikingly original. In my opinion, this rapid survey of a century and a half of literature as it confronted its immediate heirs reveals the dangers inherent in Sartre's method but promises rich rewards for future scholars brave enough to adopt it.

# CHAPTER SIX

## *The Neurotic Response (La Littérature à Faire)*

Sartre gives the name "Post-Romantic" to Flaubert's generation of writers, those who began writing just before the middle of the century. But this term is both too narrow and too broad for those whom he likes to call also the "Knights of Nothingness."[1] It is too narrow because Sartre believes that the concept of literature forged by them found its culmination in Mallarmé and was neither abandoned nor transformed beyond recognition until after the symbolists at the end of the century. It is too broad because at least some of Flaubert's contemporaries—the realists and naturalists—developed a quite different aesthetic. Sartre is not altogether clear as to the exact position of Flaubert himself in all this. It is implied that he anticipated the ideal of "art for art's sake" (*l'art pour l'art*); actually, Théophile Gautier had done so long before, though he did not use the specific phrase, in his preface to *Mademoiselle de Maupin* (1936). One gets the impression both that Flaubert was working out by himself an aesthetic which paralleled that of his contemporaries, responding to the same contradictions in the objective mind, and that his success with *Madam Bovary* was a primary influence on later developments. Or, in Sartre's terminology, we see in Flaubert a "singular universal," who may justly be called "the creator of the 'modern' novel" and may be said to stand "at the crossroads of all of today's literary problems" (1:8). Sartre stresses particularly the close resemblance between Flaubert and Mallarmé, suggesting that it was in the latter that Flaubert's ideas found their logical development. But he links Flaubert specifically, too, with Baudelaire, Leconte de Lisle, Gautier, and the Goncourt brothers.

The Knights of Nothingness rejected the real for the imaginary and created "the most beautiful works in the French language" on the basis of an "impossible aesthetics" (3:172). While paying tribute to their creations, Sartre disapproves of the authors' social attitudes and condemns their lives as lived in bad faith. We can best understand what he calls their "neurotic solution" if we consider it in the light of his summary of the heritage from the two preceding literary generations. Whatever the idea or attitude, we find it undergoing a transformation which makes it negative and unreal.

We may start with the notion of class. The writer in the *ancien régime* was convinced that neither God nor nature intended social inequities; he was proud of the fact that his recognized merit had won him the privilege of associating with the aristocracy. He was under the illusion, at least, that he had transcended his own class. The romantic, in contrast, was aristocrat by blood. Believing himself to be chosen of God (or at times of the proud Prince of Darkness), he despised the bourgeoisie who had preempted his privileges. From this second group, the post-romantic took over contempt for his own class. Like the older writers, he longed to rise above it, but this was impossible. The best he could do was elect himself to membership among "God's aristocrats," a distinction which was wholly imaginary and which he could never be sure of attaining.

For all three generations of writers, notions of class were bound up with the specific concept of "humanity": theoretically humankind, for the eighteenth-century author, meant all of us; practically, it was best exemplified in the natural state of the bourgeoisie. Human nature was basically *good.* The romantic would concede that potentially human nature was good, but he held that it achieved its full development only in a few noble souls; that is, in his own class. In the other classes it either was perverted or remained in embryo. The post-romantic identified humantiy with his own bourgeois class, as did his grandfather, but he joined with the romantic in despising this class. Therefore human nature was *bad.* His condemnation was doubly a self-condemnation: as a member of a hated class and as an exemplar of an inferior species.

In all three instances the notion of *le survol* (the overview) played an important part, but it changed its meaning. The older bourgeois writer who dined with his noble patron felt that he had won a vantage point above his class. Affiliated with none, at least in his own mind, he could speak for all. His subject was the universally human. The romantic, from his privileged position within a naturally superior class, felt that he could best comprehend humanity in its ideal relation with a harmonious universe. Detachment did not, for either of these writers, mean dehumanization. The Knights of

Nothingness tried to achieve a point of view which was nonhuman; they would have liked to deny their solidarity with the human race. This goal was obviously impossible except in imagination.

Closely connected with the stance of *le survol*, the ideal of autonomy underwent so radical a transformation as to reverse its meaning completely. In the eighteenth century it meant freedom to speak out on all subjects for the good of humanity; it was synonymous with "freedom of the press." The romantic claimed rather the privilege of expressing those truths about the All that are not available to scientific pursuit. To the Knights of Nothingness, it was the duty of not engaging oneself in any cause. Autonomy was claimed for the work of art rather than for the artist.

Ideas as to the function of the artist, his chances of success and failure, the possibility of his personal happiness, all changed similarly. In the eighteenth century the writer put his pen at the service of humanity. His public included both the bourgeoisie for whom he spoke and the aristocrats to whom he spoke. He was rewarded, not only by fame, but by the satisfaction of seeing tangible results from his efforts. He openly pursued happiness and frequently attained it to a significant degree—despite the hazards of imprisonment and personal disappointments. The romantic offered his work as a gift in a hopeless cause. To an extent he chose failure, but it was a failure consented to and partially compensated—by literature itself, if by nothing else, and a sense of mission. The Knights of Nothingness refused to serve anybody or anything. Their work was not even a gratuitous gift, for they acknowledged no public. They regarded their failure as inevitable but forced upon them and without compensation. Instead of the satisfaction derived from outside, as for the first group of writers, or from within, as with the romantic, they constituted themselves ahead of time as incapable of being satisfied. Insatisfaction became itself a value, but one which could be sustained only neurotically.

Finally, creative imagination was itself subject to changing status in these generations. For the first group of writers, it was closely allied to realistic praxis. Its points of departure and of arrival were the real world. As Sartre observes, even if Voltaire, in *Micromégas*, introduced a visitor from outer space, it was in order for him to criticize the institutions of eighteenth-century Europe. The romantic, too, asked that imagination point to what the world ought to be and possibly could be if the majority of men and women had been different. In addition imagination was to be enjoyed for its own sake but less as an escape than as an enrichment for this world. For the Knight of Nothingness Sartre claims that "imagination" became "a recourse against the impossible." Its function included but went beyond providing an escape from reality. Its task was to deny the real and to give being to the unreal, to reveal the superiority of Nothingness to Being and of the nonhuman to man. Beginning with Leconte de Lisle, we find the suggestion that what does not exist is superior to the existent—past over present, death over life, abstract over the concrete; in short, the imagined over the real. To understand Sartre's emphasis on this negativity, we may examine more closely his claim that the Knight of Nothingness expected, demanded, and nevertheless struggled against a triple failure: the inevitable failure of the man, of the artist, and of the work of art.

By the "failure of the artist," Sartre refers primarily to the rupture between the author and his public. This writer cannot hope for understanding and recognition from those he despises as philistines; his pessimistic view of human history as a continuous deterioration prevents him from dreaming that a more enlightened posterity will reverently transport his bones to the Panthéon. As writer he persuades himself that he can dispense with his public; as man he must live. Whether he is lucky enough to have inherited a small income or must work as teacher or office clerk, his outward life will be that of the neat, frugal petty bourgeois who carefully observes all the social restrictions so as to preserve his aloof privacy. His only compensation is to play the role of writer, making himself believe in the existence of an aristocratic elite of which he is a member though he has no evidence either of its existence or of his right to belong to it. Sartre compares his position to that of a man going into a monastic order with no fellow monks and no rules. Desperately he denies himself and plays the role of writer in an effort to convince himself that he merits being a creator of art.

Under the heading "The Failure of the Man," Sartre discusses the author's definition of the writer as a person. In part it is a general concept—the poet as prophet (*vates*) has given way to the poet under a curse (*le poète maudit*). In part it is a new self-image created and re-created in solitude by each one of the Knights of Nothingness. Its outlines are familiar to us from our observation of Flaubert and his self-projection in Jules. The gloriously successful poet, like Hugo, stood as a reproach rather than an incentive to his younger contemporaries. Uncertain of their own genius, they cherished the image of the lonely poet, still unread, striving to express the incommunicable to those with ears unworthy to hear. The writer felt himself incompetent in the affairs of ordinary life. Once again Sartre employs the image of the great-winged bird that cannot walk. The writer was eager to see in his own awkward steps the proof that some day one would soar. The artist will be found among society's failures (an obvious borrowing from Christian backgrounds).

Sartre's ironic description of the hypersensitive writer, "too great to be a man" is pure sarcasm. From the Goncourts to Mallarmé, he claims, one finds in all these Knights of Nothingness "the idea that the artist is prevented from acting by a hypersensitivity due to the extreme fragility but also the exquisite quality of his nervous system" (3:169). Since nervous sensitivity was popularly associated with women, incapable of masculine activities, it seemed to indicate a certain femininity in the writer's character. His artistic perceptions were at the expense of his virility. "The artist's failure is conceived as a feminization of literature" (3:169). A novelist may well have felt that it was this "feminine" side of himself that enabled him to draw convincing portraits of women. We have seen in Flaubert a certain nostalgia for androgyny. I believe that Gautier's heroine, Mademoiselle de Maupin, is a projection of the same kind of wish on the part of its author. Sartre makes it clear that this sense of possessing the qualities of both sexes in their own person did not induce in these writers any true empathy or even sympathy for women outside of fiction. "These feminized men, for the most part, were misogynists." They reproached women for not making the best use of their rich sensibility. Sartre cites Baudelaire: "Woman is in heat and wants to be screwed" (3:169). She seeks a practical outlet for her desires and is satisfied with normal affective attachments to people and to causes. By contrast, the artist rejects the passions and emotions that would attach him to the world and pours all his libidinal energy into his art. Although these writers were not noted for their warmth, as Sartre wryly remarks, they did not like to think they were lacking in feeling. They preferred to believe that they had renounced human passions because their youthful sufferings had been intolerably intense; that they remained only a burnt-out shell, so to speak, and that their exhausted, delicate nervous systems henceforth allowed only imaginary yearnings and satisfactions. (The parallel with Gustave after the crisis is obvious.)

The result is exemplified in Leconte de Lisle and Baudelaire; the human objects of desire and even the sexual impulse itself were split and kept strictly separate. Love, devotion, and the imaginative outreach of love were bestowed upon the inaccessible woman, sexual needs taken care of by prostitutes or a mistress. Attachment to the latter was viewed as an enslavement, a bond which prevented the artist from wholly transcending his pitiful human condition, one more form of failure. Another familiar pattern was more directly linked to the hidden love of failure. Sartre points out that the romantic at least believed in the lost cause to which he gave his life. In contrast the Knight of Nothingness pursued failure for its own sake—as a sign of his election and as proof of the world's unworthiness. Obviously he could do so only in bad faith, by the will to fail. Like Flaubert before his law books, he must wear himself out working to attain a goal which his accompanying conduct prevents him from achieving. Sarcastically, Sartre points out that he must not risk too much—not his livelihood or freedom of movement. Failure in love was the safest thing. It could be "radical and catastrophic; it is not dangerous" (3:177). We might add that it could be counted on to produce the kind of suffering that fed the imagination. The process was simple: begin by seeing the beloved woman as the vessel of the infinite, a defense against man's unquenchable insatisfaction; refuse to acknowledge one's secret knowledge that disillusion and disgust will inevitably follow; learn through suffering that the future artist is constitutionally incapable of sustaining human relations as others do. "The artist is a man too great to be a man" (3:177). We may note that while much of Sartre's description fits Flaubert almost too precisely, the analysis of sexual attachments does not. Flaubert himself did not indulge in either of the described perversions of love. He never idealized Louise; he claimed to be already beyond passion when he met her. Sartre does not explain why. On the basis of his own presentation of Flaubert, we may conclude that perhaps it was because as a child he felt already rejected by idealized Woman. Yet in his cynical enjoyment of prostitutes and his feeling that his too tender nature had been scarred and rendered insensitive by an old wound, he fits the pattern completely.

Finally Sartre speaks of "the failure of the work." Here he does not refer to the public's refusal to accept an author's book, but rather to the idea that the work of art must necessarily fail in its own purpose. Without a human public, the writer could write only for God, but the nihilism of the Knights of Nothingness forbade them to believe in him. Sartre observes wittily, "The major objective of the literature to be written [la littérature à faire] is to teach God that he doesn't exist" (3:181). It is easy to say, as Sartre does, that the writer as artist believed in the deity he denied as man. If so, then he wrote *as if* he believed, sustaining this fragile attitude by what Sartre calls "a hysterical process of distraction." I would find it more natural to think that the post-romantics simply assumed some sort of objective witness appropriate to their own *survol,* an imaginary, nonhuman, and more-than-human point of view before which the work as absolute art might be thought to stand judgment. In either case the "impossibility of art" derived in part from the work's being directed toward nobody and committed to nothing. (We may recall here Flaubert's wistful longing to write a book about nothing.) "The imaginary, positing itself as self-sufficient [*se posant pour soi*] claims to be the flower of Evil or better, Evil absolute" (3:181). Sartre has always shown a tendency to equate evil with nonbeing. Here the beautiful but negative works of the Knights of Nothingness are called evil for three reasons: first, they are radically pessimistic; they deny God and proclaim the total wretchedness of man without God. Second, this poisonous exposé of abandoned humanity is not offered out of concern for humankind but out of hatred; its intent is to injure. Finally, it fails to reach its own goal. The "diabolical image of our world" that it presents to us is in truth not our world but "the inconsistent outline of *another* universe which will never exist" (3:181–82).

Out of context one might take this last statement to mean simply that it is in the light of a false interpretation of the human situation that the artist rejects reality. Sartre would agree that the Knight of Nothingness neither knows nor understands our world; what he condemns is his own invention. But that is not Sartre's point here. In response to the contradictory imperatives of the objective mind, the writer is forced to conclude that "art is impossible." The impossibility is due to the artist's insistence on the wholly imaginary quality of the work of art. If it is appearance only, it "leaves intact what it denies" (3:181). In view of what Sartre has written elsewhere, one might object that this is not strictly true. Even the simple assertion of the superiority of the imaginary might well alter a reader's perception of his own real world. The problem, however, is less one of affecting this world than of providing support for what does not exist. How can one affirm nonbeing?

Sartre claims that this literature is wholly one of "allusion," that even in its failure the work claims to allude to a "being-beyond-being." I am reminded of Tillich's "God above the God of theism . . . who appears when God has disappeared in the anxiety of doubt."[2] Indeed, Sartre does not fail to compare the aesthetics of the Knights of Nothingness to the "negative theology which has wreaked such havoc in our century" (3:198). At least to the theologians this God is not imaginary; he is immanent as well as transcendent. The concept of "absolute art" posed three difficulties: how to account for inspiration, taste (aesthetic judgment), and the possibility of a world-beyond uncontaminated by ingredients from this world. The answer to all three was the book itself. The book-to-be-written exerts a demand upon the artist's imagination and sets up its own laws; it must be judged solely in terms of its intention. For us, Sartre says, this notion is relatively easy to grasp. ("*On forgera en forgeant.*") The nineteenth-century writer felt the need of an ideal externally supported. He took recourse in the notion of allusion; the book pointed to something beyond itself, to an imagined reality, intangible and inarticulable.

By definition such a world cannot be defined, and Sartre does not make the mistake of trying to analyze too precisely what it was in the mind of the Knight of Nothingness. Ultimately, the problem of the status of the imaginary and that of language become one and the same. Through style, by indirection, by invoking the silence between the worlds, by that which is not said but suggested, meanings are communicated which cannot be derived from or pinned down to words in their dictionary denotations. At times the being-beyond-being" seems to correspond to the world of the poem or book as it is imagined by its author. At other times it seems to be a universe of meanings and significances which are inscribed in all worldly objects and only gradually revealed by artists fragmentarily. Sartre quotes a passage from Mallarmé's *Autobiography* in which he says that there is only one Book, which every writer tries to write, but which cannot be accomplished by one person in one lifetime. Mallarmé can hope only that his completed fragment may authentically indicate the whole, that he may "prove by the portions achieved that this book exists, and that I have known what I shall not have been able to accomplish" (3:187). I think it matters little whether we think that the imaginary world at which all earthly meanings are directed was thought of as the same for all writers or different for each writer. In either case the problem is the same. The writer's task was to give real being to the imaginary, but in order to do so, he must use the materials of this world, not only its specific contents but the concrete langauge of his particular time or place. The validity of the written work depended on its perfect correspondence to the imagined work. The author could deliberately choose and associate words which would invoke connotations not spelled out in the literal sentence. But the silences between them are dangerous. Words have histories, a wealth of un-expected and unwanted connotations which can defeat the author's purpose.

This problem lies behind Flaubert's desperate struggles to find precisely the right word so that sound and sense may arouse the intended responses and only those. It is in back of the efforts of Mallarmé and of the circle of Parnassus to exclude all chance. Sartre contrasts this attitude with the praxis of the man of action, who has chance built into the very structure of his project. In the attempt to modify reality, he knows that the world in which he acts is ruled by chance. He tries, within certain predictable limits, both to fortify himself against adverse chance and to be prepared to utilize what is propitious. This is because the product at which he aims is worked-on matter (*matière œuvrée*) which "cannot appear in the midst of the world without forming infinite relations with the whole of materiality through the mediation of men and the whole of mankind through the mediation of materiality" (3:189). The artist, insofar as he succeeds in his task of negating the real, abolishes chance along with reality. Here we may see most clearly the absoluteness of *l'art absolu*. Insofar as a book or poem is successful, its inner integrity is such that meanings are strictly controlled, alluding not to the real world but the imagined world whose presence surrounds it like an all-but-tangible aura—or a shroud. Nothing may enter into its sphere from outside to disturb its integrity—or to enrich it. The ideal cannot be achieved, of course. The work of art is a failure, a wreck of the author's hopes. Sartre uses the word *naufrage* (literally, a shipwreck) in a deliberate evocation of Mallarmé, who recognized that finally "thought will not abolish chance." The writer is *inside* language, not outside or above it. To launch a book into the world is itself a hazardous venture. In his last poem, "A Throw of Dice," Mallarmé combined in one great image a shipwreck, the glorious failure of the poet, and the impossibility of an art pure of chance.

The Knight of Nothingness, "on strike" before the public (Mallarmé's term) knowingly tried to aim at the impossible. Negating the existing world in the name of absolute nothingness, he was like the jokester with the marble sugar cubes, one who is simultaneously per-petrator and victim of his own black humor. The ambivalence of failure is exploited to the hilt. In perpetual vacillation the writer moves back and forth between self-delusion (somehow the goal will be reached in spite of his knowing that it is impossible) and the conviction that failure is more noble than success ("*He is permitted to write books* on condition that the insatisfaction which produced them does not cease to denounce them and that the artist never regards them as other than allusive shipwrecks" [3:193]).

Sartre sums up this negative aesthetic and the triple failure in a passage which brings us back to the basic problem of the situation of the writer vis-à-vis the objective mind at the time Flaubert was ready to begin *Madame Bovary*.

> Depersonalization, a rupture with the real, solitude, hypostatized language, misanthropy, self-hatred, failure-conduct, quest of the impossible: these neurotic traits are only *the means of writing*—that is, of *continuing literature* in a period when far from finding his freedom in literary autonomy, the writer is alienated in it, a time when in everything written, writing is itself put into question, when the possibility of accomplishing a work is no longer to be counted on, when—faced with an undiscoverable public and con- tradictory imperatives—the foundation for Art must be sought in irrationality. [3:199–200]

Such an image of art and the aesthetic enterprise could be sustained by the struggling writer only by "a spontaneous imitation of autistic thought." If he is going to write, he must "play the role of writer." To what degree did he believe in the character he played? A man like the later Gide, Sartre remarks, might declare, "It is myself that I play." Here subjectivity and self-detachment are given their full weight. In the opposite case of Flaubert, there appears to be a perfect coinci- dence. Genius, Sartre concludes, depends on "the coincidence of the subjective and of the subjectivation proposed by the objective neurosis" (3:201). In his view, Flaubert anticipated the agony and public neurosis of his readers in his private existence. Diachron- ically, he prepared himself to satisfy the needs that *Madame Bovary* synchronically satisfied.

# CHAPTER SEVEN

# The Synchronic and the Diachronic

## THE PUBLIC NEUROSIS

To accomplish the controlling purpose of volume 3—that is, to show how Flaubert's personal "neurosis" and the demands of *l'art névrose* (art neurosis) coincide, Sartre feels he must analyze both the relation between this art and the reading public of the 1850s and Flaubert's precise situation in his society as artist and as person. The first of these tasks is almost as formidable and seemingly impossible as the aesthetic goals of the Knights of Nothingness. Sartre's intent is to unmask the dominating ideology of the period, not its public utterances but the deeply embedded attitudes that governed individual lives. His conclusions offer a series of paradoxes: he claims that the official optimism cloaked a deep-rooted misanthropic pessimism. The optimism scarcely qualified as an ideology and was not taken seriously by anyone. The pessimism gave rise to an ideology which was influential for an entire generation; a mixture of truth and self-deception, it effectively prevented the emergence of any true social self-consciousness. A few writers pandered to the official self-portrait. Some, like Dumas *fils*, provided light entertainment appropriate to a society disinclined to question itself; others were openly propagandistic. Du Camp, for example, in his *Chants modernes* praises progress, eulogizes the industrialists, boasts of the discoveries of technology, and proclaims, "The golden age is very near, perhaps we are already touching on it" (3:218). Ironically, these men who strove so diligently to please did not win the greatest acclaim. Instead, the public took to its heart and honored during their lifetime the writers who despised them, who refused to write for them, who, if they addressed themselves to anyone, had in mind only a hypothetical elect among posterity. To Flaubert, champion of the imaginary, his readers assigned the honorable title "realist." The

unreal world into which they entered by their reading they embraced
as their own, revealed by the pitiless scalpel of truth. Was it simply
ignorance and naïveté that made them so misunderstand the Knight
of Nothingness? No, Sartre replies. They misread the author's intention; they could not understand his negative aesthetic. But they were
bound to him by a common misanthropy; he revealed to them a truth
about themselves which they refused to acknowledge: their hatred
and their self-rejection.

By "ideology," Sartre explains, he does not mean "a philosophical
system, a rigorous construction—though one based on false premises"; he does not even refer to a vague but recognizable set of
loosely connected principles, ideas, to which every member of a class
would subscribe (3:222). What he has in mind is not a system of
thought but "an abstract model of thoughts." In other words, he is
speaking of a collection of unformulated presuppositions and attitudes which never in themselves form the content of what is proposed and debated, which may allow different, even antagonistic
elements to emerge within its compass, but which acts like a hidden
net to prevent all ideas from rising above its limits (3:223). Sartre's
thought here seems to me less clearly expressed than sometimes. At
times he appears to be speaking primarily of social attitudes. In this
sense, for example, we might note that within the ideological climate
of Greece in the fourth century B.C., Plato and Aristotle might design
quite different and quite radical patterns for an ideal state in which
the persons who made up the various classes would be selected by
merit rather than birth, but neither philosopher would question the
necessity and justification for classes as such or the assumption of
inborn abilities. At other times Sartre clearly refers to more than
social attitudes and would include all intellectual presuppositions.
Here a better example would be the inevitable differences in planning
for a Utopia which would precede or follow the industrial revolution.[1] In either case we are not dealing with an open *Weltanschauung* but with a subterranean, prelogical, unarticulated notion
of humanity-in-the-world. this ideology is not free of bad faith.
Sartre calls it a *"false consciousness*—this filter of thoughts—common
to all the individuals in a class, which springs from the impossibility
of their achieving a true class consciousness." The innate purpose of
the "false consciousness" is precisely to render a true consciousness
impossible (3:223).

Obviously no such ideology comes all of a piece, nor is there ever a
deliberate, concerted effort to formulate it. Yet Sartre thinks we can

both roughly date its beginnings and pinpoint the subgroup responsible for its development. This sort of task has always been entrusted to the "clerk." In medieval feudalism it was given to the clerics, in the eighteenth century to the Philosophes. After the establishment of Louis Philippe in 1830 it was up to the members of the professional class. Sartre calls them *"les capacités"* or *"les capables."* They were the doctors, lawyers, scientists, and technicians who made up the true "middle class" within the bougeoisie, below the wealthy industrialists, above the small shopowners and farmers. They formed, in fact, the greater part of Flaubert's readers. Until the events of 1846–48, which brought about the establishment first of the Second Republic and later of the Second Empire (1852), they tended to be "traitors to their class." Sartre points out that they invested their money, not in stock but in land, merging their interests insofar as possible with the ruling rather than the dominant class. At the same time they agitated for enlargement of the franchise. This might appear to be a move toward democratization, and so it doubtless seemed to them. But Sartre points out that they did not want universal franchise. They merely wished that the financial requirement of electors should be lowered by a hundred francs so as to include them; it was not the economic requirement *per se* to which they objected. This slight sense of disaffiliation within their class, coupled with their total refusal to align themselves with the workers, led them to attempt first to embrace an optimistic but self-contradictory humanism and then to abandon it after 1848 for a "black humanism" which was in reality a dehumanization. Obviously, Sartre could not hope to demonstrate that an entirely new ideology replaced the one that predated 1846. There must have been a gradual process in which barely perceptible modifications paved the way for attitudes which dominated later. Still, he insists that the decisive crystallization of the ideology, which was shared by almost everyone in the Second Republic and Empire, came as the result of the failed revolution and the accompanying massacres of 1848.

A bit misleadingly, Sartre speaks of a negative humanism in the eighteenth century which had to be transformed into a positive humanism to meet the needs of the succeeding century. By "negative" here he refers simply to the fact that the bourgeois class, subordinate in the *ancien régime*, used its concept of humanity as a critical weapon in its effort to gain power, whereas with Louis Philippe and thereafter it required an ideology which would justify the social order that it dominated. In the last stage of the Revolution the pros-

perous upper middle class wrote into the constitution of the year 3
provisions which would insure that the poor would no longer have
"the right to interfere in the affairs of the rich." Ownership replaced
birthright in determining who was to govern. Sartre quotes Boissy
d'Anglas:

> "A country governed by proprietors is in the social order." Which
> amounts to giving to the abstract concept of *human nature* a con-
> crete content which is nothing other than property. [3:213]

Clearly, this is inconsistent with the old humanism, which, based on
the premise that all men share a universally good human nature,
concluded that they are equal since nobody can be more or less a
man. For a time there were efforts at compromise. Society was
thought to be divided into two groups: those in whom full humanity
had been actualized, and those in whom it remained potentiality
only. Factual equality was replaced by theoretical equality. But all
were in theory "humanizable." That this view was wholly in bad
faith is quickly evident. Sartre points out that political leaders
blocked efforts to extend the education of the workers, arguing that
religious instruction was all that they needed. Casimir Perier represented a more pessimistic tendency. In 1831 he declared flatly, "The
workers must come to know that there is no remedy for them but
patience and resignation" (quoted, 3:215). Sartre adds that this view
denies even the hope of "learning to deserve Human Nature." Happiness is not possible for the worker on earth, but by patient endurance he may attain it in heaven. "On earth everything is bad. Let us
give up humanism and leave it to God; He will realize *elsewhere* if he
so desires the impossible equality of men" (3:216). The more
thoughtful bourgeois could not be satisfied with either of these com-
promises. If he abandoned the notion of a universal human nature,
he had no recourse against the aristocratic claim of superiority by
birth. If he continued to claim that all persons are equal and by
nature good, he could not justify the existing social structure.

The members of the dominant class needed an ideology which
would allow them to achieve an acceptable class consciousness and
would legitimize their power. The "clerk" must provide a new
humanism in the form of an ideology which would secure the rights
of property owners without demoralizing the proletariat or instilling
in it such despair that it would revolt. The ideology must hide the
shameful secret that the well-being of the bourgeois demanded the
pauperization of the workers. Above all, it must offer a view of a

manifest destiny in which all would participate. Only this might obscure the fact that "the class *interest* of the bourgeois is the *destiny* of the proletariat." Sartre defines "destiny" as he uses it here. Destiny means "to be subject to *another's will* as if to a natural catastrophe" (3:244).

The elite performed its task admirably; the events of 1848 enabled it to complete the job. From the beginning the well-being of the professional classes was intimately allied with that of bourgeois institutions. Scientists and practitioners depended on the wealthy industrialists for their livelihood. At this period, Sartre declares, science *was* bourgeois. It was by combining science with the myth of inevitable progress that *les capacités* laid the foundation for the new ideology. Superficially, this may sound like a reaffirmation of the faith of the Enlightenment, but it differed in two important respects: science became scientism, and progress was purely technological. Though greater affluence and ease of living could be expected for everyone, social structures were presumed to be permanent. The ideal, Sartre says, was to make the entire world bourgeois (*l'embourgeoisement de la terre*), but this did not entail either social equality or the abolition of private property. Scientism assumed that "man is not a *for-itself* but fundamentally an *in-itself* knowable in his objectivity and his exteriority" (3:225). In other words, subjectivity offered no obstacle to science; it was reducible to what could be studied by empirical observation; the observer or experimenter was conceived to be external to the experimental system. Only such a scientism could satisfy two basic needs which Sartre recognizes to be natural in all of us but particularly demanding in those who searched for an ideology which would simultaneously offer an inviting future and render present inequity palatable. The two needs are simply the desire to know and the wish not to know. Since the latter is never admissable in its pure form, it is disguised as that which is "already known." Human nature was presumed to be not only unchanging but thoroughly understood in its basic factors. The human world offered only insignificant unexplored areas—such as still unvisited spots at the poles or on the equator. In short, the human being is like all other beings—an organic machine, a thing whose properties have already been classified.

While this view of man is dehumanizing, it is not yet a misanthropy; many, I may add, have mistaken it for an optimism. It was the Revolution of 1848 that transformed it into "a black humanism." In the months preceding the outbreak of violence, a significant number of the liberally-inclined *capacités* had joined in agitation for

democratic reforms, had delivered public speeches calling for enlargement of the franchise. Terrified by mob action and—if Sartre is
correct—almost equally upset at the idea of a universal suffrage
which would include the uneducated and even illiterate, they supported the authorities who restored order, condoned the massacre of
the rebels, and even accepted Napoleon III with harmless grumbling.
The elite (*les capacités*) felt they had betrayed the workers who were
in theory their fellowmen; members of the upper bourgeoisie confronted the fact that their own welfare required that the proletariat be
kept at a subhuman level. Both groups believed that the lower classes
looked upon them with accusing hatred. We might more accurately
say that that they felt themselves *looked at* by the eyes of those they
had injured; Sartre uses the metaphor of the Look with all the implications of the subject-object conflict he described so vividly in
*Being and Nothingness*. Looking at those whom they sought to constitute as subhuman, they suddenly saw themselves regarded as objects of hate by the others. Unable to refute this judgment, they
turned it into self-hate, subsequently projecting it outward as a hate
of the entire human species. They had already despised the lower
classes; now contempt became active hatred. To universalize their
own self-hate was easy inasmuch as they had long been accustomed
to take themselves as the universal class. Human nature, they concluded, is congenitally and irremediably evil.

The new humanism is in reality an antihumanism. If Sartre calls it
a "black humanism," this is because it is against both God and
nature. Scientific progress has replaced the former; the ideal of the
new morality is an antiphysis. The eighteenth century's sentimental
portrayal of natural man as the "noble savage" was a logical corollary
to the belief that human nature is good. When human nature is taken
to be evil, the concept of "natural man" is inevitably altered. In the
nineteenth century he is one who lives only to serve his "natural
needs"; that is, on the level of animality. Sometimes the term held
connotations of the worst kind of snobbism; it referred to a man of
the people, an uneducated laborer or peasant. In a different context,
spoken cynically or with a snicker, it referred to what everyone of us
is under the skin, or would be if we did not struggle against our
nature.

Sartre links puritanism with the ideal of "distinction" as essential
to the new bourgeois morality, remarking that they spring from same
impulse. He notes that he is using the term "distinction" (the same
word in French as in English) in the sense that it holds in American

advertisements—"the man of distinction." It connotes a certain refinement and sophistication which mark one as having the qualities and meriting the privileges of a special class. In Flaubert's society, it distinguished one from the "natural man." Behind the value assigned to distinction was the aim to "constitute *culture* as the pure negation of *nature*" (3:251). The bourgeois hated in himself that animality which he shared perforce with the lower classes. Condemning self-indulgence in all human persons, he preached thrift, restraint, and self-sacrifice. The last was at the opposite pole from spontaneous generosity, being "both antinatural and self-tormenting" (3:248–49). In the professional elite dislike of the worker and shame at their own willingness to exploit him were inextricably bound together. Sartre's summation of this hate-inspired puritanism is worth quoting in full:

> It is the worker whom he hates in himself when, ill-treating his own body, by his dress, by the punishment inflicted on him by his clothes, by the abject ugliness of the stiff collars he imposes on himself, by the disgust inspired in him by his needs and by the repressive practices he exerts against them, he displays that exemplary self-hatred which must serve as the basis for the new humanism. The silent abhorrence which the proletariat directed at him after the June massacres and which the dictatorship perpetuates as a chronic evil of French society, this the bourgeois can internalize only as a self-hate; but by his distinguished manners, he turns this hatred back upon the worker by combatting in himself the grosser instincts of the populace. He is disgusted with himself for being hungry, sleepy, needing to urinate, etc. And thereby he tries to impose upon the working masses, by the example he gives to them, a negative cultural ethic; he seeks to arouse in them a vain aspiration to distinction as the essence of man; that is, a disgust with their own needs, which should have the effect of making them ashamed and restraining their demands. [3:251–52][2]

Self-sacrifice, even when it is secretly motivated by self-rejection, must be in the name of something. Sartre claims that the emerging ideology combined a narrow utilitarianism with a mystifying appeal to the future. It seemed both realistic and legitimate to assume that self-interest was the dominating force in every individual. Competition was taken to be the natural consequence of the Darwinian struggle for the survival of the fittest. (Sartre remarks on the extraordinary popular interest in Darwin.) "Nobody in this period understood that man is not the natural enemy of man" (3:277). There was, of course, at least lip service paid to the "general interest," but this was identified with the interest of those who controlled the economy. (In the

United States, we recall "what is good for General Motors is good for the country.") In short, interest was identified with profit; the goal of utilitarianism was productivity and accumulation. Man was called upon to sacrifice himself to his product; in the process he inevitably made himself (as Marx put it) the product of his product. In the resulting "ethic of effort; and religion without God," profit was the highest value. Sartre sums up its fundamental categorical imperative in two forms: The old maxim, "Eat to live, don't live to eat," is preserved but extended: "Eat to live, and live to defend your interests" (3:306). And more fully, "Act always in such a way that you treat the person in yourself and in the other as a means of realizing the human Thing and never as an end" (3:279). Antiphysis, the anti-human, and the artificial are blended in the structures and conduct of this society and in its ideals.

Can one accurately speak of "ideals" in such a context? It is precisely here, Sartre argues, that an enabling mystification enters in. This generation, which could not imagine that the *forms* of social and scientific systems might be transcended, which exchanged science for scientism, was nevertheless "mad about progress" (3:259). Projecting the ideal into the future disguised its materiality.[3] The discontent were urged to sacrifice themselves for the future of the species. Tribunes of the people, Sartre says, were replaced by social engineers. We see the fantastic culmination of this pattern in the work of Renan, who foresaw a society in which controlled eugenics would have produced a superrace of conscious beings to whom ordinary humans would be glad to pay the tribute due to gods. I cannot imagine a better combination of scientistic mystification and antediluvian sociology. Sartre sums up the artificiality of this soul-destroying ideology in a neat image of his own. After his life of parsimony, repression, and hard work, the faithful servant of the new humanism, at his death, has for his reward only the promise of becoming a thing completely.

> He passes wholly into the inorganic, his diabolical image has finally devoured him. At worst he will be one tessera among other tesserae; at best he will stand in the square, in bronze or chiseled stone, a *manufactured product*, exigence of the practico-inert, the passive symbol of a society whose members are merchandise and which is founded on human sacrifice. [3:294]

Quite obviously Sartre does not consider that nineteenth-century humanism is entirely dead even today.

In the society thus described we find three absolutes. Or as Sartre puts it, this religion without God provides a trinity: Profit for Profit, Science for Science, Art for Art (3:289). Sartre shows how *l'art névrose* and the objective neurosis reflect one another despite their profound differences. Finally, he brings us back to Flaubert, whose hegemony, according to Sartre, derived from the unique diachronic relation between his crisis of 1844 and the public disaster of 1848.

## Diachronic Relations

### The Artist and the Public

Sartre compares the Knight of Nothingness in relation to his public with the peacock which, while despising the jackdaw, provides him with his plumage (3:312). By his disaffiliation with his own class and by his refusal to communicate, the writer won for himself the very readers he rejected (3:333).

The origins of the artists' creed and of the "black humanism" were entirely different; their relation was diachronic. The formulation of "art for art's sake" was accomplished earlier. Most of the writers took no part in the events of 1848. Flaubert himself, happening to be at Paris in February, stood with Louis Bouilhet and watched some of the fighting around the Palais Royal. In *A Sentimental Education* he is content to proclaim all parties wrong. During the shooting Fréderic and his mistress take refuge amidst the historic treasures at Fontainebleau. Yet despite their contempt for their own class, Flaubert and his fellow writers, as we have seen, were forced to lead an outwardly bourgeois existence if they were to have the freedom to devote themselves wholly to art. Sartre maintains that despite their intention to denounce the real in favor of the imaginary, they provided precisely the point of view on the world which satisfied their readers. Flaubert in fact "created the need by satisfying it" (3:301).

Obviously, the public's acceptance was based on a misunderstanding; it was this that led them to label Flaubert a realist. But Sartre maintains that the misinterpretation of specific intentions could not have occurred if there had not been a basic truth which bound writer and reader together and which made possible a translation into equivalent meanings of terms superficially quite different. Misanthropy, of course, was this fundamental bond. In this connection Sartre at one point seems to be guilty of employing a circular argument. He states that the development of "art-neurosis" slightly predated the crystallization of the public neurosis. Yet in his discussion of the antihuman ideal underlying the cry of "art for art's sake," he tells us that a factor contributing to the artists' genocidal impulse was the prevailing notion of human nature as evil. On the other hand, he has traced with painstaking care the development of cynicism and contempt for humanity in Flaubert and his friends while they were still at the *lycée,* independent of external associations. In any case, the hatred of humanity that writers and readers shared, although Sartre would claim that it was historically conditioned on both sides, appeared in quite different psychological frameworks. The Knight of Nothingness was convinced that suffering and reflection had taught him a metaphysical nontemporal truth about the human species. The reader's hatred sprang from a specific dated event, but he did his best to deny its existence and to forget its origin. His feeling of guilt could be alleviated by the writer's proclamation that human nature was universally corrupt. His feeling of hatred seemed thereby to be transformed into a realistic acceptance of the fact that this is the way man is made. The author's impersonalism served to justify the proprietor's refusal to be concerned for those he exploited. Sartre claims that three other aspects of the authors' attitude could be similarly adapted by the reader to his own situation: impassivity, *le survol,* and the author's disdain for his public. The artist claimed to be no longer capable of passion; he despised in himself those human organic needs that could not be satisfied by the power of his imagination. This impassivity was easily compounded with the ideal of refined distinction. Detached objectivity, the metaphysical *survol,* was taken for the artistic equivalent of scientific objectivity. The impersonal narrator stood aloof from his characters as the experimenter fancied himself to be wholly outside the experimental system. (We may recall that some of the readers of *Madame Bovary* looked on the author as a technician dissecting a cadaver or wielding a scalpel.) Even the author's refusal to write for his public was made to serve the purpose of the new ideology. *In principle* it suited the "black humanism" to insist on the impossibility of human communication. *In fact,* the bourgeois felt that he could appropriate the author's message by the simple act of buying his book. Let the book, like a piece of private property, stand there with a placard, "Do Not Enter." The new possessor felt free to enjoy and to reconstruct it at will (3:310–11).

In describing how readers in the Second Empire took the Knight of Nothingness to their hearts, feeling that he "spoke to their condition" and at the same time managed to misread the message, Sartre returns to the question of the peculiar bond that unites the creator and the reader of any work of fiction; this time he explores in particular the possibilities it offers to one who reads in bad faith. To read fiction, Sartre says, is to participate in a "guided creation." One must use one's own imagination to construct the fictional world, but the words there on the page provide a certain objectivity. Even when author and reader are fully in accord, there is an ambivalence. Insofar as a person "falls under the spell of reading," he is like one "possessed," compelled to experience the world according to the terms set up by an Other. Still, reading remains a free enterprise; it depends on the reader to create a world out of what will otherwise remain only black marks on a sheet of paper. In Flaubert's time, Sartre claims, the reader lived his own hatred in re-creating the hate-inspired view of the world inscribed on the pages created by the Knights of Nothingness.

> The reader makes himself, openly and freely, *the man of* hate . . . in joy and terror *in order to be able* to constitute his fellowman into a man *hate-filled and hated* [*homme-haïneux-haï*] and thus to be given every reason to assassinate him. [3:326–27]

These works were not read without shock and scandal. The revelation of man as hateful, hating, and self-hating disclosed as well the secret that no true humanism can be erected on a foundation of the hatred of humankind (3:314). Still, the people championed Flaubert against the government's prosecutor. How could they both condemn and praise? First, Sartre says, it was because they could retreat into the view that the realm of literature is only *doxa*; it is neither true nor false, only appearance and opinion. At most, a book merely expresses the view of its author. The reader, after following the creator's lead to the last page, can then politely disclaim all responsibility. "It's only literature," he can say, thus relegating the book to the sphere of light entertainment, comparable, as Sartre puts it, to the chatter of cocktail conversation, talk which says nothing (3:301). In this way the reader could assuage his hate and keep it alive while denying that it was what he lived by. Even to the extent that he did allow himself to see his own portrait in the novel, he could find a source of comfort in the writer's universal denunciation of humanity. Though Sartre does not make the connection explicit, he seems to point to the same psychological process that he analyzed apropos of the boy's final response to the Garçon. The literature was by intent injurious. But Sartre observes that the acceptance of a mechanical universe without immanent or transcendent teleology does not by itself lead to moral nihilism. Aside from the possibility of working out a purely humanistic ethics, one might conclude that in such a universe the categories of good and evil simply do not apply. Such was not the conclusion of Flaubert and his confrères.

> When the Knights of Nothingness claim to refuse every norm save that of the Beautiful, they lie. Their enterprise is entirely *moral;* a black, sadistic puritanism exalts them. They preserve its ethical imperatives to the extent that these permit them to consign their fellowmen to Hell; but they reject the imperatives to the extent that a moral law founded on "You ought, therefore you can" could include within it reasons for hope, could return to man his reality as an agent, could permit him even to postulate the existence of an undemonstrable transcendent which by the same stroke would have given him commands and the means to execute them. . . . "You ought, therefore you cannot." Such is the keystone of this satanic morality whose explicit intention is to reduce to despair. [3:319–20]

Such was the intent. But it is doubtful that many of those who read the works of the Knights of Nothingness were personally demoralized. We will consider the more typical response when we examine Sartre's interpretation of *Madame Bovary*.

## Flaubert as Prophet

Sartre maintains that, "A man, whoever he is, totalizes his period to the exact degree that he is totalized by it." Yet he complains that the notion that the writer expresses his age has been oversimplified, especially by Marxist critics. The difficulty stems from the fact that humanity as such "does not exist and does not respond diachronically to any concept; what does exist is an infinite series whose law is recurrence, defined precisely in these terms: man is the son of man" (3:436–37). History must deal with broken sequences because of the discontinuity of finite lives. Strictly speaking, there is no clearly defined generation; one does not move directly from father to son but within a continuum of older and younger uncles, aunts, cousins, siblings, and children. History is finite because those who make it do so "in the perspective of its finitude (and their own) even if they claim to work for Eternity."

At this point Sartre pauses to express some interesting reflections on our finitude. The statement, "All men are mortal," he calls "a purely inductive proposition," one which truly applies only to our ancestors and ourselves. Since there has never been an exception, we tend to make of it a law for all time; but strictly speaking, it does not necessarily apply to all of the future. Our manipulation of nature could conceivably make of death a possibility rather than something inevitable. Following this remark, atypical though consistent with Sartre's open-ended view of human nature, he emphasizes that now as in the past, every human life includes death in its own definition and is an enterprise against it. A Flaubert, who dreams of literary immortality, may struggle to insure that future generations may preserve his work by making use of it (*la servant* [*en s'en servant*]). "The work but not the man. The work at the expense of the man." Like an epitaph (3:438). Other persons will struggle to initiate changes in the social structure for the good of humanity and will hope to live on in their projects. They face two alternatives, each of which underscores the agent's own finitude. If he tries to safeguard his creation by fortifying it against future changes, his work will at best endure as an anachronistic survival, already dead, until history sweeps it away completely. If he deliberately plans for it to remain as a living set of possibilities for others, the product will soon be unrecognizable as his.

Sartre introduces another, more original notion, which adds to the complexity of interpreting the relation between a writer and his period and which is of major importance with respect to Flaubert. This is the concept of "microtemporalization," which Sartre links with that of the "programmation" of a life. If we postulate, as Sartre does, that the social and material forces (i.e., the objective mind) exercise the same conditioning on the individual and on the society at large, this does not mean that the maturation in both will necessarily develop at the same tempo. "There is no reason in fact for the catastrophe of the microcosm and that of the social macrocosm to take place at the same moment" (3:440). It is possible that an individual may realize within himself a synthesis of responses to opposing elements of his situation by a process which resembles that which is taking place in society, comparable in every respect except speed (3:431). The individual may anticipate by several years, as if by a "shortcut," a totalization which in society has not come to its full term, thus "transforming a life into an oracle."

It is this kind of diachronic relation that Sartre would establish between Flaubert's crisis in 1844 and the adventure lived by the whole country in 1848. To support this claim, he must first convince us that Flaubert's solution of his family problems and his concept of the kind of artist he would be are not only connected but essentially one and the same. Gustave, who chose to retreat to the level of subhumanity in order that as the failed son he might enjoy the benefits of an artificially protracted adolescence, is inseparable from the Flaubert who had chosen to demonstrate in his writing the impossibility of man and of literature. At this point in the biography Sartre seems to have demonstrated their reciprocal reinforcement.

Everyone in France, Sartre says, had a rendezvous in 1848. Flaubert missed his (3:427–28). The decision against political involvement had been made long ago. The giant guffawed at the battles of men. The artist who survived the man did not share human aspirations. Gustave's battle on that night in January 1844 was not overtly political though we have seen that it expressed in its own way a class consciousness. If Sartre claims that it anticipated the events of 1848, the parallel lies in the consequences, not in the conflict itself. Gustave won his freedom by an act which seemed to designate that he had failed. Belief, self-loathing and guilt were inextricably intertwined. Gradually, the negative aspects were absorbed in the view that the Fall represented the sacrifice of all for art. The victors of 1848—at least the elite (*les capables* or *les capacités*)—similarly saw their liberation linked with the failure of the ideal they had supported; their shame at having betrayed the lower classes, supported by the look of hatred in the victims' eyes, filled them with self-disgust and a general misanthropy. As Gustave chose bourgeois security to enable him to escape a bourgeois career, so the elite resigned itself to an unjust society for the sake of peace and order. Gustave would sacrifice the man for the artist. The shamefaced victors would sacrifice living persons for the future of humanity. The values of the new art were ready to be incorporated into the emergent ideology almost unchanged—noncommunication and the solitude of the artist, failure compensated by derealization, the detached nontemporal point of view, a nihilism which might be readily interpreted as an acceptance of the status quo since all action ended in defeat and the corrupt nature of man left no hope of noble causes worth the stuggle. If Flaubert's family situation and protohistory and the external political events led Gustave and the French nation to their respective violent crises, externally different yet comparable, this is because the same fundamental contradictions were lived by all. Flaubert anticipated the public totalization in his own "microtemporalization."

We may grasp Sartre's point more fully and more easily by examining his notion of "programmation." He speaks of "a life program" as something which both includes and goes beyond his old idea of the "basic project," that lived choice of being or way of being which each person *is*. In referring to the "program" of Flaubert's life, he includes both the "constitution" of Gustave which has come to him from his protohistory, and the crystallized choice of his way of being, which assumed its final form following the night of Pont-l'Evêque. But the project that *is* the person Flaubert *is* also the "singular universal," the human organism that has internalized the objective mind and social pressures of a particular period and reobjectified them in his conduct. The program of this individual life will be congruent with its society so long as its totalization or synthesis, its way of being, is synchronic with that established by society as a whole—or its dominant members. Sartre's view is that Flaubert's "life program" was synchronic in only one of its three periods; that is, during the years of the Second Empire. In the last part of the reign of Louis Philippe he was "ahead of his life"; after the fall of Napoleon III, he "outlived himself." It is from this point of view, Sartre argues, that we may correctly say that someone dies "too early" or "too late," not absolutely but in terms of his "program."

Sartre sums up his thought on programmation in one of his more colorful passages.

> There are some lives which burn like nylon and others like candles, still others like a piece of coal which is slowly extinguished beneath the ashes. What counts in every case for those which are diachronically significant as retotalizing, is that whether short or long, rapid or slow, they are the period itself, from one end to the other, summed up in a program. The consequence is that the period can be completed in an individual well in advance of its reaching its end socially. For this reason even short lives may be oracular; in them the age has chosen to reveal *in reality* its meaning and the circumstances of its future abolishment. [3:442–43]

In this passage Sartre seems to say that some lives are more significant than others in summing up an age or in manifesting its qualities to contemporaries. Why was it specifically Flaubert who satisfied the needs of the new ideology even before it was formulated? Sartre attempts to answer this by a brief but fairly comprehensive comparison of Flaubert and Leconte de Lisle. The pairing of the two comes up naturally. The poetry of Leconte de Lisle certainly seems to qualify him as one of the Knights of Nothingness. Moreover, he fought in 1848 on the side of the Republicans, and thereafter, disillusioned, retreated from political life. Would it not have been more natural for the French readers to have preferred someone who had lived these events through with them? Whatever the historian may say, is not a synchronic witness more intimately allied with his contemporaries and therefore more persuasive?

Sartre's response, which in its richness and complexity merits more consideration than I can spare here, shows that Leconte de Lisle's own life program was such that despite all appearances he was not—save in actual calendar date—living the events of 1848 synchronically with his companions. He was raised on his father's estate on the remote island of Réunion, where slavery was still permissible. His family situation bore a certain resemblance to that of Flaubert in that the father was an army surgeon who married above his station. But, unlike Achille-Cléophas, who earned his respected position as one of the leading citizens of Rouen by the exercise of his profession, the father of Leconte de Lisle used the money he had earned in Napoleon's army to sail to Réunion, where, aided by his wife's name, he bought up land and established himself as if one of the nobility. Sartre speculates that if the son had not somehow lacked love, he would have accepted the inequalities in his surroundings as facts of nature. Some kind of Oedipal situation led him to revolt. Distance had effected an ideological time lag. The radical ideas that stirred the heart of the rebellious adolescent were still the revolutionary ideals of 1789. In sharp contrast to Gustave, he judged and condemned his family through the lens of bourgeois reason. We know that when in Paris Leconte de Lisle fought on the side of the people in 1848 and then later comfortably accepted a pension from the government set up in the wake of the failed revolt. He boasted that he had never sold his pen to support any cause. (Sartre remarks that a writer is paid also for his silence [3:413].) Seeking to explain the change in him, Sartre suggests that he was already disillusioned by the discrepancy between his youthful ideals of social reform and the real demands of the revolutionaries in Paris. It is one thing to free the slaves, another to have the faith in all people that would allow universal suffrage. The trouble, Sartre shrewdly suggests, was that there were not enough blacks in Paris. Trying to identify their needs with those of the workers led only to confusion. De Lisle would have been willing to grant the workers the right to vote if they were to be guided by their masters. He could not understand the dissatisfaction that led them to demand the right to work. A sense of honor, the belief that he was fighting for an ideal, led him to take part in the battle. At a deeper level it meant to him the freeing of the slaves at Réunion from the white tyranny symbolized by his father. When it was over, he felt that he had won an honorable discharge. The failure of the revolt, Sartre claims, gave him the excuse for pessimism; in reality he had lost nothing that he wanted. His despair was fake.

Leconte de Lisle was not himself neurotic, he was only formally one of the Knights of Nothingness. Yet his poetry displayed all the characteristics of *l'art névrose,* as Sartre convincingly demonstrates with abundant quotations. Misanthropy is certainly present, but it is different from Flaubert's metaphysical genocide. The good of humanity serves as a vague ideal for a distant future. Humanity at present is presented as a pyramidal hierarchy with the workers at the bottom. It is the lofty duty of the demigod aristocrat to stoop to lead his brothers upward—very slowly. Though Sartre does not mention it, this view of a humanity still potential in the lowest members of the species is reminiscent of the thought of the elite as he described it for the period just before the popular revolution. In other respects the poems are the quintessence of what later became known as Parnassan poetry. The impersonal, nonhuman *survol,* the point of view of eternity, leads to total nihilism. Action is pretense and illusion. Beauty is linked with death. The beautiful is that which does not exist. The unity of nature is not pantheism but pure emptiness. If the ancient world is seen to be more beautiful than our own, this is because it no longer exists. Sartre quotes, "The final Nothingness of all things is the unique reason for their reality" (3:373). Man's nobility is measured by his desire for what cannot be fulfilled, his unworthiness by his insistence on attainable satisfactions. Leconte de Lisle, Sartre says, was one of the first of the Knights of Nothingness to accomodate both of these aspects of humanity by recourse to the "double Eros." The wife became the angel-ideal, pure of all sexual feeling in herself and not acknowledged as the object of her husband's sexual desires; the mistress was "the beast" to whom he was goaded by his animal desires. Sartre recognizes in all this a very real misogyny, allied with but separate from a general misanthropy. It was not, he feels, as deep as Flaubert's. Possibly it was a bit less inhuman. Sartre notes that Flaubert laughed at Lisle for his refusal to visit prostitutes because they were purchased, like slaves. For himself, Flaubert objected only that his paltry finances restricted him to cheap ones (3:370).

In the middle of the century Leconte de Lisle had a clique of devoted followers but never won the public acclaim enjoyed by Flaubert. His real popularity, Sartre points out, commenced about 1875, the point at which Flaubert was regarding himself as a fossil left stranded in a world alien to him. From then on Leconte de Lisle was recognized as the first of the Parnassans.

One is inevitably struck with the feeling that there is something a little odd in Sartre's reconstruction of literary history. He claims that it is Flaubert who expressed the hidden truth of his readers' attitude toward life and that this is why they read and recognized him as one of their own, despite their false labeling of him as a realist. At the same time his claim that Flaubert stood "at the crossroads of modern literature" is based on the premise that his aesthetic and his view of the relation between reality and imagination found their logical development and culmination in the Parnassan poets and Mallarmé. Leconte de Lisle was the leader of the Parnassans. His poems have all the qualities of *l'art névrose;* they express the same world outlook as we find in Flaubert. Why then was his acceptance by a larger literary circle so long delayed? Sartre claims it was because the reading public in the Second Empire sensed that his pose as poet was not the true expression of the man, that his pessimism and misanthropy were, if not insincere, at least different in origin from their own. Even if they took him on his own terms, he was a dubious witness. His disillusion was dated, and this rendered him doubly suspect: he had fought on the wrong side; therefore he did not share their guilt. And he reminded them of the event they wanted to forget. What they needed was someone to assure them of their ontological, not their historical, culpability, someone who might "by utterly condemning *man* acquit the *men* of '48, even the murderers, of all particular responsibility. Guilty, of course, without forgiveness. But guilty *by nature*" (3:418–419).

In my opinion, Sartre's theory may have some validity in explaining the delay in the wholehearted acceptance of Leconte de Lisle. But it seems to me that there is a much more obvious explanation as to why Flaubert's novels and not Leconte de Lisle's poems were received so enthusiastically by readers in the fifties. I do not refer simply to the fact that novels are easier for the average layman, and it is not necessarily true that they offer greater possibilities for empathy. Lyric poetry, in particular, is capable of arousing a subjective identification of writer and reader. The essential point, I think, is not that Flaubert's books were better liked but that they could be misinterpreted. To my knowledge, nobody has ever called Leconte de Lisle a realist. Neurotic, and self-tormenting, hate-filled, and guilt-ridden—all these the average bourgeois may have been. But he was also, as Sartre has reminded us, one who believed passionately in science (or scientism) as a key to the future. He was practical and impatient with fantasies. If he dehumanized himself, it was in the interest of the concrete. He was not one to welcome the message that truth and beauty are only in the realm of the nonexistent or the imaginary, or that where everything is *maya,* the poem is as real as our material action. If Flaubert simultaneously satisfied both the hidden neurotic needs of his readers and their everyday practicality, this was because his overt subject-matter and superficial technique (the famous clinical analysis) were easily discernible whereas the aesthetic intention and the style, the subtle use of self-destructive language were not. To the public it seemed that the author of *Madame Bovary* was indeed portraying their own cruel, hateful world. Women tended to identify with Emma. (This was at least in part, Sartre claims, because they hated their husbands.) But if they felt, "Madame Bovary, c'est moi," they might easily add, "And there but for the grace of God go I." Even the usually perspicacious Henry James found that the novel "would make the most useful of Sunday-school tracts." He declared, "Realism seems to us with *Madame Bovary* to have said its last word."[4]

Throughout all this the author's cynicism and rejection of humanity were *felt* (Sartre might say, comprehended) rather than *known* by his readers. To the degree that one sensed the beauty of the work, this added a certain consolation to the tragic view that "life is like that" and "nothing can be done about it." Perhaps the strongest aspect of Flaubert's position at "the crossroads of modern literature" is that his influence was extended down both forks of the crossing. A superficial reading of *Madame Bovary* earned for him the unwelcome honor of being considered the father of realism, the grandfather of naturalism. In the history of literary influences the title is merited, however mistakenly it was first applied. The true line of descent, of course, proclaims Mallarmé as Flaubert's heir—spiritually and aesthetically. Recent structuralist critics have claimed that only now are we able to realize the profundity of Flaubert's concept of the function of language in imaginative literature.

In conclusion I may add that while Sartre's comparison of Flaubert and Leconte de Lisle seems to me not to accomplish quite what he claims for it, I find the encapsulated study valuable on two accounts:

first, brief as it is, the essay offers apropos of Leconte de Lisle an additional and important illustration of diachronic relations between a man and his society and indicates forcefully the complexity of the problem we confront in trying to find in an author's writing the expression of his period. Second, it is helpful to have Sartre's careful analysis of the qualities of *l'art névrose* as exhibited in the poems of a second Knight of Nothingness. Without this documentation one might be tempted to wonder whether in fact Sartre's description applied fully only to Flaubert. As it is, we have a neat demonstration of at least two responses to the objective mind which show a harmony of basic qualities in spite of the radical difference between the authors, their backgrounds, and the formal qualities of the written texts.

## THE END OF THE PROGRAM

The final section of *The Family Idiot*, "Neurosis and Programmation in Flaubert: The Second Empire," while still far removed from the sort of complete informative narration customary in biographies, at least resumes the outward form of a biographical study, which Sartre had suspended for the first two-thirds of the third volume. It is concerned with the years after the publication of *Madame Bovary*, particularly with the "liberal period" of Napoleon III (1861–70). Sartre proposes a specific thesis which he attempts to prove. In essence it is this: Flaubert's relations with the Second Empire were wholly synchronic. During the last nine years under Napoleon III he was as happy as he was capable of being. The overthrow of the Empire on September 4, 1870 killed Flaubert. "He is dead-while-alive, fossilized. He lives on for ten years; but it is a long agony, he feels himself alien to the world which surrounds him" (3:447).

In support of his position Sartre has to demonstrate ways in which Flaubert's conduct belied his verbal statements as well as to show inconsistencies in his correspondence. This is particularly true with respect to Flaubert's attitude toward Bonaparte himself. He made many slighting remarks about the emperor. After his fall, Flaubert remarked to Zola that Napoleon was "stupid"; he concluded that the years of the Empire had been "a long lie." This was after the event. His real reproach of the emperor, Sartre argues, is that he foolishly initiated the war and then lost it; in other words, his fault lay not in having established the Empire but in not having been able to sustain it during Flaubert's lifetime. As for its having been false, this, Sartre claims, is what Flaubert had found so fascinating. To mingle in the circles of such a court was to live as if in an opera, and as such it offered a particular appeal to the "champion of the imaginary."

During the early repressive period Flaubert was displeased by Napolean III's policy of allying himself with the Church. He declared that he would never forgive the government for subjecting him to the ignominious trial concerning *Madame Bovary*. Sartre argues that in both instances he sought to blame the ministers rather than the emperor himself and to see him as "the prisoner of his majority." In 1862 Flaubert was invited to the home of Bonapart'e cousin, Princess Mathilde, on an evening when the emperor and empress were to be present. From that time on he was regularly received in court circles, and he clearly gloried in it—to the extent that the Goncourt brothers mildly reproached him for showing himself too much a supporter of Napoleon III. One would not expect Flaubert to be wholeheartedly in favor of any social system, and indeed he continued to delight in examples of human baseness wherever they came from. But Sartre maintains that Flaubert could enjoy pointing out the evils and stupidity of officialdom while at the same time finding this the only society "in which Jules might feel at home." His misanthropy found an outlet in the ironic reflection that Napoleon III was exactly what the French nation deserved. Sartre goes so far as to claim that in him Flaubert tried to see a Nero, in whose exploits Gustave had reveled in the sadistic reveries of his adolescence. Bonaparte was also a "buffoon," a version of the Garçon, a demoralizer. And he was the man without genius, who won his position by hard effort—by Buffon's "long patience." Sartre hints that perhaps here Flaubert even saw a certain parallel with himself. Flaubert accepted the Cross of the Legion of Honor in 1866; that in his mind it symbolized his being made one of the emperor's knights is indicated by his refusing to wear it for a time after the latter's defeat.

It is easy to understand how Flaubert—or any writer—would enjoy being a lion and mingling with the leaders of society at parties which included other distinguished artists and intellectuals. I think Sartre perhaps is a bit unfair in saying that Princess Mathilde was the agent through whom Napolean III "bought" Flaubert. (It is not only Democrats who accept dinner invitations to the White House of a Democratic president.) Yet Flaubert's feeling that it was the end of everything good when the Empire fell seems to indicate that it had been the period during which he came into his own or, as Sartre puts it, found that his own "programmation" and society's were in full harmony. There were other reasons besides the ideological agreement we have already noted. Sartre points out that during the eight years when Flaubert was regularly received by Princess Mathilde, he finally seemed to have achieved a sense of *déclassement;* even more he was, as it were, ennobled. During the three months he spent annually in Paris, it seemed to him that he, as "the great writer," was acknowledged as "one of God's aristocrats" by the court of Napoleon III. The fact that so many of these aristocrats were not nobles of ancient bloodline made it easier to feel that he was on an equal footing with them. A certain amount of derealization was necessary to take any of it seriously, but this time Flaubert's imagination was reinforced by the collective image. Sartre elaborates on the fact that Flaubert and the Goncourt brothers were especially fond of referring to Mathilde as *"our* Princess." The pronoun expressed not only affection but the implied awareness that it was their willingness to see her as a princess that allowed her to be one.

It was the war with Prussia that brought the Second Empire to an end in 1870. Flaubert felt it was impossible to hate the Prussians enough; he declared that now at last he had become a patriot. Sartre takes all of this with a grain of salt or at least feels that we must put it in proper perspective. Flaubert did indeed resent the Prussians, particularly when they temporarily quartered themselves at his own Croisset. But he found he could blot their presence from his mind when he returned to find his possessions intact. What he really blamed them for was that they brought the old way of life to an end and ushered in a new age from which he felt estranged. His praise of the Parisians during the siege is balanced, at least in Sartre's eyes, by violent wishes that the whole capital might be burnt to the ground and by complaints against the Communards ("those mad dogs") and all who participated in what Flaubert considered the leveling process involved in setting up the constitution of the Third Republic. What is perhaps most significant, Flaubert himself drew a parallel between the events of June 1848 and the troubled months of 1871, as though the coup of December 1848, which put Napoleon in power, had provided a temporary respite before the ultimate collapse of French society. Sartre points out that Flaubert missed his rendezvous in 1848 because he was preoccupied with his own private affairs. The only specific expression of concern which we find in his correspondence is limited to two sentences: "I do not know whether the new form of government and the social state which will follow from it will be favorable to Art. That is a question."[5] This was in March, 1848. When the Goncourt brothers saw him in June of 1871, they recorded in their journal that he was still the same old Flaubert—"Literature before all" (3:539).[6] But while he was never what one might call politically aware, the Second Empire provided for him as artist the most favorable environment.

It is not my intention to try to establish the degree of correctness in Sartre's interpretation of each piece of evidence he introduces. Instead I should like to comment on four special points he brings up: the recurrence of psychosomatic reactions in Flaubert, a phenomenological sketch of mourning (or fidelity to one deceased), some remarks on the "banality of evil," and a final discussion of the interplay of reality and imagination in Flaubert. We may then conclude our discussion of the writer in situation with consideration of Sartre's claim that by juxtaposing Flaubert's private crisis in 1844 with his response to the public disasters in 1870, we may see clearly how the two lines of conditioning have come together.

*The Psychosomatic.* In the early days of the Franco-Prussian War, Flaubert, exasperated by the combination of bellicoseness and insouciance that he saw around him, wrote, "My compatriots make me want to vomit." Sartre claims that this wish was "somatized after the defeat" (3:471). In a letter to Dr. Cloquet in May 1871, Flaubert wrote, "I very nearly *died of sorrow* [*chagrin*] this winter. Nobody, I believe, was more distressed than I was. For two months I even believed I had a stomach cancer, for I had vomiting spells almost every day" (*Corr.* 4:239). Evidently, he felt that worries over recent events had precipitated in a cancer. A visit to a physician reassured him. Still, the vomitings were real. Sartre designates them, "Gustave's somatic reaction to the events. They express a refusal" (3:495). He finds in them a parallel to the reactions of certain pregnant women whose extreme and incurable nausea expresses their psychological rejection of their situation. As with many of the women, Flaubert's disgust is directed against others and the objective situation but is in part also a self-rejection. Flaubert wrote to Feydeau, "I have never had such a colossal disgust for people. I would like to drown humanity in my vomit" (quoted, 3:495–96). The imagined ulcer, Sartre says, is the result of Flaubert's internalization of September 4. The world is killing him. "The Republic is not only an external transformation of the environment." It eats him away from within. In revenge he tries to vomit himself out on the enemy. But if it is himself he vomits up, this is because he also feels guilty for having enjoyed and been an accomplice of the regime that has brought him to today's dust and ashes. He rejects both the fossil he sees himself as becoming and the deluded man who had not foreseen the outcome. He refuses his total situation. The vomitings were never explained by any physiological cause. The psychosomatic interpretation is so obvious as hardly to deserve mention. I have drawn it to our attention because it seems to me one more bit of evidence to support Sartre's claim that the more dramatic seizures of the mid-forties were also hysterical in origin. This time the body did not not cooperate to save the situation but expressed rather an utter hopelessness.

*Fidelity to the Deceased.* Refusal of the present may also take the form of clinging to the past. Flaubert did not sentimentalize or mentally reconstruct the Second Empire so as to bestow upon it a beauty it had never had in actuality. That transfiguration he reserved for his childhood. Yet he did regard the Prussian victory as marking the end of Latin culture, and he refused to be consoled. Sartre quotes a number of passages, of which the following are typical, "What agonizes me . . . is the conviction that we are entering into a hideous world from which the Latins will be excluded. Every elegance, even material, is finished for a long time." "A mandarin like me no longer has his reason for being." "Whatever happens, everything which I loved is lost." "When any hope does come to me, I try to repress it." "I roll and settle into my sorrow like a boat which *subsides* into the sea." "I am like Rachel: 'I do not want to be comforted.' I shall try to habituate myself to fixed despair" (3:495–98). This cultivation of grief with a refusal of consolation inspires Sartre to offer a brief phenomenological description of prolonged mourning or extreme fidelity to one deceased.

Sartre has always held that emotional conduct is purposeful. His early treatise on the emotions included a brief discussion of how sadness over a loss may take the form of conduct designed to resist any possibility of taking up new projects or continuing old ones in the changed structure of one's "life world."[7] Now Sartre begins his "phenomenological description" of prolonged mourning with the example of a bereaved spouse: A widow is inconsolable when she does not wish to be consoled" (3:500). At first her grief is the painful consciousness of a lack, an emptiness in her life. But this purely negative grief enfolds a positive intention of fidelity, which is addressed to the dead man, of course, but which takes the form of loyalty to a self which she has been. The bereaved wills not to become other than she has been. Suddenly shifting to the masculine pronoun, Sartre writes, "The widower will decide, therefore, that his life stopped at the death of his wife, which implies these two contradictory determinations: I will never again be the man I was (while my wife was alive); I will never be *other* (than what I am at present)" (3:500–501). What is willed to be prolonged indefinitely is not the past married life "but a certain state of widowhood with respect to that life." The resolution entails inevitably a double failure. First, the intention to continue to recall the past with all its vividness necessarily fails. This, one might say, is because memory fades, it abstracts and stereotypes and is incapable of protecting the purity of the past from present imagining. Sartre states the same thing rather differently, that failure is due to the fact that even the object recollected is revealed as an absence until finally absence itself, with its aura of disappointment, becomes the focus of the mourning consciousness. Second, the whole previous life takes on the tinge of failure since it must be viewed as leading to the ultimate shipwreck. In exchange the mourner has for consolation only "a feeling of lofty ontological dignity; that is, of immutability." Sometimes (Sartre would not malign genuine love and grief by saying "always") the time comes when it is only the self-image to which one is faithful; or at least, we might say, it is only that which still prevents any possibility of change. We may note that in those rare instances where death has been falsely reported, the bereaved has sometimes found the return of the beloved as difficult to adjust to as any new possibility.

In the case of Flaubert, Sartre observes that the refusal to countenance further change in himself is nothing new. We saw it manifested under different circumstances in the early months of 1844. In the sixties, content as he was with his own situation, he was never wholly under an illusion as to the worth of the Second Empire, but he was certain of his dislike of what followed and with the future that he foresaw. Its decline marked the end of the best he had known; hence it cast a certain grandeur over what had gone forever. His fidelity was less to Napoleon III and to imperial society than to their failure; that is, to the "moment of truth when an entire reign is totalized in a tragic, merited downfall" (3:505). Though Sartre does not make the explicit comparison, one might say that Flaubert is like the widower for whom the fact of death by itself lends stature to the deceased and renders him/her worthy of a life of mourning. Sartre carefully distinguishes between Flaubert's attitude and that of the Bonapartists who longed for and sometimes conspired to effect the restoration of the

Empire. Neither Flaubert's realism nor his pessimism allowed him that recourse. Sartre continues,

> Gustave resembles a widower who, having chosen to be inconsolable and to live henceforth only in his memory of his wife, would energetically reject her resuscitation. Because he loves her less than he claims? No, but because he loves her less than his own defeat. Or because his very love, abruptly exalted, envelops within it the defeat of his entire life as the condition of its intensity. [3:505]

*The Banality of Evil.* The last two points of Sartre's on which I wish to comment are both linked with the disillusion with which Flaubert viewed the collapse of the Empire and concluded—even while mourning it—that it had been "a long lie."

In notes which Flaubert made for a novel to be written about life under Napoleon III, he wrote down observations which throw considerable light on his retrospective judgment. What he disliked most was the smug mediocrity and hypocrisy, the lack of any real character whether good or evil. He chose for his flabby hero an opportunist who would rise to the top by a series of evil deeds "of which he was unworthy," one who would "commit all crimes from love of order." Commenting on these words, Sartre says that it is as if Flaubert had anticipated our "stupor when faced with Eichmann or a dozen other Nazi war criminals" (3:631). Evil seems to be produced everywhere without any intent to injure on the part of anyone.

Sartre in less than a paragraph offers an explanation, in terms closely linked with his *Critique,* of how this "banality of evil" is possible.[8] "Evil is in essence intentional." It is only by a particular structure of bad faith that people can continue to foster it while not finding in themselves any specific evil intention.

> They must maintain themselves in a permanent state of distraction or numbness concerning the way that the sentence of things on persons—what I call elsewhere the practico-inert—must be internalized by them, therefore *intentionalized* in the absence of any subject. Evil must come to them, and precisely as the practical meaning of the established order; that is, of disorder maintained by violence. [3:631–32]

In other words, people blind themselves to the fact that social evil is the direct result of the inequitable structures which human intentions have built into society and which its members continue to support. Evil as the meaning—or significance or inevitable consequence—of the system would not exist without its members, but as individual members they find it unthinkable; nevertheless it remains the rule of their actions and human relationships. A false consciousness, sustained by bad faith, allows them to divert themselves from the truth. What is really alienation in disorder they see as a fascination with order. "The malign intention of treating men as things" appears as "the imperious duty to preserve—even at the price of human sacrifice—the present structures of the community." Such a view of his nineteenth century could hardly have occurred to Flaubert in these terms, but Sartre feels that he was saying the same thing—"that we do Evil, and we are not wicked." Flaubert, despite his disgust with the feebleness of his contemporaries, allowed himself to be "diverted" from grasping the true explanation. He, too, was in bad faith in his shirking of responsibility. If it seemed to him that others were incapable of evil as of good, he condemned them in the name of an abstraction invented by himself.

> Evil is Beauty; that is, the impossible totalization of the *cosmos*.
> The Empire was only a beautiful dream of Evil and of Hate, which lulled the woodlice of bourgeois democracy for eighteen years.
> [3:632]

In retrospect Flaubert condemned the Second Empire for having been at heart bourgeois.

*The Final Task of Imagination.* Finally, Sartre finds in Flaubert's reactions at this period a last turn in his long struggle between the real and the imaginary. In March 1871 he wrote, "We are paying for the long lie in which we have lived, for everything was false: false army, false politics, false literature, false credit and even false courtesans" (*Corr.* 4:229; quoted, 3:491). In another person such a sentence might combine a severe condemnation of the past and an energetic awakening to the need for psychic renewal and vigorous action. But Flaubert was like one waking from a beguiling dream to a present empty of promise. Sartre endeavors to show that Flaubert was compelled to realize the falsity and inadequacy of the values by which he had lived but that he was capable only of reaffirming them—though without conviction.

To Flaubert the Prussian victory symbolized the final triumph of science over the imagination. He attributed the defeat of the French in large part to their humanistic, "Latin" education, deficient in the sciences, too much preoccupied with the cultural achievements of the past. Suddenly it seemed to him that Napoleon III, his army, his court had all been unreal, a scene from an opera or a dream. The nephew and his commanders had played the roles of Napoleon I and his marshals; his court was composed of persons with no more claim to true nobility than Flaubert, who had imagined himself "ennobled" by mingling with them. The collective dream prevented each one from perceiving his own unreality. Unfortunately, however, in this case "the dream is not the negation of the real but an *error* about reality" (3:577). The posturing of Napolean III, the whole glamorous masquerade had paved the way for the real victory of the Prussians. "It is *the Other's existence* which comes in the end to ruin every enterprise of derealization" (3:585). By choosing the imaginary, Flaubert and his compatriots had opted for the triumph of an unwelcome reality. Sartre's language here suggests the great chess image with which he sums up the message of the *Critique*. If an inexperienced player unwittingly engages in a game of chess with a professional, it seems to him that the board is filled with open possibilities and that with each move he is plotting a strategy which has reasonable chance of succeeding. His opponent can read the conclusion outlined by the pieces on the board. He predicts every step of the novice, and uses it to insure his own end.[9] One can't go on dreaming when one is an object for the Prussians (3:586).

Flaubert felt that what the Prussians had accomplished extended far beyond the terms of the humiliating peace treaty. This is the meaning of his repeated pronouncement that *"whatever may happen, the Latin race is finished."* Even beyond his dislike of what seemed to him to be the reduction of everything to mere numbers in the new democratic Republic, his apprehensions centered on the dominance of the scientific attitude. Sartre claims that the crisis had implications which touched Flaubert's personal being. The September disaster proved that the game of "loser wins" had failed. Father and his science were right. It was ridiculous to claim proudly to be "a scientist of the imagination." There was no escape from reality. The more one thought oneself to have escaped the real, the more deeply entrenched in it one became. Sartre compares Flaubert's situation to that of a person who dreams he is in a room which has caught fire. He keeps finding doors and corridors by which to escape but discovers each time that they lead him back to the same burning room (3:517). It is at this point that Flaubert particularly bemoans the futility of art; literature is but one more illusion. And if that is so, his entire life has been a failure, this time without compensation. Loser has not won but lost irretrievably.

Sartre suggests that in Flaubert's thoughts for novels which he never wrote, he perhaps believed himself to have one last card up his sleeve. Du Camp reported that Flaubert once expressed regret that he had finished *A Sentimental Education* (1869) before he had the opportunity of utilizing material from later public developments. In particular he would have liked to close the book with a tableau (wholly imaginary) of the fall of the emperor. Napoleon III would pass by a column of French prisoners who would hurl insults at him and spit at his carriage. "Motionless, without a word, without a gesture," the emperor would think to himself, "Behold those they used to call my Praetorians" (quoted, 3:505–6). Sartre makes a good deal of this reported statement. Without assuming that Flaubert would literally have liked to attach the episode to his earlier novel, he thinks he sees why Flaubert was fascinated with the idea of it. First of all, it would show how the failure of Fréderic and Deslauriers was bound up with that of society at large; it would have explained them without excusing them. Moreover, this time fiction would be seen to receive its truth from reality, the truth of "the impossibility of being man."

A further point is more complex. In this imaginary episode, Napoleon III, by the manner in which he bears his humiliation and by his ironic response, suddenly becomes a hero. "The false Bonaparte, the imposter, becomes an aristocrat in earnest at the moment that his defeat proclaims his commonness and his incompetence" (3:509). Sartre sees a double symbolism. The unredeemably worthless soldiers are *retrospectively* the falsely educated French whose inadequacies have brought defeat, and they are *prospectively* the Communards who would agitate for popular government in 1871. Napoleon III in his carriage (we can see this one coming) is Gustave, fallen to the bottom of the cart in 1844, undergoing the ennobling degradation which he had himself chosen.

But Sartre has not finished with the tableau. The sole resemblance here to the real Napoleon III is the bare *fact* of failure. Supposedly the emperor awakens to the realization of the false dream that preceded, but—as Sartre says—the awakening is like another dream. The imaginary quality of it all is revealed by the deliberately overliterary term "praetorians." At this point, Sartre claims, the writer acknowledges that all art is a lie and invites the reader to toss the book aside and return to reality. The artist announces the end of art. The writer must break his pen, for language can no longer derealize reality (3:648).

According to Du Camp, Flaubert so liked this episode that he resolved to find a place for it in the book he intended still to write on life in the Second Empire. There is one of Flaubert's sentences which Sartre finds especially revealing,

Oh! there are first-rate books to be done on that period and perhaps now the *coup d'état* and what has followed after it will have no other result in the universal harmony than to furnish interesting scenarios for good pen-promoters [*manieurs de plume*].[10]

Sartre comments on this reaction.

Art finally is this: a demand of universal harmony. Or rather it is this harmony itself inasmuch as it produces the real as a way of access to the imaginary. To write a novel is to conform to the full designs of a providence, which has realized the world only in order to provide material for derealization. [3:651]

He reminds us that "this Orphic conception of literature—the world having no other function than to furnish the material of a book or, as Mallarmé would say, of the Book, we have found already in Flaubert" (3:651). With the Knight of Nothingness, the writer's aim is always "to produce the imaginary as the permanent triumph of nonbeing over being and the systematic destruction of the human race by techniques of derealization" (3:650). But this time Flaubert's relation to his material is different.

Sartre's rather complicated line of argument runs as follows: Despite his theory of impersonality, Flaubert to some degree incarnated himself in his imaginary Napoleon III as he did in Emma Bovary and in all of his heroes and heroines. The emperor, too, was a man "too small for himself," yet one who in his glorified failure testified to the truth of his author's creed, "that there is grandeur only in insatisfaction." In his defeat, Flaubert saw also the end of *l'art absolu*. Both emperor and artist were justly punished for having created the false and cherished the imaginary at the ultimate expense of the real. Emperor, Empire, and artist died together. Still, a death notice was needed. And who could provide it? Only the artist, "a voice from beyond the tomb," one "resuscitated from the fires of Hell to bear witness." For suddenly "the miracle occurred. Appearance and being coincided for eternity" (3:652). The past, however false and imaginary it had been, had existed, at least as an appearance. It was its very quality as imaginary that had produced the real, tragic results. Without it one could not account for the Prussian triumph and the events consequent to it. But it was the artist, not the scientific historian, who was needed to portray the subtle interplay of being and nonbeing; Flaubert did not invent Napoleon III, but in his book he would have "presented the *Truth* of Napoleon III; that is, the flesh and blood usurper as imagination changed him into himself" (3:656). In so doing the author seemed to justify himself—to be transformed from accomplice to witness. For the first time Flaubert would be writing out of a sense of mission. "To save the Empire in a book seemed to him the sole justification of his having played the courtier" (3:656). "In restoring that false Empire, Art *dies in beauty*." The subsequent silence is no longer shameful (3:655).

Since Flaubert in the decade left to him did not write the projected book, one might be inclined to think that Sartre has made too much of a stray creative impulse. Yet we know that Flaubert spent considerable time working on these scenarios and seemed to feel some compulsion to realize them. Why did he never do so? Sartre observes that Zola believed it was because Flaubert felt a certain constraint owing to his having been so often the guest of Princess Mathilde. Sartre dismisses this with the observation that Flaubert did not hesitate to criticize Napoleon III and his regime publicly. The real reason, he thinks, was less a sense of guilt over his complicity than simply an overwhelming depression.

> He *loved* that imperial society; a rebound of pride enjoined upon him the order to entomb it with his own hands, but this imperative was repugnant to him. He had been bound up with the regime. He did not wish to survive it, not even to bury it. [3:658]

During his last years Flaubert wrote *The Three Tales,* a book which was the realization of a project of many years' standing—to compose a "triptych" juxtaposing themes from the ancient Near East, the medieval world, and contemporary life. At least two of them—"A Simple Heart" and "The Legend of Saint Julian the Hospitaler"—are rich in nostalgic associations with Flaubert's childhood. And he returned to his work on *Bouvard and Pécuchet,* the novel in which the ideas themselves destroy each other and intellectual enterprise is reduced to the stupid behavior of the "two old woodlice" who study everything, learn nothing, and begin and end their lives as copyists. In short, Flaubert has not changed. When his disastrous financial ruin came, it seemed simply to externalize his feeling that he had outlived himself. Everything took place, Sartre says, as though Flaubert in 1844 had chosen himself already as a subject of the Second Empire. His family situation and private neurosis had prepared him to meet the demands of the literature-to-be-written; the regime of Napoleon III provided the natural environment for *l'art absolu*. At the time of his crisis Gustave thought he had escaped his bourgeois situation; the illusion of *déclassement* was furthered by his life in the court circles. His later economic crisis and especially his panic at the threatened loss of Croisset revealed all too clearly the interdependence of his artistic *survol* and his bourgeois commitment.

# PART THREE

# The Biographer as Literary Critic

Sartre would be the last to claim that our knowledge of a writer's private life is a sure key to our understanding of his novels. And inversely, "the work *never* reveals the secrets of the biography; the book can at most serve as a schema or conducting thread allowing us to discover the secrets in the life itself." We must remember always that "there is a hiatus between the work and the life."[1] Nevertheless, the novel and the life are both objectifications of the same personality, one way or another, and Sartre does not hesitate to use either one to throw light on the other. *The Family Idiot* has been primarily concerned with ways in which the fiction can help us understand the inner life of the subject of the biography. We have seen evidence of this in his treatment of the writings of Flaubert's youth. With regard to most of the books of his maturity, Sartre is regrettably silent. He makes a few references to *Salammbô*, to *The Temptation of Saint Anthony* (particularly, however, to the first version), and to two of the *Three Tales*. These comments are for the purpose of illustrating attitudes of Flaubert's; they are of biographical interest only. Fortunately there are two exceptions. One is *Madame Bovary*. On the basis of material already published and of Sartre's notes (for the fourth volume), it is evident that he was interested in providing a full interpretation and evaluation of the novel as well as in gleaning from it what information he could find to support his portrait of its author. In other words, the four-volume sequence would have been completed with a work of literary criticism. Similarly, Sartre's discussion of "The Legend of Saint Julian the Hospitaler," which concludes volume 2, is a thorough critique of the story, one which offers an entirely new reading of the tale, both in its intention and its structure.

In considering what Sartre has done with these two works, I want to keep constantly in mind the question of whether his critical interpretation is original, sound and persuasive. If we are to accept it as valid, it must meet two criteria. First, when Sartre relates specific meanings and structures of the novel or story to the Flaubert he has portrayed, we must be convinced not only that one is consistent with the other, but that the connection is significantly illuminating. If Sartre's criticism does not lead us to read Flaubert's books in a new way, then we may suspect the legitimacy of the portrait and—at least from the point of view of literature—wonder whether the massive endeavor was worthwhile. At the same time, we must apply the reverse criterion. Flaubert's claim that a work of art must be judged solely on its own terms is one which today is generally accepted. If Sartre's interpretation is to convince us, it must be able to stand by itself, independent of all biographical reference, supported by the internal coherence of the work itself.

So far as is practical within the limitations of this study, I wish to examine Sartre's appraisal of "The Legend of Saint Julian the Hospitaler" and of *Madame Bovary* in the light of other important critical views and, in the case of the latter, to look briefly at certain post-Sartrean critics writing more under the influence of structuralism.

# CHAPTER EIGHT

## "The Legend of Saint Julian the Hospitaler"

The story of Saint Julian must have been familar to Flaubert as a child. It was depicted on a stained glass window of the cathedral at Rouen. In 1835, when he was thirteen years old, Flaubert and his classmates visited the church at Caudebec-en-Caux under the tutelage of E. H. Langlois, who published a work on the glass panes of the Rouen cathedral. At Caudebec-en-Caux there is a statuette of Saint Julian and a stained glass window representing the life of Saint Eustace, which in a number of respects is similar to the story of Saint Julian. Starkie suggests that in all probability Langlois remarked to the boys on the resemblance between the two.[1] According to Du Camp, it was on a visit which he and Flaubert made to this church in 1846 that Flaubert first conceived the idea of writing Julian's story. Ten years later, after the publication of *Madame Bovary*, he thought again of doing it, but laid it aside to work on *Salammbô*. In 1874 he mentioned it again but did not actually begin to write it until 1875. Thus there were thirty years between the initial creative impulse and its realization.

In outline, the tale of Saint Julian found in medieval legend ran as follows: Julian was the only son of noble parents. On the night of his conception his mother dreamed that from her body came forth a beast in human form which devoured her and her husband. Julian spent his youth happily, delighting especially in the hunt. On one occasion when he was about to kill a deer, the animal addressed him in human speech, prophesying that one day Julian would kill his own father and mother. Julian angrily accused the animal of lying; nevertheless he broke his bow and arrows and left home at once secretly. He consulted the pope, who bade him ignore the prediction and return to his parents. Julian insisted on becoming a pilgrim instead and departed for Jerusalem with the pope's blessing. After many years of pilgrimage and voluntary ignoble service, he interrupted the journey he was making to Saint James at Santiago de Compostela and resumed his life as a knight, winning great glory. After many adventures he married the daughter of a powerful count. One day while he was out hunting, his parents came to the door, still looking for their lost son. After a happy scene of recognition, Julian's wife put the pair to sleep in the young couple's own bed. Returning unexpectedly, Julian killed them, believing that his wife was lying with a lover. In despairing contrition he and his wife took up the life of hermits, finally spending their days beside a river where they ferried the needy across free of charge and gave them sustenance. On one stormy evening Julian rescued a leper. They fed and tried to warm him, but the leper told them that only a woman's body could give him warmth. The wife was about to lie down beside him when the leper disappeared. A voice announced to them that their sin was pardoned. Seven years later they were killed by a robber. We may note that if this Julian is guilty of anything at all, it is for interrupting his journey to Saint James—though there is no reason to believe that his going there would necessarily have prevented the accident.

Flaubert's tale is strikingly different. He lengthens the description of Julian's home. Instead of the premonitory dream, he introduces two supernatural predictions. A hermit suddenly appears to Julian's mother and prophesies that her son will become a saint; then he vanishes. An equally mysterious gypsy announces to his father, "Ah! your son! . . . much blood! . . . much glory! . . . forever happy! an emperor's family" (p. 82).[2] The most significant change is in the character of Julian himself. Flaubert carefully traces the development in him of the desire to kill. It begins when during the Mass he watches a mouse emerge from its hole near the altar. Each Sunday he waits for it with an obsessive hatred. Finally on a weekday he lures it with crumbs and kills it. Then he wreaks havoc among the small birds with a peashooter, laughing "with happy malice." He finds a voluptuous delight in wringing the neck of a wounded pigeon. Just then his father has him instructed in the art of hunting. The hunt on which he meets the deer is a true massacre. Julian has killed animals by the dozen, culminating in the shooting of the talking stag, his doe and fawn. The dying animal utters a curse along with the prophecy, "Accursed! accursed! accursed! One day, savage heart, you will slay your father and your mother" (p. 98). Julian weeps, overwhelmed by sadness, exhaustion, and disgust. But he does not leave immediately. He questions himself.

No! No! No! I could not kill them! Then, he thought: "But what if I wanted to??" and he was afraid that the Devil might implant the wish in him. [p. 99]

For three months he is ill but slowly recovers. Later Julian accidentally drops a sword, which just misses his father, cutting a piece of his clothing. An arrow which Julian aims at what he believes to be an approaching stork pins his mother to the wall by the flap of her bonnet. Then he leaves. Flaubert compresses Julian's wanderings into a few paragaphs. There is no visit to the pope, no pilgrimage. But he does win military glory, and he marries the daughter of the emperor. Flaubert's Julian has abandoned hunting, feeling that in some strange way it was connected with the prophesied killing of his parents. One day he confesses his fear to his wife. Partly influenced by her persuasion that it is unreasonable but also because "the temptation was too strong," he sets out with his weapons. On the earlier great hunt he had killed easily, "as if in a dream." Its counterpart now is a phantom hunt. His arrows are by magic deviated from their course, or they fall harmlessly when they hit. Bewildered, Julian is helpless, surrounded by a host of animals, who crowd around him, scoffing, tormenting, threatening. His frustration and murderous impulses are roused to the point where "he would have liked to slaughter men" (p. 118). At last he makes his way home to the fatal mistake and horror. Along with the death rattles of his parents, he seems to hear the braying of the stag. Unlike his sources, Flaubert has this Julian depart alone. In monk's clothing he watches the funeral procession from afar. As a wanderer he is rebuffed and insulted by those who hear his story. The animals flee his approach. At last he becomes a ferryman, rescues, and cares for the leper. Suddenly, after Julian has lain body-to-body, mouth-to-mouth with the leper in order to restore his warmth, the miracle occurs. There is the breath of roses, a cloud of incense, the waves sing, the roof flies off, and the heavens open. The leper is transformed into Christ himself, who ascends into heaven, bearing Julian with him.

Bart and Cook have effectively shown that Flaubert almost certainly did not consult the original medieval sources but drew instead on nineteenth-century versions of the story, especially on Langlois' description and interpretation of the window in the Rouen cathedral that depicted the life of Saint Julian, and on Lecointre-Dupont's adaptation of the tale contained in the Alençon manuscript.[3] In both of these the leper turns out to be our Savior; he does not, however, carry Julian and his wife to heaven. Both Lecointre-Dupont and the window in the Rouen cathedral represent the pair as being elevated later by angels. Lecointre-Dupont describes the transformation in an ending which has obviously influenced Flaubert, even in its language. The tone of Lecointre-Dupont's narrative is much more romantic than in the medieval versions. As A. W. Raitt has observed, Flaubert found ready at hand some of the emotional intensity, the "mixture of pseudomedieval simplicity and sophisticated modern psychological analysis" that characterize his own tale.[4] Yet I feel that Starkie overstates the case when she claims that Lecointre-Dupont provided the central motivation for Flaubert's story: "Julian's prowess in hunting, his blood lust and subsequent obsession with guilt."[5] Lecointre-Dupont tells us that Julian was passionately devoted to the hunt, that on the occasion of his meeting with the stag he had insisted on continuing alone when his exhausted companions wished to return home. But there is nothing resembling the wholesale massacre of animals on the first hunt and no description at all of the second one. Julian never abandons hunting or sees any connection between it and the prophesied murder of his parents. The bloodlust and feeling of guilt, which tormented Julian even before he actually committed the crime, are entirely Flaubert's contribution. The other changes which I mentioned were similarly his and not derived from either Langlois or Lecointre-Dupont. A wholly innocent accidental murderer has been replaced by a self-questioning, bloodthirsty Oedipus.

Among pre-Sartrean critics the majority have regarded "The Legend of Saint Julian the Hospitaler" as "an esthetic construction" only with no ethical implications and without significant connection with Flaubert's own life and thought.[6] Bruneau finds it unusual in this respect. "After 1845 Flaubert never wrote a line of pure imagination except for Saint-Julien."[7] There have been a few notable exceptions. As early as 1896, Marcel Schwob spoke of Julian's "criminal soul," of his "love of killing." Schwob said of him,

> He has a kind of destructive faith. Truly he touches on the sacred mystery which will make of him a saint; for are not destruction and creation sisters?"[8]

Schwob does not, however, relate any of this to Flaubert himself. Instead he generalizes. "We see the attitudes of a cruelly impassioned Julian, whose soul is very close to our own." Flaubert, with his tendency to universalize, would doubtless have been delighted with this conclusion. I do not think it will do for us.

Some critics have taken the tale as a serious admonition against the wanton killing of animals.[9] Starkie and Bart, who have offered two of the most serious and most original interpretations, have both argued that the story is significantly related to a dream which Flaubert recorded. It came to him on the journey to Italy when Gustave and his parents accompanied Caroline and her husband on their honeymoon. In the dream he and his mother were walking in a forest filled with monkeys, who crowded in upon them.

> They all looked at me, finally I was afraid. They surrounded us as in a circle. One wanted to pat me and took hold of my hand. I shot it in the shoulder and made it bleed. It uttered horrible cries. Then my mother said to me, ''Why did you hurt him, your friend? What did he do to you? Don't you see that he loves you? How he resembles you?'' And the monkey kept looking at me. That pierced me to the soul; and I woke up . . . feeling myself of the same nature as the animals and fraternizing with them in an utterly pantheistic, tender communion.[10]

Starkie points out that the description of the animals in the dream bears a close resemblance to Julian's second hunt. ''Flaubert remembered this dream for thirty years and must have felt guilt all that time for the animals he had killed, guilt which he transferred to Julien'' (p. 253). There may possibly be an element of truth in this. Flaubert, who felt that he shared a special understanding with ''children, madmen, and animals,'' may have experienced a residual guilt at the thought of animals he had been directly or indirectly responsible for killing. We have no evidence to show that it was an obsession in him any more than it is in many of us who, whether or not we hunt, do not choose to become vegetarians. To her credit, Starkie, who holds that in this story ''the moral problem is very important,'' does not consider it a work directed solely against cruelty to animals. She regards it as primarily a psychological study, and she goes so far as to argue that even ''the magical element can be interpreted rationally.'' Thus for her, the prophecies to father and mother are, as it were, hallucinatory projections of their secret hopes for their son. Similarly, I suppose the talking stag and the phantom hunt could be taken as either pure dreams or neurotic externalizations by Julian of his inner conflict. In any case, she holds that the denouement comes about not through fate but as the result of Julian's own character. This is surely correct, but Starkie gives the course of events an interpretation all her own. Julian's "evil and cruel heart" is shown in the crime itself without relation to any question of hidden antagonism against his parents.

> He jumps to the conclusion, without stopping to think, that he has a right over the life of his wife, and he is not afraid to kill her, not thinking he is destroying his own dear parents. [p. 251]

Finally Starkie finds Julian an exception among Flaubert's fictional personages, and her interpretation leads her to find the story far more optimistic than the rest of his writing.

> Flaubert generally believed that character was a man's fate or fatality ... from which he could not escape. All he could, and should do, was learn to know himself ... and how to live with himself, since he could not be changed. Julien is, however, an exception to this, and he is the one character in Flaubert's work who, in the end, redeems himself and improves himself. [p. 256]

We will find that Sartre, too, finds an unexpected optimism in the tale, but he would absolutely reject Starkie's claim that Julian's persistence and expiation had earned him merit or that the conventional Christian message can be translated into the author's psychological confidence in the possibilities of self-improvement.

Bart has been especially interested in "The Legend of Saint Julian the Hospitaler" and has commented on it on several occasions. In his book on Flaubert he devotes considerable space to the tale and gives special attention to the monkey dream, ascribing to it more significance than Starkie does and relating it more closely to the dreamer's inner conflicts. But although he recognizes the relation between the dream animals and those of Julian, his interpretation of the story is even less closely connected than Starkie's with what he sees to be the meaning of the dream. Bart remarks that the monkey dream is reminiscent of another dream in which Flaubert was walking with his mother (the one in which the mother drowned), on which Sartre commented in connection with Flaubert's passivity and secret resentment against his mother.[11] Bart thinks that both dreams point to an ambivalence which Flaubert felt toward her during his whole life, but he does not elaborate on the point. Although he deliberately refrains from giving a typically Freudian interpretation of the gun as a phallic symbol, he thinks that sexuality is a primary theme in the dream of the monkeys. He would link it with "sadism, blood lust, guilt, contrition, and the desire for absolution," all of which are present here and which he recognized to be constants in Flaubert's inner life (p. 675). Bart points out that Flaubert was fascinated with monkeys. He was struck by their resemblance to himself, but he delighted, too, in their lascivious bestiality. All of this comes out in the dream. Gustave is frightened by the monkey and shoots the one that touches him. When his mother points out that the animal is a friend who resembles him, he is heartbroken. But he wakes up feeling a pantheistic communion with all of nature, a fraternity between himself and the animals. Bart writes,

> Rephrasing only slightly, animality, and in particular sexuality which seemed frightening and yet which appealed to Flaubert, he enjoyed destroying. But then his mother, toward whom his feelings were ambivalent, told him that sexuality was his own nature and should not have been destroyed; this saddened him. But he wakened having made his peace with it all and feeling at one with it. [pp. 674–75]

Bart sees the dream as significantly connected with Flaubert's specific situation at this time, midway between the crisis of 1844 with the sexual abstinence enforced by it and the beginning of the liaison with Louise Colet in 1846. Beyond that Bart here attempts no further interpretation of the dream, and he implies rather than spells out its bearing on the story of Saint Julian thirty years later.[12] There is obviously a connection between the killing of animals and the relations of child and parent; there is a desire to kill followed by ultimate forgiveness and communion. Sexuality is not overtly present in "The Legend of Saint Julian the Hospitaler," and Bart does not incorporate it into his interpretation of the tale. He is more interested in the attitude toward animals. Flaubert, he reminds us, claimed to be particularly empathetic with animals but also with the insane. In the dream and in the short story Flaubert shows his ability both to sympathize with the animal victims and to understand their slayer.

Like Starkie, Bart finds Julian psychologically guilty, not merely the victim of fate or accident. Bart notes that it is as a punishment for his bloodthirsty cruelty that the stag specifically curses Julian (Flaubert's innovation).

> Julian now joins the long succession of men like Orestes and Oedipus, who are fated to kill their parents but must pay for their crime. Like his precursors, he will seek to evade the curse by flight, but to no avail: his own free actions will bring him to the dreaded deed. [p. 681]

Ultimately, Bart's interpretation is quite different from Starkie's.

Rather than seeking rational explanations for magical happenings, Bart argues that in Julian's world the miraculous and the realistic coexist quite naturally and that Flaubert is right in not stressing their separation. He feels that Flaubert has so closely identified himself with his hero that at one point the resemblance intrudes and mars the artistry. In Julian's first years of wandering after the crime, his misanthropic observations of the low level of human life remind us too forcibly of "the recluse of Croisset suffering the torments of a hypersensitive nineteenth-century neurotic. The anachronism breaks the reader's illusion" (p. 684). Finally Bart relates the story of Julian to the specific circumstances of the time at which it was written. In 1875 Flaubert considered himself a ruined man. He had lost almost all his wealth in a futile effort to save his niece and her husband from financial disaster. Croisset itself was threatened; he literally did not see how he was going to live. Thoughts of the past kept haunting him. It is no wonder that he turned to a legend he may have heard when he was a child; it is understandable that he might recall a dream he had three decades earlier. But how, at this period of despair, do we account for the triumphant ending? Bart finds a parallel between Julian's decision to serve others and Flaubert's willingness to come to the aid of his niece at the price of his own economic ruin. For Bart, Julian's redemption, Flaubert's sudden burst of creative energy, and the ending of the dream about monkeys are related.

> [Julian] started on the road to salvation by seeking to be at one with his fellow man. In the original dream Flaubert reached this communion without knowing how, during the moment of waking: it was the wish the dream fulfilled for him and which life itself then offered no prospect of providing. Thirty years of further living were needed before he gained the wisdom to seek this communion. Its consummation was, of course, the path he has just followed—for the first time—in helping his niece. [p. 684] [Julian's religious ecstasy] has been won at the price of sacrifices Flaubert had not known existed—until the threat to his beloved niece had made him realize that self-sacrifice was more beautiful than self-aggrandizement, even in the name of art. [p. 686]

In Bart's view it is the author who showed that he could "redeem and improve himself."

Sartre, as we would expect, claims that Flaubert has indeed objectified himself in Julian. Sartre thinks that he can understand why Flaubert wrote the story in 1875 and not earlier, and he would agree with Bart and Starkie that its conclusion is unusually optimistic. He is opposed to the idea that Julian's life represents a true repentence and earned redemption, and he stresses more emphatically than any other critic the radical difference between the moral message of the legend in Flaubert's sources and the impact of his own version.

Sartre begins by asking just why Julian is saved. It cannot be by his Christian charity and love. This is perhaps Sartre's most debatable point, but by a close reading of the text he makes a good case. People who knew Julian's story closed their doors to him and drove him off with stones. Therefore he mostly avoided them. At times, Flaubert tells us, "the need of mingling in the existence of others led him to go down into the town. But the bestial expression on the faces, the noisy occupations, the trivial chatter chilled his heart" (p. 124). Flaubert does, to be sure, add that when Julian gazed through the windows at family parties gathered around a festive table, "sobs choked him, and he went back to the country." Sartre evidently regards this statement as merely perfunctory. I would suggest that it indicates loneliness and perhaps an inability to come close to people rather than love of them. Sartre admits that Julian loves nature and watches the foals, the birds, even the insects with "transports of love," but notes also that they flee from him. Is this part of his punishment, or is it because these creatures recognize that his burning desire to kill them has been slaked only by his shedding of human blood? Sartre's most telling point is apropos of Julian's daring rescues. These are in truth disguised suicides. Flaubert writes,

> His own person so filled him with loathing that in the hope of getting rid of it he exposed it to dangers. He rescued paralytics from fires and children from the bottom of chasms. The abyss rejected him, the flames spared him. [pp. 125–26]

Then Julian resolved to kill himself. Why? Were there no more children in need of rescue? Sartre asks.

Deterred from suicide, Julian resolved to devote his life to serving others. He became a ferryman. Here, too, Sartre is skeptical. The passengers whom he transported without charge often uttered blasphemies. "Julian gently reproached them, and they replied with abuse. He was content to bless them" (p. 128). Sartre sees in this conduct a certain proud detachment. "Let them go hang themselves! God will attend to them" (2:2108). This may be going a bit too far, but I think Sartre is right in arguing that Julian keeps his contact with humanity to the minumum. I may point out that Flaubert makes no

323

mention of the hostel which, in the legend, Julian and his wife established to care for travelers. Julian lives in a tiny shack alone. There is no mention of his tending and caring for any individual until he meets with the leper, then he does so principally in obedience to his guest's demand.

Sartre asks, if not by charity, was Julian saved by faith? If we refer to orthodox belief, there is no problem. Julian had the simple, unquestioning faith typical of almost all of the saints of medieval legend. He blamed himself for having been capable of parricide; he never revolted against God for having afflicted him with this fate. But if by faith, we refer to trust and hope, the wish to be close to God, and particularly if faith is to include trust in the Church as God's representative on earth, then Sartre argues that Julian's behavior and the whole tenor of the tale are surprisingly un-Catholic. Julian never prays, never throws himself on God's mercy, does not hope or even ask for forgiveness. "Out of humility," he confesses his sin to many persons whom he happens to meet; on no occasion does he consult a priest. (I may add here in support of Sartre, that Flaubert has suppressed an important event present in all of his sources—Julian's visit to the pope.) Neither inside nor outside a church does Julian pray. Sartre concludes, "In flagrant contradiction with the principles of Catholic religion, it is because he despaired of God that Julian will be saved" (2:2114).

Other critics have observed that Julian fails to recognize signs of his approaching salvation until the ultimate moment when the leper is transformed and Julian finds himself in the arms of our Lord Jesus. Bart remarked that even when, a few minutes earlier, the water jug was mysteriously filled with wine, Julian failed to perceive the miracle and reacted almost fatuously, "What a find!" (*Quelle trouvaille!*).[13] This could be explained as a sign of his humility and sense of extreme unworthiness, a further demonstration of his merit. Sartre interprets it differently. He argues that Julian at no time *merits* salvation, that he recognizes his nature to be so radically evil that forgiveness is impossible. Therefore his supposed life of penitence is not really an atonement but self-abnegation growing out of self-disgust, a different thing entirely. Sartre claims that it is this self-abhorrence that, in highly unorthodox fashion, ultimately wins for Julian "not only his salvation but his canonization. . . . Thus the fundamental trait of sainthood will be to push to the extreme one of the primary constituted structures of *l'affectivité flaubertienne*" (2:2108).

Sartre's analysis of Julian's character and of the development of his life story includes several of the themes that Sartre has attributed to Flaubert himself. Julian is born with an evil nature; it is not the result of anything that was done to him. His bloodthirsty violence against animals, which Flaubert describes in such gory—and gloating—detail, is the surrogate for the sadistic impulses that Flaubert felt against humans. (This, I suggest, might explain why Julian can love animals after—and only after—the parricide. The extraordinary hostility toward them is no longer needed as a cover.) The stag's curse is like the paternal malediction. It is a fatum from which there is no escape; at the same time it is a formal recognition of the existing evil in the child that will lead him to the crimes for which he is responsible. Sartre recognizes the intertwining of sexual pleasure and sadism in Julian's slaughter of the animals. This and Flaubert's reference to Julian on the first great hunt as moving as if in a dream lead him to relate Julian's sadism to Flaubert's own adolescent sadistic imagining and masturbatory reveries. Sartre remarks on Julian's sense of guilt even before he has killed. His uneasy introspection marks him as an Oedipus who recognizes that the wish for what he must fear is already present within him.

> No! No! No! I could not kill them! Then he thought: "But what if I wanted to?" and he was afraid that the Devil might implant the wish in him. [p. 99]

To think that the Devil might cause him to be possessed by the wish is equivalent to admitting that he was capable of such evil. In this context the two near-fatal accidents that Flaubert introduces may well have been intended by him (in anticipation of Freud) to express repressed wishes. The pinning of his mother's bonnet Sartre finds particularly suspicious. Julian had totally abandoned hunting. Why then is he so quick to shoot, in his own garden, on a sudden impulse, at an unclear object? Julian's decision to leave home immediately seems to underscore the point. He recognizes, Sartre says, that the only fatality involved is his own nature. He substitutes physical prevention for a too weak moral resolve. Until the fatal slaying "Julian regarded himself as the unhappy product of radical Evil; now radical Evil is his product" (2:2110). We see here again the pattern we observed in *The Plague at Florence:* a prophecy which in no sense absolves the one who is guilty of fulfilling it.

Sartre views the parricide as a negative image of death and rebirth. Just as in *November,* an old man replaces the impassioned young hero. Even his vices are gone; there remains only a purified contemplation which gazes with horror on "the last recollection of his dead memory." When hazardous risks fail to bring the death he longs for, Julian in despair "sees clearly that he wants *the impossible:* one does not efface what one has been" (2:2111). Then he tries to drown himself in a pool of water but is deterred by his own reflection, which is startlingly like that of his father. It would be as though he were to kill his parent all over again. Sartre calls our attention to an odd fact. In planning the act of suicide, expressly forbidden by the Church, Julian does not appear to fear the flames of hell any more than he had hoped to appeal to heaven for forgiveness. As with Flaubert, hell is on this earth. If Julian does not leave it by self-destruction, it is because he realizes that his crime would remain, like a "statue of iniquity sculptured forever in the minerality of the past" (2:2112). Suicide is useless. After this abortive attempt Julian seems to live almost without emotions; "like a man of repetition," Sartre says.

The final episode with the leper shows in Julian the utmost self-abnegation but nothing of warmth or even sympathy. Sartre argues that we are not doing violence to the story—rather it is the only way we can fully understand it—if we see in Julian's actions a reflection of Flaubert's own self-disgust and masochism. Flaubert describes the leper in terms as revolting as possible—his sores, his stinking breath, the cavernous hole where his nose had rotted away. When Julian lies down upon him, it is not because tender compassion makes him forget any natural repugnance. Sartre says,

> It is because these sores and this oozing pus fill him with a disgust hitherto never experienced. Here is the opportunity to conquer the desperate resistance of his whole organism and to inflict upon himself the most exquisite torment, the intensity of which he measures by the repugnance which he must overcome. [2:2113–14]

There is still something more. Sartre claims that Julian wants to be infected with leprosy, "to become the rotting body which arouses his disgust." He compares this deliberate exposure to "contagion," to Flaubert's fascination and "imitation" of the epileptic. Does this go beyond what the text will support? What Flaubert has written is succinct and specific. The leper begs,

> "Warm me! Not with your hands! No! Your whole person." Julian lay spread out [*s'étala*] entirely upon him, mouth against mouth, breast against breast. [p. 134]

Sartre points to the passive force of the reflexive verb. We are told nothing of Julian's thoughts at this moment, but it does seem to me that Flaubert has emphasized the sense of passive, despairing abandon. Julian might have turned and actively taken the leper in his arms. Instead he simply lies there as if at last, in Sartre's terms, he had reached the bottom in his descent to hell. Sartre, of course, sees in the horizontal position an echo of Flaubert's preoccupation with the Fall. Certainly the absence of all reaction in Julian prevents our detecting any sign of inward transformation. The metamorphosis of the leper into Christ is external. It comes as a change of an Other's judgment on Julian, a gift of grace. Sartre states that in the triumphant ending, Flaubert has suddenly reversed the terms of his own life imagery. He quotes (Sartre's italics),

> A wealth of delight, a superhuman joy *descended* like a flood into the soul of the *fainting* Julian. . . . And Julian *rose up* toward the blue spaces, face-to-face with our Lord Jesus, who *carried* him to Heaven.

Sartre notes that the passivity is still there. It is as though Julian's soul were innundated by the celestial presence (even the level of water has been elevated!); his rapture is like a fainting (*pâmé*), he is *carried*. Verticality is here, too. But whereas in his early works, Flaubert pictured himself as escorted by Satan into the emptiness above the world in order that he might be filled with despair, this time his hero rises in joy with Jesus, into the azure spaces, to stay there forever. The subsequent fall will not take place. In Flaubert's sources for this passage, it is only the transformed leper who rises in majesty and speaks to Julian and his wife from above. Flaubert alone has Julian ascend in the arms of Christ. Sartre must surely be right in arguing that this optimistic use of the old imagery of despair is bound up with some personal hope of the author (2:2106).

At present, restricting ourselves to the story independent of its autobiographical connections, we may note that Sartre sees in Julian a man who is saved by none of the familiar Christian virtues. Indeed, his authenticity lies in his justified self-disgust. Flaubert's refusal to allow him any hope of forgiveness from God or help from His ministers or even the companionship of another feeble and repentant sinner (the wife) represents an "ultrajansenism." "To live is not only an unending, savorless unhappiness; it is a permanent crime" (2:2109). But if Julian is indeed so unworthy, why do we care about him and rejoice at his salvation? And what gives the story its charm?

For Sartre the answer lies not only in the aesthetic quality of the style, which successfully blends the naïve simplicity of legend with the subtle sophistication of self-conscious artistry and psychological understanding. There is certainly no implied message that there awaits each one of us a solution beyond our expectation or deserts. Sartre would be the first to reject this idea, and so would Flaubert. Julian is not Everyman. The secret of the story's success is its double focus, which is announced in its very title. As reader, I know that I am reading about *Saint* Julian. The point of view is that of God. Flaubert, Sartre reminds us, was writing for Christians in the Western world. And we are all, believers and nonbelievers, Christians in our heritage, especially in our imagination and sensibility (2:2124). Consequently we read the tale simultaneously on two levels. We are with Julian in his suffering, but we know something he does not: we can testify that all of this wretchedness is for his own good even though he will never recognize it on this earth. His total despair foreshadows to us the final miracle, for we know the secret that "loser wins." There is a further consequence. By a kind of trick we are forced to pity and to love Julian even when he is at his least amiable.

> Without any special sympathy for his frenetic destruction, but by our Christian education won over in advance to the author's point of view, we love him because he is loved, *without knowing it,* by an absolute love. Thus his self-hate dissolves and becomes pure merit without our ceasing to witness the havoc he piles up in our world. [2:2125]

Flaubert has tricked us, Sartre goes on to say. "We allow ourselves to be moved and to be affected with an imaginary belief in what is not believable in order to love one who is not lovable, an evil man who has turned his evilness against himself."

Critics who try to see in Flaubert's "Legend" something more than the play of aesthetic imagination naturally tend to support their interpretations by reference to details in the author's personal life and especially to the particular circumstances in which he wrote the story. We would not expect Sartre to be an exception, and he is not. The connections he establishes are inevitably different from those of Starkie and Bart as his Flaubert is from theirs. This is true apropos of Flaubert's specific situation in 1875, but even more with respect to echoes of his earlier life. In letters from this period Flaubert shows himself dwelling on the past, especially the years of his boyhood at home. Other interpreters of "The Legend" have commented on this. They have assumed that Flaubert's present unhappiness led him to seek consolation in the memories of youthful years that seemed happy in retrospect, whether or not they had been so in reality. But while they have recognized that Flaubert's interest in Julian dates back at least to 1846 and perhaps as early as 1835, they have not made either the past experiences or Flaubert's later attempt to come to grips with them an essential part of what they take to be the story's meaning. Sartre believes that Flaubert has woven into the tale his old rancors and conflicts but that in the process he has attempted to achieve some kind of reconciliation with it all.

Of prime importance to Sartre is the theme of patricide. Sartre thinks that the original fascination of Julian's story for Flaubert is precisely the fact that it tells of a man who won sainthood in spite of (or, more profoundly, because of) having killed his parents in his youth. We have already observed in Julian his sense of guilt even before the murders and his horror at having been capable of committing them. Sartre points to two details which support his contention that it is the father's death with which Flaubert was truly concerned and that the mother was included only because the story demands it, an appendage if not a cover. Sartre quotes from Flaubert's account of Julian's military ventures before his marriage.

> He protected Churchmen, orphans, widows, and especially old
> men. When he saw one of them walking before him, he insisted on
> seeing his face as if he were afraid of killing him by mistake.

The problem here is that although I have translated *les vieillards* as "old men," which is how Sartre takes it, the word could mean simply "old people" and the "him" could be generic, referring to either man or woman. It is true, however, that if Flaubert had wanted to invoke both mother and father specifically, he could have used *les vieux* and let Julian demand to see *their* faces.

Sartre's second point concerns the abortive suicide attempts. As Julian leans toward the pool in which he is about to drown himself, he sees the grief-stricken face of an old man. For a moment he fails to recognize it as his own and believes it is his father's. After that "he thought no more of killing himself" (p. 126). Why? We might conclude that his dead father seemed to bar the way, either forbidding him or indicating that no escape is possible. Sartre goes one step farther. He reminds us that by the ritualistic murder of the father, the son replaces him; that is, he becomes his father—as the reflection confirms. Thus to kill himself would be to commit patricide once again.

By insisting on a connection between Julian's crime and Gustave's disturbed relation with his own father, Sartre seeks to show that Flaubert was simultaneously doing two different things. First, he was expressing through Julian his own sense of guilt with regard to the events of the mid-forties. One passage seems to Sartre (and I am convinced that here he is right) to be a direct memory of the days that followed the crisis. Immediately after the sentence that reports Julian's fear that the devil might persuade him to wish to kill his parents, we read, without transition, "For three months his mother prayed anxiously beside his bed, and his father continually walked the corridors, moaning" (p. 99). Famous physicians were consulted in vain. Nobody could find the cause of the illness, and Julian merely shook his head in response to all questions. Julian, like Flaubert, falls ill to avoid an intolerable situation. Clearly it is his sense of guilt that keeps him silent. Similarly, Sartre argues, Gustave's illness was accompanied by a double feeling of guilt. To take refuge in a nervous crisis as the only solution to his problems was in itself a disgrace. "He was aware of . . . the profound, intolerable resentments which would make of him the principal agent of the fall of the house of Flaubert" (2:1905). But more than that he had secretly wished for his father's death, not only because it would liberate him but with all of the usual Oedipal implications. Sartre stresses the fact that belief in his wife's adultery was the precipitating cause of Julian's crime. "'A man sleeping in my mother's bed,' the classic aspect of Oedipus" (2:1901). Without claiming that Flaubert was aware of all of these implications, Sartre insists that he was conscious at least of the guilty death wish. "Freudian in advance," he knew that "the modern Oedipus is not the man who becomes a parricide without knowing it but the man who dreams of killing but stops short of the crime itself" (2:1903). In the year after his first illness, Gustave must have been aware that only his father's death would put him in a position where, in recovered health, he might stay at home and write. Sartre argues that, as has happened with thousands of neurotics, Gustave afterward secretly held himself responsible for causing the death he had wished for. Under these circumstances it is not suprising that a few months after Achille-Cléophas died, Flaubert remarked to du Camp that he was thinking of writing the story of Saint Julian. Possibly he was still too close to it all to begin writing it then. But why did he come back to it in 1875?

It is here that the notion of a reconciliation enters in. Sartre observes that the description of Julian's childhood is an idealized portrait of what Flaubert would like his own to have been, one in which the "Golden Age" had never ended. The son is the center of existence for the gentle, adoring pair. They are overwhelmed with grief at his illness; when he leaves, they spend all of their wealth and exhaust themselves in a search for him. The reflected image that Julian takes to be his father's is piteously grief-stricken, as Gustave would like his father's to have been. In short, Flaubert is recasting his own memories. I think it would be possible to see in this only a natural and harmless attempt at a moment of distress, to seek comfort in reconstructed memories of past happiness. But Sartre may be right in trying to persude us that there is something else. Flaubert, he claims, felt that his freedom to test his genius as an artist was won at the cost of his father's life. At the time it had seemed a struggle to the death between them. Thirty years later he would like to put rancor aside and come to terms with his guilt.

> Once fame has come, the black Lord [*Seigneur*] of the younger Flaubert becomes the "good Lord" of this unique son, Julian. Gustave's rancors are appeased. The ruin of the Commanville pair compels him to take refuge in his childhood; at present he wants it to have been beautiful. In Achille-Cléophas he sees nothing but the man who knew how to take leave in time. [2:1910]

In this reconstruction of the past, Sartre claims, Flaubert is trying for the first time to love himself. He does this not by a false self-portrayal but by a true one which is nevertheless designed to awaken pity. When the murderer Julian wins the compassionate love of our Lord Jesus, Flaubert in effect tells himself, "I am loved—by God the Father." In weeping over himself he comes to accept himself. Personally, I think that the description of Julian's tears for the pitiable picture reflected in the pool is better explained as an expression of this kind of self-pity than as a wish-fulfilling portrait of the grieving Achille-Cléophas, but possibly the two interpretations are not incompatible if we accept Sartre's claim that Flaubert-Julian, by the ritual murder of the Father, has replaced him.

If we are to find Sartre's reading of the story convincing, it must be in the light of his interpretation of Flaubert's reactions to his situation in 1875. Far from joining Bart in thinking that Flaubert found an inner compensation and communion as the result of his self-sacrifice, Sartre, as we saw earlier, insists that Flaubert was enraged and resentful. He did, to be sure, come to the aid of the Commanville couple out of love for Caroline and from family pride—one connected with the Flaubert family could not suffer the disgrace of bankruptcy. But he complained bitterly at the injustice of it all; he was hurt and irritated at Caroline's request that he cut down his living expenses. Two passages out of the many that might be cited from the *Correspondence* seem to me to argue convincingly against Bart's claim that Flaubert looked on his sacrifices as in any way uplifting or that his occasional doubts as to the ultimate value of art were related to a new value which he attached to human relations. In response to a letter from George Sand he writes,

> My nephew has consumed half my fortune. To prevent him from going bankrupt I have compromised all of the rest, and I don't know now how I am going to live. One can't ask any more of me. As for feeling proud after that and consoling myself with the words, "devotion, duty, sacrifice," No! No! I have become accustomed to great independence of mind, to a complete unconcern about material life. At my age you do not remake your life. You do not change your habits. My heart is crushed and my imagination beaten down. . . . I have become very fearful, very lazy, a dried up cow, a brute. [*Corr.*, Supp. 3: 214]

To Madame de Loynes he says,

> I had sacrificed everything in life to my peace of mind. That wisdom has been in vain. It is this above all which grieves me. [*Corr.*, Supp. 3:216]

Sartre finds especially significant a letter to Madame Brainne. Here again Flaubert exclaims, "I sacrificed everything in my life for the freedom of my intelligence! And it has been snatched from me by this reverse of fortune. This above all is what drives me to despair" (*Corr.*, Supp. 3:186). Sartre asks, "Sacrificed everything?" Yes, on condition that he might keep Croisset and its rents so as to have the material independence necessary if he was to devote himself to art. It is the threatened loss of Croisset that so upsets him. In the same letter, Flaubert says that if Croisset is kept safe, "existence will still be possible. Otherwise, not."[14]

This last outcry implies that there is an unfulfilled bargain, a broken contract. What is at stake is the wager of "loser wins." Here, Sartre believes, we may find the explanation of why Flaubert waited three decades to write the story of Julian. In 1875 it seemed to him that life itself had proved that "the worst is sure and the Devil always wins'' (2:2132). Humiliated by financial ruin, fearful that his changed circumstances would no longer provide him with the seclusion he felt essential for his writing, haunted by the belief that his death was imminent and that already he had outlived himself, Flaubert played his last card (2:2133). Julian's story with its implicit promise had served as a talisman. He had hugged it to his heart until the moment when he could no longer believe in it. Then when reality invaded his life, Flaubert objectified his dream in a work of art which would henceforth be a ''center of derealization'' for others.

> Saint Julian is the most intimate secret of an imaginary soul who suddenly tears it out so as to hurl it blindly into the stream of things. [2:2133]

In so doing he both bade his dream farewell and perhaps secretly hoped thereby to make it real, fascinated as always by the ambiguity of the work of art in which the imaginary becomes a ''real center of derealization.''

In Sartre's eyes, Julian's story attracted Flaubert because he could see in it both his own despair and his secret hope. Best of all, it seemed to come to him wholly from an external source, in a legend ready-made and hallowed by centuries of retelling. Flaubert wanted to preserve its objectivity and its sense of miracle. More than ever now, he resolved to write of existence as it ought to be. Therefore he would not wish to explain away the magical (as Starkie tried to do) nor would he understand Bart's objection to the way in which our belief is strained with respect to the marvelous sights in Julian's wanderings. ''The Legend of Saint Julian the Hospitaler'' is indeed a ''work of pure imagination,'' not as Bruneau believed, because it does not draw on real life, but because it reflects what Flaubert wanted to imagine his life and the world to be.

Flaubert always downplayed the importance of this tale, referring to it as a trivial work, a mere exercise, something a mother might read to her child (2:2121). (If Sartre's reading is correct, this last must be ironic!) It is possible, of course, that his deprecation was meant to hide its secret importance to him, perhaps even from himself. Sartre is careful to point out that he does not claim that Flaubert ever explicitly and with full awareness recognized the relation of the tale to the game of ''loser wins.'' But Sartre insists that even as a boy Flaubert sensed that Saint Julian was strangely important to him and that the act of writing it was not simply ''transmutation of the plastic imaginary'' (the narrative in the stained glass) into a ''verbal imaginary." Sartre believes that in the completed work Flaubert felt deeply a basic kinship between himself and Julian. There is an intimate bond between "Flaubert, unwilling atheist" and Julian, who could not believe in his God's power of forgiveness. In Julian's story Flaubert felt "something infinitely close and familiar, a sort of all pervading Grace, a nameless encouragement which came from the remote Middle Ages and yet addressed itself to him alone but without *saying* anything to him" (2:2126–28). And he was comforted.

Aside from any light it may shed on Flaubert himself, is there any reason why we should accept Sartre's interpretation of "Saint Julian" in preference to that of any other critic? In endeavoring to arrive at any such evaluation, we will find that Sartre's reading is strongly corroborated—perhaps to the point of appearing to be less strikingly original—if we look at Victor Brombert's discussion of this work. I omitted mention of Brombert in the earlier survey of critical views because of the complex interaction between him and Sartre. His study of Flaubert's novels was published several years before the appearance of *The Family Idiot*,[15] but Brombert showed himself closely acquainted with Sartre's comments on Flaubert in *Search for a Method* and with extracts from what Sartre had written earlier on *The Idiot*, which had been published in *Les Temps modernes*. In turn we may note that Sartre had read Brombert's book. The result is that Brombert makes use of Sartrean suggestions and, partly under their guidance, has worked out an interpretation of "Saint Julian" which partially anticipates Sartre's own. Brombert does not make all of the same connections with Flaubert's life that Sartre finds important— neither the specific references to the nervous illness nor to the overall theme of "loser wins." But, like Sartre, he finds "Saint Julian" "one of Flaubert's most 'personal' works" despite the impersonal objectivity of its style and form. The typical "Flaubertian themes" he identifies are those that Sartre has made central in his own analysis of Flaubert: "the fascination of the bestiary, the monastic urge, the image of the alienated saint, the temptation of despair, self abnegation as a form of self-disgust, . . . the dream of possible regeneration through copulation with Horror" (p. 218). Similarly Brombert lays stress on Oedipal implications, emphasizing "Julian's impassioned killing of his parents, in bed and in a spell of sexual jealousy" (p. 227). Brombert feels that Sartre gives too little emphasis to the role of the mother in Flaubert's life (an objection he would probably not have raised if the whole of *The Family Idiot* had been available to him), but he accepts completely Sartre's view of Flaubert's resentful, even parricidal feelings toward his father. In this connection he makes two points on which Sartre has not touched but which seem to me to lend even further support to his argument. Sartre, although he stresses the way in which Flaubert has repainted his childhood, adds,

> It is to be noted, however, that [Julian's] father does not understand him and wants to make of him a warrior (the man of action *par excellence*) whereas his mother, more sensitive, would hope that he might be a saint (an artist). [2:1905n.]

Obviously, the two predictions, both of which are fulfilled in Julian's case though not in Gustave's, suit the secret hopes of those who hear them. Brombert makes the parallel with Achille and Caroline Flaubert still closer. He notes that the doctor represented activity and worldly success, whereas his wife "stood for the monastic values of retirement, serenity, meditation and passivity" (p. 223). Following Sartre's lead in ascribing to Flaubert a guilty wish for his father's death, he concludes,

> If indeed, as is very possible, the materialistic Doctor was an impediment to his son's idealistic aspirations—if indeed, to use Sartre's image, he partly succeeded in killing "God" in him—then the theme of parricide, related to the theme of sainthood, takes on a renewed meaning. [p. 232]

To the chapter in which this discussion appears, Brombert gave the title, "Saint Julien: The Sin of Existing." The subtitle takes us all the way back to the hero of *Nausea*, who hoped through art to be "cleansed of the sin of existing.... Not completely, of course, but as much as any man can."[16] Brombert finds this kind of existential guilt deeply rooted in Flaubert. It is "not a Christian guilt" but something "almost Sartrean in nature ... which explains perhaps why Sartre has been for so long fascinated and at the same time repelled by Flaubert" (p. 229).

Brombert is content to isolate basic Flaubertian themes in "Saint Julian" rather than to offer an overall interpretation which would relate its optimistic ending to Flaubert's feelings at the time he wrote it. Indeed, for Brombert the story seems to be primarily negative in its implications. One point is especially interesting. The passage that shows Julian choking with sobs as he looks through the window at families at dinner, the grandfathers holding the little children on their knees, is passed over lightly by Sartre and dismissed as unimportant as evidence against Julian's dominant misanthropy, or at least lack of personal tenderness. Brombert, I think, correctly associates it with a passage in Flaubert's letter to George Sand, written four years later.

> I adore children and was born to be an excellent papa. But fate and literature decided otherwise! . . . It is one of the melancholies of my old age not have a little being to love and caress. [*Corr.* 8:209–10]

Through Julian, Flaubert seems to be expressing a nostalgic longing of his own. Brombert suggests (Sartre, as we observed, shares this view) that Flaubert came to recognize that his self-chosen solitude was the result of his fear of life, his having been "a coward in his youth" (p. 231). In a reference to Saint Julian in a later work, Brombert takes this a step farther: "Rejection of paternity, parricide—are these not two forms of the same refusal?"[17] That Flaubert seriously wished that he had lived his life differently I doubt very much. The regret he expresses to Sand strikes me as typical of the sort of secondary wishes many of us have—that we might enjoy in addition those things we have rejected in order to attain what we have wanted most. All the same, Flaubert clearly felt that forgoing marriage and family was one of the sacrifices he had made for art. It is a counter in the game of "loser wins," and Sartre might well have taken Brombert's point to his own account. I may add that the interaction of Sartre and Brombert in their approach to "Saint Julian" has been most fruitful. I hope it may prove to be prophetic of the way in which *The Family Idiot*, in the hands of Flaubert scholars, will continue to further and enrich our understanding of Flaubert's works.

Unaccountably, Sartre (Brombert, too) makes no reference to Flaubert's dream of his walk with his mother amid the monkeys, although it would appear to have more relevance for his reading of "Saint Julian" than it has for the final interpretations of Starkie and Bart. Two things are especially stressed in Flaubert's recollection of the dream and reinforced by the remarks that follow in his notes. These are the way the monkeys look at him and their resemblance to him. In the dream the monkeys first collectively look at him and make him afraid. Then, after his mother's reproach, the wounded animal looks at him, and he is filled with anguish. After his narration of the dream, Flaubert observes that when in waking life he looked at a monkey, he was never sure who was the looker and who the looked-at. He adds that monkeys are our ancestors. The combination of the judgmental Look and the emphasis on Flaubert's likeness to the animal that is our ancestor leads me to risk the suggestion that there is a symbolic identification between the wounded dream monkey and Flaubert's father. The association is strengthened by the fact that the look of judgment is vividly portrayed three times in "Saint Julian." The accusing stag stood before Julian "with blazing [*flamboyants*] eyes, solemn, like a patriarch and like a judge [*justicier*]" (p. 98). Later, when Julian approached his dead father, "he saw, inside the partially shut eyelids a lackluster pupil which burned him like fire" (p. 121). Finally, the leper has "two eyes redder than coals," which change when he embraces Julian into "a clear starlight" (pp. 130, 134). In these related images, animal, father, and Jesus (= God the Father) are united. That the dream should have similarly associated the looks of the monkey and the father does not seem farfetched. Julian's sufferings earned him forgiveness and redemption. What caused Flaubert to wake up with a sense of release and pantheistic tenderness? Bart believes that it was the consequence of the mother's seeming to tell her son that he should accept his sexuality, symbolized by the lascivious monkeys whom she says he resembles. This is certainly a possible interpretation and may in any case remain as a subordinate meaning. But if we identify the monkey with Achille-Cléophas, there leaps to mind an interpretation which seems to me to fit surprisingly well with both the traditional style of Freudian dream interpretations and the picture Sartre has presented of Gustave's complex relations with his parents. In the dream Gustave is first filled with fear at the monkey's look, that glance of his father which seemed to the son to pierce right through him and reveal all guilty secrets. When the animal grasps his hand, he shoots, defensively and resentfully. Reproached by his mother he is greatly distressed, but he wakes up feeling a tender, pantheistic sense of brotherhood with the animals. How do we explain the paradox of cause and effect? Sartre reminds us that even as we may fulfill a repressed wish in our dream, we may also incorporate the attitude that in waking life would accompany such an action (2:1851). Thus Gustave carries out the death wish against his father but inflicts upon himself an anguished remorse. All the same, he wakes up with a feeling of liberation. It is important to remember that the young Gustave also loved his father (the dream satisfies both the love and the resentment) and above all wished that his father might love and take pride in him. The dream mother assures her son that his father loves him and that the son is like his father. The other half of the Oedipal relation is almost certainly present, too. The gun is a destructive weapon against the

337

father, but its discharge in the presence of the mother may well have the sexual significance that the Freudians usually associate with guns. Possibly we could go so far as to say that with the gun the dreamer replaces his father as sexual partner. Thus we would pinpoint more precisely the feeling of sexual release Bart found in the dream. In addition the dream effectively restores the Golden Age of Gustave's childhood, when he felt himself to be like the animals and loved to induce in himself a pantheistic sense of merging with his surroundings. Thus it would symbolically both resolve the childhood conflicts and win for Flaubert the final deliverance from his father that he so desperately needed in 1845. The dream and "Saint Julian" deal with the same underlying conflicts and use some of the same imagery.

Brombert and Sartre alike comment on Flaubert's departure from his sources in denying Julian the company of his wife during his period of penance and attribute it to Flaubert's own essential solitude, despite the warm attachments to friends such as du Camp and Bouilhet. It increases Julian's likeness to the author. Following Sartre's lead (he himself does not suggest this), I wonder whether we could not also explain the wife's absence by reference to what Sartre has written concerning Flaubert's "femininity." It is Flaubert alone who represents Julian as borne aloft in the arms of Christ himself. It would have been awkward to represent the couple clasped thus together but perhaps not impossible. Conceivably, the suppression of the wife represents Flaubert's lurking misogyny. Yet there is something almost feminine in Julian's passivity in the embrace of the leper-Christ. Is Flaubert perhaps expressing here as well the other side of his androgynous nature? If he were acquainted with the Alençon manuscript, which Lecointre-Dupont adopted but altered, we might suspect so. There it was the wife who was expected to share the leper's bed, and the sexual connotations were clear though she was rescued in time. Bart and Cook have shown that Flaubert probably did not see this manuscript, but he may possibly have heard something of the older version.

In Lecointre-Dupont's introduction to his narrative, Flaubert must have read the sentence, "To balance the Oedipus of antiquity, the mythology of the Middle Ages can offer its Saint Julian the Beggar."[18] In that pre-Freudian era the reference would naturally not evoke the overtones it would now. Yet on Sartre's reading, Flaubert was well aware of the guilty impulses that prevented his feeling that either the legendary saint or he himself was an innocent victim. If we accept

Sartre's reading, Flaubert (not intentionally, of course) worked out Julian's redemption in a manner closer to that of Sophocles' Oedipus than to the intention of the medieval tale. The purely Christian Julian of the original story earned sainthood by his penance. Flaubert's Julian, like the Greek Oedipus, is saved and loved by God *because of* the crimes to which he was born and the suffering he endured.

# CHAPTER NINE

## Madame Bovary

In his notes for the fourth volume, which would have concentrated on *Madame Bovary*, Sartre asks, "Why write the first three volumes if one does not find them again on each page of the fourth?" It would be inconceivable for him to have meant by this that the enhancement of our understanding of *Madame Bovary* as a literary work was the sole justification of all that preceded. Obviously, he felt that if his method had been accurately applied, a discussion of the book would inevitably bring us back constantly to points established earlier. It is probably in much the same spirit that he has remarked that "anyone could write the fourth volume" by simply drawing the logical conclusions from the interpretation already laid down and continuing to apply the same hermeneutic.[1] I suspect this statement lies somewhere between false modesty and sheer rhetoric. All the same, I think Sartre perhaps does feel that the three volumes of *The Family Idiot* can be taken as constituting a unified and not obviously truncated study in a way that would have been impossible if he had been forced to stop after the first or second volume. The study of *Madame Bovary* was to have shown how the work was a totalization of Flaubert as a "singular universal" expressing his period uniquely. If Sartre's interpretation proved to be convincing, it would not only add to our understanding of the novel and its author, but would offer the test and proof, so to speak, of Sartre's method. I suspect that for devotees of literature the fourth volume might have been the most interesting of all, and some readers would doubtless have been content to enjoy the harvest without following Sartre's laborious tilling of the soil. Yet I find myself wondering if he would actually have written the final volume even if his health had not failed him. While seemingly knowing no limit in his exhaustive exploration of current projects, he never felt inclined to return for further amplification and clarification to ground already explored. The truth is that in the three existing volumes we have considerable information as to how Sartre would interpret *Madame Bovary*, both the work itself and its connection with the life of the author. His notes for the concluding volume offer certain new formulations and much elaboration, but nothing that suggests a startlingly different approach which could not have been anticipated. In this sense only I think, not that "anybody could write the fourth volume," but that any reader of the first three would know how to read *Madame Bovary* from a Sartrean perspective.

It would be idiotic to attempt to construct what the unwritten work might have been—in the manner that classical scholars try to reconstruct lost Greek tragedies on the basis of ancient plot summaries, vase paintings, etc. What does seem to me to be worth doing is to examine what Sartre has actually said about the novel, both in scattered passages in the published work and in the unpublished notes. And first I should say something about the notes. They are precisely that—*notes*. They are in no way an outline of a projected work. There are no completed sections, rarely even a fully worked-out paragraph. They are the first preliminary notations by an author getting ready to write a book which has not yet fully taken shape. They are distressingly like one's own efforts in the early, still disorganized stage of writing. The notes include comments on or by other critics and biographers of Flaubert, references to relevant passages in Flaubert's *Correspondence*, some detailed analysis of tense progressions in passages from *Madame Bovary*, a few somewhat random observations about style, descriptions, symbols, dialogue, etc. In addition and most important are interpretive observations of key points to be made concerning the characters or basic theme of the novel, repeated (sometimes in the same words) throughout the unorganized pages.[2] Obviously, any use of these notes requires the greatest caution. It would be entirely unfair to deal with these private jottings as one would with a printed passage from a completed work. Yet when important points are made clearly, more than once, and particularly when they are closely related to ideas already expressed earlier in *The Family Idiot*, it seems fair to make use of this material in an effort to understand as fully as possible Sartre's reading of Flaubert's most admired book.

We may consider Sartre's contributions from the three points of view that have interested him: first, Flaubert's intention, the meaning of the novel; second, autobiographical reflections; third, formal aspects of style and structure.

## INTENTION AND MEANING

It is true and it is an oversimplification to say that *Madame Bovary* centers on the conflict between the realistic and the romantic attitudes. Certainly Emma's foolish illusions are contrasted with Homais' unattractive and stupid realism. Neither extreme is acceptable, and Flaubert (unlike Molière) suggests no sensible middle path. Sartre has remarked that the novel is definitely post-romantic, that it is the story of "a soul brought to death by romanticism."[3] But it is a work "against Romanticism by a man profoundly influenced by it." I think anyone would agree with this judgment; it explains in part our difficulty in pinpointing Flaubert's ambivalent feeling toward his heroine. Sartre, however, makes a further observation which offers a fuller and more accurate grasp of the essential issue.

> [Madame Bovary is] less the trial of the romantic illusion than the trial of a romanticism incapable of sustaining its illusions to the end. The trial of a romanticism for which twenty years of excess have destroyed its power to believe in its own illusions, of a literature reduced to admitting that it is only literature.

This statement is fundamental to Sartre's reading of the novel—both in the interpretation of its plot and in the analysis of its sytlistic features. The essential conflict in *Madame Bovary* has nothing to do with romanticism and realism either as literary movements or as life styles. It is the tension between the real and the imaginary, which is quite a different thing.

To explain just what this difference is, I will refer to a comment by Sartre on the relation between *Madame Bovary* and *The Temptation of Saint Anthony*. It was Baudelaire who, in a review which delighted Flaubert, declared the subject matter of the two books to be the same. He declared that both the saint and Emma were tempted and harrassed by "all the demons of illusion," by all the "follies" and "lubricities" of the material world. I suggest that we may distinguish between illusions, in the sense of fantasies, and real sensory pleasures and that it is in their way of relating the two that Sartre sees the essential difference between Emma and Anthony. He says,

> Saint Anthony's temptations are imaginary. He would be damned if he took them for realities. Mme Bovary is damned because she does not remain in the imaginary, and seeks to make it real [*le réaliser*].

Emma's fault is not that she prefers the imaginary to the real, but that she betrays the imaginary by substituting the real in its place, by settling for the real in the hope that she may find the imaginary in it.

It may be helpful to contrast a "realistic" summation of the novel's theme with what Sartre is giving us. I suspect that in hundreds of classrooms intelligent but unwary teachers have presented Madame Bovary's story in some such form as the following:

> Emma destroys herself and her life by allowing her foolish dreams of passion and romance, inspired by trashy literature, to poison her life. She arouses our sympathy because the men she meets are unworthy of her and the village of Yonville would stifle any sensitive woman. If we try to imagine what might have saved her, we must postulate two things: (1) A more refined, intelligent, and perceptive husband who might have taken her to live at least in Rouen, if not in Paris. (2) A conversion on Emma's part so that she would be able to discern true worth where it existed and to be content with it. In short, we must hypothesize another woman, another life, no longer the story of Emma Bovary. As things are, her tragedy derived partly from her dreary environment, but her own foolishness was responsible for her not recognizing Charles' devotion and sterling character or even the romantic adoration of Justin. Emma Bovary might have been different if she had not read so many bad novels.[4]

Even at this level of interpretation we encounter a difficulty, for which Flaubert is responsible. Was it the particular kind of books Emma read that ruined her character, or was she destroyed by literature as such? Flaubert seems to hesitate. The novels she got from the maid at the convent were certainly pure kitsch and probably most of those from the lending library. For myself, I always imagine their authors to be predecessors of Elinor Glyn and Barbara Cartland. But Flaubert tells us that Emma also read *Paul et Virginie* and the works of Sir Walter Scott. On the boat with Léon she quoted a line from Lamartine. Sartre points out that her stolen nocturnal readings at school resemble those of Gustave and his classmates at the lycée. *They* read Chateaubriand and Byron. We are told that even before she met Charles, Emma considered herself disillusioned, with nothing henceforth left for her to learn or to feel. The description suits the adolescent *blasés* better than it does Emma. This is one place where the "c'est moi" fits a little too closely. In any case, nobody would suggest that *good* books might have saved Emma. Even within the limits of a realist interpretation, it is a confusion between the regions of the real and of the imaginary which is responsible for her unhappiness. And here we would say that her mistake lay in her inability to accept the real.

Sartre gives us an almost total transformation of the theme as just stated. I may summarize his view as follows:

> What ennobles Emma is that she cherishes a dream for something higher than this world of human mortality can satisfy. She partakes of the grandeur of insatisfaction. The cause of her suffering, that which also renders her ridiculous, is the fact that she fails to understand that what she desires is unreal and cannot be satisfied in the world. *What she betrays is not the real but the imaginary.* To have struggled to be content with Charles' devotion and Justin's idealistic adoration would have been just as much a travesty as her attempt to find fulfillment in her liaisons with Léon and Rodolphe. It is wrong to think that a different husband or a more stimulating environment would have prevented the tragedy. No man in any city could have satisfied her desire for what does not exist except in the imaginary. What *might* have saved her? That which saved Flaubert: art, which knowingly creates the imaginary and assigns greater value to the unreal than to the real. But Emma was not an artist. For her the sole solution was death. Only death and art escape the real.

Sartre notes that *Madame Bovary* and *Don Quixote* have the same subject. Other critics have recognized Cervantes' influence on Flaubert. Harry Levin states that Flaubert's target was "to set forth what Kierkegaard had spied out, to invade the continent of sentimentality, to create a female Quixote—mock-romantic where Cervantes had been mock-heroic."[5] But Sartre lays stress on the resemblance, not in the satiric intent of the two authors, but in the qualities of the hero and heroine—the grandeur of their aspirations, their fallen greatness, the tragedy that dignifies their foolishness—in short (in Flaubert's eyes, at least), their essential rightness in the face of common sense.

I think we might fairly sum up Sartre's view of the novel's theme if we said that for him Flaubert, in his story of Emma Bovary, is simultaneously making a metaphysical affirmation and demonstrating what he believes to be a psychological truth.

The metaphysical claim is one consequence of *le survol*, the *species aeternitatis*, which looks on life from the point of view of death. From this standpoint the basic polarity is seen to be not simply between Emma and Homais. In opposition to her, Sartre would pair the scientistic druggist, Homais, and the curé, Bournisien. It is they who together block off all hope of escape from the unsatisfying world of banal reality. Flaubert believed that the more sensitive of human beings yearn for a fulfilling totality, a beauty or truth or meaning which is worthy of their total devotion, which will take them out of themselves. We recall his expression of this half-pantheistic impulse in the image of the vessel of holy water, reflecting only the living colors of the light coming through the stained glass. Homais, the caricatured representative of science and rationality, denies this hope, scoffing at all mystic rubbish, jeering at any notion of God or soul. The world is only what it seems to be, and it is people like Homais who succeed in it. Bournisien is a satiric portrait of the Church at its poorest, not its best. But as Homais stands for accepted reason, so Bournisien speaks for established religion. We feel, Sartre points out, that both science and religion could have been better represented, even at Yonville, and this increases our sense of the pathos of Emma's situation. Yet the universal implication is there, too. In Flaubert's view science as such blights our highest aspirations, and religious dogma parodies our longing for the infinite by confining it in finite forms—"the black stone or the old man with a beard." The fault common to both Homais and Bournisien is their willingness to be satisfied with the human situation. Flaubert was right to juxtapose them asleep in the death chamber of the woman whom nothing could satisfy.

From the point of view of death all human enterprise is futile. At the end of the novel, Homais receives the Cross of the Legion of Honor. Otherwise, as Flaubert writes, "since the events which are about to be related, nothing has really changed at Yonville" (p. 391).[6] Sartre adds that Charles and Emma, the only ones who had wanted something better, are gone and forgotten. It is as though they had never lived. The living are nourished by the dead as Lestiboudois eats the potatoes he raises in the graveyard. Only art can incarnate the eternal unreal.

Flaubert's psychological intention may be epitomized in the key sentence that Sartre repeats several times in the notes as well as in the published volumes—"I am too small for myself." At first this may seem to be only a repetition or an elaboration of the metaphysical assertion, and indeed the two are interdependent.

Madame Bovary, who dies in horror and damned, is authentically *tragic* (and not dramatic as has been claimed) because her destiny is to live, through an intolerable experience, the radical impossibility of being human—that is, of discovering both that her desire is too great to be satisfied with the goods of this world and that she is too small for her desire (which becomes conscious of itself only through foolishness—as the religious instinct is never manifested save in the mummeries of institutionalized religion). [3:508]

Sartre finds an echo here of Flaubert's own self-doubts—his fear that he was born with creative insights without the necessary talent for realizing them, that he was like the nervous, gifted children "who would never be Mozarts," that there was a gap between the internal subjectivity he *was* and the constitution through which he had to express himself, a dichotomy between person and psychobiological character. His own solution was the catastrophic, self-imposed cure at Pont-l'Evêque, after which he hoped that by no longer living his passions, he could fix them forever, derealized and objectified in literature. Since this solution is denied to his character, Emma pursues fulfillment of her desire for the imaginary in the real world, and this is her downfall. She is too small for herself. Something in her nature impedes every step forward. And since she persists in trying to realize the unreal, Emma "at the moment she escapes banality in dream, sees her dream reapprehended by banality" (3:644). The causes and stages of Emma's gradual "degradation" are indicated by Sartre in a number of fragmentary comments, which I think may be fairly grouped under two headings. (1) She confuses, as Sartre believes Flaubert sometimes did, emotions, aesthetic reactions, and luxury. (2) She exemplifies Flaubert's objection to women: their need to sentimentalize and—as he expressed it rather vulgarly to Louise Colet—the fact that "they take their ass for their heart" (*Corr.* 2:401). Sartre maintains that Emma had only one love, which she allowed to be diverted first to one object and then another. Increasingly, she was willing to pursue purely sensual satisfaction; yearning for the infinite became lust.

Rather than following the plot step by step, I think I can best present Sartre's view of Flaubert's intentions if we look briefly at the sketch of Emma's years at the convent and then concentrate on her relations with the two lovers.

Before settling on *Madame Bovary*, Flaubert toyed with three other scenarios for a novel. One, *Anubis*, would have told the story of a deceived woman who thought she was embraced by a god when in actuality she had sexual intercourse with one of the priests. This exotic theme, much modified, was realized in *Salammbô*. The second was the tale of a Flemish virgin, which Flaubert outlined in a famous letter to Mlle Leroyer de Chantepie: the story of a provincial woman, growing old in bitterness but attaining to the highest state of religious mysticism and purely imaginary physical passion (*Corr.* 4:169). The third, *Don Juan*, was to deal with both heavenly and earthly love as Don Juan united with a nun, he seeking in her something more than the physical, she hoping to find in him something substantial to fulfill the sensual impulse that formed part of her passionate reaching toward God but was never appeased. Sartre, like other critics,[7] recognizes that all three projected novels have the same theme: love that cannot be satisfied. He finds echoes of the second two in *Madame Bovary;* in this connection he has offered what I believe is an original reading.

Sartre remarks that Emma and Charles are both inferior to their education. (I doubt that anyone would seriously maintain that *Madame Bovary* is a critique of French schooling, though Flaubert did on one occasion, in a letter to his mother, deplore the way in which women were generally educated.) So far as religion is concerned, Flaubert is careful not to blame the teaching sisters. Emma is at first attracted to the religious life, falling into a sort of "mystic languor" which is evoked by the flowers at the altar, the incense and candles, the music, the softly moving, pale-faced nuns, the erotic imagery of the Catholic service. Her teachers hope that she might have a vocation, but they are disappointed. Emma is impatient with doctrinal instruction and rebels against discipline. Of course, the later woman is here in embryo, and we could say that she has already revealed to us her shallowness and her inability to separate spiritual aspirations from sensuousness. True, but that is not the whole story. Bart, apropos of this passage, reminds us that on his expedition to Normandy Flaubert had commented on the mingling of religion and the erotic in the cult statues and in the worshippers' attitude, particularly toward the Virgin.[8] To him it seemed inevitable, and in that setting he did not condemn it. The story of the Flemish Virgin would have made this insight a part of its central theme. It is subordinate in *Madame Bovary*, but it is there. And it is important for Sartre's point—that in Flaubert's view any aspiration toward the infinite was diminished and distorted the moment it was incarnated in finite myths, doctrines, or forms of ritual. We see this happening with Emma several times and especially on two occasions. During her serious illness after Rodolphe's departure she seeks the consolations of religion but is quickly put off by the shallow religious books that the curé procures for her. On her death bed, she bestows on the crucifix her "fullest kiss of love." Even at this "purified" moment Flaubert forces us to feel that the spiritual and sensual impulses are inextricable.

Where Sartre departs from other critics is in his insistence that Emma has but one love. He attributes to Flaubert a view that is the precise contrary to Freud's concept of the libido and sublimation. Freud sees in sublimation a higher, disguised, and less direct satisfaction of a purely biological need. Flaubert feels that there is in us an impulse which is originally directed toward something totally beyond the human and finite but which inevitably falls back to the limitations of the animal human if we try to express or realize it in any sphere but that of the imaginary. I think Sartre is correct here. Flaubert never suggests that Emma is to be condemned for adultery per se. What he cannot forgive is her fatuous, if temporary, belief that Charles or Léon or Rodolphe or anyone could be the fulfillment of what she desired.

Sartre makes considerably more of the significance of Flaubert's plans for *Don Juan*. In the notes he states that the theme of the two kinds of love has been embodied in Emma. Considering the way in which she herself lived the adulterous affairs with Léon and Rodolphe (*not* the quality of the men themselves), Sartre claims that her liaison with Rodolphe represents heavenly love, the amour with Léon the earthly. He argues that Emma loved Rodolphe, but that what she felt for Léon was at first purely imaginary (before he went to Paris) and afterward only lust; that the relation with Rodolphe was founded on truth while the intrigue with Léon was based on a lie (she did not tell him about Rodolphe); that her sexual union with Rodolphe was "natural" whereas her relation with Léon involved an exchange of sex, a perversion, depravity.

I believe that if we examine Flaubert's account of Emma's involvement with the two lovers, we will find evidence for Sartre's overall interpretation of Emma and of Flaubert's intention concerning her. I do not think we will find support for such an overneat contrast in her relations with the two men. In fact, I believe that Sartre is in error because of a mistaken emphasis, which I will now explain.

Flaubert, with artistic economy, has used two characters where an inferior novelist might have employed three or even four. To use Flaubert's term, Emma's "sentimental education" progressed through four definite stages, which I will indicate by referring to Léon 1, the timid clerk at Yonville; Léon 2, the self-confident clerk who returned to Rouen after Paris; Rodolphe 1 in the period leading to Emma's cooling toward him and their near break; Rodolphe 2 after the fiasco of the club foot operation had brought Emma back to him. When Sartre contrasts Emma's relations with the two men, he tends to concentrate almost exclusively on what I have called Rodolphe 1 and Léon 2, ignoring evidence from the early days with Léon and the later ones with Rodolphe. In doing so he not only does violence to the text, but also misses evidence which might provide further support for his major thesis: that Emma increasingly betrays the imaginary for the real.

What Sartre says about the stage I have called Léon 1 is not consistent with the sharp contrast he has indicated. In volume 1 and again in the notes he makes three basic observations: (1) Emma's never consummated love remains wholly in the imaginary. (2) There is some true communication between the two, which is expressed nonverbally. (3) What is communicated—in addition to unacknowledged sexual desire—is their common and commonplace romanticism.

Since Léon at this period never found the courage to declare himself, any expression of his or of Emma's feelings must of necessity be indirect. They are conveyed to us by descriptions of small actions and gestures. That these do indeed speak is proved by the fact that Emma herself interprets Léon's behavior and is sure that he loves her. Numerous passages show us that messages are sent and received. For an example I may quote one of those to which Sartre refers.

> They were talking about a group of Spanish dancers who were expected soon at the theatre in Rouen.
> "Will you go?" she asked.
> "If I can," he replied.
> Did they have nothing else to say to each other? Yet their eyes were full of more serious talk; and while they forced themselves to find trivial sentences, they both felt the same languor creep over them; it was like a murmur of the soul, profound, continuous, which dominated over that of their voices. Surprised and marveling at this unfamiliar sweetness, they did not think of speaking of it to one another or of tracing its cause. [pp. 411–12]

Comparable passages might be found in other authors, but usually they will be accompanied by words that by a hint or *double entendre* reflect inner feelings more explicitly. The significant point here, as Sartre reminds us, is that Flaubert always distrusted the verbal expression of emotions. What is genuine is expressed nonverbally. The passage quoted suggests that what Léon and Emma felt for each other in this early period was real.

Most of the time, however, Emma and Léon chattered incessantly, at the inn on the night of their meeting, in their whispered conversations as Léon and Homais dozed by the fire after the card games. Concerning the first of these occasions, Sartre commented in some detail early in volume 1 in discussing the child Gustave's disorientation in language. In this context Sartre wrote,

> Let us say that he looks on words *from the outside*, as things, even when they are in him. . . . Vocables are at first sensible realities; their connections are effected outside—accidents, customs, institutions; meaning comes third, the strict consequence of the first two moments but in itself *anything whatsoever*.

Sartre uses the first encounter of Emma and Léon to prove his point. They had spoken of travel, of music and reading, and especially of nature. But the literal content of their conversation was not its meaning. Sartre says,

> Emma and Léon will speak of nature because the situation requires—by social custom—that it be spoken of; not that there is any logical reason for it; it is simply that Nature is invoked at a certain stage in sexual relations. At the same instant thousands of couples are saying the same things in the same terms. It is essential for these still platonic lovers to feel, thanks to this silly prattle, a "communion of souls" with their future mistresses. In short, the verbal connections are physical, they are modulations of a chant. The purpose of this conventionalized lovers' speech is to replace caresses, impossible at this stage, to prepare them, and by this communication of breaths before embracing, to awaken a feeling of reciprocity. The meaning is there in the vocables, prefabricated. It is needed not *for itself* but in order that the future lovers, in sharing a taste, may create the equivalent of a shared desire. [1:27]

I think we may say that there are at least three layers of meaning in the lovers' conversation as we read it: the literal statements, the erotic, of which Sartre speaks, and the author's ironic commentary. In the notes Sartre makes a further point. The romantic longings that Emma and Léon express are reminiscent, even in the specific details and actual choice of words, of the lyrical utterances of the hero of *November*. Flaubert is mocking himself as well as his characters. Sartre's attitude toward the pair is mostly cynical, but he does acknowledge a certain reciprocity. Is he correct, then, when he says in the notes that Emma never loved Léon and that before Léon went to Paris, hers was a purely imaginary love? What drew them together was their romanticism. We may call it shallow and false. But Flaubert suggests that as human loves go, it was real. Emma did not immediately try to see Léon as a romantic hero as she did with the viscount at the ball. Indeed, she was slow to recognize her own feelings as Flaubert tells us in a homely, tender image.

> She did not question herself to know whether she loved him. Love, she believed, must arrive suddenly, with great explosions and lightnings—a hurricane from the skies which falls upon a life, overturns it, sweeps away wills like leaves, and carries the whole heart into the abyss. She did not know that on the terrace of houses, the rain makes lakes when the rainspouts are choked. [p. 416]

I am surprised that Sartre, instead of insisting that Emma never really loved Léon, did not make positive use of his insight that at this early stage she kept her feeling for him in the realm of the imaginary. Flaubert tells us that inwardly Emma seethed with hatred of her husband and desire for Léon. The role she chose to play was that of the inaccessible, loyal wife. "I am a virtuous woman," she said to her reflection in the mirror, and this was the image she offered to Léon up to the moment of his departure. We may sneer at her for cowardice; we may even argue that if Léon had been bolder, she would have put up little resistance. The fact remains that, with Léon 1, she has not yet betrayed the imaginary by taking steps to make it real. After he goes, she is embittered and frustrated; she is not wholly disillusioned. Sartre seems to recognize this when he observes that her dreams of what might have been make the reality of Yonville unbearable.

Sartre is primarily interested in contrasting Emma's and Rodolphe's liaison with the fulfillment of her passion for Léon after his return from Paris. Flaubert has provided numerous details to show that he clearly wanted to stress the parallel development of the two affairs. The question is whether he wished primarily to contrast them or to play up their similarity. Is his intention to mark Emma's degradation or to stress the meaningless repetition of patterns that is inherent in human endeavors? Sartre stresses the former almost to the exclusion of the latter; I think there is evidence that Flaubert was doing both.

Sartre makes his most impressive point in a long and truly brilliant discussion of the contrast between the two scenes in which Emma first gives herself to her lovers. With Rodolphe it takes place in the woods. Sartre does not deny that Rodolphe is a cheap seducer nor that Emma is in bad faith. Yet he feels that when their union is first consummated, the author's irony is momentarily suspended. Flaubert's description suggests that Emma's sexual fulfillment is in harmony with surrounding nature; there are pantheistic overtones.

> She surrendered herself. [Most translators say "She gave herself to him." But "lui" is not there, only *elle s'abondonna.*] The shadows of evening were falling. The horizontal sun, passing through the branches, dazzled her eyes. Here and there, all around her, in the leaves or on the ground, luminous spots were quivering as if hummingbirds in flight had scattered their feathers. Silence was everywhere; something sweet seemed to come forth from the trees. She felt her heart, whose beats were beginning again, and the blood circulating in her flesh like a river of milk. Then she heard from far off beyond the woods, on other hills, a vague, prolonged cry, a voice which was long drawn out, and she listened to it silently, as it mingled like music with the last vibrations of her throbbing nerves. [p. 472]

This time Emma has not been talking about nature, but its presence is felt. There is no human chatter. As Sartre puts it, "she has no words in her head." It is in total silence that she is aware of the sights and sound that seem to mingle with her own being. Sartre finds a beauty and innocence in it all that seem to absolve Emma. He says of Rodolphe, "This deceiver is the dupe of the world, its chosen instrument whereby it may, on the occasion of a totally maculate conception, attain in this woman a self-awareness." As for Emma, she "is very close to realizing the prayer of the last Saint Anthony: 'to be matter'" (2:1283).

Sartre thinks that Flaubert sustains the sense of authenticity until Emma stands before her mirror at home that night. Even here the subtle movement from the indirect reporting of her reactions (*le style indirect libre*) to direct speech protects the genuineness of what has occurred. Emma recalls the fields, the surrounding trees, the rustling of the foliage and calls of the birds. She wonders at her own reflection. "Never had her eyes been so large, so black, of such depth" (p. 473). The indirect style leaves us uncertain, Sartre says, as to whether her reflected face is really modified by the experiences she has undergone or whether she imagines it. Suddenly she speaks aloud.

"I have a lover! a lover!" Now all is altered. She sees herself, not as she was in the forest, but as in a book, one of the countless heroines whose passions she wanted to experience as her own. She has become unauthentic.

Still, there are moments which seem to repeat the first occasion. I may add in support of Sartre that the development of the story of Emma and Rodolphe continues to stress the association with nature. When he comes to her, they meet in the garden at night. When she sometimes makes a surprise visit to him at dawn, she comes with the freshness of the morning dew on her hair. "It was like a spring morning entering his room" (p. 475). Flaubert goes on to say, "Something stronger than herself impelled her to him." Sartre feels that at this point something of a "heavenly love" remains in Emma's impulse, even if it is kept alive through the imaginary—or perhaps for that very reason.

In sharp contrast with the forest scene, Emma's and Léon's first sexual union takes place in a tightly curtained cab (*fiacre*). Sartre claims that Flaubert has deliberately made the lovers ridiculous by an abrupt change in point of view. We as readers are almost violently moved from participation to extreme detachment as the author forsakes gentle irony for savage satire. In the hotel room the previous evening we were still very close as we observed the two trying to idealize each other and their love. By an effort of imagination, Sartre says, each one tried to deny the primacy of carnal desire, to transcend the physical toward beauty and purity.

> In order to reassure her of the purity of his intentions, the young clerk transforms his desire to make her an adulteress into an inconsolable regret at having been unable to marry her. Two sister souls, meant to soar together, frustrated by evil chance: in short, they are *already* married. [2:1276]

Of course, deception and self-deception are present. Flaubert writes, "She did not confess her passion for another; he did not say that he had forgiven her" (p. 537). This is the lie that Sartre claims rests at the basis of their relation. Yet one feels that there is a truth here, too. In the midst of their talk occurs one of Flaubert's significant nonverbal exchanges, which Sartre does not mention.

> They were no longer speaking; but looking at one another they sensed a humming in their heads as if something resonant had reciprocally escaped from the fixed pupils of their eyes. They had just joined hands; and the past, the future, reminiscences and

dreams, all were mingled and confused in the sweetness of this ecstasy. [p. 540]

Shortly thereafter Léon leaves. Sartre points out that during the whole evening the two strove valiantly to support each other's self-image and their mutual dignity as free beings not at the mercy of generic, biological impulses. In terms suggesting that he is recalling his own intentions in *No Exit* (as well as in *Being and Nothingness*), he says that the task was made easier in that no Look of a third person was there to destroy their fragile intersubjectivity. They were not *seen*.

> This isolated intersubjectivity they take for their absolute being: You desire me, therefore I am. I desire you, therefore you are. No wonder if each one is convinced of his transcendence by the faith which his partner reveals to him. [2:1276–77]

The scene next morning at the cathedral is deliciously comic, but in the beginning we are still near to Emma and Léon as individual persons pursuing their ends in the fashion of their own determining—Léon proffering the gift of violets, Emma offering and then taking back the letter of farewell, Léon furiously impatient with the beadle's sightseeing tour, Emma clutching at it with relief, clinging to "her expiring virtue."[9] Once they have entered the cab, everything changes.

> What does Flaubert do? He obeys his creatures. They have drawn the curtains so as not to be seen by anyone? Very well, then. Nobody shall see them. Not even the author. [2:1277]

But the cab will be seen by everybody in Rouen. Flaubert makes the couple ridiculous by an excess of impersonalism which dehumanizes. Sartre links Flaubert's "impersonality" in this passage with his own theory of the laugh. "Since the laugh is a refusal to understand and to participate, he will render them *objectively laughable*" (2:1284). Léon and Emma are not henceforth mentioned in this episode. We are told nothing of their feelings. A voice directs the coachman, once a bare hand reaches out, finally a veiled woman emerges and walks hastily down the street. We do not see the man.

The narrator, who has been so near to his characters, suddenly merges with the point of view of all Rouen as the populace sees the closed vehicle move round and round crazily, passing and repassing the same spots in apparently random motion. The demoralization of the coachman, so comically described by Flaubert, is obviously a source of delight to Sartre, who seems to be trying to do him one better in his analysis of the scene. At Paris, Sartre observes, the driver would know what is going on and relax in the expectation of a large tip. At Rouen he is simply bewildered. What so distresses the driver is that he sees the cab stripped of its normal function, which is to convey persons as directly as possible to a chosen destination. The vehicle is suddenly a monstrous mechanism to be moved by a mysterious interior voice. The driver would like to stop, to satisfy his hunger and thirst, to rest a bit, but he must keep on like a machine himself. He cannot understand this "frenzy of locomotion." Sartre points to the *double entendre* in the words and adds that the joltings of the cab are obviously meant to suggest the movements of intercourse.

> Thus the two lovers, transformed into a furious vehicle, are more naked than in a bed since they no longer have anything to protect them. Their "sexual embrace"[10] is public. . . . As the driver, unguided, continues to repass the same places, the copulation which they wished to hide is transformed into an obscene exhibition. [2:1281]

The satire extends beyond the couple inside; it is directed at the whole human species.

To point up the contrast with Emma's first love scene with Rodolphe in the woods, Sartre comments on the symbolism of the closed curtains. This pair is totally isolated from nature. Sartre takes special pleasure in one detail of the cab's journey.

> It is a stroke of genius to have the cab pass "behind the hospital gardens where in the sun old men in black coats walk the length of the terrace all green with ivy." The fiery flash of grotesque and finally desperate *furia* traverses the mortuary calm of old age, of repetition without hope, of ancient and taciturn nature. But inversely the poignant poetry of this terrace disqualifies the two lovers because they, wholly occupied in mingling their sweat, *do not see it.* Drawn curtains: Communication refused. It is the opposite of the *"baisade"* with Rodolphe. [2:1286n.]

I am surprised that Sartre does not mention a still more obvious symbol. At one point the cab is going along a field of red clover. A hand reaches out and scatters tiny pieces of paper. The fragments of Emma's farewell letter float through the air and come to rest on the flowers "like white butterflies."[11] These broken resolutions are Emma's sole contact with nature on this occasion.

Sartre's contrast of the two seduction scenes is very persuasive, and I would not argue that Flaubert did not mean to suggest a certain moral decline in Emma. Yet Sartre seems to me to have weighted the scales a bit by discussing the evening preceding the seduction by Léon and omitting a comparable preliminary scene for Emma with Rodolphe—their meeting at the agricultural fair. Certainly the counterpoint in this passage where Flaubert interlaces the sentences, even the phrases and words, of Rodolphe's insincere protestations with the high-flown rhetoric of the politician's speeches is more openly mocking than the later conversation in the hotel room. That the scenes are deliberately parallel I grant. In fact, Sartre has commented, apropos of Emma and Rodolphe, that in this scene, there is one moment of silent communication. Flaubert writes,

> Rodolphe was no longer speaking. They looked at one another. A supreme desire made their dry lips tremble; and slackly, effortlessly their fingers intertwined. [p. 462]

Sartre finds it significant that this nonverbal moment of true feeling is put side by side with the announcement of the name of the old woman who was to receive a medal for fifty-four years of service at the same farm. Possibly so. I find the close resemblance, including even the detail of the clasped hands, to a similar moment in the later conversation between Emma and Léon still more impressive.

One can find other small points that underscore the parallel in the two relationships. Some of these certainly suggest a deliberate contrast. Sartre notes that, while Emma embarrassed both men with her presents, it was to Rodolphe that she gave the hand-sewn cigar case that, in her own mind, identified him with the Viscount and herself with the Viscount's mistress. I may mention in addition the contrast between Emma's morning visits to Rodolphe, when she seemed to bring with her the spring morning, and her theatrical gesture of buying roses to throw over Léon as he lay in bed. There is a marked difference, too, between the unexpected, stolen meetings with Rodolphe and the regularly scheduled Thursdays with Léon. Sartre points to a progressive use of the mirror as symbol. At the time of Léon 1, Emma murmured to her reflection, "I am a virtuous woman." After she has first given herself to Rodolphe, the words are, "I have a lover." In a passage which Flaubert later deleted, Emma, in Léon's room, "undresses brutally" before the looking glass. This example certainly indicates a downward movement, but it is significant that Sartre must refer to the two phases of the relation with Léon to make his point, which weakens his contrast between Emma's two loves.

Other parallels stress sameness rather than difference. For example, Sartre notes that the decisive stroke in persuading Emma to get into the cab is an appeal to her "snobbism"—"It's done in Paris." He does not mention the obvious parallel: when Emma demurred at the plan of going riding with Rodolphe, it was the promise of a new riding habit that decided her. What seems to me most important, however, is what Flaubert has done with the later part of Emma's liaison with Rodolphe, which I have referred to as the stage of Rodolphe 2. The relation of the two now is so altered that, as I suggested earlier, another author might have felt it necessary to introduce a new character. Yet Flaubert is convincing in indicating that it all stems from a change in Rodolphe's attitude. Earlier, partly under the spell of Emma's idealistic romanticism, he had restricted his love-making to "respectful forms." Very delicately, Flaubert shows us how now, more openly sensual, Rodolphe introduced Emma to new expressions of eroticism. Sartre remarks that the conventions of the day forbade Flaubert to be explicit in physical details. "Like Celia, Emma does not shit." Artistically, this was fortunate. No explicit description in the modern style could possibly convey the depths of depraved sensuality expressed in the sentence, "He made of her something supple and corrupt" (p. 500). In short, Emma shows herself ready to settle for lust. She "takes her ass for her heart." Flaubert has included one passage which seems to me to be a deliberate travesty of the half-pantheistic ecstasy she experienced in the scene in the forest. Note the juxtaposition of the two sentences.

> He made of her something supple and corrupt. Hers was an idiotic
> sort of attachment, full of admiration for him, of voluptuousness
> for her, a beatitude that benumbed her; and her soul sank in
> this intoxication and drowned in it, shriveled up, like the duke of
> Clarence in his butt of malmsey. [p. 500]

The image is especially appropriate if one recalls that malmsey is a sweet, heavy wine. In my opinion, the contrast with the first love scene with Rodolphe is at least as striking as that between the forest setting and the cab.

In the notes Sartre lays special emphasis on the point that Emma's relation with Rodolphe is the perfectly natural one between man and woman whereas with Léon there is a change of sex, a perversion. (I will not take up the question of whether Sartre may or may not betray here a certain prejudice as to just what the approved pattern of man-woman relations should be, but at least we may acquit him of puritanism. When he speaks of "perversion," he is not making a moral judgment. He defines the term as "taking to the limit an erotic image which is based on the imaginary.") Without question Flaubert has included a masculine element in his portrayal of Emma, which is never more evident than in her relations with Léon. I shall return to this point in my discussion of the autobiographical implications of *Madame Bovary*. At present I will simply argue that Sartre is certainly right in finding an intensification of sensuality and masculinity in Emma in the episode with Léon 2, but that the difference between this and the period of Rodolphe 2 is not so clear-cut as he would have us believe. Sartre acknowledges that Rodolphe 2 "prepared Emma" for Léon 2, but adds that whereas she was the pupil to Rodolphe in the art of corruption, she was teacher to Léon. This is correct, and it is true also that Flaubert tells us that Léon "was becoming her mistress instead of her being his" (p. 578). Sartre observes, too, that at the masked ball with Léon, Emma wears the costume of a man; it is on the morning following this occasion that she realizes the full extent of her degradation, that she was in the company of "women of the lowest class." Emma maintained the aggressive role with Léon. Sometimes, however, she played at being his mother, assuming an air of great authority and experience, calling him child. It is not wholly a matter of reversing the male and female roles. Moreover, it is not only with Léon that Emma's "masculine side" is emphasized. Sartre himself notes that she regularly wore a monocle "like a man," and he comments on the way Flaubert describes Emma and Charles as seeming to have exchanged the usual roles of man and woman in their manner on the morning after their wedding night. "It was he whom you would have taken for the virgin of the evening before while the bride allowed nothing to be revealed from which you could guess anything" (p. 352). And during the period with Rodolphe 2 she once scandalized the people of Yonville by holding a cigarette in her mouth as she walked with him and by one day wearing a waistcoat cut like a man's.

To sum up, I think Sartre is right in saying that Emma's love affairs show in her a steady deterioration, but I do not think the evidence will sustain his claim that, as anticipated in the somewhat different plan for the heroine of *Don Juan*, Emma experienced with Rodolphe and Léon respectively a heavenly and an earthly love. If I have devoted so much space to the matter, it is not that I consider it of great importance to prove that Sartre is mistaken in a single point of interpretation, offered chiefly in unpublished notes. It is rather that examination of the arguments he presents, put side by side with Flaubert's own account, seems to me to result in overwhelming support of his major claim—that Emma's sin is her increasing betrayal of the imaginary by seeking to make it real.

In volume 2 Sartre gave another explanation of Flaubert's lack of sympathy with Emma's liaison with Léon, one which is not bound up with any notion of heavenly and earthly loves.

> Life appeared to Flaubert as a cycle of involutive repetitions; everything always recommences but by ceaselessly degrading itself. Thus he would willingly apply to the events of an individual life the remark which Marx will make a little later concerning the great events of history: facts reproduce themselves; the first time they are true and tragic, the second burlesque. . . . Thus in giving herself to the young clerk Emma parodies herself. This sexual intercourse is a caricature, the hysterical imitation of the unique instant, forever lost, when a movement which, managing to overleap its finite determination, reintegrated her with the infinite, while, by a reverse movement, the macrocosm entered into her and was made whole there. [2:1284]

I think we must be careful not to misunderstand or to make too much of this one ecstatic moment. Flaubert is certainly not suggesting (nor is Sartre implying that he does) either that sex with the right person at the right moment or a mystic union with nature represents a genuine fulfillment of our aspiration for the infinite, as though after all there might be a way to overcome the "being too small for oneself" and to appease the unsatisfiable desire. Emma's experience in the forest does indeed bear a resemblance to Djalioh's melting into nature, to Jules' ecstatic moment of insight, and to Gustave's childhood trances. But Flaubert sternly refused to entertain pantheism on the level of true concept or philosophical truth. All of these experiences (save possibly that of Djalioh, who is not fully human) depend heavily on the imaginative insight of the subject. Even in the case of Emma, it is important to remember that she did not yield to Rodolphe until after he had returned to the romantic words that he knew she wished to hear. If this moment was privileged, it was not because it revealed a truth about the human being's relation to the surrounding world but because illusion and the natural surroundings for once worked together to create a moment of beauty.

Emma is ridiculous because she thinks the infinite and unreal can be grasped in the finite relationships in the real world. Yet clearly

Flaubert feels that she is better than the mediocre men she tried to love. Sartre observes that even at the end, when she begs both of them for money, she asks nothing of them that she would not have been willing to do herself—for them and for love. She would gladly have stolen for Léon, she would have sold her own possessions for Rodolphe. But "Léon was a coward, and Rodolphe was stingy." Furthermore, Sartre points out that Emma was never really cured. Even after Rodolphe's refusal, she leaves, more hurt in her love than in her disappointment at not having got the money. She still feels that if Rodolphe had not refused her, all might have been well. "She still believes in Prince Charming."

Flaubert's irony is a bit heavy-handed at the death bed as he describes how the priest annointed the eyes, nose, hands, and feet of the body that had taken such delight in adulterous pursuits. Is he ironic still when he tells us that Emma bestowed upon the crucified Christ "the fullest kiss of love that she had ever given"? It is hard to be sure. Possibly her fervor and sincerity are greater here because it is a symbol she kisses and not even she can take it for a reality. In any case the effect is negated by the final song of the blind man. Emma dies with a disillusioned laugh at the blighting of *all* dreams of love and fulfillment. Sartre says several times in the notes that if Emma had not happened to find Justin alone so that she could procure the poison, the ending would have been different. "She would not have committed suicide a day later." He gives no explanation for this judgment. Presumably it is because he feels that since she was not cured, she would have found some other form of dream to support her. Or perhaps, like Flaubert in the seventies, she would have "outlived herself." But then Emma did not have art. In any case, Flaubert does not end the book with her death but goes on to tell us of the destinies of the other characters and particularly of the death of Charles.

Sartre writes particularly sympathetically of Charles and assigns him a slightly different role in the novel than the one critics have generally allotted to him. He is described by Sartre as the man of no imagination who was doubly destroyed by imagination. During Emma's lifetime, it is an imaginary woman he lives with, not the real Emma. Since he does not understand Emma, he is easily mistaken in thinking that because he is content, he is making her happy. Yet his love is his whole life. Lack of imagination does not prevent depth of feeling. (While Sartre does not say so, I may suggest that possibly Flaubert is making the point that it is precisely the people without imagination who are capable of loving without reservation or question.) After Emma's death, when Emma, in Flaubert's unforgettable words, "corrupted him from the grave," Charles tried to become the man she wanted, to live by her values. We may say that he died of a broken heart, or, less sentimentally, that he no longer had the will to live. The fact is that Charles died the "death by thought" that Flaubert awarded his young hero of *November*, there—but not in *Madame Bovary*—adding that such deaths are possible in fiction only. There may be deliberate irony in assigning this romantic fate to the bumbling, ordinary, rather stupid country doctor. But Sartre believes that Flaubert wanted us "to weep for Charles," to feel that his death, like Emma's, was truly tragic. Flaubert himself has said that Charles was more like Léon than appeared on the surface. Sartre notes a small resemblance to Rodolphe. Both men, he comments, wore boots "they considered good enough for the country." Understandably, Sartre does not press the similarity. His reading of the scene in which Charles, after discovering the truth, finally meets Rodolphe is different from the usual critical view. Charles pronounces the one fine phrase of his life. "It is the fault of fatality." Rodolphe, who complacently feels that he has managed to arrange the fatality, finds what Charles has said quite comic. Critics tend to feel that Rodolphe has the last word.[12] Sartre disagrees. If one really understands what has happened, Charles is right (1:333). It was not Rodolphe but fate that destroyed Emma, the same fate of human circumstances that blights all aspirations for something beyond the wretched condition to which we are born, and the fate that seemed to Flaubert to blight his own existence as a younger son.

Flaubert once remarked that his Emma Bovary was now weeping in twenty villages in France. But it would be a mistake to see her either as a victim of a social milieu or as a recognizable type of discontented woman, a never matured, romantic, adolescent girl. She is more universal than that. Anyone who has experienced a desire for more than this world can offer may say with Flaubert, "Madame Bovary, c'est moi." Flaubert projected an important part of himself into his created character and thereby avoided what might have been a fate comparable to hers. If Emma was destroyed by literature, Flaubert saved himself by it. Sartre's attitude toward that is ambivalent, to say the least.

## AUTOBIOGRAPHICAL REFLECTIONS

The significant connections between *Madame Bovary* and its author fall into two groups: those that seem to throw light on Flaubert's relations with other members of the family, and those that show him projecting aspects of himself in his characters, not only in Emma but also in Léon and, if Sartre is correct, even in Charles.

Looking first at reflections of his family relationships, we come immediately to the problem of Dr. Achille-Cléophas Flaubert. Obviously, Charles is not to be taken as a portrait of Gustave's father (or brother either), but Sartre thinks that Flaubert was not above taking a certain pleasure in making the dim-witted Charles a representative of the medical profession, even if he never qualified as a full-fledged physician. There is at least one parallel between Charles and the director of the hospital at Rouen: it appears that Achille-Cléophas, too, once attempted unsuccessfully to operate on a clubfoot.[13] The portrait of Dr. Larivière, who is called in for consultation when Emma is dying, is almost certainly based on Gustave's father, and most critics have taken it to be a flattering one, a tribute offered by filial piety. Sartre finds this incredibly naïve. Who is right? On the surface, at least, the description seems wholly admiring. We are told that the doctor was one of the old-time philosophical physicians, who disdained honors, who were fanatically devoted to the art of medicine, which they practiced "with enthusiasm and wisdom." His students so revered him that they imitated him down to the details of his clothing. But even in this laudatory paragraph, there is a suspicious hint of self-complacent arrogance.

> And so he went his way, full of that *majesté débonnaire* which is given by the consciousness of a great talent, of fortune, and forty years of a hard-working, irreproachable existence. [p. 618]

Almost everything here is potentially two-edged. *Débonnaire* can mean "meek" (it is so used to translate the key phrase in the third Beatitude), but frequently it is closer to the idea of "goodnatured" or "easygoing." With the word *majesté* it conveys the idea of "condescending." *Fortune,* in French as in English, may refer to either luck or personal wealth. Flaubert's choice of words is a bit dubious if he intended an unalloyed compliment. Sartre argues that if Flaubert had wanted to pay tribute to his father, it would have been more natural to introduce the doctor in a situation where he could effect a cure. As it is, the great doctor is brought into a situation where he is helpless to do anything. Then there is the statement that after talking with Charles, Dr. Larivière left with Dr. Canivet, "who didn't care either" (i.e., who also did not want) to see Emma die under his hands. But Sartre omits to mention that Dr. Larivière, witnessing Charles' distress, could not hold back a tear, which fell on his shirtfront (1:454 ff.).

Is Flaubert making little digs which perhaps he would not acknowledge even to himself? I suggest that our answer depends on how we respond to the account of the doctor's dinner with Homais. Dr. Larivière certainly sums up the druggist when he reassures Mme Homais' anxiety for her husband's health by saying, "It is not his blood that is thick." Are we to think that at this meeting we have the true scientist contrasted with the pseudoscientist who makes a travesty of all science? Or is Flaubert saying that both represent that shallow rationalism which can neither understand nor help those whose souls cry out for something more than science? We may note that there is no suggestion that Dr. Larivière's sympathy for Charles and Emma in any way prevented his thorough enjoyment of the delicacies Homais ordered for their dinner.

Baudelaire, in his review of *Madame Bovary*, recognized both that Flaubert had incarnated himself in his heroine and that in so doing he bestowed upon her certain masculine traits. Insofar as possible he "stripped himself of his own sex and made himself a woman." In her energy and ambitions, and even as "dreamer," "Madame Bovary remained a man. Like Pallas in armor sprung from the brain of Zeus, this bizarre androgynous being retained all the seductions of a virile soul in a charming feminine body."[14] In *Search for a Method* Sartre indicated that in a study of Flaubert, it would be important to make a phenomenological study of Emma Bovary in order to understand the meaning of Flaubert's metamorphosis of himself into a woman.

> [We must ask,] what the artistic transformation of male into female means in the nineteenth century (we must study the context of *Mlle de Maupin*, etc.), and finally, just who Gustave Falubert *must have been* in order to have within the field of his possibles the possibility of portraying himself as a woman. The reply is independent of all biography, since this problem could be posed in Kantian terms: "Under what conditions is the feminization of experience possible?" [p. 141]

While Sartre has not been able to carry through with all of his ambitious program, the published volumes include considerable discussion of Flaubert's "femininity" and its presence in *Madame Bovary*, and Sartre has given a few hints at least on how all this would be related to the social milieu.

We have already considered Sartre's view of Flaubert's sexuality as connected with his constitutional passivity, his desire for the "phallic mother," and the accompanying nostalgia for androgyny, expressed both in the wish-fantasy of his romantic hero (in *November*) that he might have the experience of being a woman and in Flaubert's equally unrealistic wish that Louise Colet might be at once woman and man. The most obvious reflections of all this in the novel are to be found in the episodes with Emma and Léon. In Sartre's discussion of these what emerges most strikingly is the fact that to some degree Flaubert has alternately—sometimes perhaps even simultaneously—identified himself with both Emma and Léon. Baudelaire claimed that Emma was masculine in her sensuality and her pursuit of pleasure. Possibly from the nineteenth-century male's point of view this was so. Sartre, as we have seen, takes the same attitude, viewing the entire relation of Emma to Léon as based on a "perversion" of their natural sex roles. Speaking for myself, I find all of this comment on Emma's "masculinity" a bit exaggerated. That she would have had a wistful yearning for the more free and adventurous life that she imagined to be open to a man is only natural for any woman in a society which opens more doors for men than for women. This is especially true for Emma, who always believed that an alteration in her situation—whether another man or a different city—would perhaps allow her to realize her dreams. Flaubert explicitly says this in the course of describing Emma's pregnancy.

> She wished for a son; he would be strong and dark, and she would call him George; and this idea of having a male as her child was like a hoped-for revenge for all her past impotences. A man, at least, is free; he can explore passions and countries, overcome obstacles, taste the most distant pleasures. But a woman is continually held back. [pp. 405–6]

When she learns that she has borne a girl, Emma faints. Decades before Freud, Flaubert writes of a woman who, frustrated in her own desires, hopes to compensate by vicariously living the life of her son. The motivation he supplies is a cultural one, not the famous "penis envy" hypothesized by Freud. The passage shows also a sensitivity on Flaubert's part to circumstances not resembling his own which

Sartre is reluctant to recognize and which, it must be admitted, is seldom present in Flaubert's attitude toward women outside of fiction.

There is nothing masculine in Emma's relations with Rodolphe. The only suggestion of an exchange of sex roles with Charles is the description of the pair on the first morning after the wedding night, and this quite clearly refers solely to their respective reactions to their first sexual union. If Charles, rather than Emma, resembles the newly awakened deflowered virgin, this is because the experience meant more to him than it did to her. Like the wedding guests, we may wonder why but cannot know. Inasmuch as Charles certainly had full sexual relations with his first wife, I think the text, as concerns him, refers to enhanced emotional experience or what we might call erotic rather than sexual in the narrow sense. Sartre refers to a notation in Flaubert's plans for the novel, which says that Emma received no pleasure from her husband. We may easily believe that the experience was disappointing to her whether there was technically a physical satisfaction or not. The point is not important for our concern here. Nothing on that morning after suggests that she was the aggressive partner. With the weak and relatively inexperienced Léon, Emma, the pupil of Rodolphe, naturally dominates, but this is hardly to say that she does not remain fully feminine unless one is to cling to an outmoded view of what feminine sexuality is. I agree, however, that what Flaubert has told us of the quality of Emma's and Léon's amorous relations is important, and it is legitimate to ask whether we may find here reflections of Flaubert himself.

Insofar as the identification with Emma is concerned, Sartre does not emphasize the explicitly sexual. To the degree that he was fascinated by the idea of living in imagination the life of any of his characters, Flaubert may have derived a particular satisfaction from imagining as fully as possible what it would be like to be a woman. The conventional equation of femininity and passivity may have held a special appeal for him. Beyond what Sartre has pointed out apropos of Emma's union with Rodolphe in the forest, we might find a special significance in the fact that the pantheistic aspect is inextricably linked with a feminine sexual fulfillment. Once again, I think passivity is the essential thing here. But it is possible that in Flaubert's mind passive receptivity to these visionary moments and his imaginary femininity were closely associated. On the whole, however, it is his deepest aspirations toward beauty, the eternal, and the more than humanly real that he both incarnates and to some degree ridicules in Emma. To put this self in a woman may reflect a feeling on Flaubert's part that this aspect of his character was more feminine than truly virile. We recall his complaint that women possessed a large degree of the artist's innate special sensitivity, but that they almost inevitably betray it by linking it with the particular erotic. This is Emma's error. I cannot go so far as to agree with Sartre when he says in the notes that "the subjectivity of Emma is not that of a man but of a man who believes himself a woman." He adds that a woman would have portrayed Emma differently. True, and so would a different man. I agree that if Flaubert's own psychological traits had been different, he would not have been able to give us Emma. But that Emma as a character is "a disguised man" I cannot accept. The question of how much in her is also Flaubert is a quite different thing.

Sartre lays more stress on the degree to which Flaubert has identified his own sexual inclinations with Léon's. He does not mean, of course, that Flaubert has modeled Léon as a person after himself. Sartre observes that Flaubert disliked Léon, partly perhaps because he resembled Ernest Chevalier, who also posed as a romantic in his youth but later became a typical bourgeois. But Léon in bed with Emma offers some interesting parallels to what we know of Flaubert. Léon is indeed a male who plays a role closer to that conventionally assigned to women.

To Léon Emma was the Angel and the Mistress. At times he felt uneasily that he was the one possessed by her, but this half-resentful attitude belonged to reflective moments away from her. In her presence he experienced the same kind of self-effacement, the fulfilling loss of self that Emma felt with Rodolphe.

> Often in looking at her, it seemed to him that his soul, escaping toward her, spread out like a wave above the outline of her head and descended, drawn down into the whiteness of her breast.
> [p. 567]

What is different here is the sense of being absorbed into the other or blended with her, and—though Sartre does not comment on it—there is something faintly reminiscent of the symbiotic relation of mother and infant.

At other times Flaubert describes something almost frenetic in their relations, especially on Emma's part, and Léon is put off.

> There was on that brow, covered with cold drops, on those trembling lips, in those distraught eyes something extreme, vague and

mournful, which seemed to Léon to slip subtly between them as if to separate them. [p. 583]

Sartre finds in these descriptions echoes of both Flaubert's imagined sexual fantasies and his actual relation with Louise. In Emma, Léon has found the dream mistress of the hero of *November*, the woman adored and feared, who ruins men with her whims, who devours her lover with kisses that suck out his very soul. There is a still an older echo. Flaubert shows Emma liking to play the role of mother. Sartre claims that Léon fulfills, so far as is consistent with Flaubert's surface realism, the dream of the phallic mother. He is like the dependent male child, roused to virility, so as to penetrate and possess the caressing mother.

Sartre sees one very specific connection between art and life in the cab episode, and he believes that it helps to explain Flaubert's mockery of the lovers. The Goncourt brothers recorded in their journal an occasion in 1862 when Flaubert told them about the beginning of his involvement with Louise. He described how it all took shape in a ride in a cab, with him playing the role of one disgusted with life, filled with Byronic gloom, yearning for suicide. The game so much amused and disgusted him that from time to time he stuck his nose out the door so as to give himself relief in laughing (2:1269). The Goncourts looked on all this quite unfavorably and Sartre declares flatly that Flaubert's recital was the act of a cad. He and Louise (even after the affair was over) moved in the same circles; he could count on the two Goncourts to repeat the story, and the now well-known cab scene in the novel would add to the hilarity. What Sartre thinks Flaubert was doing, both in his conversation and in the novel, was to give vent to a rancorous memory. A carriage ride with Louise shortly before his first night with her played an important part in their sentimental history. The love-making was purely verbal or implied. Louise's child was present, and there were probably no closed curtains. But Sartre believes that the "line" Flaubert describes to the Goncourts was in all probability his timid attempt to reveal to Louise something of himself, either as he was or as he had been in the past. It may have been partly role-playing, but at least the role was one that Gustave had played for himself for some years. In a letter to Louise which Sartre cites, he speaks of having "begun by showing her his wounds." At twenty-five, Flaubert, though he had considerable experience with prostitutes and a glamorous courtesan in Egypt, was unsure of himself with a woman of Louise's social standing. Sartre notes that

Flaubert was inadequate their first night together though he easily made up for it on subsequent occasions. Sartre claims that the memory of his lack of assurance rankled and that it was this that led him to introduce an altered version of the ride in *Madame Bovary*. In the cab in Paris there may have been some question as to who was seducing whom. At Rouen, Léon is the aggressor, Emma the dupe. But both are the objects of the scornful laugh of the giant who looks down from above on all this sorry foolishness of the human species. The laugh is also that of the Garçon and the jeering schoolboys at the lycée.

In the *Critique* Sartre indicated that if we are to understand the meaning of a male author's imaginative metamorphosis of himself into a woman, we must learn what this would mean in the context of his particular society, one which had produced, among other things, Gautier's *Mademoiselle de Maupin*. In his discussion of the Knights of Nothingness, he gave part of the answer: the artist's feeling that aesthetic sensitivity required a certain feminization, linked with the idea that success as an artist must be paid for by failure as a man. The mention of *Mademoiselle de Maupin* suggests to me something else. The novel concerns a young woman who enjoys sexual relations with both another woman and a man, who have been lovers of each other. The suggestion is that each of the pair could experience complete love only with a person who combined the essential qualities of both male and female beauty and personality. Their relation with each other, we are led to believe, will be enriched by their mutual adoration of the androgynous ideal. Mlle de Maupin herself, of course, enjoys the fulfillment of both sexes, albeit in perverted form (I use the adjective in the Sartrean sense). At the end of the book the heroine leaves both her lovers after a single night and goes on, in the same disguise, to pursue more adventures. She is the all but literal fulfillment of the fantasy of the hero of *November* and, if Sartre is right, of Flaubert. More than this, she satisfies, insofar as is possible, the desire for an impossible totality of experience. We should be careful, however, not to confuse this androgyny with that sometimes proposed today as an ideal. There is no reformist tendency, no intent to question prevailing attitudes as to what properly constitutes male and female or to suggest that they be merged in a new concept of the person. Mademoiselle de Maupin first takes up her disguise in an effort to know what men really are apart from the roles they play in women's presence and to see if one of them might be worthy of her as person. She continues her disguise because she learns that no man respects women or can be trusted in his relations with them, and she admits that most women are what men believe them to be. At best, she stands for an unreal, purely romantic escape from the limits of our real human condition. She is a male artist's projection of himself in a female body, and she is closer to Plato's double sexed creature in the *Symposium* than to a real man *or* woman in the nineteenth century or in our own.

Sartre has noted a number of autobiographical details in *Madame Bovary*, many of which have been mentioned by other biographers and do not seem to me of great significance either for our understanding of Flaubert or of Sartre's own intentions. There are two groups of observations which are original and more important; the first of these concerns Emma, the second refers to Charles.

Any reader of *Madame Bovary* must be aware of the consistent pattern in Emma's responses to her great disappointments. On each occasion there is a repetition and an intensification. After the ball at Vaubyessard, which both illumined her life and poisoned it by seeming to reveal a real world in which romantic dreams might be satisfied but one closed to her, she falls into a psychosomatic decline, a mental torpor with real physical symptoms of ill health. After Léon leaves for Paris, the same thing happens; Flaubert himself points up the parallel: "The bad days of Tostes began again" (p. 438). When Rodolphe leaves her, Emma nearly dies of "brain fever." At the end, she commits suicide. Critics have pointed out that just before she goes to get the poison, she experiences a sense of disorientation, with hallucinations of fiery balls exploding in the air, which seems to recall Flaubert's seizure at Pont-l'Evêque. Sartre recognizes all this, remarking on the psychosomatic implications, with obvious reference to Flaubert's own life. He comments particularly on Emma's illness after Rodolphe's departure and links it with Flaubert in two ways. Emma reads Rodolphe's parting letter alone in the attic. Looking out the window, she is tempted to kill herself. The abyss before her, the glancing light and blue heavens, the ground of the square below that appears to be moving, the floor that seems to dip "like a tossing boat," all impel her to let herself go. She is stopped by the sound of Charles' voice calling her. Sartre thinks that this near suicide is a recollection of a similar experience of Flaubert's. We know he had thought of suicide during those early years in Paris; Jules comes close to throwing himself off a bridge. Sartre relates the passage to one in *November*, which, like this, merges the idea of death with overtones of the childhood sense of being lost, or dissolved in nature (2:1722). The young man lies down near the sea and is tempted to let the waves wash over him. "The voices of the abyss were calling him; the waves were opening like a tomb ready then to close over him and to wrap him in their liquid folds" (p. 468). Both the "abyss" and the "sea" have been retained in Emma's near delirium even though she stands in an attic overlooking the village square. Sartre calls to our attention, too, the significance of Emma's being at a height from which she would throw herself down—Flaubert's old theme of verticality and fall.

Sartre finds an echo of Flaubert's own fall in Emma's subsequent illness. Flaubert tells us that she developed "brain fever," a nineteenth-century designation for any illness which involved loss or distortion of consciousness, particularly when it followed after some kind of psychic shock. What happened first with Emma was that she cried out and fell prostrate, rigid on the floor. Obviously the description evokes the memory of Flaubert's fall in the carriage. Sartre brings the parallel still closer and uses it as evidence that Flaubert was fully aware of the response of his own body to his psychological dilemma and recognized that his seizure and illness were a response and an adaptation. Sartre writes,

> The proof of this is that his Madame Bovary later on will make explicitly a somatization-response. Abandoned by Rodolphe, she falls ill, a terrible bout of fever seems to put her life in danger; and then, at the end of some weeks, she finds herself cured of fever and of love, both at once. Or, if you prefer, love *is made into a fever* in order that it may be liquidated by means of psychic disorders. [2:1810]

Sartre points to one other, less dramatic resemblance between Gustave and his heroine: their love of luxury. Flaubert is quite explicit in showing how Emma's dreams of love were inextricably bound up with longings for luxurious surroundings. In a sense, the ball at Vaubyessard awakened her to the possibility of the real existence of both love and luxury and intensified their interdependence. Flaubert himself did not live in luxury, but Sartre argues that he envied those who did. We have observed how the word "mistress" conjured up for him associated ideas of passion and wealthy splendor. He longed to have the superfluous in order that he might be freed from the power of need. Sartre claims that in his nostalgic regrets at the collapse of France in 1870 there was a barely concealed longing for its past luxuriance. "Even every material elegance is finished for a long time" (quoted, 3:495).

With respect to Flaubert's self-identification with Charles, we must be very careful. Obviously Sartre does not intend to take this very far. In the opening pages of the novel, "Charbovary" is clearly contrasted with the "we" of the rest of the class. In passages that Flaubert decided not to include, the separation is stressed still more. In fact, it was by a negative portrait of Charles that Flaubert described himself and the others. "How little he resembled all the rest of us!" Charles did not read late at night, long for Paris, and strike Byronic poses (2:1353). Still Sartre believes that the picture of Charles' isolation as the sorry butt of the other pupils may represent in exaggerated form Gustave's recollections of himself in the early days when he felt himself to be misunderstood and ridiculed. Even the mumbled "Charbovary" may reflect the young Gustave's feelings of frustration apropos of language. This view, of course, fits in with Sartre's feeling that Flaubert wants us to "weep for Charles"—with more sincerity, I suggest, than was in Dr. Larivière's solitary tear. I think one cannot go very far with the Flaubert-as-Charles notion. And indeed Sartre, too, notes the several times that Flaubert describes Charles' love in terms suggesting nutrient—making love regularly as one takes dessert after dinner, enjoying his remembered joy as one has the aftertaste of truffles, hardly images to apply to a sensitive hero. But it well may be that Flaubert retained a certain sympathy with a man who felt deeply without trying to express himself in words and who was therefore credited with no depth of feeling.

For Sartre, however, the autobiographical significance of *Madame Bovary* is found not only in incidental reflections of episodes or in Flaubert's attributing to one of the characters particular attitudes of his own, whether sexual or intellectual. What is essential is that his overall intention in the book and the life project of Flaubert himself are—if not identical—closely harmonious. This will become more evident if we look at Sartre's plans for analyzing the form and style of the novel.

## STYLE AND STRUCTURE

While I would never say that Sartre's interpretation of *Madame Bovary* is due to the influence of Baudelaire, it is amazing how much of what he has said could be viewed as an elaboration of points made in the poet's famous review of the novel. We have already remarked on

Flaubert's projection of himself in his heroine, Emma's "masculinity," and the similarity of theme in *Madame Bovary* and *The Temptation of Saint Anthony*. There is another passage which may serve as an introduction to our present discussion; this one, however, will show us Baudelaire's limitations as a critic as well as his gifted insight. He imagines Flaubert as having said to himself:

> I do not need to concern myself with style, with picturesque ordering, with the description of places; I possess all these qualities to a superabundant degree; I shall proceed relying on analysis and logic, and I shall prove that all subjects are indifferently good or bad according to the way they are treated and that the most commonplace can become the best. [p. 652]

Baudelaire recognized that the true subject of the novel was something more than the chronicle of the affairs of a "provincial adulteress" (p. 650); what he failed to see was that Flaubert effected his transformation, not by analysis and logic, but precisely by his deliberate, highly conscious, and careful concern with style—in descriptions and in his ordering of every paragraph and sentence. It is style that allows him, as Sartre puts it, to seem to be treating one reality while actually writing of another.

"*Madame Bovary* is a metaphor for *The Temptation of Saint Anthony*." This mingling of the realistic concrete with the metaphysical both gives the novel its value and, Sartre admits, results in the "falsity" of its style.[15] In moving from the trials of the saint to the story of the "provincial adulteress" and her unfortunate husband, it is as though Flaubert said to himself—or perhaps, as Sartre suggests, someone else said to him—"Instead of imagining the imaginary, imagine the real." For Flaubert, "to imagine the real" would be to *derealize* an actual event (whether specific or typical) by giving it a meaning which it did not have for those who lived it, to make it serve as a vehicle to convey a more universal truth perceived by the author. Above all, it would be to tell a story in which the most important things were those that were not said, in which *l'indisable* would be communicated. All of this must be done with no distortion of everyday reality in the details of the narrative and without moral commentary by the author, who must remain impersonal. It can be accomplished only by *style*, which Sartre himself has defined as a way of saying three or four things at once, of providing in a single sentence a plurality of meanings, some of which may be contradictory.[16] In the hands of a Flaubert, style may lead us to hold two points of view at once without fully realizing that we are doing so.

Flaubert once expressed the wish that he might write a "book about nothing" (*Corr.* 2:345). This disdain for subject-matter and specific content reflects his wish to substitute imagination entirely for reality and to keep art free of material restrictions. We have observed his feeling that words betrayed poetic vision and genuine emotion. Sartre claims that Flaubert's style originates precisely in this resentment against words.

In the notes Sartre make some general statements about how Flaubert conveys his sense of two realities, and he provides numerous examples of detailed analyses of stylistic points. Flaubert liked to think of himself as a "writer" rather than as a "novelist." Sartre suggests that perhaps one reason for this was reluctance to consider himself a mere "teller of tales." "The novel will be the mirror of the world." It must tell a story, but "this story must be at the same time a totalization of the world. This is the case with Madame Bovary. The world reveals its nothingness in her and in her death." The author "will show that every life which elects to live is a Fall and suffering [*mal*], by two examples: Emma and the realist Charles who has no imagination but who is devoured by the imagination of a dead woman." *Madame Bovary* is a "novel of failure and of fatality. It presents not causes but maturations." As a story the book unfolds a clear temporal sequence; as a totalization it seems to deny the passage of time. "Since the events about to be recorded here, nothing has changed at Yonville" (p. 391). The tale seems to be told us long after the central characters are dead. The last sentence, which informs us of the honor Homais has just received, is in the present tense; this is the laugh that eternally mocks all higher aspirations. At one point Charles feels as if he were surrounded by evil influences. In the midst of her happiness with Rodolphe, Emma asks herself why she should feel so sad. Death and emptiness are present everywhere. Sometimes the narrative and style seem to be at odds with each other; ultimately they come together. One of Sartre's compressed notes sums it up as follows:

> Thus the adventure of the Bovary couple is seen from two points of view: (1) Metaphysically: movement is annulled, rest remains. (2) Socially: they were unable to adapt. Two times: the immutable and the time of degradation.

Emma herself is not just a "provincial adulteress"; she is, Sartre says, Saint Anthony, and she is "a myth." Like Flaubert, she is an "imaginary person," but she lives in a world as real as the author could make it, the "invented real." The world of the novel is not actually our world, but it resembles ours. This is why, Sartre seems to tell us, the story of Emma and Charles is offered to us as our own story—in metaphor.

Sartre has said that volume 4 would have been mostly a stylistic analysis. He has stated also that he intended to use certain "structuralist techniques," which he felt would be compatible with his own method if they were properly applied. He added that for the most part he looks with disapproval on current literary research, which is overconcerned with formalism and rhetoric. Both structuralists and linguists, in his opinion, treat language too much as something external, divorced from human intentions.[17] There is nothing in the notes that indicates just how Sartre held his intended procedures to be related to structuralism. Most of what he does seems to me not radically different from the approach used in pre-structuralist criticism. Yet there is a certain similarity between some of his analyses and the kind of linguistic investigation employed by a few recent Flaubert critics who have been influenced by structuralism. Even here, however, one will find Sartre relating particular uses of language to what he believes to be Flaubert's subjective intention rather than to the requirements of the text as a strictly objective, created work of art.

Sartre's specific observations on the structure and style of *Madame Bovary* may be grouped under three headings: the problem of narrative point of view; the author's attitude toward his characters, which includes both a consideration of irony and the problem of language as communication; descriptions of places and things.

*The Narrator.* Although Sartre gives no indication of having read Wayne Booth's *Rhetoric of Fiction,* he is clearly aware of the problem of what Booth calls "the authorial voice." The "omniscient author" may reflect the writer's ideas, but author and narrator are not the same. This, Sartre explains, is "because the author as person *invents* whereas the narrator tells *what happened.* . . . The author invents the capricious narrator who merely tells a story." As Booth has pointed out, the narrator, whether he intrudes with "dear reader" commentary or purports to be as impersonal as he is omniscient, is always a unique creation for the specific book in which he appears. He (or she, for the authorial voice need not be sexless simply because it is not individualized) sets the tone for the book and *is* the point of view as surely as if we were dealing with a fictional first-person narrator. Any narrator, Sartre says, is a mediator who stands between the

book's "environment" and the reader. We may note that the narrator
who most closely resembles the author still communicates to us only
that aspect of his or her self which the author chooses to offer. In the
case of someone like Flaubert, who has resolved "not to write himself
in," the ideal of total impersonality is already betrayed in the choice
of the narrator who is assigned the role of chronicler.

Of course the problem of the narrator in *Madame Bovary* is a complex one. Most of the time he seems to be the typical omniscient
recorder of both outward events and internal reflection, the pure
"authorial voice." But when we first meet him, he is presented as an
eyewitness, one of "us" who were in the classroom on the day of
Charles Bovary's first day at school. There is a suggestion of the
relaxed tone of one who talks with us; indeed, Sartre claims that the
novel as a whole shows traces of an oral style (1:885). What is the *real*
identity of this man who first speaks to us? Sartre tells us that he is
the second narrator of *November*. I think this insight is particularly
apt. The dry tone, the irony (much further developed, of course, in
*Madmae Bovary*), the hidden sense that even in her romantic foolishness and falseness, his poor heroine is better than the people who
surround her, and (most important of all) the way in which the narrator is sometimes outside as a mere acquaintance and then again
privy to the most secret feelings of the character—all of these things
are common to both narrators. If we accept Sartre's claim that the
second narrator of *November* represents already the role that Flaubert
had chosen for himself in contemplating his own life and past, then
we may conclude that the resemblance is neither coincidental nor
insignificant. Possibly it explains why Flaubert continued to be fond
of this work of his adolescence and to allow some of his friends in
later life to read it.

This is not to overlook the fact that there is considerable shift in
narrative point of view beyond the initial movement from "we" to
omniscient author. Sartre notes that we have two forms of the present witness even in the opening pages. At first the narrator seems to
be one of the boys in the class at Rouen who see Charles as a new
student and stranger. Then suddenly we are given a quick survey of
his family background and childhood, something which might just
possibly have been provided by a member of the class who later
became more closely acquainted with the Bovary family. Then come
the words, "It would be impossible for any of us now to recall anything about him" (p. 332). After which, as Sartre points out, the
narrator proceeds to tell us very intimate things about Charles,

whom he knows very well. It is as though an impersonal "we" (what in English we call the "editorial we") had emerged out of the personal "we" of the schoolroom. But the chatty citizen of Rouen returns from time to time. He is implied in the sentence "Nothing has changed at Yonville," and is probably present in the last sentence of the book: "He has just received the cross of honor." Sartre points to other discontinuities. There is an unidentified "you" (*vous*) when we are told at the scene of the fair that "the housewives bumped into you with their big umbrellas, their baskets, and their babies" (pp. 449–50). To whom does the "you" refer? "It is the readers, not as they sit reading the book but as if they had been present." Sartre cites another example of lack of precise placement: at the ball the viscount and Emma dance down to the end of a long gallery and disappear. "From whose point of view?" asks Sartre. Then there are the many modulations of tone. The book is "polyphonic," Sartre says, in that Emma's is not the only point of view that is important; we must see things through Charles' eyes as well and occasionally through those of Rodolphe or Léon or one of the other characters. But even when seeming to be inside the same character, the tone may change. We saw one example in the cab scene, but there are numerous less extreme examples where the narrator, who has been very close, will suddenly seem to hold his heroine at a distance, will move from reflecting her thoughts to commenting on them.

Sartre, like other critics, notes Flaubert's predilection for the indirect reporting of Emma's reactions (*le style indirect libre*). Rather than giving us internal monologue or stream of consciousness, he will tell us about her thoughts and feelings in such a way that one cannot quite be sure what is fact, what is Emma's own reflection, what is narrator's commentary. When Emma, the evening after being with Rodolphe, looks at her altered reflection in the mirror, the indirect style seems to give authenticity to her perception. In the statement, "She longed to die and to live in Paris," we obviously have the narrator's ironic summation of the contents of her reflections. And what of such a sentence as we find, for example, when Emma is desperately wondering to whom she might turn in order to prevent Charles from discovering that her financial recklessness has ruined him.

> The wish came to her to return to Lheureux: What good would it do? To write her father; it was too late; and perhaps now she began to repent of not having given in to the other [the notary].
> [pp. 603–4]

In this particular instance the uncertainty of the "perhaps" may be the perfect description of Emma's state of mind. As applied to the narrator, it raises a question. Sartre points out that on many occasions the narrator will profess not to know the real reason for his character's reaction. He will tell us that Charles disapproves of Homais, possibly for one reason, possibly for another. Or he says that Emma herself does not know . . . "But if she doesn't know," asks Sartre, "is this any reason why the author should not know?" Or the omniscient narrator? Everything seems calculated to throw us off base, to prevent us from knowing exactly from what angle we are viewing what we read.

Sartre would explain this deliberate ambiguity and discontinuity as the result of Flaubert's insistence on maintaining the point of view of *le survol*. As author he assumes the stance of one who is viewing events from a vantage point outside time and space. Consequently he comprehends all points of view at once and will not allow his narrator to be restricted to one angle. Could he not have gained the same result by using simply the "omniscient author" without resorting to the "we" in the first chapter? Sartre does not take up this question directly. I would suggest that there might be two reasons for what Flaubert has done. First, we may note that the person who speaks to us out of the "we" is never individualized. He represents a collective point of view on how Charles looked to his peers—just as later we are told how Emma's conduct is regarded by the gossips in Yonville. Not formally but practically it is little more than an extended use of the indirect style applied to a group. As such it amounts to simply one more of the viewpoints that add up to constitute the all-embracing comprehension of the impersonal observer. It is important that *le survol* should include all points of view, not become simply one more of them. It cannot be allowed to seem to give unity and coherence to a reality that lacks them. Second, if we raise as a difficulty the argument that one cannot be simultaneously inside and out, Sartre might reply that this was something that Flaubert never recognized. The narrative point of view in *Madame Bovary* is the artistic development of Flaubert's form of revery when he simultaneously suffered and triumphed in the schoolroom at the lycée.

Jonathan Culler, in a study of Flaubert that acknowledges a heavy debt to Sartre and *The Family Idiot*, argues that already in his juvenile works, Flaubert recognized a basic dilemma: if he maintained a purely authorial stance, his *exempla* were obviously instances created to prove a point, hence carried no authority; a first-person confessional, on the other hand, could express only a biased judgment, therefore could not pronounce objective judgment on reality as a whole.[18] In one sense, then, we may say that *Madame Bovary* is the solution. The author, by alternating between complicity and detachment, presents simultaneously a subjective, temporal experience and an impersonal nontemporal judgment on all human affairs. Culler goes a step farther. Just as he argues that the comment at the end of *November* is a mocking reminder that only in novels is it possible to "grasp this life as a meaningful whole," so we are not allowed to achieve a single, unifying point of view on events in *Madame Bovary*. The inconsistencies (as a realist would call them) are a deliberate means to force upon us the constant realization that we are reading a novel and that a real life cannot be read as a novel any more than Emma could realize her dreams as the literary heroines did. Shifts in narrative point of view force us to recall that we are reading a work of art just as, Culler argues, Flaubert's sentences are deliberately designed to call attention to themselves as language.

Are Culler's and Sartre's explanations mutually exclusive? In principle I do not think so. Sartre, too, recognizes that Flaubert wishes us to realize that unity, eternal meaning, and beauty belong in the realm of the unreal. But he is concerned with the question of *why* Flaubert is so insistent on the superiority of the imaginary. One particular passage in Sartre, however, has been sharply attacked by both Culler and Dominick LaCapra, who claim that Sartre's biographical interest in Flaubert has led him to make a false critical judgment. This is in the context of Sartre's interpretation of the cab episode. Culler writes, quoting from Sartre directly,

> Sartre judges the episode a failure because the shift in perspective "refers us to the malignant intention of the author. . . . It's the end of dramatic illusion: there are no longer characters, just puppets manipulated by a director." It is not a little ironic that Sartre, whose greatness derives from his overpowering theatrical sophistication, should condemn *Madame Bovary* in the name of dramatic illusion and the theory of the novel it implies. . . . The thematic projects which Sartre correctly identifies depend, in large measure, on the techniques of displacement and fragmentation which he finds disturbing. The reader would not be demoralized, after all, by a tale told from the point of view of an order which he could identify and adopt as his own. [p. 122]

This last sentence is certainly true, and I think Sartre would agree.

But I believe that Culler has misread Sartre's intention. Sartre does not condemn *Madame Bovary* nor even say that the passage in question is a failure in itself. Specifically, he claims that Flaubert has failed to achieve a particular end which he had set for himself. Sartre defines it in the form of a question:

> Has he succeeded, while remaining himself invisible, in sending an anonymous laugh, without laughers, to run from one page to the next, imposing itself on the readers without the author's emerging from his "impersonalism" and without having done anything but to deliver to them the itinerary of a particular cab during the afternoon of a particular day in a particular year? [2:1285]

Obviously he has not. Flaubert forces us to view the lovers' afternoon, not as they experience it or even as the reader might be inclined to see it, but as he himself wants to see it. But this is consistent with what he has done elsewhere in the novel. It is the juxtaposition of the author's immediate subjectivity and *le survol* that partially accounts for the sense of "two realities" and allows the shadow of one to fall upon the other. But *le survol* is always itself a fiction. If Sartre intended to leave the impression that Flaubert's personal malice had intruded so as to ruin the scene, Culler's criticism would be justified. But if he meant only that the presence of the giant and Gustave Flaubert is more apparent here than elsewhere and that we know the reason for it, I think Sartre is entirely right. I certainly cannot agree with LaCapra's statement: "The fiacre scene seems to be written from no one's point of view: it is almost 'pure' text, writing itself."[19] To accomplish this aim would have required the suppression of the coachman's comic bewilderment and indeed to make the description nothing but the itinerary of a coach on a certain day in a particular place, and it would hold no interest.

*Attitude toward Characters.* Sartre has expressed what I think is typical of readers' reactions to the characters in *Madame Bovary*.

> Reading Flaubert one is plunged into persons with whom one is in complete disaccord, who are irksome. Sometimes one feels with them, and then somehow they suddenly reject one's sympathy and one finds oneself again antagonistic to them.

Sartre explains this as the result of Flaubert's self-dislike. As his own creations and at times his self-projections, they are subject to the same sadomasochistic attitude he sustained in his personal relations with the world.

> He tortures them because they are himself, and also to show that other people and the world torture him. He also tortures them because they are not him and he is anyway vicious and sadistic and wants to torture others.[20]

Although the last sentence may be an overstatement, it does seem that Flaubert's characters (including the good Félicité) are punished by sufferings in inverse proportion to their merits. It is also true that Flaubert's irony, in *Madame Bovary* at least, prohibits any total empathy with any of the characters. Sartre has not elaborated on the manner in which the irony is sustained, perhaps because this subject has already been thoroughly discussed by critics. Culler points out that Flaubert preferred "verbal rather than situational irony."[21] This is true, and I have noted that on the rare occasions when he does provide an ironic situation, he sometimes seems impelled to call our attention to it with an authorial comment, almost as though he could not let the situation speak for itself. For example, when Emma, just after refusing to sell herself to the notary, resolves to appeal to Rodolphe, Flaubert tells us in so many words, that "she was running to offer herself to that which had just now so outraged her, totally unaware of her prostitution" (p. 607). Usually the irony is much more subtle and is a function of the style itself, resulting from the deliberate use of words and sentences with a plurality of meanings. At times it is so delicate one can hardly be sure that it is there. A word or image will have the effect of slightly undermining the mood or tone of a passage, like the self-deprecating smile of one who puts himself forward. My own favorite example comes from the very passage that I quoted earlier to illustrate the nonverbal communication between Léon and Emma on the first evening at the hotel. The moment of silence is filled with an infinite sweetness, and the prevailing tone is one of tenderness. Yet it includes an image so strange as to be almost bizarre. "They sensed a humming in their heads as if something resonant had reciprocally escaped from the fixed pupils of their eyes" (p. 540). The mixture of auditory and visual, the overprecise localization of sensation and origin becomes ludicrous if one stops to analyze. Is this Flaubert's intention? I suspect so, and think that he also intended that it would be so without spoiling the dominant effect of the passage when read quickly. The ambivalence is characteristic of the entire novel.

In the notes Sartre makes several references to the lack of communication that generally exists between characters and that paradoxically is conveyed by means of their conversations. Direct speech is comparatively rare. When it occurs, Sartre says, we do not have true reciprocal dialogue, but rather "an alternation of monologues," at best "a simultaneity of discourse not understood rather than communication." Mostly it is at cross-purpose. Emma's abortive visit to the curé is one example, when the curé interprets her *"je souffre"* as referring to purely physical ailing and tells her to ask help of her husband. Emma and Charles outdo each other in offering to take on the burden of the trip to Rouen to consult Léon about the power of attorney. And so on. Most of what is said is insincere— Rodolphe's wooing at the fair, his impassioned protestation on their last night together, which owes its unusual intensity to his secret resolve to leave her. When a true message *is* conveyed, it is by means of a hidden conversation which has nothing to do with the actual words spoken; for example, Emma's first meeting with Léon. Sartre notes that there are a few occasions when the words are sincere, but then they are not taken as such—as when Rodolphe fails to believe in the depth of Emma's love for him because he has heard the same banal phrases from other lips obviously false. In the characters' relations with one another words destroy; only the rare nonverbal moment of communication unites. The author's words simultaneously describe a world which the overtones, the "silences between the words," undermine.

*Descriptions and Objects.* Sartre observes that Flaubert has a way of introducing descriptions just when something is about to happen. He "keeps us on the edge of the event" just long enough so that what finally happens seems somehow diminished. "It is the descriptions which prepare the event and annul it because they suggest to us that which makes us fall into revery." Landscapes, he says, serve less as an environment for the characters than to refer us to a cosmic emptiness. They seem almost to annihilate persons and events. Sartre notes the several occasions in which Flaubert uses the word *vide* (empty) in describing his settings, usually for sky or meadow, once for Emma's room at Yonville. More specific descriptions emphasize the seeming inexhaustibility of what is observed. Sartre cites from Flaubert's letters a number of his comments concerning concrete objects. On first reading they might seem contradictory. Some of them indicate a fascination with things as they are in their separate, impenetrable existence. For example, "I know nothing more noble than the ardent contemplation of the things of this world" (*Corr.* 4:357). The context of this remark is his professed admiration for science, but Sartre is probably right in assuming that Flaubert would hold the same attitude with respect to his writing. On another occasion we find, "Art is a representation: we must think only of representing" (*Corr.* 3:21). These and comparable passages would suggest that he thought of himself as the literary equivalent of a realist painter, a Courbet. Indeed, the challenge of conveying in words the quality of physical things always appealed to him as one worthy of the artist's powers. Other remarks suggest that it is not the object per se that is important but the subjective relationships imposed upon it. In a very late letter Flaubert writes, "Have you ever believed in the existence of things? Is not everything an illusion? What is true is only 'relations'; that is the way in which we perceive objects" (*Corr.* 8:135). And again, "The True does not exist. [*Il n'y a pas de Vrai.*] There are only ways of seeing. Is a photograph a resemblance? No more than an oil painting, or just as much" (*Corr.* 8:370). The use of the photograph as an example shows that the two sets of remarks are not really contradictory. For Flaubert any form of *mimesis* is a transformation of the real into the unreal, and this is precisely the artist's task. "Poetry is only a way of perceiving external objects, a special organ which filters the material and which, without changing it, transfigures it" (*Corr.* 3:149). Objects are the material out of which the imaginary world is created and made to appear real. But while Flaubert was interested in the problem of how style could be used to convey a quality impossible to express directly, the "taste of a plum pudding," for example, Sartre recognizes that descriptions in the novel are never there for their pictorial interest and only partially for the sake of guaranteeing verisimilitude. In one of his notes Sartre sums up Flaubert's method by referring to music.

> All objects are nothing more than collected impressions ready to be modulated according to the rhythm of the sentence. . . . All things appear then as musical notes on which one will only have to compose the symphony, things which will be orchestrated into a totality, a correspondence between objects and minds which will make the very story, *this novel,* this poem.

This purpose of descriptions is aesthetic, of course, but it is half-philosophical as well. They do not represent the focus of the characters' attention, but are a means whereby the author directs the reader's response.

> [Description] becomes for Flaubert the unique experience by which it seems possible to express the movements of life. It is analysis and expression of feelings which things symbolize, or support, the two being confused with one another. It is objects which carry the story insofar as they are seen by us, presented to arouse our emotion, our memories, and our revery.

Flaubert's use of objects as symbols has long been recognized. The cigar case, the greyhound, Hippolyte's wooden leg, the statue of the curé which breaks during the move from Toste to Yonville are among the most famous examples. My own favorite is the *Hirondelle*, the coach which first brought Emma to Yonville, which took Léon away from her when he left for Paris, which later carried her to him in Rouen. Its name, "The Swallow," is gently incongruous; it symbolizes ironically Emma's longing to soar, to fly from banality to a world in which dreams are fulfilled without travesty. The awakened memories, of which Sartre speaks, may refer to connotations for the reader which come from outside the novel, but may also be echoes of earlier passages. To give again an example of my own choosing, there is Flaubert's use of Emma's parasol in two deliberately contrasted passages in part one. The first occurs very early when Charles still comes only as her father's physician. There is a thaw, everything is melting.

> The parasol, of dove-colored shot silk through which the sun shone, lighted the white skin of her face with shifting hues. She smiled beneath the tender warmth; and drops of water were heard, falling one by one on the stretched silk. [p. 341]

Nothing is spoken, all is tender, warm, gentle; the tension is only of burgeoning promise. One day, after her marriage, Emma goes for a walk out to a deserted pavilion. The walks are moldy, the shutters rotting on their rusty bars, nettles surround the stones amid the remains of the garden. She gives vent to her inward tension by making sharp jabs in the ground with the tip of her closed parasol and asks herself, "My God, why did I marry?" (p. 365). It is no accident that Emma carries her umbrella on both occasions.

Sartre lists a number of objects that add overtones of broken hopes, futility, despair by their reappearance in the story, e.g., the arbor, the greyhound, riding whips, and, of course, the bridal bouquet, the cigar case, and the mirror. He points to symbolic associations connected with levels in the house and with windows (borrowing here, I think, from Brombert's discussion of Flaubert's use of imagery). His more original contribution, however, concerns the extended descriptions of the physical environment. He claims that these are centrifugal, leading us away from the characters, forcing upon us a detachment that breaks our empathy with them, and introducing the chilling gaze of *le survol*. Unfortunately, Sartre himself has provided no example. Jonathan Culler, however, seems to have taken Sartre's lead and has provided substantial documentation for this immediate point of Sartre's, though Culler's ultimate conclusion as to why Flaubert's descriptions are as they are differs somewhat from Sartre's explanation.

From Flaubert's initial description of Yonville, Culler quotes two sentences which he feels "might well stand as touchstones of Flaubert's revolutionary achievement."

> The thatched roofs, like fur caps pulled down over the eyes, come down over a third of the low windows, whose bulging panes of old glass are decorated in the middle with a boss, like the bottoms of wine bottles. On the plaster wall, which is diagonally traversed by black beam-joists, a withered pear tree sometimes clings, and the ground floors have at their door a little swinging gate to keep out the chicks, which come to pick up, on the threshold, bits of wholemeal bread dipped in cider.[22]

Culler, in a detailed analysis which I will not try to reproduce here, shows that these sentences are marked by three anomalies: first, their function is not truly grammatical. Especially in the first sentence he argues, "The point of arrival has nothing to do with the point of departure." Each sentence "appears to fritter itself away, as it runs down toward the minute and trivial." There is "no obvious thematic purpose." Second, "the sentences have no apparent function." They give us a collection of disparate facts. They tell us nothing to differentiate Yonville or to serve the story. Finally, the particularity of details suggests immediate and specific observation, but the mode is one of generalization—the withered pear tree that "sometimes clings," the chicks that regularly come to pick up the cider-soaked bread. No narrator seems to hold this all together. It is "a written text, which stands before us cut off from a speaker" (pp. 76–77). Culler finds here the real meaning of Flaubert's impersonality. "One should always be in a position to claim that a description fell off a lorry." Or perhaps one has surreptitiously removed it, for Culler relates this notion to Sartre's claim that Flaubert's project was to "steal language from men" (p. 78).

Culler quotes a number of other passages from Flaubert's novels that show this same kind of movement "into inanity." Typically, the details in descriptions are presented without highlights to indicate what is important, almost in a flat listing. The piling up of items that are neither unified nor meaningful, that neither set a mood nor reveal a character, nor establish a definite perspective is certainly centrifugal, as Sartre says. Why is Flaubert so addicted to these descriptions? What purpose do they serve? One obvious answer Culler treats as obvious and rather unimportant. The impersonal, objective descriptions give a sense of reality.

> In so doing they reveal one of the basic conventions of post-seventeenth-century European culture: that "reality" is opposed to meaning. It consists of discrete concrete objects and events prior to any interpretation, and therefore to give a sense of "the real" one must offer details which have no meaning. [p. 76]

I would not dismiss the matter so quickly. It is hardly a convention of the last two and a half centuries that reality allows no human meanings to be imposed upon things. It has been the common assumption of novelists, confirmed recently by phenomenologists, that every one of us inhabits a "life world" overlaid with meaningful connections. To convey the quality of the world as lived by unique individuals has been a major concern of fiction writers. In reality, as Sartre has reminded us, one never encounters the material world without meanings—except abstractly.[23] What is different about Flaubert is that he tries to look at the world as no individual, real or fictional, would ever look at it but rather as it would be seen by a nonhuman observer who comprehended human activities without sharing human interests. Culler understands this. The difference between his explanation of it and that given by Sartre comes out most clearly in his comment on Sartre's description of the Flaubert sentence.

Long before he had settled down to writing *The Family Idiot*, Sartre remarked on the peculiar deadening intent of Flaubert's style.

> His sentence closes in upon the object, seizes it, immobilizes it, and breaks its back, wraps itself around it, changes into stone and petrifies the object along with itself. It is blind and deaf, bloodless, not a breath of life; a deep silence separates it from the sentence which follows; it falls into the void, eternally, and drags its prey

down into that infinite fall. Any reality, once described, is struck
off the inventory.[24]

Opposing Sartre, Culler argues that the sentence does not actually
destroy the object; rather, "The passivity of the sentence . . . suggests
to us an unconcern with the objects which it goes beyond and leaves
behind it as the jetsam of this formal quest" (p. 205). Herein lies the
source of its charm for the reader, in Culler's opinion, and he says,
"Calling attention to themselves as language, the sentences produce
a discrepancy between novelistic signs and novelistic function" (p.
206). This is the essential point for Culler. Flaubert at all times wants
to keep his readers alert to the fact that they are contemplating a work
of art, not immersing themselves in life. Flaubert's novels "are
novels" and must be "read as novels," Culler insists. "The novel is
writing, not a world" (pp. 229–30).

In contrast with Sartre, who says that *Madame Bovary* treats of two
realities, Culler might say that it refuses to be about any reality. Yet
Culler, like Sartre, recognizes that even in his persistent contrast
between the novel and real life, Flaubert comments on the nature of
our relation to the real. Consider the question of Charles Bovary's
famous headpiece: Sartre, avoiding the elaborate allegorizing of
some critics with regard to this ludicrous creation, says of it simply
that its "mute ugliness has depths of expression. [It] is an image of
Charles, and a sign alluding to his parents." Culler would avoid even
this. He sees in this description the writer mocking his own enterprise as though searching for symbols which could not be found.
"We follow the adventures of a language attempting to capture the
world and make it signify but experiencing defeat before the particularity of an object about which one could go on and on without
getting anywhere" (p. 93). Even if we were to say that Culler and not
Sartre is right in this particular instance, I think myself that Flaubert
is making a comment both on the limitations of language and reality.
Culler would not necessarily deny this: LaCapra has criticized him
for appropriating and developing Sartrean insights while contesting
"Sartre's interpretive strategy."[25] In my opinion, Culler, as much as
any other critic in the period since *The Family Idiot* was published,
has proved the fruitfulness of Sartre's work for Flaubertian studies.
He explores, in a way that Sartre has not, some of the specific ways in
which Flaubert has exploited "the uses of uncertainty" in narrative
technique and in language itself. But he never denies that Flaubert's
attitude toward the world and his personal project were divorced

from his intentions in writing the novel. LaCapra, who is much more committed to contrasting Sartre's "totalizing dialectic" with a structuralist textual criticism, goes so far as to say that the fourth volume might have shown up the failure of the Sartrean method. *"Madame Bovary* as a text might have deconstructed the very type of discourse with which Sartre apparently would have tried to comprehend it" (p. 200). This view seems to me to rest on the mistaken belief that one can legitimately read a book by Flaubert as if it were written by Alain Robbe-Grillet or Michel Butor. To wish that one might write a book about nothing is not the same as to decide to write a work in which the text itself is the subject.

In the notes and earlier, too, Sartre indicated his intention of analyzing smaller units of Flaubert's sentences, especially verbs. He has emphasized especially Flaubert's extensive use of the passive voice and preference for iterative verbs and the imperfect tense. The passive voice, Sartre believes, reflects Flaubert's own personality as a "passive agent" and his propensity to see himself and others as victims of a "fatum," whether characterological or cosmic. Sartre has analyzed several passages in terms of tense usage, noting that Flaubert not only prefers the imperfect on occasions in which there is a clear choice between it and the simple past, but even on some occasions in which he is describing a single action or event. The effect, Sartre claims, is to suggest a feeling of endless and futile repetition, to deny temporality, to evoke "the ontological sense of life." In addition, Sartre had planned to include a comprehensive discussion of metaphors in a chapter on the processes of creative imagination. If he had been able to carry through successfully, he would have been able to demonstrate his argument and basic theme: that every line of *Madame Bovary*, if fully understood, would lead us back to Flaubert, the "singular individual" and the period that made and was modified by him. And we would have seen the first three volumes at the margin of every page of the fourth.

# CONCLUSION

## The Verdict on Literature

Adapting Baudelaire's title for his poetry, Sartre sarcastically calls Flaubert a "flower of the least evil" (3:487). The specific reference is to the pessimism that led Flaubert to reject any hope of a good society and to accept all too easily the Second Empire as the least bad of possible alternatives. Sartre extends the notion, declaring that a mandarin of Flaubert's type springs from the manure of an already constituted society whose ends he refuses to share; he is a man who uses all its resources in order to destroy the human order "by the production of that aggressive inutility, the work of art, as a center of derealization" (3:610). Sartre continually refers to the world of literature as unreal, to beauty as nonbeing; he insists that to be a writer, in Flaubert's case at least, was to choose the imaginary and to prefer art above life. His diatribe against the Knights of Nothingness includes the grudging admission that they have produced some of the most beautiful works in the French language. Even as he praises the socially committed Philosophes of the eighteenth century, he points out that some of their purely literary efforts—e.g., the plays of Voltaire—are embarrassingly bad. One senses that there is a divorce between the creation of beauty and the aims of praxis. All of this, along with Sartre's account of the devastating effects of romantic literature on the boys in the lycée at Rouen, has inevitably led some to conclude that the object of the attack is not just Flaubert or the Second Empire but literature itself. I think this reaction is understandable, but it is not correct.

As to the *purpose* of literature Sartre and Flaubert disagree radically. Demoralization is the intent of one and revolution the aim of the other. Flaubert hoped that art might deliver him from the world;

388

Sartre wants literature to deliver the world to us. Detachment, impersonalism, noncommitment, the desire to show the futility of all action, Flaubert's imaginary *survol* are at the opposite pole from Sartre's engaged writer, inviting us to act, carrying concern with social message to the very brink of that chasm which divides art from propaganda. Flaubert disdained his public—or all but the very few devoted like himself to art for art's sake. Sartre emphasizes not only communication but reciprocity. Flaubert, Sartre claims, liked to think of the artist as a member of an unacclaimed but precious elite, as one of "God's aristocrats." Sartre longs for a future age when there will no longer be professional writers because everyone will write.[1] Flaubert's "absolute art" is its own end and reason for being. It seeks to lift itself above its period, to be universal and eternal. "We write for our own time," declares Sartre.[2] Literature is a means; at its best it is a form of praxis.

We observe that these differences have nothing to do with the definition of literature or with the nature of its appeal and power. That Sartre has modified his original view with respect to this question may be seen by comparing his earlier and later pronouncements on Flaubert. In the first number of *Les Temps modernes,* Sartre wrote, "I hold Flaubert and Goncourt responsible for the repression which followed the Commune because they did not write a line to prevent it."[3] Here Flaubert's sin is one of omission. He is guilty of having done nothing when action was called for. One is reminded of Sartre's claim in those days that "not to choose is already to have chosen." The accusation in *The Family Idiot* is stronger but quite different: Flaubert contributed heavily to the formation and reinforcement of the ideology that led to and supported the Second Empire. Granted, it was a misunderstanding which resulted in his being branded a realist. This is an example of how individual intentions are deviated in the practico-inert, of how "the world steals my action from me." But more profoundly, Flaubert revealed and satisfied his readers' need. He "spoke to their condition." The unreal had real effects. At the very least Sartre's book is an effective proof, by negative example, of the power of a work of fiction to affect the world. I would go farther than this. In *The Family Idiot* Sartre has attempted to come to grips with the ambivalent attitude toward literature that he has held for several decades. I will not say that the book provides a synthesis which wholly resolves the tension in his thought. I believe it does offer a reconciliation of sorts, that it stands in itself as a demonstration of what Sartre believes literature can and should do, and that this is closely bound up with what have been called the book's novelistic qualities.

The basic paradox—if it is not a contradiction—was already apparent in *The Psychology of Imagination* (1940). Most of that book was devoted to proving that the image is unreal. Its status is like that of a perception in that it is an act of consciousness intending an object, not the object itself; unlike the perception it is unreal, regardless of whether its object exists or has once existed (an absent friend) or has never existed (the centaur or my walk on the moon). As compared with the perception, the image is impoverished. I have no inner eye which can return to it to check details and glean new information: the image contains only what I have put into it. I cannot learn the number of the columns on the front of the Panthéon by counting them in my image. Were Peter's eyes brown or blue? I can imagine them either way, but the image provides no evidence. The face and figure are a generalized Peter of no particular time or place. If I try to analyze the image, it is revealed as a nothingness. I can only manufacture a new image in its place. The image is too poor; at the same time it is too rich. If I am afraid of something I imagine, this is because the image suggests far more than it clearly offers. It carries with it the illusion of hidden depths. It is "suspicious." Or, if it is positive, it seems to point to riches it cannot deliver. Furthermore, when I want to enter into an image I must make myself unreal. Only an imaginary "I" can step on the imagined moon just as it is only the dream self that moves in the landscape of a dream. At times Sartre's tone is almost denunciatory.

> The act of imagination is a magical act. It is an incantation designed to effect the appearance of the object of thought or the thing desired—in such a way that one can take possession of it. In this act there is always something imperious and childish, a refusal to take distance into account, or difficulties.[4]

The choice of the imaginary is not a preference for a richer life, but for a poorer, more secure one; it is revealed as a preference for imaginary feelings directed toward imaginary objects which one can control because they lack the unpredictability and inexhaustibility of real presences. In all of this discussion Sartre seems to bestow upon the life of the imagination a strictly limited value. It allows one to relax in the enjoyment of imitative entertainment such as impersonations and pantomimes. Certain imagistic schemata may serve as a step toward clarifying thought. Images may fill our idle moments with harmless fantasies as dreams occupy us in our sleep. Finally, aesthetic appreciation depends on our ability to cancel out the real materiality of canvas, ink, or vibrating piano strings so as to reconstruct the imaginary creation behind them. All of this is at the expense of the real, and Sartre never in these pages hints at any constructive effect which the imaginary might have on the real as one inevitably returns from image to perception. Even at the very end of the book, when he discusses briefly the status of the work of art, he stresses the aesthetic as an escape.

> Aesthetic contemplation is an induced dream, and the passage to the real is an actual awakening.... Nothing more is needed to arouse the nauseating disgust which characterizes consciousness confronting the real [*conscience réalisante*].

But unexpectedly, in the conclusion Sartre pulls a volte-face. Imagination, he says, is not a contingent enrichment; it is essential to consciousness. He describes it in terms that seem almost to equate it with the nihilation that is synonymous with conscious process. It is by imagination that consciousness goes beyond its immediate situation to posit a different one, by imagination that we can project a future for ourselves and the world which will not be mere repetition. Imagination, while seeming at first to be the opposite of rational thought, turns out to be its necessary accompaniment. Without it there would be no freedom, no possibility of change. We would be on the level of the other animals. This paradox—that imagination is an escape from reality and that it is essential for creating a better reality—is only partially resolved by differentiating oneiric or artistic imagination from the nihilating vision that is a necessary ingredient of praxis.[5] If they are kept altogether separate, we lose any hope of explaining how the unreal can have real effects. Sartre's plea for an engaged literature implicitly assumes a necessary passage from the first to the second, but in *What Is Literature?* he did not explain satisfactorily what is achieved in the first step. Except in the discussion of poetry, which Sartre exempted from his claim that the primary aim of all writing is communication, the book is almost without reference to the peculiar function of literary language or to imagery.[6] The aesthetic object remains unreal and is evoked by the guided recreation of the world of events that the author had imagined. But since its ultimate reference is to the real world, the work serves as a critical mirror of society. It is not surprising that Sartre argues that the best style is like clear glass which reveals without being noticed.

Implicit is the suggestion that it should introduce no distortion. To see things as they are—but as if held a little at a distance—is the first step toward wanting to alter them. The aim is lucid communication; the appeal is primarily to our intellectual faculties. Sartre does not try to explain how or why a work of fiction communicates differently from an explanatory treatise on geography, for example, or a well-reasoned sociological article. One gets the impression that the engaged writer of imaginative literature tries to accomplish indirectly what the social activist does more effectively. No wonder that Sartre soon decided, not only that the writer is not privileged, but that literature is a luxury which our oppressed society can ill afford. How can I read Robbe-Grillet, Sartre asks in effect, when millions of people in the world are starving?[7] Robbe-Grillet's mirror may be reflecting only in segments, but Sartre seemed to feel for a while that nobody should be fiddling with mirrors while the world is burning.

Sartre claims that Flaubert turned to literature because he was ill at ease with language. Sartre's own interest in the unique possibilities of language as used by the creative writer developed after he became concerned with the way in which words frustrated and deviated thought. His first relevant work here was his introduction to *Black Orpheus*, an anthology of poems in French by black writers.[8] Compelled to use the language of their oppressors, these poets wrestled with words that were the means of their own alienation. The truly revolutionary poetry they produced was the result of the poets' deliberately doing violence to words, wrenching them from their normal usage, "stripping them of their white underclothes," forcing them to express what they were never intended to say. Here for the first time Sartre suggests that communication may be achieved, not by means of, but in spite of the precise significations of words. In a series of later essays and lectures published in the sixties and seventies, Sartre extends the idea to language as utilized by the prose writer, whether revolutionary or not. The clean window pane as the ideal image of style has given way to stained glass. *The Family Idiot* is the culmination of this line of thought.

Sartre points out that words (like the image) are both too poor and too rich.[9] They are too poor because they are the result of earlier fixed determinations and are not designed to express something new. They cannot express what is unique in a concrete example, nor can they convey the nuances of sensations and confused feelings. As Flaubert discovered, words cannot directly communicate either the beauty of a particular woman or the flavor of a plum pudding. In despair he confessed, "The inadequacy of vocabulary is such that I am very often forced to change the details" (*Corr.* 4:287). Words are also too rich. Their long history has given them a concretion of connotations which cannot be suppressed. We recall Sartre's discussion of Mallarmé's attempt to exclude all chance associations and echoes save those desired. But while one can never predict the throw of the dice, the writer may still play the richness against the poverty of words so that in their association they express more than they denote. Thus style speaks by means of silences. The "unsayable" is expressed by what is not said. This is Sartre's view. He claims it is also the essential discovery of Flaubert. That he is right is supported by Flaubert's famous statement that "style is as much *beneath* the words as *in* the words. As much the soul as the flesh of a work" (*Corr.* 4:315).

In describing how the literary writer is a specialist in ordinary language, utilizing words for the maximum of misinformation they can be made to convey, Sartre relies on a distinction between *sens* and *signification*. Although both words can be translated as "meaning," *sens* refers to "meaning" in a sense broader and richer than the purely denotative, whereas *signification* is strictly denotation. In English perhaps we might use "meaning" exclusively for *sens* and the cognate for *signification*. In differentiating them, Sartre employs the same distinction that he originally offered for sign and image (in *The Psychology of Imagination*).

> An object is signifying when one intends through it another object. In this case the mind pays no attention to the sign itself. . . . [An example of signification would be the direction given on a highway marker.] Meaning [*le sens*] is not distinguished from the object itself. . . . I shall say that an object has a *meaning* when it is the incarnation of a reality which goes beyond it but which cannot be grasped outside of it and that its infiniteness does not allow it to be expressed adequately by any system of signs. It is always a matter of a totality: the totality of a person, of an environment, of a period, of the human condition.[10]

Obviously a technical treatise always and a philosophical essay ideally (at least according to Sartre) would employ, insofar as possible, significations only. The literary writer, while he needs a certain "precise structure of language" if he is to communicate at all, is concerned primarily with *le sens*.[11] We may note, however, that whether Sartre is speaking of images or art objects or the molding of words into style, two quite different points are involved. First, the suggested meaning is a reference to something which, as a totality, is more than the sum of its parts, which is given all at once, which can be sensed but not adequately denoted in words. I grasp as *le sens* the essential quality of Maurice Chevalier in the impersonator who imitates him, perhaps better than I could in a photograph or even in a quick glance at Chevalier himself. The Renaissance is present in Michelangelo's statue of David more vividly than in a three-tome study of the age. Beyond the sentences of *Madame Bovary* is the cold eternity of a world inimical to human hopes, already dead. What is conveyed is not knowledge; it is nothing conceptual. It is something communicated as lived experience—*le vécu*. As such it is not abstract, and this brings us to Sartre's second point. The image or the style that evokes *le sens* has a certain materiality. Just as the image, in contrast to the sign, is not wholly effaced before the object it signifies, so the materiality of words (their sounds and their physical shape on the page) is integrated into the meaning they express. An example of this is seen in Sartre's analysis of Flaubert's sentence about longing to die of cholera in Calcutta or Constantinople. Of course, sense is involved as well as sound; one could hardly substitute Chicago and Cannes. But the letter clusters add to the meaning beyond the signification. Again Sartre sees the printed letters of "*sans mâts*" in Mallarmé's poem as evoking a visual image. As Howells points out, this is a visual device to play *sens* against *signification*. [12] The materiality of words in every instance is an essential ingredient in communicating *le vécu* in contrast to information and ideas.

Sartre's attitude toward this concern with words for their own sake has been somewhat ambivalent. At times he links it with the failure to recognize that the true purpose of language is reciprocal communication. This realization, he believes, is not there at the start but is something we learn later. Language is not in us, we are in it.

> Language is a kind of immense reality which I would call a whole of *practico-inert*; I am constantly in a relation with it—not insofar as I speak, but precisely insofar as it is first for me an object which surrounds me and from which I can take things; only subsequently do I discover its function as communication. [13]

Initially, words for Sartre, as he claims they were for Flaubert, were like things, and his first relation to them was one of appropriation. He wanted to create from words the equivalent of a child's sandcastle, for the beauty of the thing itself, something that could stand for itself. (There are overtones here of Sartre's discussion, in *Being and Nothingness*, of creation as both an appropriation of the world and an extension of myself in an object which I make, something which is both me and not-me.) Flaubert, Sartre says, never abandoned the ideal of creating a "wordcastle."[14] Sartre may have had in mind a letter in which Flaubert, after referring to the profound effect upon him of the sight of a bare wall on the Acropolis, exclaimed, "I wonder if a book, independently of what it says, could not produce the same effect" (*Corr.* 7:294). But Sartre, while he insists that it is an illusion to think one can possess things by means of words and that in any case it is *what* is communicated that is finally most important, acknowledges that in any writer there is still some remnant of the child who aims at creation-appropriation.[15]

He elaborates on this same point in commenting on the distinction made by the structuralist critic, Roland Barthes, between *l'écrivant*, one who writes, and *l'écrivain*, the writer. The first writes simply to transfer the information; the second "produces a certain verbal object by working on the materiality of words, taking significations for a means and the nonsignifying for the end."[16] Sartre's view is that only structuralist critics can be *écrivains* in this sense. A creative writer must be both *écrivant* and *écrivain*. Flaubert may have wished that he could write a book about nothing which would be supported only by the internal force of its style (*Corr.* 2:345) or one in which all that he had to write was sentences (*Corr.* 3:248). He recognized that he could not do so. If *Madame Bovary* is a book about two realities, this is because its most significant communication is expressed by the *sens* behind the *significations*. Flaubert and Sartre would agree that even when the author refuses to write himself in, his invisible presence is everywhere felt. Sartre, of course, is quite different from Flaubert in putting the accent on reciprocal communication and positive social commitment.

In *The Family Idiot* Sartre finally devotes careful attention to the question of how the unreal can have real effects. He introduces two new concepts: the work of art as "a real and permanent center of derealization" and the "social imaginary," both of which we have considered apropos of the actor and in the context of the schoolboys' reading in the lycée. Sartre develops more fully than he has ever done before the way in which the material of the analogue determines the quality of the unreal aesthetic object—as in the example of the marble Venus. More relevant to our immediate purpose, however, is his discussion of how the materiality of the book, the objective reality of its printed pages, gives the illusion of independent and real existence on the part of the social imaginary. To know that all of my companions have imagined the event described on page 176 seems to make it a part of our common and real experience. Sartre, of course, will not allow that either the character or his adventure is real. Yet there has been a succession of real happenings: each of us, in response to the same analogue, has derealized himself or herself so as to create roughly similar imaginary experiences. It seems difficult not to attribute some kind of objective being to this "social imaginary," but why will Sartre not allow that it is real? The answer lies in the question. The imaginary is not real, but it does have being. If we understand this, we can see how and why the unreal has real effects.

Sartre's language is regrettably the source of some confusion. At times he uses "unreal" and "nonbeing" as if they were synonyms. This is true particularly when he speaks of beauty or of Flaubert's desire to escape from the real world by creating an imaginary one. But the logical inference, that we are to equate real and being, is not valid if we consider Sartre's ontology as a whole. He tends to use "real" as a nonphilosophical term referring to what can be given temporal and spatial location (not to exclude, of course, a physical sensation or a specific emotional impulse). In *Nausea* real objects and specific persons have existence; in contrast, being is ascribed only to such things as mathematical constructs (the circle) and imaginary aesthetic objects—a narrated adventure, a melody, or the novel Roquentin will write. Sartre has always put the psychic on the side of being-in-itself, not of consciousness, and the experience of an individual consciousness depends on its relations with its objects, with Being. The ego itself, in Sartre's view, is a psychic structure, the result of the activity of consciousness in organizing its own experiences and self-reflections. It stands as the background of every conscious act; it holds the residue of my past. In *The Psychology of Imagination* Sartre stated that memory tends to confuse real and imagined things.[17] This is because in the past both have become Being, and consciousness must intend them in a new act. Since consciousness always chooses and initiates action in response to its objects, a remembered or imagined object may result in a modification of conduct just as well as an encounter with the real. We can all recall instances in which our feelings and even our behavior in the presence of real persons have been colored by our memory of our being with them in a dream. The social imaginaries of literature exert an even stronger influence. For most tourists the sense of the past presence of Agamemnon and Clytemnestra at Mycenae is at least as vivid as that of Pericles on the Acropolis.[18]

All of this has been brilliantly worked out by Sartre in his analysis of the way in which the boys identified their own egos with the fictive ego of the romantic hero. My encounter with the fictional becomes part of the being of my past. In my present action we see its real effects. We recall Sartre's description of how Chatterton seemed to stand there as a reproach to the boys' bourgeois enjoyments. He might have said that Chatterton had become their common ego ideal. This by itself may go a long way toward explaining the power of literature to influence the action of individuals and of groups. I should add "either for better or for worse." Sartre, however, in this context has emphasized only the negative, partly because he disapproves of the *Weltanschauung* of the romantics and partly, I suspect, because this kind of reading is so uncritical.

Two essays in which Sartre tries to answer the questions of *why* one writes and *why* one reads, are much more positive. Once again he emphasizes that what is communicated in literature is not—save incidentally—knowledge. It is nonknowledge, feeling, meaning, lived experience, and it is expressed by the materiality of words, by the invocation of *sens* beyond the *significations*. *Le vécu* can be expressed only by art, by literary language, not by reasoned argument. Thus imaginary literature may convey a truth which would be lost or distorted in factual statements. Its power to influence rests on the fact that *le vécu* becomes part of my being, not merely an object posited by my thought. The idea that the transmission of nonknowledge is the unique aim of literary language turns out to be essential to Sartre's final justification of literature. For although he declares that "writing is a craft like any other," he allows that it can do at least something of importance which no other skill can.

In an interview in 1960 Sartre discussed the problem from the point of view of the writer. He disclaims his earlier extravagant hopes.

> I have quite lost my literary illusions: that literature has an absolute value, that it can save a man or simply change men (except under special circumstances)—all that seems to me long out of date.[19]

But if literature does not have an absolute value, it has a unique value. Everyone feels the need to write, Sartre claims. This is because people want to bear witness to their lives, to find meaning. "You don't live tragedy tragically or pleasure with pleasure. In wanting to write, what you are attempting is a purification." By itself this statement suggests escapism, a wish to turn life into literature, which Sartre has always condemned. But what Sartre means here is that the would-be writer seeks to clarify his life, to discover its unique features, to understand the forces that have stunted him, his relations with being. Before one can communicate, one must clarify what is opaque in oneself. In short, one writes in order to discover meanings by expressing them.

> Each of us wants to write because each has the need to be *signifying*, to *signify* what he *experiences*. Otherwise everything goes too fast, you have your nose to the earth like the pig which is forced to dig up truffles. There is nothing.

Still the writer needs a reader.

> The "written cry," as Cocteau calls it, cannot become an absolute unless memories preserve it and others can integrate it into *the Objective Mind.*

In all of this Sartre seems to be implying certain absolute values: self-understanding, heightened awareness, an almost aesthetic pleasure stemming from my self-conscious "carving out my being in the world." While not objecting to any of these, I may point out that they all are highly individualistic. Sartre as social revolutionist might well wonder whether society could at present afford to support such luxurious psychic well-being for its writing minority. Indeed, in this interview the most Sartre offers for the community at large is the precarious hope that in the far-off better future everyone will write and there will be no need for professionals. One wonders who will read.

In a debate in 1964 on the subject "What Can Literature Do?", Sartre spoke from the point of view of the reader. In reading, a person seeks a meaning which he/she feels ought to be found there, but which is lacking. This is not just because "this life is for everybody badly made, badly lived, exploited, alienated, mystified," although we who live it know that it *could* be something else.[20] It is also due to the fact that what meanings people do manage to give to their lives are partial and fragmentary. The unity of meanings which they cannot find in their individual lives may be freely and personally realized in reading a book, which gives a meaning (not to be confused with purpose) to the life of man in the world.

In still another essay, "A Plea for Intellectuals," Sartre elaborates and clarifies his intention with respect to both reader and writer. Everyone has something to say, he reminds us, but there is a feeling that there are some things that only the writer can say. This idea appears paradoxically in the common experience of recognized authors to whom someone may say, "If only I could tell the story of my life. It is a novel! Look here, you are a writer. I'll give it to you, and you can write it."[21] Sartre observes that this is to imply that the writer has nothing to say, that he uses his technique to express whatever content happens to come to him. But more subtly, the speaker thinks that the writer will be able to incarnate and to communicate the nonknowledge, *le vécu*, in such a way as simultaneously to preserve its uniqueness and link it with the totality of life in this world. For ultimately, Sartre believes,

> the writer aims at communicating the incommunicable—lived being-in-the-world [*l'être-dans-le-monde vécu*] by exploiting the portion of misinformation [*désinformation*] contained in the common language and maintaining the tension between the part and the whole, the totality and the totalization, the world and being-in-the-world as *le sens* of his work. [p. 454]

This time Sartre uses the word *sens* with the broadest possible intention. Lived experience always has both a subjective and an objective side. Insofar as documentaries suppress the subjective side, what they reveal is a less complete truth than we find in the superficially fictionalized film *Holocaust*. Each of us exists as a singular universal. Sartre maintains that the subject of every writer worthy of the name is ultimately the human person's insertion in the world.

> A work is valid only if it accounts for *the whole* in the mode of nonknowledge, of *le vécu*. The whole—that is the social past and the historical conjuncture insofar as they are *lived* without being known. [pp. 452–53]

An author today does not need to mention the bomb; its existence will be manifested in "a vague anguish trailing along from page to page." A particular book reflects only one subjectivity in its insertion in the world as a singular universal, but the reader, on the level of nonknowledge, grasps the effort at totalization and glimpses, on the horizon, as it were, some sort of universal *sens*. It is an experience, Sartre seems to be saying, which illuminates one's comprehension of what it means to be an individual subjectivity in a world, independent of one's particular experiences.

Malraux's statement, "A life is worth nothing, and nothing is worth a life" may express very well the ambivalence which is at the basis of the literary work. It unites the viewpoint of the world as background (indifferently producing and crushing out each life) and the viewpoint of the singularity which hurls itself against death and affirms itself in its autonomy. [p. 454]

Unlike Flaubert, who believed that some things must always be relegated to the region of *l'indisable*, Sartre insists that on principle nothing is incommunicable. It is only a matter of finding the right means of expression.[22] Sartre would explain this difference in point of view by Flaubert's and his own respective political commitments. Bourgeois ideology rests on the notion of isolated molecules where personal privacy and untouchability are the subjective equivalents of private property and true community is impossible because of the built-in restraints of human nature. Sartre, despite his philosophical commitment to the ontological separation of consciousness, cherishes the ideal of a day to come when "two people will no longer have secrets from one another because nobody will any longer have any secrets, because the subjective life as well as the objective life will be entirely offered and given."[23] This somewhat dubious ideal of total transparency Sartre believes to be necessary for social harmony in that distant society to be established after a social revolution has wiped out all oppression, exploitation, and alienation. Self-clarification and reciprocal communication are essential ingredients for that "we of humanity" of which Sartre speaks wistfully in the *Critique*. It appears that the language of literature will be forever useful in order to express *le vécu*. At present it is a necessary requisite for all attempts at greater openness. Sartre suggests that today when "we know ourselves very little and are still unable to give ourselves without any holding back," perhaps the best way a writer can express the truth of himself is to portray himself in "a work of fiction which is not a fiction." By contrast, he has granted that *The Words*, overtly an autobiography, was in a certain sense a novel.[24]

*The Family Idiot*, whatever else it might be, is avowedly an attempt to come to grips with the meaning of the human person's insertion in the world. Sartre uses every device available to him as writer to convey to us the quality of Flaubert's lived experience in the nineteenth century, to express *le sens* of Flaubert and of the period. At the same time, as he says must happen in any literary work, we sense the author's presence on every page and the outlines of his own world—and ours—on the horizon. Sartre, too, speaks in the silences between the words. We must ask ourselves now about *le sens* and *les significations* of this biography.

## THE SUBJECT OF THE PORTRAIT

In our survey of Sartre's discussion of Flaubert as man and writer, I have raised the question of the validity of specific claims by Sartre, testing them by what Flaubert himself has recorded, or his contemporaries, and on occasion comparing them with the views of certain other critics. A thoroughly documented and detailed evaluation of the biography would require a work longer than *The Family Idiot* itself, a project of dubious value even if one felt qualified to undertake it. Yet I want to state at least my own response to the questions raised in my introduction: Has Sartre presented to us a Flaubert who, within the limitations inherent in any psychological biography, rings true as the real Flaubert? Or do we have a fictional character invented by Sartre or—worse yet—an elaborately disguised self-portrait by Sartre? In the terms I used earlier, is *The Family Idiot* finally a biography, a novel, or an autobiography? Is there truth in it? And what kind of truth?

Sartre has said that fascination with a personality so totally the opposite of himself was one of his reasons for choosing to write about Flaubert, but he added that his antipathy had given way to empathy. He believed that in seeking to understand Gustave from within, he was able to suspend judgment sufficiently to allow a personal sympathy to become dominant so that he found himself taking sides against those he finds responsible for Flaubert's unhappiness.[25] Some reviewers maintain that the antipathy was never overcome; these tend to read the work as a novel in which Flaubert is the antihero, if not the villain. Others argue that empathy has been carried to the point where it defeats its original purpose. Sartre may have derived the concept of *empathie* from the German *Einfühlung* or from our frequently used "empathy." (Neither Larousse nor Robert gives the word.) Webster defines "empathy" as the "imaginative projection of one's consciousness into another being," an operation difficult to perform without introducing antibodies. The problem is whether Sartre's imagination has succeeded in viewing the world with Flaubert's eyes or "imaginative projection" has become self-projection. Fabre-Luce declares flatly that Sartre's empathy is that of the ventriloquist.[26]

Taking up first the question of the autobiographical aspect of *The*

*Family Idiot*, we may observe at the outset that the book reflects Sartre's own philosophical commitments and rightly so. It would be highly regrettable if he had produced an impersonal study of documents from no definite point of view. One expects and wants to learn about Sartre as well as about Flaubert. But are the two distinguishable? There are certainly points of resemblance between the author of the biography and its subject, but this does not necessarily mean that the so-called portrait is really a self-portrait. I think it is important to distinguish among the various kinds of similarities we find in Sartre and in Sartre's Flaubert.

To start with, we find certain obvious parallels in their objective situations and expressed attitudes which Sartre clearly has not invented and which may help to account both for his initial fascination and for his later empathy. A list of those that come quickly to mind is impressive. The first, which Sartre has himself remarked, is their social class. Both writers expressed in violent terms their hatred of the bourgeois class into which they were born, and neither was able wholly to escape from it. Flaubert believed that he had done so, but politically and economically his existence, Sartre says, remained eminently that of the petty bourgeois. The income of Croisset supported his life as an artist. People who know Sartre as a social activist might think that he had broken away; he himself recognizes that at most he is a bourgeois who has sided with the workers. Differently, but still comparably, his life as an intellectual sets him apart from those whose interests he would serve. His books are read by the educated bourgeois, not by the masses. *The Family Idiot* is itself an indication of Sartre's inability to free himself of his commitment to the life of the intellectual, and his attitude toward the work is ambivalent. Its method, he believes, is relevant and useful to the contemporary world, but the content, its concern to reconstruct an individual life in the nineteenth century, seems to him to represent a form of personal escape. Perhaps, he adds, that is one reason why he was able to feel empathy for Flaubert.[27] Roquentin's solution at the end of *Nausea* is almost identical with Flaubert's commitments to *l'art absolu*. Sartre, too, has to some degree retreated from the present real to the imagined past.

Second, despite the radical difference between the careers of the two men, their lives show certain common patterns. Neither Flaubert nor Sartre ever married or raised children; both as young men saw in this refusal a form of protest against bougeois expectations. Each one entered into a significant relation with a woman writer though I hasten to add that the quality and history of those relationships were as different as Simone de Beauvoir is from the notorious Louise Colet. Again, though I would not press the parallel too closely, there is a similarity in the way in which each man looked at his own life. Flaubert felt that his existence had broken into two, that the man who emerged from the nervous crisis had replaced rather than developed from the earlier Gustave. Sartre speaks of two "conversions" in his life—the first his renunciation (at about 1960) of the idea that the engaged writer was privileged by a special mandate, the second his radicalization in 1968. Sartre uses the word neurosis to describe both Flaubert's and his own (temporary) preference for literature over life.

A third bond between the two is their attitude toward literature. Though Sartre ultimately abandoned the idea that literature is a salvation and the writer privileged, by his own reckoning, he cherished the ideal for almost fifty years. Conversely, Flaubert held that art alone was worthy of a lifetime's devotion, though at certain moments he doubted its absolute value. Both began to write and dreamed of literary glory while they were still children. Flaubert was one of the great "Immortals" on the Schweitzer bookshelf into whose ranks Jean-Paul longed to place himself.

Fourth, Flaubert's neurotic fears and the abnormal mental states associated with the nervous crisis are not altogether without parallel in Sartre's experience. In a depressed period in his early thirties, following a laboratory experiment with mescaline, Sartre suffered for some months from monstrous hallucinations and was seriously afraid that he was doomed to insanity.

Finally, each man, toward the end of his literary career, embarked on an extensive if not impossible project which exploded the form with which he worked. The unfinished *Bouvard and Pécuchet*, the plot of which concerns the futile effort to totalize our entire intellectual life, is as preposterous for a novel as Sartre's incomplete *The Family Idiot* is for a biography.

Of course, one might object that these similarities are far less significant than the obvious contrasts between the two writers. I agree and would point out that, even in what I have called parallels, the surrounding circumstances, motivations, and reactions are more important than the core of resemblance. Sartre, for example, insists that the emotional environment of the two child prodigies was radically different; furthermore, he believes that he has effectively cut himself off from the child he had been whereas he claims that in Flaubert the unhappy child remained at the heart of his basic orientation. The abrupt volte face is one of the distinguishing traits of Sartre's career; critics have commented on the steadfastness of basic themes in the work of Flaubert. My point, of course, is not that in the final analysis Sartre and Flaubert are significantly alike but that accusations that Sartre has illegitimately projected himself into Flaubert must at least recognize genuine points in common.

There are a few more questionable examples. I have said that I think we must acknowledge Sartre to be in error when he attributes to Achille-Cléophas and his wife the ideological division that existed between Sartre's grandfather and the women of the household. Some have viewed with suspicion the parallel between Sartre's portrayal of his own mother living like a child in her father's house and Caroline Flaubert's relation to her father-husband. But here I am not sure that Sartre is so obviously wrong. What we know of Dr. Flaubert's behavior toward his fiancée and later wife suggests that there was never between them any of the camaraderie and approximation to sharing which is characteristic of what Sartre calls "the conjugal marriage." Furthermore, he has emphatically not extended the parallel to include the siblinglike relation that he claims existed between himself and his mother. The point is hardly important in any case. But there is one other obvious similarity that is more significant: the likeness between Achille-Cléophas and Sartre's grandfather as depicted in *The Words*.[28]

Sartre claims that his grandfather so resembled God the Father that he was sometimes taken for Him. The arguments that this thoroughly Protestant patriarch conducted with the Catholic women of the family convinced Jean-Paul that "neither of these persuasions had any value."[29] We have heard the echo of these debates at the Flaubert dining table where Sartre represents the doctor fulminating against the ridiculous tenets of the Church. Of course, the results were not the same. Jacqueline Marchand has made the perceptive observation that Flaubert reproached himself for his lack of faith and still waited for Godot whereas Sartre congratulated himself on his escape.[30] This is quite true, and I do not think it unreasonable to suppose that the agnostic doctor was partly responsible for his son's ambivalent attitude. The real problem is not the question of whether there was as much likeness between the two fathers as Sartre suggests, but the whole theological framework that he imposes on Gustave Flaubert's life history.

Despite his rejection of God and religion, Sartre has long been accustomed to employ the language and concepts of Judaeo-

Christianity as essential tools to express his thought. With respect to his own life he tells us that after getting rid of God the Father, he cherished the Holy Ghost within him for many years in the form of a sacred mandate (his commitment to literature). *Being and Nothingness* describes our pursuit of the missing God. The passion of "Saint Genet" is a drama in Christian costume even though it is a Black Mass that is being celebrated. Now Sartre ascribes to Flaubert a longing for a mandate and ultimate judge (for art) and speaks of the difficulties of his finding them in the absence of God. Sartre tells us that Gustave felt himself to be the son cursed by the father as Cain was cursed by God. The child's Fall from the Golden Age is a replay of the expulsion from the Garden of Eden. In the game of "loser wins" we find a subtle interplay of Christian ideas: that self-sacrifice will be rewarded, that the gift of grace will be bestowed on even the most unworthy sinner if his sufferings and silent devotion to an impossible quest have been great enough, that God the Father will always hold his arms open to the prodigal son—in short, that "the last shall be the first." Sartre clearly finds it meaningful to use theological notions in interpreting secular experience, but is it fair to attribute this way of thinking to Flaubert? It is not only Christian metaphors that are introduced as explanatory structures. "Loser wins" itself is something which, outside the religious context, Sartre had already used extensively—especially and explicitly in *The Condemned of Altona*, actually titled *Loser Wins* in the translation published in England. When it is made the keystone of Flaubert's life strategy, our natural reaction is to feel that Sartre himself has stepped onto the stage where the play is being performed.

It is these intellectual habits of thought that constitute the real problem and not the supposed factual similarities. I think we must believe Sartre when he says that in personality structure he and Gustave are opposites, that they have very little in common.[31] The history of their emotional development as children shows one to be almost the reverse of the other. Jean-Paul knew that he was loved; Gustave was *un mal-aimé*. Spoiled by his grandfather, adored by grandmother and mother, Jean-Paul was made to feel that he was indeed the center of a fostering universe and a sovereign agent. No reading problems for him! And I think no one has ever discerned in him any passivity or lack of aggression. Moreover, he was an only child with no older brother of whom to be jealous, no unborn sister, whose place he had usurped, or living one who was given a welcome denied to him. If later he came to hate his childhood, it was not because of resentment toward any of the members of his family. The truth is that, if *The Family Idiot* is in any sense an autobiography, it is not because of an identification between its author and its hero. This I think even Sartre's severest critics would be forced to recognize. The question remains as to whether Sartre's way of looking at Flaubert distorts what he sees and whether in this sense the book tells us more about Sartre than about Flaubert. But at this point we move to the other charge—that the biography is really a novel in which Sartre has created a hero (or antihero) to demonstrate a thesis.

Sartre quite clearly wanted to grasp "the truth of Flaubert" and believed that he had arrived at it. Many years of careful research have gone into these volumes. Sartre has examined unpublished material from the period as well as all of the published work of Flaubert himself. As Rybalka has observed, *The Family Idiot* is the most fully documented of Sartre's books since his student thesis on the imagination.[32] If his references to other biographers and critics are sparse, this is not because he has not read them. Sartre does not claim to have introduced new evidence as to the major events of Flaubert's life. He assumes our knowledge of such significant developments as the liaison with Louise or the financial debacle brought on by the nephew's mismanagement; he does not narrate them. What is new is the interpretation of the meaning and the internal unity of the experiences.

In my opinion, the specific factual errors of which Sartre has been guilty are not essential.[33] If, for example, Achille-Cléophas was in truth an elector, this does not alter the fact of his being by birth an outsider to the class in which he moved as an adult, or the instability of the distrustful alliance of the bourgeois and the governing aristocrats. If Gustave's mother was not a believer, the child nevertheless must have felt the tension between his intellectual acceptance of his father's scientific agnosticism and his emotional inclinations toward some form of pantheistic fulfillment. While the willingness or reluctance of Flaubert scholars to accept Sartre's conclusions does not actually prove anything, we have noted that some of those writing since Sartre's work on Flaubert first appeared have accepted or reinforced much of what he has said.[34] It seems only reasonable to conclude that whatever judgment may finally prevail, *The Family Idiot* will direct the course of Flaubert studies for a long time to come.

Still, we can hardly ignore Benjamin Bart's aggrieved exclamation, "It is a very fine book, but it has nothing to do with the man named Gustave Flaubert."[35] The odd thing is that one can find in Bart's biography mention of almost all of the individual traits that Sartre attributes to Flaubert, including the negative or neurotic ones: melancholy, pessimism, self-doubts, an early inclination to sadistic fantasies, the conviction that "life was hideous," an uneasy sexuality related to a disturbed relation with his mother, etc. Bart does not, any more than other non-Sartrean biographers, attempt to find some underlying pattern that would unify these qualities along with others and would relate them to Flaubert's determination to write, his aesthetic creed, and the books themselves—style as well as content. In trying to do precisely this, Sartre has made his most important and unique contribution to Flaubert studies. But it is this also that has led Bart and some other critics to charge him with having *imagined* Flaubert.[36] Since nobody has suggested that he has invented events, conversations, or letters in the way that the historical novelist might do, the accusation can refer only to two things: Sartre's hypotheses regarding Gustave's early relations with the members of his family and Flaubert's totalizing project; that is, the unifying thread of his life history, including the half-theological, half-feudal framework, the game of "loser wins," the entire "strategy" centering on the crisis of Pont-l'Evêque.

Without repeating what I have said already in earlier sections of this study, I may sum up my own conclusions as follows: To leap to the heart of the matter, I find Sartre's central thesis convincing: that he has traced a unifying pattern of development in Flaubert's life history which finds its climatic moment in the crisis of 1844 and spreads its consequences over the future as the rivulets of water trace their way to the shore from the breaking wave. At the very least Sartre has effectively demonstrated the essential and inextricable internal relationships of the following: Gustave's feeling (well developed in early adolescence and never abandoned) that this life is unadmirable and nonfulfilling, that the universe is indifferent, that reality and the limitations of human nature frustrate all attempts to achieve the impossible ideals that some few among us can imagine; his growing conviction that the artist, combining his creative imagination with the imaginary *survol*, could give being to his impossible dreams of absolute beauty and harmony and in so doing rise above the horror and the triviality of the real world; his determination that he would *be* a writer; the psychosomatic pattern of behavior leading up to the crisis, a desperate strategy intended to free him from a hated professional career so that he might devote himself to art; the conviction that his aim could be accomplished only by the sacrifice of one part of himself; the final liberation at the time of his father's death and his own subsequent cure; Flaubert's ambivalent attitude toward Napoleon III, his delight in moving in court circles and his disillusioned despair at the demise of the Second Empire; his feeling at the end that he had outlived himself. To this extent at least Sartre has demonstrated that we need not concede that the detailed study of this man's life has revealed only "heterogeneous and irreducible layers of significations." To my mind he has successfully interwoven this individual thread with the strand of literary history and the surrounding social fabric. His accomplishment is splendidly evident in the discussion of the way in which the public accepted *Madame Bovary*, responding to the book's inner meaning yet distorting it by proclaiming its author a realist. Despite my criticism of certain points in Sartre's discussion of the literary tradition, I believe he has succeeded admirably in showing how Flaubert's personal conflicts and literature itself find their solution in the aesthetic creed that, in opposition to the realists, lead us to Mallarmé and the twentieth century. Whether or not one is willing to accept everything that Sartre says about Flaubert, his society, and the literature of the period, I think nobody can well deny that he has brought them all together. He has made good on his promise to describe how a particular person is inserted in his period, how he both reflects and modifies it, how he is "a singular universal."

"What do we know of Flaubert?" Sartre asked in the preface, and the answer to this question is supposed to aid us in coming to grips with the larger one, "What can be known of any person?" The joint approach of existential psychoanalysis and Marxist sociology seems to me to have proved fruitful overall, but can we accept those novelistic techniques that Sartre calls "imaginative hypotheses"? These are of two sorts. First, there are those intellectual schemata to which I referred earlier—the feudal-theological coloring that Sartre imposes on Gustave's inner life and whose traces he thinks he can see in Flaubert's life history. I have indicated my own dissatisfaction with Sartre's imposition of feudal structures upon the Flaubert household, which seems to me to be carried too far and sometimes to lead him astray, for example, in the discussion of Gustave's early relations with his sister. Yet I am far from believing that there is no truth in this insight of Sartre's, and I suspect that the family tale of the child Gustave's "presentation" to the duchesse de Berry may in truth have its secret connections with Flaubert's pleasure in being received by Princess Mathilde. The theological interpretation, if we take it literally, is worse than exaggerated; it is false. But, of course, Sartre never intended to say that Flaubert in his self-reflections explicitly formulated his experiences in these terms or deliberately, in full awareness, acted in accordance with these categories. The feudal and the theological images are two sustained metaphors; at the same time they are explanatory devices. Sartre employs them in order to convey to us the inner meaning (*le sens*) of Flaubert's life. By evoking all of the overtones associated with this elaborate imagery, he hopes to recreate and to convey to us the flavor of Flaubert's lived experience as it would have been for him. But he is also trying to let us understand the meaning and evolution of the developing life in an appraising totalization such as the one who lived it would not have been able to achieve. To put it another way, Sartre wants to offer to us both *le sens* and *les significations* of Flaubert. From one point of view he does what Faulkner does in *As I Lay Dying*. In certain of the passages in which we are inside the mind of the characters, especially those concerning Dewey Dell and Vardaman, Faulkner uses his own language (not the limited speech of Anse and his family) to communicate the nonverbal experiences and inner quality of the person.[37] Sartre wants us to comprehend Flaubert simultaneously from inside and from without, a comprehension which stands midway between the sort of knowledge a psychoanalyst would attempt to convey in reporting a completed case history and the intimate understanding lovers seek of the beloved. In *Being and Nothingness* Sartre declared that "man is a useless passion." Later he reproached himself for resorting to to this literary phrase in a philosophical context.[38] I cannot share his regret. I think that, properly understood, the sentence expresses an insight which pages of reasoned argument can further explain; they would never quite be its equivalent. I think that the use of feudal and theological metaphors in the biography of Flaubert must be regarded in much the same way.

It may be helpful at this point to recall Sartre's remark that *The Words* might be considered a novel. He did not explain his statement. Quite obviously, he did not mean it in the sense that his mother is reported to have said with regard to the book, that her son did not understand anything about his childhood.[39] Perhaps the easiest way to grasp what he did mean is to place *The Words* alongside Simone de Beauvoir's *Memoirs of a Dutiful Daughter*. The latter is autobiography pure and simple, a detailed record of the events of her childhood and adolescence, reporting what she can remember of her own reaction to them. Her adult judgment enters in, to be sure, but only by way of occasional commentary. Where de Beauvoir's account is a recollection, Sartre's is a distillation. Indeed, the title (more properly, simply *Words* rather than *The Words*) indicates that he is more interested in examining what he believes to be the dominating theme of his life than to give us information about the happenings of those early years. At every instant we are aware that the mature adult is using all of the resources of language to enable us to capture simultaneously the meaning of the young life as it was lived by the child and as it is understood, explained, and judged by the adult. Thus for all the paucity of detail, a total life is offered to us. What Sartre had attempted to do for himself he tried to do for Flaubert.

Someone might say, "Very well, we will accept the Sartrean formulations as interpretive schemata and novelistic devices. But what about the hypotheses concerning the infant Gustave's relation with his mother and the whole drama of the child's conflict with father and brother? Here we are not dealing with hermeneutics but with the simple issue of truth versus fiction." Personally, I do not think that Sartre's account of Gustave's troubled relations with father and brother needs any defense. One may disagree, of course, as Bruneau does,[40] but here Sartre has interpreted, not invented. The evidence he has adduced from the juvenile writings and the correspondence seems to me entirely persuasive. The theme of sibling rivalry is blatant in the stories. Relevant passages from *Madame Bovary*, if not conclusive, certainly seem to suggest the uneasy mixture of admiration and resentment that Sartre claims Gustave felt toward his father. The case of the mother is different. We cannot possibly know what mother and child felt toward each other in the first few years, and Sartre admits it. Yet paradoxically the cluster of attitudes and behavior patterns that, according to Sartre, stems from the disturbed relation with the mother—the passivity, the femininity, the ambivalent relation with Louise Colet (both as it was in actuality and as it was reflected in Emma and Léon), the tendency to idealize and to love in imagination while satisfying sexual needs with prostitutes, perhaps an inability to love, onanistic inclinations and fetishism, his horror at the idea of becoming a father and raising a family—all of this has been recognized by other critics, even those hostile to Sartre, to originate in the psychological bond between mother and son.[41] In this connection I find a particular significance in an episode not mentioned by Sartre but cited by Bart.

One day Dr. Flaubert tried to surprise his wife by giving her a most expensive new carriage which he had ordered specially from

Paris for her. Alas, a glance sufficed to turn her against it: she found it ugly, uncomfortable, and too small for their large family. But it was not her way to say so to her husband, and she held her peace. Her habitual migraines and insomnias, however, re-doubled—until her eldest son, now mature enough to intervene, explained matters tactfully to his father. The first carriage was sold, a second was purchased more to her taste, and Madame Flaubert's migraines and insomnias subsided to their normal levels.[42]

Bart uses this episode as an example to support his claim that Madame Flaubert's "strength was of that indomitable sort which comes from ruthlessly using alleged weakness to get one's way, always." What strikes me is that here we see the mother employing exactly the sort of active passivity, with an accompanying psychosomatic pattern, that Sartre ascribes to her son. Did Gustave learn the strategy of "loser wins" from his mother? Did he, as a Freudian would say, identify with her, introjecting her, so to speak, and attempting to become like her? Everything suggests that some sort of explanatory hypothesis is necessary. If Sartre had postulated an Oedipus complex, a too loving mother, an overdependent son, nobody would raise an eyebrow. But this, too, would be no more than conjecture. Sartre argues that if we reject his hypothesis, then the burden of proof rests on us to offer and defend an alternative one. The facts are there to be accounted for. Speaking for myself, I think that Sartre's reconstruction is plausible enough. It seems to account for the specific quality of Flaubert's sexuality and associated re-actions better than the more general concept of the Oedipus complex. What is most important, however, is to recognize that whether Flaubert's mother loved him too much or too little, the traits that Sartre attributes to Flaubert's affective constitution are perceptible in his earliest writing as they are in his mature work and have presum-ably been developed in response to earliest conditioning.

How much can we know of a person? Sartre would have us achieve for Flaubert something midway between conceptual knowledge and carnal knowledge. *Le sens* of Flaubert will be a little different for anyone who reads him. Yet I think it is fair to ask in a general sort of way whether the Flaubert of *The Family Idiot* sufficiently resembles the man as his close associates saw him and whether Sartre has accounted for all aspects of him or has given us only a partial picture. What I myself find lacking is an appreciation of Flaubert's talent for friendship. Sartre has stated that he would find Flaubert a boring dinner companion,[43] a compliment which I am sure the host at

Croisset would heartily return. But others enjoyed him despite his sometimes behaving like the Garçon at parties. He was rich in close personal friends, both men and women. George Sand had to coax him for years before he finally visited Nohant; she was eager to have him come again. A quick glance at the record of their friendship may be illuminating. There is certainly no suggestion of lord and vassal even though he did like to address her as "Dear Master." Close to twenty years older than he, she might have been like a mother to him, and indeed she does sometimes worry and fuss over him like a mother. But he preferred to refer to the two of them as "two old troubadours together." Both of them occasionally use the masculine pronoun with regard to her. One wonders whether in this nonerotic relation Flaubert finally felt he had discovered the androgynous being he vainly sought in Louise. Their letters are full of tender protestations of affection and eagerness to assist each other—even financially. If his complimentary remarks on her novels are insincere (and they could hardly be otherwise), his overall respect for her must be genuine. She liked to analyze his personality in her letters to him. Often she speaks of his goodness and his generosity. More often she scolds him for his negative traits. "Your sadness, your weeks of spleen, I do not understand them, and I reproach you for them." She feels that he has isolated himself too much from the bonds of life. She writes, "You do not want to be a man of nature, so much the worse for you!" She objects that the characters of *A Sentimental Education* are too passive, and she makes the acute observation that Flaubert himself secretly liked to be ruled. She reproaches him with loving literature too much and carrying his hatred for the imbecility of the human race too far.[44] On one occasion he apparently felt stung enough to defend himself.

> No! Literature is not what I love most in the world . . . I am not such a pedant as to prefer phrases to existences [*des êtres*]. [*Corr.* 6:356]

This exchange was the result of his having written in his last letter, "Nothing interests me but sacrosanct literature" (*Corr.* 6:353). Which statement was closer to the truth may be discerned by comparing them with a sentence written years before to Louis Bouilhet. "My mother, about six weeks ago, said a marvelous thing to me, 'The passion for phrases has dried up your heart.'" Had he remembered it so long because it was "*un mot sublime*" or because he was pierced by its truth? (*Corr.* 4:78–79)[45]

The Flaubert-Sand correspondence seems to me to reinforce most of what Sartre has said even though it reveals more of gentleness, delicacy, and sympathetic understanding than we might expect if we had read only *The Family Idiot*. My own experience has been that when I return to Flaubert—either his literary works or his correspondence—I find everywhere new details to support Sartre and, perhaps more important, the feeling that they are intimate parts of the person I have come to know. For me the biography is not a novel in the pejorative sense. Its truth is *le sens* of Flaubert.

## LEAVING *THE FAMILY IDIOT*

Sartre claims that it is philosophy, his "philosophy of the age," that unifies all of his work—fiction and formal treatise alike.[46] *The Family Idiot*, too, he considers at heart a philosophical work. As such it stands as an ultimate synthesis, a definitive statement for his views on man-in-the-world, ontologically and sociologically. There is a proverb which Sartre is fond of quoting: "The more we change, the more we remain the same." Both the style and the content of *The Family Idiot* echo the manner and thought of the man who, in his early thirties, was simultaneously working on a treatise on the nature of the ego and writing the novel *Nausea*. Whether he writes about Roquentin or Flaubert or impersonal consciousness, Sartre's subject is human freedom struggling to realize itself in a world both all encompassing and alienating, a contingent being thrown into a universe that is "allergic to man." Yet Sartre's thought, without this last major work, would appear far less complete and with many problems left unresolved. Here he has done more than to tie up loose ends; he has introduced entirely new concepts. Some of these, as I have tried to show with regard to his theory of language and literature, have served to reconcile—in part, at least—what had seemed to be discrepancies. Others, while they may develop further implications of ideas inherent in earlier works, carry us so far in a new direction that they raise the question as to whether Sartre's position is any longer consistent with the fundamental ontology of *Being and Nothingness*.

A comparison with Sartre's biographical study of Genet is inevitable. There are many parallels in detail that testify to the predilections of the biographer. The titles of the first two chapters of *Saint Genet* are revealing by themselves.[47] The first—"The Melodious Child Dead in Me Before the Axe Slices Off My Head." For both Genet and Flaubert Sartre seeks to reveal the psychological damage done to the child by adults. The second—"A Dizzying Word."

Although the consequences were as different as the pronouncements, Sartre in each case attributes a decisive impact to a
single sentence which he assumes was spoken: "You are a thief" to
Jean Genet; "You would make an excellent actor" to Gustave
Flaubert. Again, each small boy is pictured as having at one stage
resolved to be what those who condemned him expected him to
be—but against them. Of course, the two subjects are radically different, but in both books Sartre is concerned with role playing, with
the sense of alienation from one's own ego, with ambivalences of
hatred and longing for acceptance. In each one he employs, both
rhetorically and interpretively, categories of being and nothingness,
of real and unreal, and equivalences of evil, nonbeing, and beauty.
Of course, both books denounce the injustice, oppression, and
hypocrisy of respectable bourgeois society. Despite all this the two
works are not really similar. Beside *The Family Idiot, Saint Genet* appears strangely abstract. The man himself may seem to live for us,
but he appears to move in no specific time or place—in spite of the
occasional factual documentation.[48] It is difficult to recall any person
present there except for Genet. Flaubert is firmly ensconced in his
family, his school, his literary and historical period. In the biography
of Genet Sartre shows us how after society made Genet a thief, he
made himself a poet. There is nothing comparable to the step-by-
step exploration of the early stages of "Constitution" and "Personalization." Sartre did not make any serious attempt to see Genet as "a
singular universal." Genet's struggles are viewed as a conflict with
the forces of society; we are no longer on the level of the battle
between individual subject and the abstract "Other" in *Being and
Nothingness*. But while Sartre's analysis is more concrete, and
although he shows himself much more aware of the alienating power
of human institutions, *Saint Genet* does not (like the *Critique*) stand as
a milestone in the development of Sartre's philosophical theory. It
does not offer significantly new conceptual tools nor synthesize
views on psychology, sociology, and literature as *The Family Idiot*
does. Quite obviously it is not yet the result of Sartre's carefully
thought out progressive-regressive method.

So far as the method itself is concerned, I believe that Sartre has
eminently proved its success if we interpret it in terms of its overall
intention and procedure. It does indeed unite psychoanalysis and
sociology. Its scope is overwhelming. Sartre has steadfastly combined analysis of the documentary evidence on a given point with
the search for a synthesizing hypothesis which will unify the data

and explain its origin. He has sought to reveal all the "horizontal" implications of Flaubert's life in relation to the world around him, and he has painstakingly examined the way in which both Flaubert's psychological development and the historical evolution of society have brought each to the conjuncture. The guiding principles of these procedures are carefully described, and Sartre is at pains to situate himself with respect to them. Yet as he himself admits, it was impossible for him to keep the analytic and synthetic phases entirely separate. The truth is that the farther one reads, the more one forgets that a special method is being employed, and Sartre no longer bothers to indicate at which stage we are. The novelty lies less in formal method than in the philosophical principles on which Sartre is working.

I think that one feels closest to the Sartre of *Being and Nothingness* in the phenomenological sketches he has interpolated—discussions of the laugh, the actor, the comic, practical jokes, mourning, the notion expressed in "I am too small for myself." All of these, though they may involve my relation with the Other, belong in the domain of individual psychology; the problems are those of the single consciousness trying to make its own being. If gathered together, they might form an appropriate appendix to *Being and Nothingness*. Everywhere else one is very much aware that *The Family Idiot* is a sequel to the *Critique*. In saying this I mean to point to more than the obvious fact that Sartre is concerned with social conditioning and the evolution of ideologies considered from a Marxist point of view. Perhaps the most striking characteristic of his thought in this work is the degree to which he emphasizes the importance of physical matter in human development. The *Critique*, of course, gave what Sartre felt was its due weight to matter as well as to consciousness, especially in exploring the practico-inert, which gradually took over the function formerly assigned to being-in-itself. In *The Family Idiot*, except for the tantalizing passage in which he hints at an evolutionary stage in the development of consciousness (I refer to his discussion of the bored dog, which seems to leap toward and to fail to achieve a self-consciousness), Sartre makes no attempt to relate us more meaningfully to natural processes. He is not interested in a metaphysics of nature. But materiality is essential to his fully developed aesthetics and to his brilliant discussion of the objective mind and of programmation.[49]

A new dimension to Sartre's concern with the material aspect of human experience is the heavy emphasis he gives to the body. It would not be fair to accuse him of having neglected the body in his former work, though Merleau-Ponty evidently thought so. In *The Transcendence of the Ego* the body as the domain of the psycho-physical is an important element in the formation of the "I-concept." The body is essential to Sartre's early essay on the emotions. Eye movements and kinesthetic reactions play an important part in his theory of how we form images. In *Being and Nothingness* Sartre insists that consciousness and body are inseparable. In a breathtaking sentence he declares,

> The body is what this consciousness *is;* it is not even anything except body. The rest is nothingness and silence. [p. 434]

Even so, and in spite of the important role played by the body in Sartre's discussion of the Look and of the caress, the for-itself appeared almost to make its choices independently of the body's influence. Neither genes nor natural mental endowment nor endocrinological secretions, not even illness entered into account. Sartre has never acknowledged the existence of such things as native intelligence or innate I.Q. As we have seen, he insists that intelligence is the result of the way that a society regards and develops the potentialities of its members. In this respect he has moved entirely onto the side of environmental rather than genetic conditioning. Almost everywhere else the body has become an essential ingredient of Sartre's discussion of personal development. He attributes the nature of a person's affective constitution to the infant's awakening to a sense of its own body at the hands of its mother—or whoever cares for it in the first years. Flaubert's passivity, a new and important concept by itself, was the result of this first body experience, and it colored the history of his entire life—sexually, emotionally, intellectually. Love is an imperative for the fostering of a free and active agent, and it is expressed by the voice, touch, and physical movements of the adult body in relation to that of the child.

At this point one might well feel that the determining constitution and the early process of personalization, to which Sartre attaches equivalent importance, must be taken as a repudiation of his earlier claims for freedom. Strangely enough, it is his discussion of Flaubert's psychosomatic reactions that reinstates the notion of individual self-direction. This is particularly evident in his analysis of Flaubert's failure-conduct at the time he was studying law. The "will to fail" is a complex pattern of bad faith, a lie to oneself which, at least in Flaubert's case, could not be adequately convincing without an accompanying psychosomatic structure. Avoiding any recourse to a Freudian type of unconscious, Sartre demonstrates how the elaborate strategy that carried Flaubert to the crisis at Pont-l'Evêque and determined the style of his future existence was accomplished "intentionally but not knowingly" with the body as instrument. Passive activity and autosuggestion achieved Flaubert's purpose while appearing to thwart it.

Nevertheless, it would be a mistake to equate Flaubert's neurotic solution with the full realization of an unlimited freedom. Sartre does not, in this book, address freedom directly as a philosophical problem. Everything depends on the assumption that Flaubert's crisis was not an accident but the consequence of a basic choice. To this extent freedom must be allowed. Yet one feels that even if Flaubert came to live in a prison of his own making, he was forced by prior conditioning to build it. In commenting on *The Family Idiot* Sartre has somewhat clarified his position, though it seems to me that he still does not quite adequately distinguish between what might be called "existential freedom" and "practical freedom." The first requisite for acting free, he implies, is the belief that one is free. With remarkable simplicity, Sartre maintains that one feels free when one's childhood has been without family conflicts and one has been loved by one's mother. Hence Sartre has always felt himself to be free whereas Flaubert did not, and the fact that he did not was due to circumstances beyond his control. Within these limitations Sartre states that Flaubert had some measure of freedom.

> Flaubert was free to become Flaubert, but he did not have so many possibilities outside of that. There were some: that of being nothing but a bourgeois, or that of being a poor physician, and that of being Flaubert.[50]

Flaubert had only conditional options. And so, Sartre argues, it is for all of us, *at least today*. He prefers to speak of "predestination" in place of "determinism." He will not say that we are given no choice. We have to choose. "But you know that in choosing you will not realize what you have chosen." At present we are not free because we are alienated:

> One is always lost in childhood; the methods of education, parent-child relationships, instruction, etc.; all this creates a self [*moi*], but it is a lost self.[51]

Sartre surely implies that in a world with better social structures a

417

genuine freedom may be realized. In that sense human reality is existentially free. But a given individual at a particular date cannot be said to be entirely free psychologically if the fundamental project which he *is* has been restricted like the wings of a newly emerged moth confined in a matchbox. More than ever before, each freedom finds its one obstacle to be the freedom of others, but now the very movement of consciousness itself is affected. Freedom is a goal to be realized after long and dubious battle. Meanwhile it remains present within us in embryo.

In 1971, on the day that the first two volumes of *The Family Idiot* were published, Sartre said in an interview, "If I were fifty today, I would not begin the *Flaubert*."[52] Given the length of the work, many persons who have read it, and still more who have refused to read it, have felt that writing it was an act of self-indulgence on Sartre's part, that he had no right to expect any reader to devote so much time to a book needlessly extended beyond all reasonable limits. I do not deny that these three volumes would be more improved than impaired by some degree of condensation. The same might be said of *Saint Genet* and the *Critique*. Yet while judicious cutting of a few pages here and there would not significantly mar the work, it would be impossible to remove any complete section without serious loss. Furthermore, some of the parts which theoretically are most extraneous to the central subject are among those which one remembers with particular pleasure and sense of enlightenment. In my slow perusal of it, I frequently found myself, even in the midst of deploring its unmanageable mass, regretting that Sartre had not discussed just a bit further a particular insight he had introduced without developing it. Whatever Sartre may think, those who have found in his philosophy an illumination of our period and of our human condition will not regret that he wrote *The Family Idiot*, even though they may recognize that it would take a lifetime to arrive at a full appreciation and worthy appraisal of this totalizing culmination of Sartre's life work.

# NOTES

INTRODUCTION

1. The question of factual errors will be taken up later.

2. "Sartre parle de Flaubert," interview with Michel Sicard, *Magazine littéraire* (November 1976): 99. Unless otherwise stated all translations are my own.

3. Jean-Paul Sartre, *Being and Nothingness*, trans. Hazel E. Barnes (New York: Washington Square Press, 1972), p. 734.

4. Sartre, "Sur *L'Idiot de la famille*," *propos recueillis* par Michel Contat et Michel Rybalka, *Situations* 10 (1976): 92.

5. "Itinerary of a Thought," (interview) *New Left Review* (November-December, 1969): 50–51.

6. Sartre, *L'Idiot de la famille* (Paris: Gallimard, vols. 1 and 2, 1971; vol. 3, 1972). In references to this work I will use simply the volume and page number.

7. Sartre, *Search for a Method*, trans. Hazel E. Barnes (New York: Alfred A. Knopf, 1963), p. 56.

8. Ibid., p. 142.

9. "Sartre parle de Flaubert," p. 97.

10. Sartre, "Itinerary of a Thought," pp. 52–53.

11. *Sartre*, the text of a film made by Alexandre Astruc and Michel Contat, with the participation of Simone de Beauvoir, Jacques-Laurent Bost, André Gorz, Jean Pouillon (Paris: Gallimard, 1977), p. 60.

12. Sartre, "Itinerary of a Thought," p. 65.

13. Ibid., p. 55.

14. Sartre, "Sur *L'Idiot de la famille*, p. 94.

15. Some examples of the two attitudes are the following: Benjamin Bart, "This is a very fine book, but it has nothing to do with the man named Gustave Flaubert." ("Interventions," following a paper by Michel Rybalka, "Sartre et Flaubert," *Langages de Flaubert: Actes du Colloque de London, Ontario*, 1973, ed. Michael Issacharoff [Paris: Lettres modernes-Minard, 1976], p. 231); Harry Levin, "We learn much less about Flaubert than we do about Sartre." "A Literary Enormity: Sartre on Flaubert," *Journal of the History of Ideas* (October-December 1972): 647; "Flaubert, c'est moi," title of *Times Literary Supplement* review of vol. 3, September 29, 1972; Ronald Aronson,

"There is not enough grounding in reality, not enough rooting in facts and evidence. Gustave Flaubert—and Sartre may indeed understand him—becomes too much a construct of Jean-Paul Sartre's imagination." "*L'Idiot de la famille*: The Ultimate Sartre," *Telos* (Summer 1974): 106. But consider also the following from the opening and closing paragraphs of a three-week series of articles by Pierre Daiz: (1) "[The book] is a new type of novel, a way of putting into language the reality of a man, a man who has actually lived; who is also a character, not only because he is a writer but because he is a writer who continues to communicate with us. With Sartre pre-eminently." (2) "One comes out of *The Family Idiot* impregnated by the characters as one comes out of *Madame Bovary* or *A Sentimental Education*, but with something more. As if Sartre had succeeded in adding something real to Flaubert." *Lettres françaises*, May 16 and 19, June 2, 1971.

16. Rybalka, "Sartre et Flaubert," p. 219.
17. "Sartre parle de Flaubert," pp. 97–98.
18. Ibid., p. 99.
19. Sartre, "Sur *L'Idiot de la famille*," p. 95.
20. Claude Burgelin, "Lire *L'Idiot de la famille*?", *Littérature* (May 1972): 119.
21. Sartre, "Sur *L'Idiot de la famille*, p. 103.
22. Ibid., p. 92.


CHAPTER ONE

1. Gustave Flaubert, *Ecrits de Jeunesse*, Préface et notes de Maurice Nadeau (Lausanne: Société Coopérative Editions Rencontre, 1964), pp. 146–47. (All page references are to the first volume.)
2. Flaubert uses this instead of the standard *l'indicible*. Sartre thinks it may have been a local variant. This is certainly possible, but Flaubert was also capable of coining words, at least in his informal correspondence if not in his novels.
3. Sartre's accuracy has been challenged here. I shall return to this point later.
4. Sartre reaffirms this conviction in speaking of his own life. "You feel free when you have no family conflict as a child—I had none—and when you have been loved by your mother and, in short, have been created in a certain world in which you become indispensable; that is, your family treats you in such a way that you believe yourself to be indispensable to it, so that you feel yourself to be one of the generous ones, who fulfill it, etc. And in fact, for quite a long time I confused freedom and generosity." *Sartre*, film, p. 32.
5. *Being and Nothingness*, p. 534n. Sartre has stated explicitly that his discussion of human relations in *Being and Nothingness* refers to the consequences of the project, in bad faith, to realize the missing in-itself-for-itself. Preface to a book by Francis Jeanson, *Le Problème moral et la pensée de Sartre* (Paris: Editions du Myrte, 1947).
6. To say that consciousness is nothing except body has, of course, a special significance for Sartre, who defines consciousness as a process of nihilation. Consciousness *is not* its body in the same way that it *is not* any of its

objects. But it has no existence separate from that of the body. I have discussed this point in an article, "Sartre as Materialist," to be published in a forthcoming volume in the Library of Living Philosophers series.

7. We may recall that Emma Bovary's greyhound was named Djali and that Emma tries to ease her own unhappiness by seeing in Djali someone like herself and pretending to console her.

8. R. D. Laing, *The Divided Self* (Baltimore: Penguin, n.d., first published by Tavistock, 1959), p. 77.

9. Barnes, "Sartre as Materialist."

10. Sartre, *Being and Nothingness*, p. 790.

11. "The Son as Father of the Man," *Times Literary Supplement*, Friday, September 24, 1971.

12. Harry Levin, "A Literary Enormity: Sartre on Flaubert," p. 649. Taken as a whole, this is the most hostile attack on *The Family Idiot* I have seen; it is not, in my opinion, a fair or well-considered review.

13. Jean Bruneau has claimed that he can prove that Dr. Flaubert did hold the electoral privilege. If Sartre is wrong on this point, it does not affect his basic argument about social mobility or the difference between the doctor's origins and those of his influential patients. "Interventions," in *Langages de Flaubert*, p. 230.

14. Sartre, "Sur *L'Idiot de la famille*," p. 98.

15. There is a remarkable resemblance between this anecdote from André Gide's *Journal*, dated October 26, 1924, and Thomas Mann's description of Aschenbach's encounter with the gondolier in *Death in Venice*, published in 1911. One wonders whether Gide's reaction might have been unknowingly influenced by Mann's story. I suspect that Sartre has merged the two accounts in his memory. Aschenbach's gondolier took him across the lagoon, Gide's to a deserted canal within the city.

16. Sartre, *The Transcendence of the Ego*, trans. Forrest Williams and Robert Kirkpatrick (New York: Noonday Press, 1957), pp. 65–68, 76–77.

17. Sartre discusses this incident (1:600). Flaubert relates it in a letter written in 1846. He adds that this was the one occasion when he had rendered his father proudly happy. *Correspondance* (Paris: Conard, 1926–33, 9 vols.; and supplement, 1954, 4 vols.) 1:355.

18. Sartre cites as evidence for this feeling Flaubert's early unfinished short story, *Un Secret de Philippe le Prudent Roi d'Espagne*, in which a father secretly spies on his son, who somehow senses it and feels that his father wants to ferret out even the most secret of his son's thoughts and feelings (1:397). I think Sartre has been influenced also by the sketch of Dr. Larivière in *Madame Bovary*, which is generally taken to be a disguised portrait of Gustave's father. Flaubert writes, "His look, more penetrating than this lancets, descended straight into your soul, through all excuses and reservations, and dissected every lie."

19. Bruneau, "Interventions," p. 230. Levin, "A Literary Enormity: Sartre on Flaubert," p. 645.

20. "Les Ecrivains en Personne," an interview with Madeleine Chapsal in 1960. *Situations* 9 (1972): 32.

21. Philip Spencer quotes the following from Gertrude Collier's *Memoir*: "I delighted in startling father and son into loud discussions. What surprised

me was the noise, loudness and want of courtesy with which they carried on conversation, particularly Gustave. His voice seemed to drown every other voice." This description appears to be at variance with Sartre's picture of Gustave as quietly submissive, but we cannot tell whether in these discussions he actually contradicted his father. Sartre might argue that his violence indicated an unspoken resentment behind the actual words spoken. Spencer, "New Light on Flaubert's Youth," *French Studies* (April 1954): 104.

22. The most important study is by Jean Bruneau, *Les Débuts littéraires de Gustave Flaubert: 1831–1845* (Paris: Armand Colin, 1962), with which Sartre was well acquainted. Although Bruneau has thoroughly explored the sources for these very early works, he acknowledges their degree of originality and the significance of recurring themes. It is worth noting that Bruneau, in the same discussion in which he points out certain disagreements with Sartre, speaks approvingly of his treatment of this material. "Interventions," in *Langages de Flaubert*, p. 231.

It is interesting to observe the degree to which Flaubert has added his own coloring even in a school assignment, an essay in history. Julia Bloch Frey has demonstrated this in her discussion of a manuscript recently discovered. "Un inédit de Flaubert: *La Lutte du Sacerdoce et de l'Empire (1837)*, scheduled for publication in 1980 in an issue of *Revue de l'histoire littéraire de la France* devoted to Flaubert.

23. All page references in this section, unless otherwise indicated, are to Flaubert's *Ecrits de Jeunesse*.

24. The statement is reported by Sully-Prudhomme, quoted by Sartre (1:444).

25. Actually it is the hero of *November* who does this, not Flaubert himself, but I suspect Sartre is right in attributing the reaction to Gustave.

26. Sartre derives this idea from *The Temptation of Saint Anthony* but believes that it represents Flaubert's own thoughts (1:402).

27. Marcel Eck, "*L'Idiot de la famille*. I. La psychanalyse de Flaubert selon Sartre: A propos de l'ouvrage de Jean-Paul Sartre," *La Nouvelle presse médicale*, March 4, 1972.

28. Jonathan Culler, who is mostly sympathetic toward what Sartre has done in *The Family Idiot*, has written an interesting study of Flaubert's attempt in these first works to overcome the difficulty of maintaining simultaneously the point of view of the confessional and the authority of the author who gives *exempla* to prove a point. *Flaubert: The Uses of Uncertainty* (Ithaca: Cornell University Press, 1974).

CHAPTER TWO

1. One may question whether it was quite this early. At any rate, it was not long afterward, for at age ten Gustave wrote that he had thirty plays, many of which he and his sister had acted out (1:661, 774).

2. Sartre adds that Gustave wrote also to Ernest Chevalier, "Look at yourself in the mirror and tell me if you don't have a great desire to laugh. So much the worse for you if you don't" (1:681). On this occasion Flaubert was

urging his friend not to take himself and his profession too seriously.

3. Sartre has no firm proof that Caroline was her mother's favorite or treated as such. He quotes as evidence that Gustave was second best a statement by the niece, who wrote, "My mother's marriage and her death coming so shortly after that of my grandfather left my grandmother so griefstricken that she was happy to keep her son near her" (1:723).

4. J. Laplanche and J. B. Pontalis, *The Language of Psychoanalysis*, trans. Donald Nicholson-Smith (New York: W. W. Norton and Company, 1973), p. 160.

5. Philip E. Slater, *The Glory of Hera: Greek Mythology and the Greek Family* (Boston: Beacon Press, 1971), chap. 11, "Maternal De-Sexualization: Perseus."

6. Flaubert, *Ecrits de Jeunesse*, pp. 268–69.

7. Benjamin F. Bart, *Flaubert* (Syracuse: Syracuse University Press, 1967), p. 226 and again on p. 385.

8. Sartre, *Search for a Method*, pp. 140–42. Sartre's reference to the doctors is inexact. The source must be a letter to George Sand. Flaubert says that he is going to Saint-Moritz on the advice of Dr. Hardy, "who calls me an hysterical old woman.—'Doctor,' I said to him, 'you are right.'" *Corr.* 7:137. The letter to Sand, from which I have quoted, is in 5:268. Sartre quotes from the letter to Madame Brainne without page citation (1:687). It is in 4:287.

9. Flaubert, *Souvenirs, notes, et pensées intimes*, Avant-propos de Lucie Chevalley Sabatier (Paris: Buchet/Chastel, 1965), p. 105.

10. Enid Starkie, *Flaubert: The Making of the Master* (New York: Atheneum, 1967), p. xiv. Sartre explicitly rejects Starkie's view, believing she has misinterpreted the letters in question (1:687). Bart believes there was no overt manifestation of homosexuality in Flaubert's relations with his closest friends though he thinks there may have been a hidden tendency in him toward it (*Flaubert*, pp. 225–26). Homosexuality is not an important aspect of Flaubert as interpreted by either Bart or Starkie.

11. It seems to me that this statement to Bouilhet is sufficient evidence to refute Starkie's claim that the two were lovers.

12. My evidence is from Bart, who refers to letters not included in the standard *Correspondance* (*Flaubert*, pp. 42, 751).

13. Laplanche and Pontalis, *The Language of Psychoanalysis*, p. 309.

14. Sartre makes a good deal of the fact that Flaubert resisted all of Louise's requests to meet his mother and broke with her soon after Louise, on her own initiative, made an unexpected visit to their home at Croisset. In one of his letters trying to dissuade Louise, Flaubert writes, "I do not like this confusion, this marriage [*alliance*] of two feelings from a different source" (1:707).

15. Neither here nor later in discussing the plays that the children put on at home does Sartre consider that Caroline was anything more than passive audience or an obedient performer who carried out directions. I cannot believe that she did not enter to some degree into the more active game of make-believe. If she did, this would not invalidate Sartre's claim. To have induced someone else to act as if the imaginary were real would strengthen Gustave's inclination to become a "creator of images."

CHAPTER THREE

1. Sartre, *Critique de la Raison Dialectique* (Paris: Gallimard, 1960), p. 246.

2. Sartre, "L'Ecrivain et sa langue," *Situations* 9:56.

3. Sartre notes that Flaubert's niece reported that the children presented tragedies as well as comedies, but he attributes this statement to her snobbism. In his letters to Ernest, Gustave lists only comedies (1:810).

4. Sartre denounced "the spirit of seriousness" in the last pages of *Being and Nothingness*. His best fictional representations of "serious men" are *les salauds*, whose portraits are hung in the art galley in Bouville (*Nausea*), and the adults in the house of the hero of "The Childhood of a Leader."

5. *Sartre*, film, p. 85.

6. Sartre, "Autoportrait à soixante-dix ans," propos recueillis par Michel Contat, *Situations* 10:226.

7. I think this statement is true, though one must remember that the individual's suffering may not result from his own actions. Even on a narrow and literal reading of *Oedipus the King*, one which would hold Oedipus himself innocent, his parents were not. Thomas Hardy might seem to be the obvious exception, but the famous chance that appears in his novels works hand and glove with the psychological qualities of the victims.

8. We will return to this point in the section "From Actor to Artist."

9. Flaubert, *Ecrits de Jeunesse*, p. 264.

10. Sartre draws here from a longer passage eventually excised from the final version of *Madame Bovary* (2:1202).

11. His niece states in her *Souvenirs* that Flaubert's record at school was mediocre, an opinion which should prevent our attaching too much weight to the prizes he received. Enid Starkie, finding Madame Commanville's report strange in the light of what Gustave was writing during his years at school, suggests that the curriculum at the lycée was such that his talents were simply not recognized (*Flaubert: The Making of the Master*, p. xii).

12. One is inevitably reminded of Lucretius' opening lines in book 2 of *De rerum natura*, where the poet tells us how pleasant it is to view from afar the struggles of the ignorant who have not attained through knowledge to our safe vantage point. The difference, of course, is that in the evangelist of atheism the suggestion of smug complacency is counterbalanced by a genuine concern and desire to help humanity.

13. Among biographers, René Dumesnil seems to me to be the only one, other than Sartre, to recognize the equivocal nature of the Garçon and his importance for our understanding of Flaubert's character. Dumesnil speaks of the invention of the Garçon as a "mythic creation" and says that the Garçon is "a kind of Hercules of stupidity and ignomity." *La Vocation de Flaubert* (Paris: Gallimard, 1961), p. 45.

14. Anyone in France would, of course, understand that reference is made to the Saint Bartholomew's day massacre, the revocation of the Edict of Nantes, and the persecution of the Huguenots by Louis XIV.

15. Edmont and Jules de Goncourt, *Journal: Mémoires de la vie littéraire. 1858–1860* (Monaco, Fasquelle and Flammarion, 1956), vol. 3, pp. 247–48.

16. Bruneau calls Sartre's picture of life at the school at this period "ex-

trêmement fantaisiste." "Interventions," p. 230.

17. Sartre discusses at some length a disagreeable episode in which Flaubert took the lead in publicly tormenting and ridiculing a boy for his commitment to the Church (2:1206 ff.).

18. Sartre, *Being and Nothingness*, p. 784.

19. I would challenge Sartre's statement that in a dream one cannot deliberate over possibilities. In my own nocturnal dreams, I am frequently faced with the necessity of choosing between two possible courses of action, and I feel all the sense of strain and uncertainty that accompanies a comparable experience in waking life. It is true, of course, that as the dream develops, the decision may never be made or, if made, will entail no logical consequences. I would not argue that the possibilities are real, but only that they exist in the same way as any other ingredient of the dream. I think that Sartre is probably right in claiming that possibles are excluded from pathological autism.

20. Sartre, *L'Imaginaire: Psychologie-phénoménologique de l'imagination* (Paris: Gallimard, 1940), p. 91.

21. Sartre's interpretation of romanticism is open to question. I will return to this subject in chapter 5.

22. When Sartre speaks of Chatterton, he is thinking less of the actual poet than of the myth of Chatterton, particularly as exemplified in the comte de Vigny's play.

23. Sigmund Freud, *Group Psychology and the Analysis of the Ego*, trans. James Strachey (New York, Bantam, 1965).

24. Sartre raises this question specifically in his unpublished notes for the fourth volume. He does not attempt to provide an answer in general terms.

25. It is interesting to note that Rimbaud, in his poem "Voyelles," calls *a* a black vowel and reserves white for *e*. Donald Sutherland called my attention to the poem.

26. An example in English might be "Constantinople." Besides the obvious echoes derived from the founder Constantine and history, it might evoke overtones, of *constant, noble, stand*, possibly even ant, apple, etc.

27. The theory, of course, is Sartre's not, Flaubert's. The relation between Flaubert's aesthetics and Sartre's theory of language will be discussed in the conclusion.

28. At the end of *Un Parfum à sentir, Ecrits de Jeunesse*.

29. Sartre, *L'Imaginaire*, p. 244.

30. Sartre states that it is only on the recognition of universal human need that a humanism can be established (1:1081). *Le besoin* as the starting point of our society of exploitation is the cornerstone of Sartre's argument in the *Critique*.

31. We may note that whether or not he is correct in attributing to Gustave an erotic impulse toward Alfred, this does not contradict Sartre's earlier argument that passivity, rather than homosexuality in the usual sense, is primary in Flaubert. The attraction, if indeed it existed, would have been at the period when Gustave's relation to Alfred was still that of chosen vassal to suzerain.

CHAPTER FOUR

1. Sartre has taken "Elbenhon" from the name of a character in Mallarmé's *Igitur*. As he has acknowledged, it is misspelled. It ought to be "Elbehnon." "Şur *L'Idiot de la famille*," p. 93.

2. René Dumesnil, *Flaubert: Son Hérédité—Son Milieu—Sa Méthode* (Paris: Société Française d'Imprimerie et de Librairie, 1903), pp.86–105. Dumesnil has restated this position in *La Vocation de Flaubert* (originally published in 1912), p. 65n. Bart, *Flaubert*, pp. 93–97, 752–53; Francis Steegmuller, *Flaubert and Madame Bovary: A Double Portrait* (London: Macmillan, Revised Edition, 1968), pp. 5–6, 11–15, 34–35; Philip Spencer, *Flaubert: A Biography* (London: Faber and Faber, 1953), pp. 61, 70–71; Victor Brombert, *Flaubert* (Paris: Seuil, 1971), p. 24; Marcel Eck, in a quite hostile review of *The Family Idiot*, argues for epilepsy, perhaps arising on a background of hysteria, and disputes any suggestion of psychosomatic factors. "*L'Idiot de la famille*. 2. La maladie et la personnalité de Flaubert selon Sartre: A propos de l'ouvrage de Jean-Paul Sartre," *La Nouvelle presse médicale* (March 18, 1972): 825–27.

3. Starkie, *Flaubert: The Making of the Master*, pp. 103–4.

4. Flaubert, *Souvenirs, notes et pensées intimes*, p. 63.

5. Bruneau, *Les Débuts littéraires de Gustave Flaubert*, p. 320.

6. Flaubert, *Ecrits de Jeunesse*, p. 469.

7. Since the publication of *The Family Idiot* two critics have taken issue with Sartre's explanation of the second narrator. Marie J. Diamond objects that Flaubert is not really as detached as he seems and that he shares many of the hero's attitudes. Actually, Sartre recognizes this point, which seems to me to strengthen his view rather than to weaken it. Diamond thinks that Flaubert realized that he had not succeeded, either artistically or emotionally, in separating his two selves and that he acknowledges his failure "when he questions the emotional authenticity of the first narrator and reveals that the truth originally claimed by the second is only a contrived and artificial fiction." *Flaubert: The Problem of Aesthetic Discontinuity* (Port Washington, N.Y.: Kennikat Press, 1975), pp. 68–74. Jonathan Culler also thinks the important point is not the "death by thought" but the admission that the story is only fiction. Believing that Flaubert consciously tried to avoid precise themes and meanings, he argues that the penultimate sentence deliberately undermines what has preceded. Flaubert "confronted his readers with the mocking cry: 'So you thought you could grasp this life as a meaningful whole, did you? That only happens in novels.' Successful employment of the confessional form would be a Romantic solution and could not satisfy." *Flaubert: The Uses of Uncertainty*, pp. 47–48. I do not think that Culler's view and Sartre's are incompatible.

8. Flaubert, *Ecrits de Jeunesse*, p. 464.

9. I have discussed this point more fully in "Sartre, Flaubert et Shakespeare," trans. Nicole Leconte, *Obliques* 18–19 (1979): 199–209.

10. Sartre anticipates our asking what would have happened if the chain of events had been different. Suppose Flaubert had not gone to see Hamard or with Achille to Deauville. Suppose the other driver had not been there. He thinks it most likely that another assembly of factors would have emerged,

and been utilized. In any case "the profound results would not have been different" (2:1834).

11. Simone de Beauvoir, *La Force de l'âge* (Paris: Gallimard, 1960), pp. 216 ff.

12. What Flaubert actually wrote was "La main que j'ai brûlée." Sartre remarks on the awkwardness of the expression. One would expect either "la main que mon père m'a brûlée" or la main que je me suis brûlée." Although *avoir* could have replaced *être* in local usage, it also enabled Flaubert to hedge between revealing the truth and betraying it (2:1885n.).

13. Sartre's reference is incorrect. The letter from which he quotes is in *Corr*. 3:270, not in vol. 1.

14. Flaubert, *L'Education sentimentale (Version de 1845), Oeuvres de jeunesse inédites* (Paris: Louis Conard, 1949).

15. Neil Hertz, "Flaubert's Conversion," *Diacritics* (Summer 1972): 7–12.

16. Bruneau rejects L. Bertrand's view that the episode is wholly hallucinatory. He does not find very helpful D. L. Demorest's suggestion that the scene is "an example of Flaubert's symbolism, a 'fusion of reality and of dream'—like the stumbling of Bovary's horse" when Charles first rides to Bertaux. He agrees with A. P. Coleman that Jules saw a real dog and that it served much the same function as the poodle in *Faust*, which also signified the start of a new existence for the hero. He approves of L. P. Shank's claim that the dog represents the past and that acceptance of one's past is the only condition for recovering it. He accepts part of Bonwit's interpretation. She saw in the episode not only a psychological significance, but the emergence of Flaubert's aesthetic theory, especially insofar as Flaubert (like Jules) was going beyond subjectivism toward artistic impersonalism. Bruneau accepts her conclusion that in this episode we see Jules not only rejecting the fantastic, but refusing "to project his own thoughts and visions on the outside world," thus keeping the author as man separate from the artist. But he does not agree with her postulation of two Juleses when she writes, "Jules of the past, accustomed to project his personality upon his surroundings, sees his own sadness in the tired animal. . . . The new Jules observes the sick dog clinically."

17. Sartre accepts this view, noting that Flaubert remarked to Louise that he had had "curious" encounters with "the children, idiots, and beasts" who seemed to want to attach themselves to him (2:1927n.). Sartre, however, goes beyond Bruneau in associating the encounter with the nervous crisis.

18. Hertz, ibid.

19. Diamond, *Flaubert: The Problem of Aesthetic Discontinuity*, pp. 85–88.

20. Culler, *Flaubert: The Uses of Uncertainty*, pp. 62–66.

21. I find a parallel so striking that it can hardly be purely coincidental between the structure of the last part of the first *Sentimental Education* and Aldous Huxley's *Time Must Have a Stop*. Huxley's novel is, among other things, the story of the passional and spiritual education of an artist, the poet Sebastian. There is an abrupt break before the "Epilogue" in which an utterly transformed Sebastian leafs through his journal; this is not a narration but a series of thoughts about spiritual discipline (like Jules' reflections on art). At the very end Huxley, like Flaubert, returns to the narrative so as to tie

together the loose ends of the story. Sebastian's reflections, too, stress the need of an inward retreat from life. His mentor, Bruno, speaks disparagingly of the lives of the poets as compared with their poetry.

CHAPTER FIVE

1. It is the concluding clause of the sentence that would not be accepted by the English romantic Keats in his famous identification of truth and beauty. Also that beauty *is* truth is not quite the same as that beauty *serves* truth.

CHAPTER SIX

1. Joseph Halpern picked up this designation for one of the early articles to appear on *The Family Idiot*, "From Flaubert to Mallarmé: 'The Knights of Nothingness.'" *Diacritics* (Fall 1973): 14–17. The article has been incorporated in a later book, *Critical Fictions: The Literary Criticism of Jean-Paul Sartre* (New Haven: Yale University Press, 1976). Halpern notes, "For the sake of variety, Sartre offers us a number of versions of his formula: the Barons of Non-Humanity, the knights of Non-Being, the knights of Absolute Negation, the knights of the Imaginary and the Impossible, the misanthropes of Art-Absolute, the pioneers of Art-Neurosis, the prudent Templars of Nothingness, the Artists of Hatred" (p. 157). Halpern finds the repetition of such terms irritating and suggests that the name-calling "makes proof seem superfluous" (p. 158).
2. Paul Tillich, *The Courage to Be* (New Haven: Yale University Press, 1960), p. 190.

CHAPTER SEVEN

1. W. K. C. Guthrie and F. M. Cornford apparently had something of this sort clearly in mind with regard to the period of the early Greek philosophers. Quoting from Cornford (*The Unwritten Philosophy*), Guthrie says, "In addition to the vagaries of individual temperament, there is another type of presupposition to which men are born, and which finds expression in the very language which they are compelled to use—'that groundwork of current conceptions shared by all men of any given culture and never mentioned because it is taken for granted as obvious.' These traditional conceptions (or it may be a new outlook moulded by the pressure of recent history, as in some of the forms taken by existentialism after the war of 1939) are powerful in every age." *A History of Greek Philosophy* (Cambridge University Press, 1962), vol. 1, p. 118.
2. Sartre speaks primarily of France but points to "Victorian cant" as another illustration of the common origin of "puritanism" and "distinction" (3:245). More generally we may note the close association of puritanism and the Calvinist work ethic in both England and America.
3. Sartre has an interesting footnote in this connection. He observes that still today economic and social planning. while taking into consideration all

other sorts of changes, assumes that the existing social order is to be preserved. By contrast, science fiction writers, who carry the notion of scientific
progress to its ultimate limit, frequently use it not to justify contemporary
ideology but to condemn the human species (3:284n.). A good example is
Huxley's *Brave New World*.

4. Henry James, *French Poets and Novelists* (London: Macmillan and Co.,
1884), pp. 200, 202.

5. Sartre's citation for this letter is inaccurate. The statement may be found
in *Corr.* 2:80.

6. The account is recorded by the Goncourts in their *Journal*, vol. 10, pp.
18–19.

7. Sartre, *The Emotions: Outline of a Theory*, trans. Bernard Frechtman
(New York: Philosophical Library, 1948), pp. 64–66.

8. Obviously Sartre has borrowed the expression from Hannah Arendt.

9. Sartre, *Critique de la raison dialectique*, p. 750.

10. Sartre quotes this from Durry's *Flaubert et ses projets inédits* (3:506).

PART THREE (Introductory Section)

1. Sartre, *Search for a Method*, p. 143.

CHAPTER EIGHT

1. Enid Starkie, *Flaubert the Master* (New York: Atheneum, 1971), pp.
244–45.

2. Flaubert, *Trois Contes* (Paris: Editions Garnier Frères, 1961).

3. Benjamin F. Bart and Robert Francis Cook, *The Legendary Sources of
Flaubert's "Saint Julian"* (Buffalo: University of Toronto Press, 1977).

4. A. W. Raitt, "The Composition of Flaubert's *Saint Julien l'Hospitalier*,"
*French Studies* (October 1965): 367.

5. Starkie, *Flaubert the Master*, p. 246.

6. The statement is made by Victor Brombert, who does not, however,
agree with the prevailing view. *The Novels of Flaubert: A Study of Themes and
Techniques* (Princeton: Princeton University Press, 1966), pp. 221–22. I will
return later in this chapter to Brombert's own view.

7. Bruneau, *Les Débuts littéraires de Gustave Flaubert*, p. 481.

8. Marcel Schwob, *Spicilège* (Paris: Société du Mercure de France, 1896),
pp. 178, 182.

9. Benjamin Bart cites two of these, Josiah Combs and Harry Levin, who, in
their editions of Flaubert's *Tales*, have pinpointed the theme of cruelty to
animals as central to his purpose. "The Moral of Flaubert's *Saint-Julien*,"
*Romanic Review* (February 1947): 26.

10. The dream is recorded in Flaubert's *Notes de Voyages* (Paris: Louis
Conard, 1910), vol. 1, p. 15.

11. *Mémoires d'un Fou, Ecrits de Jeunesse*, pp. 268–69. Bart, *Flaubert*, pp.
673–74.

12. In a later article Bart discusses Flaubert's dream further and connects it
more closely with the story of Julian. He retains the idea that animality is

closely associated with sexuality in Flaubert's mind but gives much more weight to Flaubert's ambivalent attitude toward nature and his desire to be reconciled with it. "After murdering his parents, Julian must learn, through his penance, what the Anthony of 1874 knew, to which will be added, even more overtly, the sexual component present in *Salammbô*. He must integrate his body and his soul and accept his own place in a nature no longer conceived as inanimate, but rather understood pantheistically as one and all, animate." "Psyche into Myth: Humanity and Animality in Flaubert's *Saint-Julien*," *Kentucky Romance Quarterly* 3 (1973): 336.

13. Bart, "The Moral of Flaubert's *Saint-Julien*," p. 32.

14. Sartre quotes other letters showing Flaubert's grief and sense of self-sacrifice. He does not cite the passages from the letters to Mesdames Loynes and Sand, which I have added as further support for his argument.

15. Brombert, *The Novels of Flaubert*, published in 1966.

16. Sartre, *La Nausée* (Paris: Gallimard, 1938), p. 221.

17. Brombert, *Flaubert*, p. 146.

18. The text of Lecointre-Dupont's adaptation of the Alençon manuscript is given by Bart and Cook in appendix B of *The Legendary Sources of Flaubert's Saint Julien*.

CHAPTER NINE

1. "Sartre parle de Flaubert," p. 94. In this, his most carefully considered statement, Sartre qualifies by adding, "Actually that is not true." By which he seems to imply that his statement was not entirely true but not wholly false either.

2. Occasionally I have found a remark which is clearly an aside, not intended for inclusion in the work to be written. The most amusing of these is a comment apropos of Rodolphe to the effect that one seduces women by talking to them of themselves, not of oneself. "Rod. does the opposite. Because Flaubert is not a seducer." And is Sartre?

3. Unless otherwise indicated, all quotations without page references in this chapter are taken from Sartre's unpublished and unnumbered notes.

4. Naturally, I do not mean to say that eminent Flaubert critics have restricted themselves to so simplistic a reading of the novel as I have given here, though some of the best (including Henry James) would not essentially disagree with it. The vast number of publications on *Madame Bovary* forbids me to attempt even the limited survey of pre-Sartrean critical opinion which I offered for "Saint Julian." I may merely mention a few of those whose views I have introduced earlier in this book. Starkie, for example, introduces a slight variation on the realist interpretation by putting it in psychological terms. "Emma Bovary does not know what her possibilities are nor what she is capable of achieving, and that is her tragedy.... All Flaubert's characters... possess this failing; and their view of themselves and their ambitions is far beyond their possible powers of achievement, so that they can never attain happiness or content (*Flaubert: The Making of the Master*, p. 299). Bart reads the book as antiromantic but stresses that while Flaubert castigates Emma for her false dreams, he is even more scornful of the bourgeois society

that produced and damned her. He comes very close to Sartre in recognizing that Flaubert "believed that life was hideous and to be avoided by living in art, in the incessant search for the true perceived through the intermediary of the beautiful," a possibility not open to Emma (*Flaubert*, p. 337). Spencer observes that while Flaubert "discarded the immature Romanticism which, in his view, culminated in unhappiness and disaster," he preserved certain elements of romanticism such as "love of fine language," irony, the "conception of fate," distrust of a hostile world, and scorn for what society called success (*Flaubert, A Biography*, p. 131). Brombert is more concerned with Flaubert's novelistic method than with basic meanings but sees, as Sartre does, that Emma's greatness and her foolish dreams are inextricably linked. "At the moment of her complete defeat in the face of reality, she acquires dignity and even majesty" (*The Novels of Flaubert*, p. 87). R. J. Sherrington, like Sartre, is interested in the devices Flaubert employs to prevent our sustaining an empathetic or even consistent point of view with regard to any of the characters or the narrator, but he does not attempt to relate this procedure to Flaubert's intent to demoralize or to the author's own attitude. Sherrington appears to have exerted considerable influence on the post-Sartrean critics whom I have mentioned. *Three Novels by Flaubert: A Study of Techniques* (Oxford: Clarendon Press, 1970).

5. Harry Levin, "The Female Quixote," "*Madame Bovary and the Critics: A Collection of Essays*," ed. B. F. Bart (New York: New York University Press, 1966), p. 109.

6. Flaubert, *Madame Bovary*, vol. 1 of Flaubert's *Oeuvres*, Texte établi et annoté par A. Thibaudet et R. Dumesnil, Pleiade Edition (Paris: Gallimard, 1951).

7. Bart is particularly perceptive (*Flaubert*, pp. 234–36).

8. Ibid., pp. 116–67.

9. Sartre notes that the humor of this scene is augmented by the phallic imagery of the cathedral. Other critics have commented on the irony of Emma's looking at the scenes of the Last Judgment as she delays the moment of her adultery. I think it is possible that Flaubert had still one other thing in mind. He did not sneer at the half-aesthetic, half-religious emotions stimulated by the music and the splendor of ritual in the cathedral; these were genuine witnesses to our thirst for the infinite. But Emma here is oblivious of the aesthetic in visual art, just as her response to the opera had been not aesthethic but a reaction in terms of her own emotional life as compared with that of the fictitious characters.

10. Sartre uses the word *baisade*, which is not in decent use in French even though it appears at least as early as the Journal of the Goncourt brothers, who use it in referring to Flaubert's early relation with Louise. The obvious vulgar translations in English seem to me not to have quite the same flavor.

11. Flaubert had used the image of *black* butterflies in describing Emma's burning of her bridal bouquet. Here the connotation is rather of dreams that have been killed.

12. Cf., for example, Culler, who argues that Charles' cliché, because of its banality, serves Flaubert's ironic intention and prevents us from thinking of Emma's fate as tragic (*Flaubert: The Uses of Uncertainty*, p. 143). The truth is that Flaubert, as pointed out earlier with regard to Emma and Rodolphe, felt

that genuine feelings and truth frequently are not communicated for the very reason that they can be expressed directly only through the limitations of banal phrases.

13. My source is Brombert, who cites an earlier article by Jean Pommier. The important point is that the book by Duval that Charles ordered so that he might study the procedure before the operation was a real work by Vincent Duval, "Traité, pratique du pied-bot." This mentions that Dr. Flaubert treated a child's clubfoot unsuccessfully. Brombert believes that Bruneau's attempt to prove, against Sartre, that Flaubert "had a deep love for his father" is unconvincing though an "understandable reaction to Sartre's excessive affirmations" (*The Novels of Flaubert*, pp. 73, and 224–25).

14. Charles Baudelaire, *Oeuvres complètes*, Pleiade Edition (Paris: Gallimard, 1961), p. 652.

15. "Sartre parle de Flaubert," p. 101.

16. Sartre, "Autoportrait à soixante-dix ans," p. 137.

17. Sartre, "Sur *L'Idiot de la famille*," p. 110.

18. Culler, *Flaubert: The Uses of Uncertainty*, pp. 37 ff.

19. Dominick LaCapra, *A Preface to Sartre* (Ithaca: Cornell University Press, 1978), p. 203.

20. Sartre, "Itinerary of a Thought," pp. 52–53.

21. Culler, *Flaubert: The Uses of Uncertainty*, p. 188.

22. Ibid., p. 75. In this instance only I have used Culler's translation, p. 240.

23. Sartre, *Critique*, p. 247.

24. Sartre, "Qu'est-ce que la littérature," *Situations* 2 (1948): 172.

25. LaCapra, *A Preface to Sartre*, p. 244, n. 10.

CONCLUSION

1. Sartre, "Les Ecrivains en personne," p. 36.

2. This is the title of an essay published in *Virginia Quarterly Review* (Spring 1947): 236–43.

3. Sartre, "Présentation des *Temps modernes*," in *Situations* 2:13. Christina M. Howells makes this same contrast, though she handles the problem somewhat differently. "Sartre and the Language of Literature," *The Modern Language Review* (July 1979): 572–79. Howells has a longer work on this subject: *Sartre's Theory of Literature* (London: The Modern Humanities Research Association, 1979).

4. Sartre, *L'Imaginaire*, p. 161. Thomas R. Flynn has an excellent article on the relation of this book to the development of Sartre's aesthetic theory: "The Role of the Image in Sartre's Aesthetic," *Journal of Aesthetics and Art Criticism* (Summer 1975): 431–42. In another article Flynn stresses the continuity between *L'Imaginaire* and *The Family Idiot*: "Sartre-Flaubert and the Real/Unreal," *Existence and Dialectic: Contemporary Approaches to Jean-Paul Sartre*, ed. Hugh J. Silverman and Frederick A. Elliston (Pittsburgh: Duquesne University Press, 1980).

5. We have noted that Sartre later concluded that imagination can provide "truth on the level of structures." He distinguishes between purely fictive imagination and that which is "retranscriptive" but points out that even a

fictive imagination may contain elements of truth. For example, the imagined centaur in my mind is based on a Greek social imaginary which historically was objectified by representation in numerous works of art ("Sartre parle de Flaubert," p. 98).

6. A seeming exception is Sartre's discussion of how the name "Florence" is inevitably both city and woman with echoes of floral, flower, etc. But the context here is concerned with poetry where the poet uses words as a painter employs colored pigments. It is only later that the same idea is applied to the prose writer's use of language. Significantly, however, even in this example Sartre adds that his own private connotations have enriched the word for him, independently of its context ("Qu'est-ce que la littérature?", p. 66).

7. An interview with Jacqueline Piatier, "Jean-Paul Sartre s'explique sur *Les Mots*," *Le Monde*, April 18, 1964. To be exact, Sartre's statements at this time still retain a bit of the old distinction between engaged and noncommitted writers. But this was the beginning of the break that was completed after 1968 when he proclaimed that in the present period, since the revolution was already underway, a leftist writer should write only revolutionary tracts.

8. I have discussed this point in *Sartre* (New York: J. B. Lippincott, 1973), pp. 143–47. Howells notes that both "Black Orpheus" and *Saint Genet* are early explorations of the alienating power of language," and she gives special emphasis to Sartre's concern, in the *Critique*, with the power of language to impede praxis. She writes, "Having recognized the extent of language's power to alienate, he became increasingly sensitive to the ways in which the writer succeeds in overcoming this alienation. As a result, his conception of the nature of literary communication underwent a radical transformation" ("Sartre and the Language of Literature," p. 573). "Orphée noir" is in *Anthologie de la nouvelle poésie nègre et malgache de langue française*, ed. Léopold Sédar Senghor (Paris: Presses Universitaires de France, 1948).

9. Sartre, "Plaidoyer pour les intellectuels," in *Situations* 9:434.

10. Sartre, "L'Artiste et sa conscience," in *Situations* 4 (1964).

11. Sartre, "A Structure of Language," interview with Jean-Pierre Berckmans, *Politics and Literature*, trans. J. A. Underwood and John Calder (London: Calder and Boyars, 1973), p. 70. The interview was first published in *Le Point* 8 (February 1967).

12. Howells, "Sartre and the Language of Literature," p. 577.

13. Sartre, "L'Ecrivain et sa langue," in *Situations* 9:40.

14. Ibid., p. 43.

15. Ibid.

16. Sartre, "Plaidoyer pour les intellectuels," pp. 436–37. Sartre refers to this same distinction in "in L'Ecrivain et sa langue." It is here that he insists that a writer cannot be either *écrivain* or *écrivant* without being the other as well (pp. 45 –46).

17. Sartre, *L'Imaginaire*, p. 178.

18. In *The Family Idiot*, in a somewhat different context, Sartre refers to tourists who try to revive the living quality of the Roman arena by recalling scenes from *Ben Hur* (2:1951n.).

19. Sartre, "L'Ecrivain et sa langue." This and the following quotations from the same interview are pp. 38–39.

20. Sartre, *Que peut la littérature?* présentation par Yves Buin (Paris: L'inédit 10–18, 1965), p. 122.

21. Sartre, "Plaidoyer pour les intellectuels," p. 433.

22. Sartre, "L'Ecrivain et sa langue," p. 65, and "Sur *L'Idiot de la famille*, p. 128.

23. Sartre, "Autoportrait à soixante-dix ans," p. 142.

24. Ibid., p. 146.

25. Sartre, "Sur *L'Idiot de la famille*," p. 97.

26. Alfred Fabre-Luce, "Sartre par Flaubert," *Revue des deux mondes* (October 1972), p. 60.

27. Sartre, "Sur *L'Idiot de la famille*," pp. 114–15.

28. The Father in *The Condemned of Altona* is a somewhat comparable patriarchal figure. The play involves also a younger son who feels resentful that his brother is the favorite.

29. Sartre, *Les Mots*, p. 14, and "Les Ecrivains en personne," p. 32.

30. Jacqueline Marchand, "Sartre, Flaubert et Dieu," *Raison Présente* (March 1975), p. 76.

31. Sartre, "Sur *L'Idiot de la famille*," p. 103.

32. Rybalka, "Interventions," p. 227. Rybalka says that almost all of Sartre's library consists of books by and about Flaubert. In the notes for the fourth volume Sartre has page references to numerous biographers and critics, very few of whom are mentioned in *The Family Idiot*.

33. Ibid., p. 231. Sartre gives as examples of errors the misspelling of "Elbehnon" and the fact that he credits Dr. Flaubert with having written a treatise on philosophy rather than physiology. "Sur *L'Idiot de la famille*," p. 93.

34. This is particularly true, as I have shown, in the work of Brombert, Culler, and, to a lesser extent, Hertz.

35. "Interventions," p. 231.

36. Rybalka expresses the positive view, "Sartre et Flaubert," pp. 223–24. Bart says, "C'est le fond même qui est imaginé." "Interventions," p. 231. Aronson calls *The Family Idiot* an "imaginary study of the interior of an imaginary person." "*L'Idiot de la famille*: The Ultimate Sartre?", p. 107.

37. In these passages Faulkner does not use dialect unless words are meant to be taken as spoken aloud or represent the sudden verbalization of hitherto nonverbal awareness—as if, for example, one might after a period of vague discomfort suddenly say to oneself, "My tooth aches."

38. Sartre, "Autoportrait à soixante-dix ans," p. 139.

39. Reported by Axel Madsen, *Hearts and Minds: The Common Journey of Simone de Beauvoir and Jean-Paul Sartre* (New York: William Morrow and Company, 1977), p. 231.

40. Bruneau, in a discussion with Rybalka, stated that Sartre's depiction of Flaubert's relations with father, mother, and brother was "completely false . . . but not necessarily important." When pressed, he admitted that the account of Gustave and Achille, for example, was not necessarily false but that the evidence allowed different interpretations. "Interventions," p. 231.

41. E.g., Bart, *Flaubert*, p. 674.

42. Ibid., p. 9.

43. Sartre, "Sur *L'Idiot de la famille*," p. 102.

44. References are to *The George Sand-Gustave Flaubert Letters*, trans., A. L. McKenzie (Chicago: Academy Chicago Limited, 1977), pp. 279, 323, 347, 288, 330.

45. The French is richer in overtones: "La rage des phrases t'a desséché le coeur."

46. *Sartre*, film, p. 42.

47. Sartre, *Saint Genet: Comédien et martyr* (Paris: Gallimard, 1952). Although the titles are suggested by words written by Genet himself, Sartre's selection of them is significant, representing an emphasis and interpretation which are his and not Genet's.

48. Sartre recognized this fact. "The study of the conditioning of Genet at the level of institutions and of history is inadequate. . . . The main lines of the the interpretation, that Genet was an orphan of Public Assistance, who was sent to a peasant home and who owned nothing, remain true, doubtless. But all the same, this happened in 1925 or so and there was a whole context to this life which is quite absent. . . . Genet is a product of the twentieth century; yet none of this is registered in the book" ("Itinerary of a Thought," p. 51).

49. The "objective mind," as a term, is obviously taken from Hegel. In making use of it, however, Sartre has indeed "stood Hegel on his head." Instead of abstract Spirit making itself concrete in the temporal process, Sartre's objective mind is the reification of past thoughts with which new thought must contend and which it must surpass.

50. *Sartre*, film, p. 76.

51. Sartre, "Sur *L'Idiot de la famille*," p. 99.

52. Ibid., p. 115.

# BIBLIOGRAPHY

Aronson, Ronald. "*L'Idiot de la famille*: The Ultimate Sartre." *Telos* (Summer 1974): 90–107.

Barnes, Hazel E. *Sartre*. New York: J. B. Lippincott, 1973.

———. "Sartre, Flaubert et Shakespeare." Translated by Nicole Leconte. *Obliques* 18–19 (1979): 199–209.

———. "Sartre as Materialist." In forthcoming volume on Sartre in Library of Living Philosophers series.

Bart, Benjamin F. *Flaubert*. Syracuse: Syracuse University Press, 1967.

———. "The Moral Of Flaubert's *Saint-Julien*." *Romanic Review* (February 1947): 23–33.

———. "Psyche into Myth: Humanity and Animality in Flaubert's *Saint-Julien*." *Kentucky Romance Quarterly* 3 (1973): 317–42.

Bart, Benjamin F., and Robert Francis Cook. *The Legendary Sources of Flaubert's "Saint Julian*." Buffalo: University of Toronto Press, 1977.

Baudelaire, Charles. *Oeuvres complètes*. Pleiade Edition. Paris: Gallimard, 1961.

Beauvoir, Simone de. *La Force de l'âge*. Paris: Gallimard, 1960. In English, *The Prime of Life*. Translated by Peter Green. New York: World Publishing Co., 1962.

Brombert, Victor. *Flaubert*. Paris: Seuil, 1971.

———. *The Novels of Flaubert: A Study of Themes and Techniques*. Princeton: Princeton University Press, 1966.

Bruneau, Jean. *Les Débuts littéraires de Gustave Flaubert: 1831–1945*. Paris: Armand Colin, 1962.

Burgelin, Claude. "Lire *L'Idiot de la famille?*" *Littérature* (May 1972): 111–20.

Culler, Jonathan. *Flaubert: The Uses of Uncertainty*. Ithaca: Cornell University Press, 1974.

Daix, Pierre. "Le Flaubert de Sartre." *Lettres françaises* (May 16 and 19, June 2, 1971).

Diamond, Marie J. *Flaubert: The Problem of Aesthetic Discontinuity*. Port Washington, N.Y.: Kennikat Press, 1975.

Dumesnil, René. *Flaubert: Son Hérédité—Son Milieu—Sa Méthode*. Paris: Société Française d'Imprimerie et de Libraire, 1903.

———. *La Vocation de Flaubert*. Paris: Gallimard, 1961.

Eck, Marcel. "*L'Idiot de la famille*. 1. "La Psychanalyse de Flaubert selon Sartre"; 2. "La Maladie et la personnalité de Flaubert selon Sartre." *La Nouvelle presse médicale* (March 4, 1972): 685–88; (March 18, 1972): 825–28.

Fabre-Luce, Alfred. "Sartre par Flaubert." *Revue des deux mondes* (October 1972): 44–61.

Flaubert, Gustave. *Correspondance*. Paris: Conard, 1926–33, 9 vols.; and supplement, 1954, 4 vols.

————. *Ecrits de Jeunesse*, Préface et notes de Maurice Nadeau. Lausanne: Société Coopérative Editions Rencontre, 1964.

————. *L'Education sentimentale (Version de 1845), Oeuvres de jeunesse inédites*. Vol. 3. Paris: Louis Conard, 1949. In English, *The First Sentimental Education*. Translated by Douglas Garman. Berkeley: University of California Press, 1972.

————. *Madame Bovary*, vol. 1 of *Oeuvres*, Texte établi et annoté par A. Thibaudet et R. Dumesnil. Pleiade Edition. Paris: Gallimard, 1951.

————. *Souvenirs, notes, et pensées intimes*, Avant-propos de Lucie Chevalley Sabatier. Paris: Buchet/Chastel, 1965. In English, *Intimate Notebook 1840–1841*. Translated by Francis Steegmuller. Garden City, N.Y.: Doubleday and Co., 1967.

————. *Trois Contes*. Paris: Editions Garnier Frères, 1961.

"Flaubert, c'est moi." London. *Times Literary Supplement* (September 29, 1972).

Flynn, Thomas R. "The Role of the Image in Sartre's Aesthetic." *The Journal of Aesthetics and Art Criticism* (Summer 1975): 431–42.

————. "Sartre-Flaubert and the Real/Unreal." In *Existence and Dialectic: Contemporary Approaches to Jean-Paul Sartre*. Edited by Hugh J. Silverman and Frederick A. Elliston. Pittsburgh: Duquesne University Press, 1980.

Freud, Sigmund. *Group Psychology and the Analysis of the Ego*. Translated by James Strachey. New York: Bantam, 1965.

Frey, Julia Bloch. "Un inédit de Flaubert: La Lutte du sacerdoce et de l'Empire (1837)." In forthcoming issue of *Revue de l'histoire littéraire de la France* (1980).

Goncourt, Edmond and Jules de. *Journal: Mémoires de la vie littéraire*. Monaco: Fasquelle and Flammarion, 1956.

Guthrie, W. K. C. *A History of Greek Philosophy*. Vol. 1. Cambridge, England: Cambridge University Press, 1962.

Halpern, Joseph. *Critical Fictions: The Literary Criticism of Jean-Paul Sartre*. New Haven: Yale University Press, 1976.

————. "From Flaubert to Mallarmé: 'The Knights of Nothingness.'" *Diacritics* (Fall 1973): 14–17.

Hertz, Neil. "Flaubert's Conversion." *Diacritics* (Summer 1972): 7–12.

Howells, Christina M. "Sartre and the Language of Literature." *The Modern Language Review* (July 1979): 572–79.

————. *Sartre's Theory of Literature*. London: The Modern Humanities Research Association, 1979.

James, Henry. *French Poets and Novelists*. London: Macmillan and Co., 1884.

Jeanson, Francis. *Le Problème moral et la pensée de Sartre*. Paris: Editions du Myrte, 1947.

LaCapra, Dominick. *A Preface to Sartre*. Ithaca: Cornell University Press, 1978.

Laing, Ronald D. *The Divided Self*. Baltimore: Penguin, n.d., first published by Tavistock, 1959.

Laplanche, J., and J. B. Pontalis. *The Language of Psychoanalysis*. Translated by Donald Nicholson-Smith. New York: W. W. Norton and Co., 1973.

Levin, Harry. "The Female Quixote." In *"Madame Bovary" and the Critics: A Collection of Essays*. Edited by B. F. Bart. New York: New York University Press, 1966, pp. 106–31.

————. "A Literary Enormity: Sartre on Flaubert." *Journal of the History of Ideas* (October-December 1972): 643–49.

Madsen, Axel. *Hearts and Minds: The Common Journey of Simone de Beauvoir and Jean-Paul Sartre*. New York: William Morrow and Company, 1977.

Marchand, Jacqueline. "Sartre, Flaubert et Dieu." *Raison Présente* (March 1975): 65–77.

Raitt, A. W. "The Composition of Flaubert's *Saint Julien l'Hospitalier*." *French Studies* (October 1965): 358–72.

Rybalka, Michel. "Sartre et Flaubert." *Langages de Flaubert, Actes du Colloque de London, Ontario*, 1973. Edited by Michael Issacharoff. Paris: Lettres modernes-Minard, 1976, pp. 213–25, followed by "Interventions," pp. 226–33.

Sartre, Jean-Paul. "L'Artiste et sa conscience." Preface to a book of this title by René Leibowitz, 1950. In *Situations* 4 (1964).

————. "Autoportrait à soixante-dix ans." Interview with Michel Contat. In *Situations* 10 (1976). In English, "Self-portrait at Seventy." In *Life/ Situations: Essays Written and Spoken*. Translated by Paul Auster and Lydia Davis. New York: Pantheon Books, 1977.

————. *Critique de la raison dialectique* (précédé de *Question de méthode*), vol. 1, *Théorie des ensembles pratiques*. Paris: Gallimard, 1960. In English, *Search for a Method*. Translated by Hazel E. Barnes. New York: Alfred A. Knopf, 1963. *Critique of Dialectical Reason*, vol. 1, *Theory of Practical Ensembles*. Translated by Alan Sheridan-Smith, edited by Jonathan Ree. Atlantic Highlands: Humanities Press, 1976.

————. "L'Ecrivain et sa langue." First published in *Revue d'esthétique* (July-December 1965). Texte recueilli et retranscrit par Pierre Verstraeten in *Situations* 9 (1972). In English, "The Writer and His Language." In *Politics and Literature*. Translated by J. A. Underwood and John Calder. London: Calder and Boyars, 1973.

————. "Les Ecrivains en personne." Interview with Madeleine Chapsal, 1960. In *Situations* 9. In English, "The Purposes of Writing." In *Between Existentialism and Marxism*. Translated by John Mathews. New York: William Morrow and Company, 1976.

————. *Esquisse d'une théorie des émotions*. Paris: Hermann et Cie., 1939. In English, *The Emotions: Outline of a Theory*. Translated by Bernard Frechtman. New York: Philosophical Library, 1948.

————. *L'Etre et le néant*. Paris: Gallimard, 1943. In English, *Being and Nothingness*. Translated by Hazel E. Barnes. New York: Washington Square Press, 1971.

439

————. *L'Idiot de la famille*. Paris: Gallimard. Vols. 1 and 2, 1971; vol. 2, 1972.

————. *L'Imaginaire: Psychologie-phénoménologique de l'imagination*. Paris: Gallimard, 1940. In English, *The Psychology of Imagination*. Translator anonymous. New York: Philosophical Library, 1948.

————. "Itinerary of a Thought." Interview with the editors, *New Left Review* (November-December 1969): 43–66. Later French text, "Sartre par Sartre." In *Situations* 9. Also in *Between Existentialism and Marxism*.

————. "Jean-Paul Sartre's explique sur *Les Mots*." Interview with Jacqueline Piatier. *Le Monde*, April 18, 1964.

————. *Les Mots*. Paris: Gallimard, 1964. In English, *The Words*. Translated by Bernard Frechtman. New York: Braziller, 1964.

————. *La Nausée*. Paris: Gallimard, 1938.

————. "Orphée noir," preface, *Anthologie de la nouvelle poésie nègre et malgache de langue française*. Edited by Léopold Sédar Senghor. Paris: Presses Universitaires de France, 1948. In English, *Black Orpheus*. Translated by S. W. Allen. Paris: Présence africaine, 1963.

————. "Plaidoyer pour les intellectuels." In *Situations* 8 (1972). In English, "A Plea for Intellectuals." In *Between Existentialism and Marxism*.

————. "Présentation des *Temps Modernes*." In Situations 2 (1948).

————. *Que peut la littérature?* présentation par Yves Buin. Paris: L'Inédit 10–18, 1965.

————. *Saint Genet: Comédian et martyr*. Paris: Gallimard, 1952. In English, *Saint Genet: Actor and Martyr*. Translated by Bernard Frechtman. New York: Braziller, 1963.

————. "Sartre parle de Flaubert." Interview with Michel Sicard. *Magazine littéraire* (November 1976): 94–106.

————. *Sartre: Un film* réalisé par Alexandre Astruc et Michel Contat avec la participation de Simone de Beauvoir, Jacques-Laurent Bost, André Gorz, Jean Pouillon. Texte intégral. Paris: Gallimard, 1977. In English, *Sartre by Himself*. Translated by Richard Siever. New York: Urizen Books, 1978.

————. "A Structure of Language." Interview with Jean-Pierre Berckmans. In *Politics and Literature*. The interview was originally published in *Le Point* (February 1967).

————. "Sur *L'Idiot de la famille*." Interview with Michel Contat and Michel Rybalka. In *Situations* 10. This first appeared as "Un Entretien avec Jean-Paul Sartre" in *Le Monde* (May 14, 1971). In English, "On the Idiot of the Family," in Life/Situations.

————. "La Transcendence de L'Ego: Esquisse d'une description phénoménologique." In *Recherches Philosophiques* 6 (1936–37). In English, *The Transcendence of the Ego*. Translated by Forrest Williams and Robert Kirkpatrick. New York: Noonday Press, 1957.

————. "We Write for Our Own Time." *Virginia Quarterly Review* (Spring 1947): 236–43.

Schwob, Marcel. "Saint Julien l'Hospitalier." In *Spicilège*. Paris: Société de Mercure de France, 1896.

Sherrington, R. J. *Three Novels by Flaubert: A Study of Techniques*. Oxford: Clarendon Press, 1970.

Slater, Philip E. *The Glory of Hera: Greek Mythology and the Greek Family*. Boston: Beacon Press, 1971.

Spencer, Philip. *Flaubert. A Biography*. London: Faber and Faber, 1953.
————. "New Light on Flaubert's Youth." *French Studies* (April 1954): 97–108.
Starkie, Enid. *Flaubert: The Making of the Master*. New York: Atheneum, 1967.
————. *Flaubert the Master*. New York: Atheneum, 1971.
*The George Sand-Gustave Flaubert Letters*. Translated by A. L. McKenzie. Chicago: Academy Chicago Limited, 1977.
"The Son as Father of the Man." London. *Times Literary Supplement* (September 24, 1971).
Tillich, Paul. *The Courage to Be*. New Haven: Yale University Press, 1960.